THEORIES OF LEARNING

For Neil, without whose support this project would not have been completed. I am grateful for the innumerable conversations about progress throughout the construction of the manuscript.

THEORIES OF LEARNING

Tools for thinking about practice

DEBRA MCGREGOR

1 Oliver's Yard
55 City Road
London EC1Y 1SP

2455 Teller Road
Thousand Oaks
California 91320

Unit No 323-333, Third Floor, F-Block
International Trade Tower
Nehru Place, New Delhi 110 019

8 Marina View Suite 43-053
Asia Square Tower 1
Singapore 018960

© Debra McGregor 2025

Apart from any fair dealing for the purposes of research, private study, or criticism or review, as permitted under the Copyright, Designs and Patents Act, 1988, this publication may not be reproduced, stored or transmitted in any form, or by any means, without the prior permission in writing of the publisher, or in the case of reprographic reproduction, in accordance with the terms of licences issued by the Copyright Licensing Agency. Enquiries concerning reproduction outside those terms should be sent to the publisher.

British Library Cataloguing in Publication data

A catalogue record for this book is available from the British Library

Editor: James Clark
Editorial assistant: Esosa Otabor
Production editor: Nicola Marshall
Copyeditor: Niketha
Proofreader: Girish Sharma
Indexer: TNQ Tech Pvt. Ltd.
Marketing manager: Maria Omena
Cover design: Sheila Tong
Typeset by: TNQ Tech Pvt. Ltd.

ISBN 978-1-4462-5313-7
ISBN 978-1-4462-5314-4 (pbk)

CONTENTS

About the Author	vii
Acknowledgements	ix
Preface	xi
Chapter 1 Introducing How Learning Is Talked About	1
Part 1 Introducing Theories of Learning	17
Chapter 2 Introducing Behaviourism and Information-Processing Theories	19
Chapter 3 Introducing Constructivism and the Agentive Mind	44
Chapter 4 The Importance of Language and Meaning-Making	69
Chapter 5 Introducing Social Constructivism and Socioculturalism	97
Chapter 6 Thinking Further About the Social and Cultural Aspects of Learning	125
Part 2 Applying Theory to Make Sense of Practice	151
Chapter 7 Classroom Cases Featuring Aspects of Behaviourism and Information Processing	155
Chapter 8 Classroom Cases Featuring Aspects of Constructivism	181
Chapter 9 Classroom Cases Featuring Aspects of Social Constructivism	210
Chapter 10 Classroom Cases Featuring Aspects of Socioculturalism	234
Conclusion: What Is the Use of Theory and Why Does It Matter for Practice?	260
Index	273

ABOUT THE AUTHOR

Professor Debra McGregor currently works at Oxford Brookes University. She has worked in education for nearly 40 years. She has taught in primary and secondary schools and various university settings in the United Kingdom, Europe and the United States. She has led various research projects across many contexts up and down the country and within Europe. She has published many papers and books concerned with teaching and learning, the performing arts, cognitive development, the nature of creativity and close to practice research. She remains passionate about supporting education to provide the best that is possible for teachers and their students.

ACKNOWLEDGEMENTS

To Patricia Murphy, without whom this whole project would not have been possible. I am indebted to her support and wisdom.

Also, to James Clark, a most supportive and constructive editor. His consistent encouragement to complete the project has been very much appreciated.

PREFACE

There are several books that have been written about theories of learning which describe the many views, models and perspectives that have evolved over time. However, there is no one universal theory that all educationalists agree on, so this book is intended to help you consider what the different theories mean and how they may be helpful for you to develop your practice. This book is not concerned with simplifying theories of learning (Bates 2023). It is written to explain straightforwardly how theories of learning are complex. Neither is the book written to describe a diverse range of theories (Aubrey and Riley 2022). It is concerned firstly with explaining how foundational theories have developed over many decades; secondly, why theories of learning are useful for you as a teacher, and thirdly, how the theoretical perspectives could be applied to inform happenings in classrooms and even suggest ways that your practice could be developed to achieve different outcomes with your learners and their learning.

EXPLAINING THE FOCUS OF THE BOOK

Current practices involving many formulaic approaches, like, for example, how to teach phonics and times tables, suggest that specific kinds of learning experiences should be followed by all pupils. This one-size-fits-all approach risks alienating some learners, so the ways that practice influences the learning experience for classes of pupils is of concern in this book. There are also many aspects of learning that are talked about in vague ways. Depending on the way in which a teacher has generated the opportunity for learners to talk about ideas, discuss perspectives or elaborate on their thinking will influence the learning that is possible. Consider, for example, pupils verbally reading aloud, reciting a memorised poem or discussing a Shakespearean play they have just watched, all three activities involve dialogue that serves quite different learning purposes. Thinking about how learning happens and theorising about such processes can bring into existence and make explicit forgotten or overlooked assumptions we often hold about education. Although we now know much more neuroscientifically about the physical nature of the brain, we still do not know exactly how an individual's experience, memory and learning are linked. There remain ongoing debates about many aspects of learning including whether nature or nurture is the most important influence and the extent to which innate ability counts, how far learning is a social or an individual process and what part society and the local or global community plays in the process of learning. These and many other questions are addressed throughout the book.

It is clear from many studies that learning is a complex phenomenon (Qvortrup et al. 2016) and that theorising about such a fundamental human process is not straightforward. Therefore, before exploring what theories of learning state about the ways that humans learn, it is useful to consider why they can be useful in educational situations. To answer this, practitioners need to have a view about what theories are and what purposes they serve. A theory is described by Mercer (1995) as a simplified explanatory model. He suggests how a theory is derived from observations of the real world to help explain it. Theorising is a very human response to trying to make sense of our complex world. Theories can help us to see the wood for the trees. Jerome Bruner, an eminent educationist and theorist, described how 'our interactions with others are deeply affected by our everyday intuitive theories about how other minds work' (Bruner 1996: 45). Everyone develops personal theories (sometimes knowingly, sometimes unconsciously) that inform what they do and how they understand what others do. For example, you may hold a view that 'the more homework children do, the better they will perform in school examinations'. However, homework can take many forms, ranging from committing to memory formulations or concepts, practicing previous examination questions or re-presenting information in various mind or theoretical map formations. The point is, these are different ways 'doing homework' can be practiced or enacted. Theories of learning are often distinguished from practice, but they can also be seen as being interlinked with a teacher's practice. To consider this relationship briefly here you also need to have a view about what is meant by 'practice'. Typically, it is a word used to mean what people do or how they act. In this book, actions are not considered separate to knowing so practice and theory are not understood as a dichotomy. For teachers, their specific practices are concerned with how to support learning and assess it. Teachers as practitioners are concerned to understand how what they do affects the learners that they support. To reflect on the effectiveness of their practice though requires analytical tools to make sense of why certain ways of doing things in schools for certain learners result in particular outcomes. Theories can help teachers answer reflective questions about interactions between peers and between pupils and themselves such as 'Why did it happen in that way?' and 'How could I have behaved or done things differently?' Thoughtful reflection can help you to recognise what is effective practice and the ways that successful teachers enact particular practices. Theories along with evidence from practice are the main tools that support reflection about teaching and learning. The theories considered in this book are long held, well-established perspectives that explain how learning arises. The chapters have been developed to consider increasingly complex theories and the ways they could be used as tools for thinking about practice. It is intended that these theories as tools for thinking help readers and practitioners better understand how their practice affects learners and influences learning.

Confusingly, sometimes, the theories that resonate with your concerns and ways of seeing the world might be quite different to those embedded in policy or in school practices or those of your colleagues.

WHO THE BOOK IS INTENDED FOR

A key intention of this book is to help educators appreciate how theories of learning differ and that practices associated with each of them impact on learners and learning differently.

Engaging with theories that might challenge how you practice is potentially useful as it offers a way of clarifying the perspectives you value and why. It can also open up and render more obvious possibilities for different ways of teaching. In a similar way, understanding the implicit theories in educational policies about teaching and learning can help explain why they resonate or not with how you teach. In this way, it is argued that theories are important tools for reflection, evaluation and development of practice.

Consequently, the narrative in this book is constructed to help and support you understand various theorical movements and the ways associated concepts might offer insights about yours and others' practice. Contrasting theories of learning assume different interpretations of the processes that affect an individual's capability of coming to know something new. The discussions about the theories make clearer how they each differ in the kinds of activity learners engage in, the nature and purpose of dialogue involved and the extent to which particular kinds of interaction are is important. These influence differently individual and even cultural development. How the nature of knowledge and knowing varies across the different perspectives is also considered. So, too, is the way that agency and identity, society, community and culture are acknowledged and understood differently. These and other concepts associated with the various learning movements are explained, considered and contrasted for each perspective.

In Part 1, the ways different theories of learning have been understood over the years are described. The book is particularly concerned with theories that have longevity and have prevailed for many decades. The evidence these theories have been based upon is discussed and considered to highlight how they are currently applied or displayed in classrooms today. In helping readers to appreciate how various concepts within theoretical movements can, and are, applicable to classroom practice, a range of teaching metaphors are drawn on. The intention is that the metaphors render more explicit nuanced and less obvious aspects of practice that sometimes go unnoticed or are overlooked in discussions about learning.

Part 2 then presents narrative construals of moments from classrooms where aspects or concepts within a theoretical movement are discernible. The text throughout the book is written to engage the reader in reflexively considering how these theories are applicable to their own classroom situations and contexts and even inform how they might resolve challenges their learners face.

Although this book has been intentionally written for teachers, the discussions about different theories of learning are applicable beyond school situations. The book is, therefore, also useful for researchers examining aspects of learning and teaching that require theoretical underpinnings to inform the approach they are assuming or the 'lens' they are adopting. Throughout the chapters, there are also sections where policy is analysed to understand the inferred theory of learning adopted. This book, therefore, may also be useful for those responsible for generating educational policy.

THE CONTENT OF THE BOOK

To help you as a reader to understand how the book is constructed, the following paragraphs detail how and why the chapters are organised as they are.

Part 1, *Introducing theories of learning*, provides clear, evidenced and well referenced explanations of enduring theoretical movements. These include behaviourism; information processing; constructivism; cognitivism; symbolic interactionism; social constructivism and sociocultural theories of learning. The various concepts like, for example, nature of activity, type of social interaction or ways learners are positioned to learn, associated with each theoretical movement are also introduced and explained.

Part 2, *Applying theory to make sense of practice*, extends consideration of the theoretical movements introduced in Part 1. Excerpts from moments in practice are brought to the fore. These moments are presented as narrative construals which offer examples of ways particular concepts (within theoretical movements) are made available for you, the reader, to reflect upon. These moments invite readers to consider the influences of both policy and practice on learners and learning.

Chapter 1 is an introduction to the ways that learning is talked about and understood. The discussion highlights how individuals personalise their theoretical perspective of learning as a result of their particular experiences. The ways that teaching and learning are different and distinct but related processes is explained. The relational connection between learning, pedagogy and practice is also introduced and explained. The limitations of thinking about one aspect of a theory which does not take into account all of the associated concepts and assumptions carried with the long-held perspectives are also considered. Metaphors that characterise different aspects of teaching approaches are introduced to more clearly demonstrate contrasts between theories of learning. Consideration of the metaphors is extended to their application as tools for thinking about practice and how it supports and influences the ways that learning can happen for different learners.

Part 1, comprised of five chapters (2–6), introduces the features and origins of well-established and long-held theories of learning. The historical perspective details how the theories came to be and highlights the associated concepts, some of which are often overlooked in educational literature. This set of chapters differs to Part 2 where application of the theories informs ways of looking at practice in classrooms.

Chapter 2 introduces behaviourism and information processing theories and considers the ways they continue to influence policy and practice today. The metaphors of *lion tamer* and *petrol pump attendant*, for example, that characterise practice supporting behaviourism are contrasted with those of the *parent-bird* or *watch-maker* that demonstrate aspects of information processing.

Chapter 3 introduces constructivism and the agentive mind and considers how cognitivism challenges behaviourist assumptions. This chapter also discusses how learners, mind and development are characterised within Piagetian theorising. The ways that different views of learning imply different understandings of the mind are explained. In particular, the learner as agent of learning which suggests a particular way of thinking about how the 'mind' develops is discussed. Later the mind as brain, mind as agentive and mind as distributed are considered. The role of activity and curricular imperatives is explained to invite the reader to think about implications for learners. The shifting role of the teacher from an authoritarian controlling learning to the metaphor of *gardener* or *facilitator* is also deliberated upon.

Chapter 4 considers further the role of language and meaning making in learning and sets out to explain the meaning of 'social' in theories of learning. Vygotsky's views of the zone of proximal development (ZPD) are reviewed in a differentiated way. First, the context of learning (and features of tasks) is considered, then the context of the classroom as a micro-culture is discussed and third, mind as distributed is explored, all with different dimensions of the ZPD in mind. The role of language and the extent to which intersubjectivity (i.e. how we come to understand others' minds) and culture (the ways in which societal traditions and customs) may influence how we learn and what we learn is also appraised. Contrasts between Piagetian and Vygotskian theorising are deliberated upon. Metaphorically speaking, the teacher as *scaffolder* supporting learning is considered.

Chapter 5 introduces social constructivism and socioculturalism. This chapter considers the different ways that various social dimensions can influence learning. The ways that differential social interactions influence the ZPD are discussed, and how this results in tensions between relativist and realist ontologies are thought about. Ideas about identity and agency are presented. Consideration of the usefulness of the metaphor of *tourist guide* and *sherpa* introduces further thinking about teacher enactment in classrooms.

Chapter 6 considers social and cultural influences on learning further. The ways that context, community, culture and history matter in this kind of theorising are explained. Participation, activity, identity, affordance and agency are other concepts within this movement that are also discussed. The social and cultural aspects of learning described and considered serve to demonstrate the multidimensional and complex way in which particular sociocultural perspectives may overlook some influences on learning.

Part 2, comprised of four chapters (7-10), is focused on drawing from the theories introduced in Part 1 to make sense of everyday practice that supports learning in classrooms today.

Chapters 7-10 offer narrative construals of moments in primary and secondary school classrooms across mathematics, English, science and other disciplines. The intention in these chapters is to make available a range of real classroom situations and use the theories as tools for thinking about practice and the impact it can have on learners and learning in those particular moments. In so doing, the discussion attempts to highlight for the readers the consequences of different practice directions and the alternate ways that teachers can support learning.

Chapter 7 considers enactments of aspects of behaviourism and information processing within a phonics, mathematics and English classroom. In each case, it is clear that acquisition of particular skills is priority for the teachers. Transcripts presented offer construal of a range of situations for the reader to think about. Practice is described for the reader to consider the extent to which the teacher demonstrates aspects of the metaphoric *lion tamer, petrol pump attendant* or *sculptor*. Parallels with the *parent-bird* and *watch-maker* metaphors are also considered.

Chapter 8 considers enactments of constructivism within science, mathematics and English lessons. Across the cases, curricular policy and the inferred theory of learning are considered as well as identifying different features of the constructivist movement highlighted in the lesson descriptions. Of particular note are the ways that extrinsic motivation and resources are made available for learners to influence the nature of learning; the extent of social interaction and the nature of the activities engaged in affording opportunities for agentive action. Finally, discussion about the usefulness and applicability of the metaphor of *gardener* is considered.

Chapter 9 considers enactments of a variety of different practices that characterise ways of supporting interaction and dialogic exchange within an historical, scientific, mathematical and English lesson context. Across the cases, the different ways that practice promotes social constructivism and extends the ZPD for learners is discussed. Finally, for each case, the ways that the teacher enacted features of practice as *modeller, guide* or *scaffolder to* influence agentive learning opportunities are considered.

Chapter 10 discusses the ways in which practice can promote sociocultural dimensions of learning and teachers position learners for learning. There is consideration of the extent to which dialogue, thought and action are inter-related when learning socially. The ways that a classroom, group or community culture could influence how mind-as-distributed emerges is considered across the cases of a mathematics, history, science and forest school context. Finally, the ways that a teacher as *tourist guide, sherpa or even co-adventurer* offers ways of thinking about learning are reflected upon.

The final chapter concludes the book by summarising how the various concepts within the different theoretical movements differ. This chapter also considers the usefulness of applying metaphors to help teachers think about their practice, learners and their learning to consequently consider future directions for development.

ADDITIONAL READING

Aubrey and Riley (2022) in their book, *Understanding and Using Educational Theories* provide straight forward descriptions of prominent theorists' lives and work. They then present aspects of each theorist's view to describe how their perspectives can be linked to classroom practice.

Illeris (2018) entitled *Contemporary Theories of Learning. Learning theorists…In their own words* collates a comprehensive range of chapters written about learning by many eminent theorists including Engestrom, Hattie, Gardner, Bruner, Usher, Wenger and Biesta.

Qvortup et al. (2016) discuss concepts related to the phenomena of learning in an attempt to understand the complexity of its relationship to teaching. The book considers conceptualisations and provides deep contemplations in conversation with established scholars about the empirical phenomena of learning.

REFERENCES

Aubrey, K. & Riley, A. (2022) *Understanding and Using Educational Theories.* 3rd ed. London: SAGE.

Bates, B. (2023) *Learning Theories Simplified and How to Apply Them to Teaching.* 3rd ed. London: SAGE.

Bruner, J. (1996) *The Culture of Education.* Cambridge, Massachusetts: Harvard University Press.

Illeris, K. (2018) *Contemporary Theories of Learning. Learning Theorists in Their Own Words.* 2nd ed. Abingdon, Oxon: Routledge.

Mercer, N. (1995) *The Guided Construction of Knowledge. Talk Amongst Teachers and Learners.* Clevedon: Multilingual Matters.

Qvortrup, A., Wiberg, M., Christensen, G. & Hansbøl, M. (2016) *On the Definition of Learning.* Odense, DK: University Press of Southern Denmark.

1
INTRODUCING HOW LEARNING IS TALKED ABOUT

CONTENTS

Introduction to Thinking About Learning	2
Developing a Theory About Learning Through Your Personal Experience	4
Theorising About Learning to Drive	5
Underpinning Assumptions	7
What Do Students Say About Coming to Know Something?	7
Other Ways Learning Is Talked About	8
Thinking Further About How Learning Is Talked About	10
Experiences of Learning Depicted by Metaphors	12
Interpreting Views About Learning	14
Summary	15
Additional Reading	15
References	16

Chapter Aims

After reading Chapter 1, you will have considered that:

- there is significant variation in the ways that learning is understood and thought about;
- there is no common theory that explains learning;
- personal theories about learning may be informed by individuals' experiences of learning;
- characterising the nature of learning is complex;
- teaching and learning are different and distinct but related processes;
- metaphors emphasising key features of contrasting teaching processes can demonstrate differences in theorisations about learning;
- theories as tools to think with can demonstrate how learning can be thought about and understood in different ways.

INTRODUCTION TO THINKING ABOUT LEARNING

It is challenging to readily define learning because it is a dynamic and ongoing process. It applies to everyday tasks such as cooking, driving or even communicating on social media. It is also integral to leisure pursuits, such as learning how to play a particular sport, speak a new language or learning how to play a musical instrument. In everyday life, we also learn how to manage a household budget to balance income and expenditure at home. Interestingly though, learning is most commonly thought about in relation to specific planned experiences, such as lessons in schools, workshops at college or lectures at university.

Traditionally, learning has been narrowly defined, restricted to concerns focused on academic knowledge and achievements. It is often assumed to include processes which facilitate new accomplishments, attainment or understandings that were believed to be previously lacking or non-existent. Achieving a high class degree, good examination results or performing well in a test, for example, has long been understood and celebrated to be the successful acquisition of knowledge which consequently demonstrates successful learning. These accomplishments have been long regarded as individual intellectual endeavours that are demonstrable and measurable, over time, through formal (and informal) educational assessments of progress. Learning to attain formalised qualifications is highly prescribed and carefully scheduled for in schools, colleges and universities. In these kinds of institutions it is typically organised chronologically and in countries like England it is expected to develop and progress in groups (or classes) of similar aged peers. What is to be learnt has been pre-determined by national or state curricular schemes of work, textbooks or lecture programmes and specified assessment criteria. The guidance for how it is learnt has been strongly underpinned by an assumption that material should be presented by expert teachers to learners, who are expected to absorb and then retrieve or recall the information given to them.

Learning, relating to pre-school or early education, is described by Pritchard (2009) as almost imperceptible. Humans, as babies or young children innately, that is, biologically determined or through actions mimicking others, illustrate what they have learnt. Prichard expresses this kind of development in early childhood as unplanned developmental learning. Learning which appears to happen quite naturally, like a toddler learning how to crawl or feed themselves materialises slowly and incrementally and is not apparent until reflecting back to assess the extent of personal improvements made over a period of time. This perspective assumes that learning is an innate capability and that learning can happen unaided. Interaction with the environment is not acknowledged in this view. Others, however, may see development such as this as experiential learning, that is, the young child interacts with the world around them, adapting to it. A young child presented with a toy rattle, given to them by another, is likely to respond to the noise it makes, grasp the object and even attempt to shake it to re-create the sound. This is an example of the child interacting with the world (or environment) around them.

As a child matures and learns at nursery or primary school though play, learning is often perceived to emerge naturally. The child, like a 'lone scientist' (Alexander 2010: 90), is assumed to learn by interacting with things rather than people. Later in more formalised classroom settings, learning processes involve more direct interaction with the more knowledgeable teacher and learning outcomes are more narrowly focused, with more subject (or skill) specificity. Learning in school is usually designed to achieve very clear academic objectives. Learning in these kinds of classrooms often becomes more highly specialised with teachers providing clear steerage and guidance about what should be learnt. There is also an expectation that learners will interact and work with others in the classroom in a variety of ways to develop knowledge about the subject matter of concern.

Historically, learning was thought to emerge from innate ability, genetically determined, in early life. The educative process was (and still is by many) understood to be pre-dominantly about learning through play whilst children are young, then as they mature and attend school, their learning is directed and shaped by more knowledgeable teachers. Unfettered individual interaction with the environment to learn has been assumed to recede as learning becomes more social in nature as a child progresses through school. This reflects to some extent the nature–nurture debate, whereby the influence of nature recedes as maturation proceeds, and nurturing or directing learning becomes more conspicuous. Those who take the view that behaviours and characteristics are only determined by nature or natural processes (i.e. via inheritance) are known as nativists. The nature–nurture debate is more commonly referred to when discussing the concept of ability and whether it is innate and determines what is possible for an individual to learn. The concept of 'ability' is examined further in Chapter 2.

DEVELOPING A THEORY ABOUT LEARNING THROUGH YOUR PERSONAL EXPERIENCE

Many adults engage in lessons beyond school, for example, when they embark upon being taught to learn to drive. Listening to others' narratives about how they learnt to drive, it becomes clear that individuals think differently about their learning experience. To introduce different ways of thinking about how learning happens, consider how you learnt to drive and successfully pass both the theoretical and practical aspects of your test.

When you learnt to drive and came to understand what the rules of the road were, what kind of learning experiences did you engage in? How did you know what was expected of you? What did you *do* to learn? What did your instructor *do* to help you learn? How did you learn through interaction with others? How did you become knowledgeable about the legalities of driving, develop understanding about how to control a car and hone the skills you needed to become a proficient driver? How did you know you made progress in your learning? How were you judged to finally have passed the theoretical and practical parts of the test?...and how far did passing the test prepare you to become a competent driver in any weather or road conditions?

Your view about how you learnt to drive will differ to others. Consider here two contrasting views from Pritpal and Sally. They each become proficient drivers, but recollections of their experience of learning to drive differ. Their views are offered here, for you, the reader, to think about. Although Pritpal and Sally achieved similar learning outcomes, they perceived they progressed through quite different learning experiences.

Pritpal recollected:

> I just followed what the instructor told me to do and learned by trial and error. I tried doing what I was told and if it didn't work or went wrong I changed it. I remembered things he told me, such as the mirror, signal, maneuver, for example. I also copied what I'd seen him and other drivers do too. When I did something correct he said 'good' or 'well done', so I knew when I had learned something. I wanted to be able to drive well, which meant knowing what the road signs signified and being able to control the car to get from A to B quickly.

Sally recounts:

> I was guided by the instructor. He asked me lots of questions before I carried out any actions. He questioned me about any experience I had handling and driving cars previously. He also asked me what I already knew about the highway code before my lessons began. After each session he asked me what I thought I had learned and what I thought I needed to concentrate on when I practiced in between my lessons. I was fortunate I could practice all my newfound skills driving with my father in his car. I thought good driving was all about arriving safely at the destination you were travelling to.

Although both Sally and Pritpal have achieved passing a standardised national qualification. They each articulated how they learnt quite differently and they both focused on different aspects of the process. They both needed to master motor skills (e.g. managing clutch control and changing gear to increase and decrease the speed of the car), recognise and respond to road signals (e.g. slow down at double dashed lines across the road to give way) and react appropriately to unpredictable happenings (e.g. emergency stop when encountering an obstruction in the road), but they didn't recollect a similar learning experience to achieve similar outcomes.

Task 1.1

Consider Pritpal and Sally's recollections of learning to drive. Think about *how* they indicated they learnt, *what* they particularly noticed about their learning experience and *how* they remembered they were taught (i.e. what their driving instructor did). What do you recollect about your learning to drive experience. Can you sketch a diagram that models how you or they [Pripal and Sally] theorised their experience of learning to drive.

THEORISING ABOUT LEARNING TO DRIVE

In Pritpal's view, he indicates how he thinks learning to become a driver involved mimicking or replicating successful actions (of others) and following his instructor's directions. He appears to hold the instructor's behaviours as exemplary performances that he must emulate. This could arguably be seen as a mastery perspective of achievement. The nature of the interactions between himself as learner and the instructor appears to be asymmetrical, that is, instructions are directed towards him (from the experienced driver) and he passively absorbs and emulates behaviours that are expected. In the process of accumulating the repertoire of consummate actions behind the wheel, he perceives that he has learnt by trial and error and regularly rehearsed what was deemed 'good' by the instructor.

Consider how far Pritpal's view of learning resonates with Ofsted's (2022) view of the quality of education. Ofsted (2022: 13) states,

> teachers present subject matter clearly [...] They check learners' understanding systematically, identify misconceptions accurately and provide clear, direct feedback. In doing so, they respond and adapt their teaching as necessary, without unnecessarily elaborate or differentiated approaches.

Pritpal recalls how he absorbs directions from the instructor and if things didn't work, it was his fault and he must adapt and copy better. He does not question the exemplary performance of his instructor. He appears to assume his instructor's driving performance is what he should aim for. His view of successfully learning to drive appears to include being able to control his car to reach his destination swiftly and remember what road signs represent. Figure 1.1 offers a way of theorising Pritpal's view of his learning.

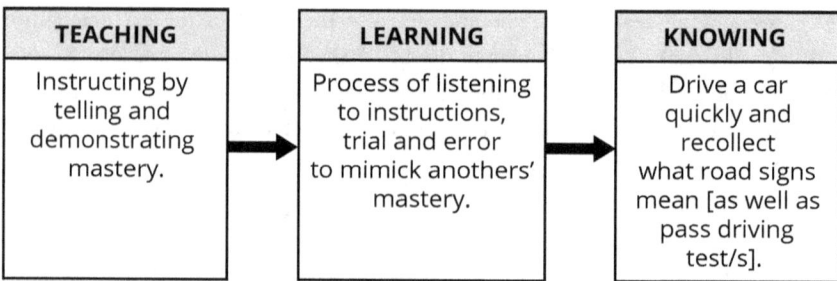

Figure 1.1 The Relational Connections Between Teaching, Learning and Knowing Inferred From Pritpal's Perspective

From Sally's perspective, her recollections highlight how the driving instructor appears to guide rather than constantly direct her about what to do. She indicates there is more discussion, and from her perspective, the process appears not to be as didactic as Pritpal's. The instructor questions her to elicit details about her previous relevant experiences. This indicates the instructor considers that what she already knows (and has done) matters. The second instructor's approach appears to differ to that which Pritpal's tutor advocates. Sally appears to also take some responsibility for practising between lessons. This could indicate that her view is that she needs to experience a wider range of contexts than just those presented in a driving lesson. She also appears to value time behind the steering wheel to build her confidence and competence in driving to arrive safely at her destination.

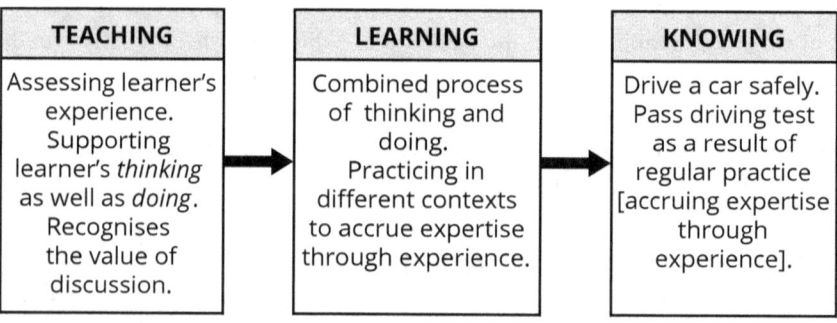

Figure 1.2 The Relational Connections Between Teaching, Learning and Knowing Inferred From Sally's Perspective

Figures 1.1 and 1.2 offer two distinct personalised theories about learning to drive, each informed by inferences from learner's recollected experiences. These models suggest how individuals can theorise about learning by drawing on personal experiences and what appeared to matter to them. These models or views are not necessarily generalisable and applicable to a wide range of learning situations for other people. However, prevailing theories that have been long accepted and widely influenced policy and practice in education *are* presented in the next few chapters of this book.

UNDERPINNING ASSUMPTIONS

A general underpinning assumption applied throughout the book is that learning, knowledge or knowing and pedagogy are inter-connected, and that these related entities affect the nature of practice a teacher enacts. This is because the way learning is theorised necessarily brings with it an associated view about how we come to know something and what that knowing means. Teachers hold views about what they wish to achieve in classrooms (intentions) and adopt particular approaches (e.g. lecturing, demonstrating) to achieve such. Pedagogically, therefore, their approach will be informed by curricular imperatives, learning and assessment activity they think appropriate and the kind of 'manner' (e.g. authoritarian, democratic) they wish to adopt in the classroom. What emerges (as indicated in Figure 1.3) is the practice they enact as the lesson progresses. These three relational aspects, learning, knowledge and pedagogy, consequently inform the teacher's practice that learners experience and are expected to respond to in the classroom.

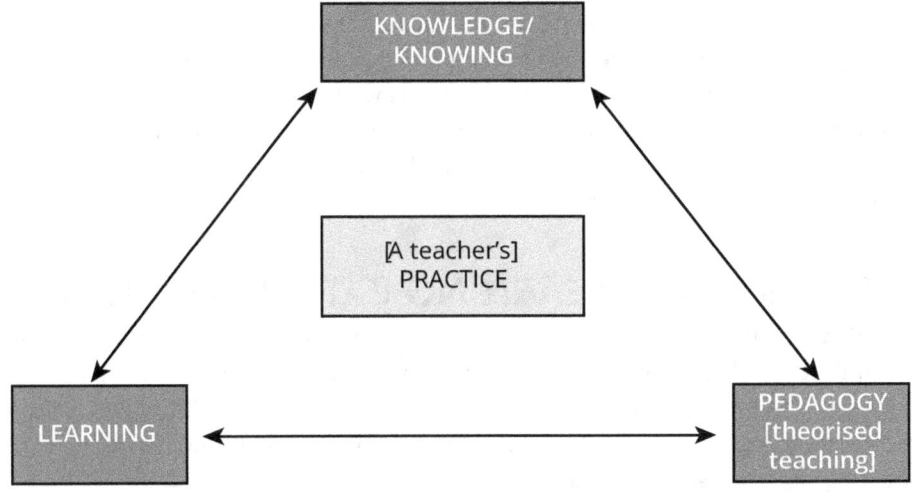

Figure 1.3 Relating Learning, Knowledge, Pedagogy and Practice

WHAT DO STUDENTS SAY ABOUT COMING TO KNOW SOMETHING?

In a recent study of 1,250 undergraduates, Flaherty (2023) suggested that the largest proportion of students in higher education claimed they learnt best and retained information in interactive lectures. That is, they valued specific tasks that required them to actively engage with material they were being lectured about. Although being active might at first suggest to an observer a constructivist approach to learning was being enacted, it very much depends on the nature of the tasks. If the students were practising a particular skill over and over again until they could master it or if they were being asked to discuss in a small group what each individual interpreted from a case study, the learning encouraged could be defined as a behaviourist approach (discussed further in Chapters 2 and 7) or a social constructivist approach (discussed further in Chapters 5 and 9). Without more details of the context, what the teacher did, how the activities were framed, how the students were invited to engage with the tasks and the aspects of learning what was paid attention to by the tutors, it is difficult to discern which theoretical movement (and associated concepts) were enacted in the active phases of the lectures.

Questioning school-aged children, James et al. (2007) carried out surveys to elicit how 1,700 primary and secondary pupils indicated they perrceived they learnt. Depending on the age of the pupils they were asked between 25 and 75 questions. The older pupils (aged 15 years) were given more questions than the youngest pupils (aged 10 years). Included in the surveys were questions that asked them whether they liked to use their own ideas; be told exactly what to do; be given lots of decisions to make about what to do; and be told the answers to questions or work things out for themselves. Findings (Alexander 2010: 148) suggested that children liked challenge, exciting, varied and active 'hands-on' kinds of learning activities. They disliked mundane, repetitive, 'drill-and-practice' tasks. Although the responses to these questions might suggest how pupils generally prefer to learn, it is unclear exactly how a teacher's practices might offer the kinds of experiences valued. With little detail about contexts, the nature of activities and tasks and clarity about the ways that teachers and learners interact it can be difficult to discern which theoretical movements (and associated concepts) were enacted.

OTHER WAYS LEARNING IS TALKED ABOUT

The following descriptions of learning are introduced briefly here and then re-considered later in the book. The following quotations (1-8) are concerned with attempting to define what learning is. Think about how far each of these quotations resonate with your own view about learning and consider how helpful they could be to you as a teacher in ways they suggest how learning arises and how it can be supported.

1 Jarvis (2018: 18) suggests that 'it is the changed person who is the outcome of learning'.
2 Kyriacou (2009: 3) describes three psychological conditions that appear to be crucial for learning as:
   The pupil must be attending to the learning experience;
   The pupil must be receptive to the learning experience;
   The learning experience must be appropriate for the desired learning to take place.

3 James et al. (2007: 3) convey that learning is about 'using knowledge' and 'the ability of people to respond flexibly and creatively to demands for new knowledge, skills and dispositions'.
4 Illeris (2017: 3) describes learning as 'any process that in living organisms leads to a permanent capacity change and which is not solely due to biological maturation or ageing'.
5 Pritchard (2009: ix-x) highlights how 'Learning in schools does not happen by chance, though children will learn many things that are not planned for'. 'Effective learning is [...] lasting and capable of being put to use in new and differing situations'.
6 Allen (2010: 3) describes how learning arises as 'people reflect upon their past life experiences when devising their mental models or constructions. In order for a new fact or concept to make sense it needs to fit in somewhere with an already-established model that has been previously constructed, and if it fails to do so it is less probable that the learner will be able to recall the new information at a later date'.
7 Hodkinson and Macleod (2010: 174) propose that,

> Learning is a conceptual and linguistic construction that is widely used in many societies and cultures, but with very different meanings…..[..] learning does not have a clear physical or reified identity in the world. Rather, learning is a concept constructed and developed by people to label and thus start to explain some complex processes that are important in our lives.

8 Sfard (2016: 333) in defining the most basic form of learning that constitutes the primary goal of schooling suggests it is:

> the process by which one turns into one's own some of the patterns of acting that already exist in society. In this process the learner may become able to perform competently, and on her own accord, such historically shaped activities as preparing food, dressing, communicating with others, solving mathematical problems or doing biological research. If we think about learning in this way, *interactions with people come to the fore as the primary source of learning.*

Task 1.2

Consider your own learning in and out of school and consider how far it resonated with the views described above? How helpful are these views for you in thinking about your own personal theories of learning?

Each author, above, emphasises different aspects of learning. Some accentuate the biological influence or the psychology (the cognitive) aspect, whereas others highlight interaction with the environment or others. Many see these various influences on learning as related and inseparable.

THINKING FURTHER ABOUT HOW LEARNING IS TALKED ABOUT

Thinking about how others describe learning can help you discern what you consider it is and is not. The different questions posed below are presented to help you consider what resonates (or not) with your personal theory of learning.

Jarvis's (2018) quotation signals how it is an individual's experience in the world that changes them in some way that consequently results in learning. He discusses, too, how learning can involve adapting to your environment and that resultant changes can be cognitive, emotional or practical in nature. This perspective is considered further in Chapters 3 and 8.

> **Question for Consideration 1.1**
>
> Does learning arise through direct experience or is reflection required?

This resonates with Kyriacou's view of learning which he defines as 'changes in a learner's behaviour or observable actions which take place as a result of being engaged in an educational experience' (Kyriacou 2009: 22). He subsequently discusses distinctions between reception and discovery learning, as well as rote and meaningful learning. These contrasting perspectives are considered further in Chapters 2, 3, 7 and 8.

> **Question for Consideration 1.2**
>
> Is learning only evidenced through observable changes in actions?

James et al. (2007) argue that prior knowledge is important. They acknowledge that what is already known (or previously learnt) is important, as well as being able to respond flexibly, seek out new information and ways of doing things. These ideas are explored further in Chapters 3 and 8.

> **Questions for Consideration 1.3**
>
> What are the implications for teachers if learner's prior knowledge is to be taken account of?

Illeris (2009) highlights that learning may be biological and psychological, that is, what is genetically inherited or biologically determined matters as well as what happens in the mind too. Quotations i, ii and iii do not emphasise to the same extent that what goes on in the head is important. Illeris implies that learning is what arises over and above normal maturation (which Pritchard has suggested is more gradual, such that it is almost imperceptible in early childhood).

Questions for Consideration 1.4

Is learning the result of only biological mechanisms?

Illeris's view suggests that learning is a permanent capacity advancement which arises through intervention or augmentation of natural maturational processes. His view indicates he sees learning as a change in being. This view of learning emphasises the long-term changes in the head, that is, learning as a psychological phenomenon. Long-held views have endured that resonate with Illeris's view about individual's psychological processes leading to knowledge acquisition. Often described, as Kyriacou outlines, in a straightforward, three-phase view of learning:

I   Transmission (training, teaching, inculcation)
II Input (storage in memory, internalisation of what's transmitted)
III Retrieval and transfer to problem-solving in new situations.

This linear view about learning and the implications for practice are discussed further in Chapters 2 and 7.

Questions for Consideration 1.5

How can learning become robust and transferable with such a simple model?...what are the implications for teaching?

Pritchard (2009) recognises the long-term process of learning that begins well before anyone starts school and continues throughout life after school. He explains how effective learning is not fleeting; it is concerned with gaining knowledge or how to do something and is sufficiently robust to be practically applied to fresh or existing situations.

Questions for Consideration 1.6

If learning requires both the mind and body, what does this mean for teachers?

Jarvis (2018) does not specifically highlight learning as happening only in the head, but that it effects a transformation in the whole person. He expands on this view to say that 'Human learning is the combination of processes throughout a lifetime whereby the whole person – body and mind – experiences social situations, the perceived content of which is then transformed cognitively, emotionally or practically or through any combination and integrated into the individual person's biography resulting in a continually changing or more experienced person' (Jarvis 2018: 19). This additional perspective from Jarvis extends the previous views to acknowledge the importance of both the body and mind and that learning should be able to be practically applied to different contexts and enable learners to act appropriately in new situations. These ideas are explored further in Chapters 5, 6, 9 and 10.

Questions for Consideration 1.7

To what extent is learning a physical phenomenon?

The range of views considered so far highlight biological and the psychological influences on learning. Hodkinson and Macloed (2010) consider further learning as a phenomenon that doesn't have a physical reality. They also discuss the difficulty in conceptualising a commonly held view of learning. They and Sfard (2016) indicate how learning emerges through different kinds of activities involving social interaction. It is the way that different folks, engaged in varied activities, talk about it that bring it into existence and reify what is valued through dialogic (and actional) exchanges. This is in contrast to the earlier descriptions of learning which imply learning clearly does physically exist *and* involves the body, biological mechanisms and something a little less tangible that is more psychological and includes the brain. Purposely, the perspectives offered here raise dilemmas about *what* learning *is* as well as *where* and *how* it *occurs*.

EXPERIENCES OF LEARNING DEPICTED BY METAPHORS

To help you understand how experiences of learning can be characterised differently, two metaphors are offered here for consideration. These metaphors are described and explained so that you can then consider whether they are useful in helping you discern how you have learnt various things in school or even mastered driving.

As Sfard (1998) explains, metaphors offer a way of using everyday language to talk about a concept in a systematic way. The concept concerned may be rather complex, like learning, so metaphors can utilise everyday life experiences to communicate about such sophisticated ideas. To introduce symbolic or representative metaphors as a way of thinking about learning, consider the following descriptions that Sfard (1998: 5) provides regarding two distinct views of learning. She adopts an acquisition metaphor (AM) and a participation metaphor (PM) to emphasise particular characteristics of contrasting perspectives of learning processes. Consider how they offer you another way of thinking about Pritpal and Sally's views of learning to drive.

Acquisition Metaphor

This is presented as related to the act of gaining knowledge. Learning in this metaphor assumes concepts are mentally accumulated (like wealth or material goods), personally owned or grasped, accrued in one's cognitive structures. That is, it is concerned with gaining possession over a commodity such as knowledge or a range of concepts. Traditionally, this has been held as a widely accepted view. This perspective of learning as *having*, contrasts with the PM, related to *doing* and *knowing*.

Participation Metaphor

This alternate perspective embraces entities such as reflection, dialogue, collaboration and community of enquiry. This metaphor embraces 'knowing', rather than acquiring abstract facts, indicating the ongoing nature of 'learning activity that is not considered separately from the context in which it takes place' (p. 6). Learners in this metaphor are assumed to engage with others to learn, that is learning as participation is implied (Table 1.1).

Table 1.1 Summary of Metaphoric Mappings

Concept	Acquisition Metaphor (AM)	Participation Metaphor (PM)
Learner	Recipient	Apprentice
Learning	Acquisition of something	Becoming a participant
Teacher	Provider or facilitator	Expert participant, preserver of practice/discourse

Source: Adapted from Sfard (1998: 7).

Reflecting back on Pritpal and Sally's recollections of learning and the quotations i-viii, do these metaphors help you think about the ways that others think about learning differently?

You might consider how Pritpal described his experience as one which resonates more with the AM whereas Sally's recollections about learning resonate a little more closely with the PM. In both cases, however, we are inferring from a limited amount of data and we would really need more information about the context, the nature of dialogic exchanges, the ways that the instructors supported learning to drive as well as Pritpal and Sally's responses before we could discern more exactly the extent to which either metaphor was enacted.

The use of metaphors is continued throughout the book to help you as a reader to think about learning from different perspectives. There are also more detailed excerpts, in Part 2, that are narratively construed from moments in practice that can enable you to consider which metaphor might be appropriate to help you think about learning differently in that particular educational situation.

INTERPRETING VIEWS ABOUT LEARNING

The Office of Qualifications and Examinations Regulator (Ofqual 2021) published a review of their research about learning in England during the pandemic. They indicated that they were concerned with 'the scale and nature of learning losses' and the ways that 'barriers' had prevented learning. These 'losses in learning' reported by the Office for Standards in Education (Ofsted 2020) differed across primary, secondary and special schools. The 'recovery curriculum' (Ofsted 2020), however, was noted to mean different things across schools and phases. Reading, phonics and mathematics were noted to be of concern in primary education and language and communication were priority in special schools. Secondary school heads reported a focus on 'important building blocks' for each subject, dropping 'option' subjects, prioritising what could not be taught effectively through remote learning and even extending teaching time for examination classes to 'catch-up with their learning'.

> **Task 1.3**
>
> How can the AM and PM metaphor help you discern the assumptions about learning in these comments?

Drawing on the metaphors introduced to think about the ways that national bodies or educational organisations discuss learning can be helpful to better understand the views of the policymakers. Talking about 'losses' in learning conveys a view that learning is understood as knowledge acquisition (Sfard 1998) and that learning does not happen outside of a formal school situation. There appears to be an assumption that learning processes are concerned with accruing concepts and knowledge. So communicating subject matter is understood to be unproblematic as students (or learners) are seen as collectors of information. Teachers considering how they act in classrooms to facilitate or enable either AM or PM learning can consider these alternate theoretical ways of looking at their practice to reflect on what they are doing that affects the processes their students are engaged in. The AM and PM metaphors in full are a little more complex than outlined here, but it is suffice to say they offer a theoretical perspective about learning that can help teachers 'see' their practice differently and consider whether and how they may wish to change it. As Sfard (2016: 326) explains, metaphors can be used as a discursive device to objectify actions. Reporting on what kind of 'online' learning was possible (Ofqual 2021) during the pandemic and the kinds of activities engaged in 'offline', they suggested that without access to electronic devices, the internet and a quiet study space at home, 'there were still many [students] who were not able to access their learning'. Reflecting on these kinds of statements, and applying Sfard's AM and PM metaphors, you can begin to 'see' what assumptions can be inferred about the way that learning is talked about by Ofqual and others. Later in the book, you are invited to consider how the ways that curriculum documents are written reveal different theoretical perspectives, whether implicit or explicit, that inform what is valued knowledge. The inferences from these kinds of documents are also discussed to convey how students are assumed to learn and what being educated means.

The intention of this book, therefore, is to invite you, the reader, to think about learning by applying theoretical movements (associated metaphors and concepts) to make sense of the process from different perspectives. Applying different theories or concepts that have been adopted over time can provide educators with alternate ways to interpret what national policies, curricular resources and everyday people assume about learning and learners.

SUMMARY

This chapter began by introducing personalised views of learning, particularly learning to drive. You were invited to consider ways of beginning to theorise about the learning process. A wide range of different views about learning were introduced to you to demonstrate the variations in ideas held by others. The series of quotations presented suggest how defining such a complex process is not straight forward, but presents dilemmas for educators about *how* and *where* learning arises. The idea of metaphors was introduced to offer everyday ways of thinking about the nature of learning, how it is talked about and understood.

In Chapter 2, theories of learning centred on behaviourism and information processing are considered and two particular questions that challenge assumptions about learning and learners are discussed:

- What kind of knowledge is valued?
- How far do these approaches prepare learners for the variety of things they need to learn in life?

ADDITIONAL READING

Illeris, K. (2018) *Contemporary Theories of learning*. Learning theorists in their own words. Abingdon: Routledge.

This book provides a rich collection of chapters written by various theorists about their views of learning. The theorists include Engestrom, Merriam, Hattie, Donoghue, Gardner, Bruner, Usher, Wenger and Biesta, amongst others.

Sfard, A. (1998) On Two Metaphors for Learning and the Dangers of Choosing Just One. *Educational Researcher*, 27(2).

This article argues why metaphors help understanding more abstract ideas in learning. The two contrasting metaphors discussed demonstrate how two distinctive perspectives of learning are characterised differently.

Rogoff, B. (1999) Cognitive Development through Social Interaction: Vygotsky and Piaget. in Murphy, P. (ed) *Learners, Learning & Assessment*. London: Paul Chapman & Open University pp. 69-82.

This chapter provides an excellent discussion introducing the contrasting Piagetian and Vygotskian theories of learning and the differences in the social aspects of their views. This chapter offers useful prior reading for the next few chapters.

REFERENCES

Allen, M. (2010) *Misconceptions in Primary Science*. Maidenhead: Open University Press.

Alexander, R. (2010) *Children, Their World, Their Education*. London: Routledge.

Flaherty, C. (2023) How college students say they learn best. Available at https://www.insidehighered.com/news/2023/04/05/survey-how-college-students-say-they-learn-best. Accessed 20/05/24.

Hodkinson, P. & Macloed, F. (2010) Contrasting concepts of learning and contrasting research methodologies: Affinities and bias. *British Educational Research Journal*, 36(2), 173–189.

Illeris, K. (2009) *Contemporary Theories of Learning* London: Routledge.

Illeris, K. (2017) *How We Learn: Learning and Non-learning in School and beyond*. London: Routledge.

Illeris, K. (2018) *Contemporary Theories of Learning*. Abingdon: Routledge.

James, M., McCormick, R., Black, P., Carmichael, P., Drummond, M-J., Fox, A., MacBeath, J., Marshall, B., Pedder, R., Swaffield, S., Swann, J., and William, D. (2007) *Learning How to Learn*. Classrooms, schools and networks. Routledge: Abingdon.

Jarvis, M. (2018) Learning to be a person in society. Learning to be me. In K. Illeris (Ed) *Contemporary Theories of Learning*. London: Routledge.

Kyriacou, C. (2009) *Effective Teaching in Schools Theory and Practice*. Cheltenham: Nelson Thornes.

Ofqual (2021) *Learning during the Pandemic: Review of Research from England*. Available at https://www.gov.uk/government/publications/learning-during-the-pandemic/learning-during-the-pandemic-review-of-research-from-england

Ofsted (2020) *Covid-19 Series: Briefing on Schools September 2020*. Available at www.gov.uk/ofsted

Ofsted (2022) *Education Inspection Framework*. July 2022. Available at www.gov.uk/ofsted

Pritchard, A. (2009) *Ways of Learning*. 2nd ed. Abingdon: Routledge.

Sfard, A. (1998) In two metaphors for learning and the dangers of choosing just one. *Educational Researcher*, 27(2), 4–13.

Sfard, A. (2016) An interview with Anna Sfard. In Ane Qvortrup, Merete Wiberg, Gerd Christensen & Mikala Hansbel (Eds) *On the Definition of Learning*. University Press of Southern Denmark.

PART 1
INTRODUCING THEORIES OF LEARNING

INTRODUCTION

This part of the book presents five chapters (2–6) that introduce the nature and origins of long-held theories of learning. Each theoretical movement is introduced with an historical dimension that explains for the reader how the ideas came into existence. Within each chapter the key aspects associated with it are described and explained. Chapter 2, for example, focuses on behaviourism and ways that learners are characterised as passive receivers, their ability is assumed to be innate, they learn by reacting to the environment and their learning involves forming habits. These features and those of an information processing theory are substantiated from research evidence. Chapter 3 introduces constructivism and the agentive mind informed predominantly, but not solely, by Piagetian theorising. Chapter 4 bridges between constructivism and social constructivism by identifying the way that language and meaning making are more prominent in a Vygotskian theory of learning. Chapter 5 introduces features of social constructivism and socioculturalism including differential views of the zone of proximal development, for example. Chapter 6 considers further social aspects of learning including situated learning, communities of practice, identity and agency across different cultural settings. In each chapter the discussion highlights important features of each of the enduring theories that still prevail today and are regularly mentioned in educational literature (across the domains of policy, practice and research). The discussion also presents how in professional and academic literature the characterisations of these theories are often assumed or only some features are paid attention to. It is not always made explicit, either, in educational policies and materials related to educators' practices exactly which aspect of a theory is being drawn from and how. General educational discourse that centres on theorising learning is often not clear. It is often ambiguous and inaccessible for teachers such that they are often challenged to think about the complexity of learning and the influence/s of their practice on learners. In this part of the book, however, the theories are clearly explained, referenced and illustrated so that readers can begin to understand them and consider how they might be informative to think about development of their practice.

2
INTRODUCING BEHAVIOURISM AND INFORMATION-PROCESSING THEORIES

CONTENTS

Talking About Learning and Mind	21
Theorising Teaching: Relating Pedagogy and Practice	24
A Science of Behaviour	25
The Emergence of the 'Conditioned Learner'	26
Behaviourist Teaching – The 'Controller' of Learning and Knowledge	27
The Emergence of the Passive Imitative Learner	28
Behaviourist and Transmission Views of Knowledge	30
From Behaviourism to Information Processing	33
Implications for Practice	35
Theories About Ability	35
Comparing Features of Behaviourist and Information-Processing Theories of Learning	39
Summary	40
Additional Reading	41
References	41

Chapter Aims

After reading Chapter 2, you will have considered:

- how people talk in the everyday about learning and mind including your personal experiences of this;
- behaviourist theories of learning and how they characterise teaching;
- the relationships between behaviourist and information-processing theories of learning and mind;
- the relationship between theories of ability and behaviourist and information-processing theories;
- how aspects of theories endure and continue to influence policy and practice.

Mercer (1995) describes theories as simplified explanatory models used by people to make sense of a complex world. The role of theories in helping 'make sense' is central to the aims of the book. Mercer argues that whilst theories simplify real life, they can also help us 'see the wood for the trees' (Mercer 1995, p. 64). This chapter and Chapters 3-6 that follow begin to consider how ways of theorising learning have also led to different ways of understanding and guiding practice, enabling teachers to develop a critical awareness of what they do. The chapters distinguish between theories about learning, which are developed by theorists to explain and generalise about learning beyond the here and now and are explicit in articulating concepts and relationships between them, and those theories that each and every one of us develops to make sense of the world. The former are developed through researching into human behaviours and activities. The latter, often referred to as intuitive or 'folk theories' (Bruner 1996), are developed by people based on their experience of being in the world.

In looking at theories and analysing policy and practice, the chapters use the relational framework offered in Chapter 1, where theories of learning and of knowledge and pedagogy are linked. *Epistemology* is the term used to describe theories about how we come to know what we know. It is the study of our coming to understand the world as we do. These theories try to explain such questions as what is knowledge, how do we know things, are there different kinds of knowledge and what kinds of knowledge enable us to act productively. *Ontological* theories are concerned with what we understand about the social and physical world. As Thomas (2009) puts it, ontology is concerned with:

> The kinds of things that we assume to exist in the world and how those things should be viewed and studied...[Ontology] helps us to understand that there are different ways of viewing the world. (Thomas 2009: 86)

Theories about existence or being (ontology) that are relevant to educational enquiry concern how we understand learners and what should be studied in the process of supporting learning. Differences and similarities in ontological and epistemological positions between theories and within policy and practice and how they relate to theories of teaching – *pedagogy* – will be identified throughout the chapters in this book.

Behaviourist theories about the nature of the human mind have been very influential in the past and continue to shape policy and practice in current educational settings. This theory over time has become related to some pervasive views about learners. What is often neglected when using these ideas to describe learners and how to teach them is the theoretical roots of these core ideas and this is what the chapter explores.

TALKING ABOUT LEARNING AND MIND

> Question for Consideration 2.1
>
> How do I talk about learning?

In Chapter 1, we discussed how people recognise learning in quite simple ways, such as when a certificate for a qualification is achieved or when they can do something that they could not do before. In schools, this can be achieving right answers, but if students are not sure how they got the answer or why they got a high mark, it is often not clear to them just what that learning might be. As one 16-year-old student described her experience:

> ...I was so surprised with how well I did. If I got that [grade] when I don't seem to understand anything, then I wonder what I would have been like if I would have had set [ability] teaching so that I could have come with all 'As' in all of them [subjects]! (Sharp 2003, unpublished thesis)

This observation reflects how little marks or grades convey to learners about the achievements that lie behind them. It also hints at how students see decisions by others about their ability affecting what is possible for them to learn and achieve.

> Question for Consideration 2.2
>
> How do I recognise when I have learnt?

There is also much 'learning' that is not recognised. Successfully cooking a new recipe, for example, or setting up and using a new mobile phone. You could add to the list just by thinking of things you have 'managed' in your daily life over the last few weeks. These may not be recognised because they are not seen as significant or valued as *academic* learning; they are just things anyone can learn to do. Hodkinson and Macleod (2010) in Chapter 1 describe learning as a 'conceptual and linguistic structure' that is widely used across cultures and societies. This suggests common terms or linguistic structures are used by all people, but meanings differ because what is valued as knowledge differs across cultures and societies (pp. 174-5). Varied forms of knowledge and ways of doing things are considered more or less important than others (discussed throughout this book) and some of these may appear more difficult to achieve. Consideration of who is involved and how suggests that learning becomes talked about in terms of status and effort, and importantly, in terms of which people are associated with it.

D'Abreu and Cline (2003) refer to this as the social value attached to roles and activities. In their research study, they used pictures to represent different social practices and different people engaged in them. They found that the schoolchildren in their study assumed maths was important in a shop assistant's job but not at all important in a taxi driver's job, even though both roles shared the need to exchange money for services or goods: the activity and the person influenced their judgements. One 11-year-old Pakistani boy explained why he thought a man in one of the pictures was good at maths:

> Because look at him [office administrator], all wearing flashy clothes and like he looks like a rich....and he's got such a good job, and him, he's ...nothing he has to do taxi Like if he ain't good at something he'd have been like him [taxi driver], like he's probably not good at anything. (De Abreu and Cline 2003: 23)

One of the points De Abreu and Cline (2003) make is that living in a society, people become accustomed to what learning means through the values accorded to different things.

An important, but often unacknowledged, attribute of learning is the lack of physical reality and this influences how it is talked about and how people come to understand it (Hodkinson and Macleod 2010). Words and phrases are used to project meanings for learning and these become part of 'taken-for-granted' shared meanings in daily conversations. For example, when someone is referred to as 'brainy' or a 'brain box', it is generally understood to mean that they are good at school learning.

Questions for Consideration 2.3

Where do I think?
What helps me think?
How do I know what I know?
Can I keep on learning?
What might limit me learning?

In Task 2.1, you are asked to reflect on these 'taken-for-granted' phrases used to describe learning and to think about the meanings associated with each.

Task 2.1

When you think of the 'brain', what do you imagine?
When you think of 'mind', what do you imagine?
Think of phrases where 'brain' and 'mind' are used to describe something about learning or its absence.

Discussion about the 'brain' is often taken to indicate the *potential for learning*. When the word is invoked, it is often about this potential or its lack and so 'brainy' is applied to describe significant academic achievement. Having a 'brainstorm' suggests that someone is thinking creatively and effectively. When actions are described as 'brainless', it suggests someone has acted without thinking. The brain has a physical reality frequently portrayed in pictures, in text books and in posters on walls of classrooms. It is, therefore, commonly where learning and thinking are imagined to happen and where knowledge is thought to reside. The brain has been, and continues to be, a source of explanations or theories about learning. In the 19th century, for example, brain size became the focus of research to justify the belief in male superiority and the male domination of public life from which most women were excluded. It was also the case that male brains were found to be about 10% larger than female brains. However, brain size was found not to predict achievement. In addition, research into sex differences demonstrated more similarities than differences between the capabilities of males and females (Halpern, 2000; Gipps and Murphy 1994). As a consequence, interest in the correlation between brain size and ability to learn, that is, 'the how much brain' explanation or theory of learning, faded. Yet there are still popular books published that imply significant biological differences between men and women. For example, 'Why men don't iron' and 'Men are from Mars and Women are from Venus'.

Another word perhaps more widely used every day as we talk about learning and thinking is 'mind'. These are some of the everyday expressions where the word 'mind' is used:

'mind your step'; 'make your mind up'; 'mind over matter';
'I'm mindful of what you say'; 'I hope you don't mind'; 'what I have in mind';
'he has lost his mind'; it blew his mind'; 'free your mind';
'I am in two minds'; 'a meeting of minds'; 'you don't know your own mind';
'my mind is working like clockwork'; 'it's at the back of my mind'.

These phrases all suggest something about a person that is not physical but is conscious and guides actions. 'Mind' is a metaphor for something that cannot be seen and is commonly used to describe something about how human nature and existence are understood, which distinguishes people from other animals. The notion of 'mind' tends to be used in talk about the 'brain', assumed to be in action as it 'learns' (Lave 1988; Wertsch 1991). For Bruner (1996: 8). A theory of mind to be useful educationally should contain some specification for 'how its functioning can be improved or altered in some significant way'. This idea of the usefulness of theories is something that will be returned to throughout the book. How mind, its location and relation to the brain, is understood will influence what theories of learning you have sympathy with and what kind of teacher you aspire to be or might wish others to be. 'Beliefs' if not made explicit and available for reflection may unconsciously shape what you think and other teachers or practitioners do. Consequently, practice may not realise teaching intentions and there may be unintended consequences for learning (Grady et al. 2010).

THEORISING TEACHING: RELATING PEDAGOGY AND PRACTICE

Pedagogy involves the beliefs and theories of teaching and is distinguished in this book from *practice* which involves putting those beliefs and theories into action with learners to achieve particular ends. Pedagogy reflects the thinking behind teachers' intentions, whereas practice is what emerges as those intentions are enacted with learners. It was mentioned before how beliefs can unconsciously shape what teachers do, but as a school student once yourself, you might well remember how your peers, other students, can influence and change teachers' intentions. This will happen whether purposive or not because the students will bring to lessons their own beliefs and expectations about learning, which will affect the ways they participate and respond to teachers and others in the classroom.

An example of this was observed in an English lesson where the task for the 14- to 15-year-olds was to write three novel openings from a range of genres (Murphy and Ivinson 2005). In one of the classroom events, the teacher took time for selected students to read out examples of their writing, these students were mainly girls, and many of their examples were in the romance genre. Directing the girls to read out their examples was one way the teacher modelled what was a 'good' response; it also legitimised the girls' choices. Yet the boys typically avoided the romance genre. In talking to the students about their choices, the following boys' explanations reflect how other students influence what they feel able to do:

> Lawrence: because if you like something [the piece of writing] that is [judged] not good and it is bad but he's tried it as a Romantic novel and it is pretty bad and the girls think it is bad then they [the girls] are going to think that he didn't have any clue at all about relationships and the boys are going to crack up at him and they are just going to really, really embarrass him.

> James: I think it's harder to write about real things because if you were writing about them, then if people read them they would like know what your thoughts were about, things that were actually happening to you. But if it just a fantasy thing it is not going to reveal anything unless you want to reveal it. (Murphy and Ivinson 2005, 194-5)

The boys typically produced writing about 'adventure', 'crime' and 'horror'. So rather than extending their engagement with different 'genres', the teacher's intended task was reformulated with other students in mind and most boys stuck to what was familiar and safe. Findings such as these are why we distinguish between pedagogic intention and what emerges when it is enacted in settings with students, that is, *practice*. It is also important to note that not all boys or girls will react to their peers in the same way, so their subjective views about their experience of practice will vary. The means used by teachers to enact their pedagogy are often referred to as methods, or *practices*, such as group work, brainstorming and demonstration, for example.

Teaching is about enabling learning. How this role is imagined by individuals suggests something important about how learning and learners are understood. There are many theories of learning, but few theories of teaching as these are typically implied by the former. To characterise approaches to teaching Guy Claxton (1990) offered a number of metaphors to represent what teachers do.

A *metaphor* is helpful for carrying meaning(s) from one context to another. It can highlight an important similarity between apparently quite different things.

Task 2.2

When you think about, teaching how would you characterise the role to someone else?
Can you think of a metaphor that sums it up for you? This can reflect either your experience of being a teacher or your experience of being taught and what, if you are starting out as a teacher, you imagine yourself becoming.

In this chapter and the four following chapters, you will have opportunities to consider how your characterisation or metaphor for teaching aligns with different theories of learning. In this chapter, the focus is on behaviourist theories of learning and how teaching is characterised within it. The section continues by relating behaviourist characterisations of teaching to current pedagogical approaches.

A SCIENCE OF BEHAVIOUR

The origins of theoretical perspectives on learning are often attributed to the ancient greeks. However, Behaviourism or learning theory took hold in educational thinking when scientific enquiry came into ascendancy. Scientific enquiry had been disallowed and devalued and held no place in universities and school curricula for many centuries. It wasn't until the Clarendon Commission in 1864, for example, that some science was introduced into the public school curriculum in England (Ivinson and Murphy 2007). What altered the position of science was the rapid growth of technological development in the 16th and 17th centuries in the drive to access the earth's resources and combat the devastating effects of natural disasters and disease. In the United Kingdom (and beyond), these directed human enquiry towards finding the means to control the outside world. The discourse about science that emerged at this time invoked notions about nature being constrained and controlled by man for the human good (Ivinson and Murphy 2007: 18). Scientists in this discourse were represented as heroic figures who used the scientific method to create true knowledge. Later in the 18th century, technological developments enabled the beginnings of mass production of goods (through the invention of the steam engine, the coming of the railways and the construction of factories). A little after this, aligned with evolutionary thinking, Darwin's *On the Origin of Species* was published in 1859, which suggested that humans were not radically different from other animals. This reinforced the possibilities and indeed the need to apply scientific enquiry to understand human learning. This view that scientific enquiry is the best way of establishing rigorous and generalisable findings about learning continues to dominate educational policy construction and the funding of educational research (see for example Hammersley 2007; Ellis and Moss 2014; Edovald and Nevill 2020).

Many commentators describe how psychology 'lost its mind' when influenced by scientific ways of looking at the world (Richardson 1998: 2). Applying scientific enquiry to human learning justified a shift away from trying to understand 'inner knowledge and mental functions' (Richardson 1998: 50) as these were unobservable and unverifiable, both important requirements of scientific research. A scientific approach to learning, as it was then understood, legitimised behaviourists' methods which entailed looking at observable behaviours in animals and how to control them and extrapolating from these findings to generalise about human behaviours and learning. Human learning and development were reduced to 'conditioning'. Classical conditioning emerged from Pavlov's work with dogs. In 1927, he demonstrated how dogs could be conditioned, that is, learn to associate a ringing bell with food and to salivate eventually on just the ringing of the bell. Other research developed from Pavlov's work across a range of animal species looking at a wide variety of behavioural responses that were conditioned to many types of stimuli and reinforced in different ways. The intention was to find laws about the most effective way to produce and sustain learning that applied across species to develop a science of behaviour. Behaviourism or learning theory with its roots in biology brought to the fore biological explanations for how people learn.

THE EMERGENCE OF THE 'CONDITIONED LEARNER'

Skinner (1968) in his work introduced 'operant conditioning' as he found that shaping animal behaviour to produce a particular response and to maintain it involved a complex relationship between response and reinforcement. He argued that for teaching to be effective, teachers needed to use 'schedules of reinforcement' that focused on what children know and can learn rather than the focus of the education system as he saw it on what children do not know and cannot do (Skinner 1968). This view suggests that schoolchildren's potential to learn could be judged by what they were successfully conditioned to do. Failure is attributed to the learner, but what was made available for them to learn was also limited.

> **Questions for Consideration 2.4**
>
> Do people want to learn?
> Is it part of being human?
> What motivates people to learn?

The mind and its complex processes were unacknowledged by behaviourists. They assumed that if rewards and sanctions determine human development, the mind functions purely by association between ideas which over time operate automatically. This mechanistic view of mind reinforces the view that students need *extrinsic motivation* and positions them as *passive* in the learning process.

The metaphors and ways of understanding teaching discussed next can be related to behaviourist theories to varying degrees. They share commonalities about learners, learning and knowledge and how teaching is understood.

BEHAVIOURIST TEACHING – THE 'CONTROLLER' OF LEARNING AND KNOWLEDGE

Two related metaphors for the teacher that closely align with behaviourist theories of learning, where humans are not distinguished from other animals in the way they learn, are those of the *sculptor* and *lion tamer*. These metaphors position learners as raw material to be shaped, tamed and disciplined. The belief that a goal of education was to discipline young people can be traced back to the roots of education when it was controlled by the Church.

> **Questions for Consideration 2.5**
>
> Is learning only about thinking and not doing?
> Does it happen just inside the head?

Disciplining the body was an essential aspect of education for the male elite to free the mind from bodily concerns in order to think, creating the longstanding hierarchy and divide between theory and practice and mind and body, respectively. This relates to the widely used everyday phrase 'mind over matter' where the 'mind' can overcome physical limitations like an athlete or a mountaineer.

For schoolchildren, behaviourism put into practice by a teacher as a *sculptor* or *lion tamer* (applying the metaphors) suggests how learning is about 'forming habits' and more complex learning occurs as these habits, reflexes, become linked. Biological, or genetic, learning potential determines which learners acquire the most links and, therefore, which achieve the most useful and valued knowledge and skills.

The learner in these metaphors must be motivated by external factors or stimuli, the crack of the whip and the reward of the pork chop for the lion or the stick and the carrot for the student. This is what is meant when motivation for learning is explained in theories of learning as being *extrinsic* to the learner. In behaviourism, learners react to the environment, the stimulus, and through the practices of *drill* and *repetition* they learn. Teachers, in this view, have all the responsibility as well as the control of learning as they create the conditions for learning, maintain learners' motivation and keep them on task.

THE EMERGENCE OF THE PASSIVE IMITATIVE LEARNER

Behaviourism declined in influence in the second half of the 20th century, but as Wood (1998) notes, Skinner's work spawned a 'vast technology of experimental studies of learning' (Wood 1998: 4). Such a legacy does not disappear; it shapes educational thinking and can be seen to resurface in numerous ways in:

- the practices that are considered effective for learning for some children;
- how learners are understood and positioned in classrooms and lecture halls;
- how knowledge is understood to be structured and acquired.

Traces of behaviourism can be seen in certain enduring practices. For example, in Askew et al.'s (1997) research into effective teaching of numeracy, teachers whose practice reflected a belief in rote learning particularly for some children were identified. For example, Elizabeth, talking about her children aged 9-11 years old, explained how she dealt with children experiencing difficulties in learning maths:

> A lot of them learn by rote ...one who needs extra help, I will stand behind him when he is doing it and actually work with him for a long time long time....so they [the weakest] get a lot more of my help. Minus minus something really, I teach it by rote... (Askew et al. 1997: 40-1)

It is through drill and repetition that basic skills are believed to combine to make a more complex whole. This is what Claxton refers to as the 'switchboard' view of the mind (Claxton 1990). The more often the links occur, the stronger the association between them. This view of mind is implied in policies that advocate that basic skills must be acquired first. This belief underlies the rationale for the current focus on phonics in literacy lessons for schoolchildren aged 4 to 6 years old in England (Ellis and Moss 2014; National Reading Panel 2000).

Another legacy of behaviourism is the continuing belief that the:

- teacher 'controls' learning;
- learners are *passive imitators* in the teaching and learning process;
- learning is a process of inputting knowledge and skills from teacher to student.

In this view, the teacher has agency, that is, the capacity to act to structure learning resources and habitualise ways of learning. The learner receives 'knowledge' imparted by the teacher. Teaching as *transmission pedagogy* is characterised by a number of related metaphors. The metaphor of the teacher as *petrol pump attendant* (Claxton 1990) represents knowledge, as the petrol, pouring forth from the teacher, the expert and controller of the flow. In this representation of teaching, *the learner is the passive recei*ver like the car, and *the teacher* is the *source of knowledge*. These passive learners must orientate themselves towards the teacher and make what they think and do *contingent* upon the teacher's thinking and intentions (Wood 1998: 204).

Implied in this metaphor is that the location of learning is the *brain*, represented as the petrol tank. The predominant teaching process in this metaphor is the handing over or *transmission of knowledge* which is uncontested and unchanging. This view of knowledge as *pre-given* or *pre-determined* stems from Platonic views that knowledge was derived from God and was 'brought out' for learners through education. Transmission views of learning, which overlap with a behaviourist perspective, assume an *input–output view of the teaching and learning proce*ss, rather than stimulus-response conditioning. A slight modification of the image of the teacher as *petrol pump attendant* recognises that the knowledge to be handed over must be transformed in some ways to make it more accessible for learners *prior* to input. This is the teacher as the *parent bird*, regurgitates knowledge broken down into forms that the learner can 'manage'. Here the teacher's role is more demanding as the knowledge out there must be interpreted, but there is still the sense of an input-output view of the teaching and learning process.

What is shared between behaviourism and transmission pedagogy is the view of the passive imitative learner, the reduction of the teaching learning process and the continuing belief that human development and learning follow a biologically pre-determined path. The role of the environment and nurturing does not influence or alter the course of learning in any substantive way.

Question for Consideration 2.6

Are mind and brain the same?

Task 2.3

Reflect on your response to Task 2.2. Do some of the metaphors discussed overlap with your own views of the teacher's role or your experience of it?
In Chapter 1, you were asked about the source and location of learning.
In the above metaphors for teaching, where do they suggest learning is located?
Reflect now on your own thinking about 'mind'. What does it mean for you?

In these metaphors for teachers and teaching, there are some common ontological beliefs about learners:

- they are not unique but assumed to be essentially the same;
- they are the subjects of teaching and not participants in the process;
- mind is located in the brain, and mind and brain are assumed to be the same.

Other commonalities between these views include:

- a hierarchal relationship between teachers and learners with the teacher as the authority and the learners as dependent;
- knowledge is the property of the teacher;
- learning does not vary in kind only in quantity, or in how well subject matter is recounted;
- knowledge exists external to the learner although its source has shifted from God to the gene.

BEHAVIOURIST AND TRANSMISSION VIEWS OF KNOWLEDGE

In behaviourist and transmission views of learning, knowledge has to somehow 'pass' from the teacher into the individual student and become deposited in the brain, laid down like an imprint that remains metaphorically like a finger print pressed into wax. Phrases used by people when trying to remember something such as 'searching my mind' and 'it's at the back of my mind' suggest this idea of knowledge being 'stored' and located within a person's head.

> Questions for Consideration 2.7
>
> Do I know in the same way as everyone else?
> Why do things make sense to some people and not to others, were we in the same lesson?

This 'knowledge' which is deposited in individuals' heads remains *unchanged* in its nature. If this view is taken up by a teacher, it is possible to assume that what is taught and, therefore, known is common across learners. Any perturbations arise either because the knowledge has not been acquired or it has been forgotten as the metaphoric wax is worn away or laid over with other memories. This has implications for how learning is assessed and how students are taught. For example, all students can be treated the same by a teacher or a tutor if they believe that knowledge is acquired in the same way. It is also why many recent policy interventions to 'drive' or 'move' learning forward assume the 'same size' pedagogy 'fits all' students and teachers.

In behaviourist views of knowledge (i.e. epistemologically), it is assumed that through drill and repetition, basic skills combine to make a more complex whole. The metaphor of the teacher as a *watchmaker* recognises this as these teachers must provide not just the components of knowledge but ensure that they are arranged and connected in the right order. Learning here is a construction process, requiring the teacher to involve the learner, engaging them in tasks that increase in complexity. The *watchmaker* view of teaching also assumes that there is a pre-given order for organising learning, like a jigsaw to be put together. This order is assumed to function similarly across learners and relies on a systematic hierarchical relationship within knowledge structures. In this view, knowledge is understood as building blocks that must be put together in ways that ensure the building emerges and is stable and sustainable.

The issue of how children learn to read is a contentious one. The role of, and approach to, phonics instruction (discussed further in Chapter 7) is central to this ongoing debate. Whilst the professional community generally accept that phonics instruction is important, there remains some disagreement over its significance in learning to read (Ellis and Moss 2014). In England, in 2012 (retained in the current curriculum), the government mandated that a specific strategic approach, systematic synthetic phonics, must be taught in all state schools and university teacher education programmes. The following information communicated for parents was based on the claim that:

> Research shows that when phonics is taught in a structured way – starting with the easiest sounds and progressing through to the most complex – it is the most effective way of teaching young children to read. It is particularly helpful for children aged 5 to 7.
>
> Phonics is a way of teaching children to read quickly and skilfully. They are taught how to: recognise the sounds that each individual letter makes; identify the sounds that different combinations of letters make – such as 'sh' or 'oo'; and blend these sounds together from left to right to make a word. Children can then use this knowledge to 'de-code' new words that they hear or see. This is the first important step in learning to read (DfE 2013: 1).

Task 2.4

Consider the previous information to parents and the following policy extracts about teaching reading from the Programme of Study of the 2014 National Curriculum document for 5- to 6-year-olds in England.

Can you discern traces of behaviourist views of learning? Think about how the learners' experience is being structured and what that says for how they learn and what they learn about reading.

> During year 1 teachers should [be] making sure that pupils can sound and blend unfamiliar printed words quickly and accurately using the phonic knowledge and skills that they have already learnt. Teachers should also ensure that pupils continue to learn new grapheme-phoneme correspondences (GPCs) and revise and consolidate those learnt earlier. The understanding that the letter(s) on the page represent the sounds in spoken words should underpin pupils' reading and spelling of all words. This includes common words containing unusual GPCs. The term 'common exception words' is used throughout the programmes of study for such words.
>
> Alongside this knowledge of GPCs, pupils need to develop the skill of blending the sounds into words for reading and establish the habit of applying this skill whenever they encounter new words. This will be supported by practice in reading books consistent with their developing phonic knowledge and skill and their knowledge of common exception words. At the same time, they will need to hear, share and discuss a wide range of high quality books to develop a love of reading and broaden their vocabulary. (DfE 2014: 20)
>
> Pupils' vocabulary should be developed when they listen to books read aloud and when they discuss what they have heard. Such vocabulary can also feed into their writing. Knowing the meaning of more words increases pupils' chances of understanding when they read by themselves. The meaning of some new words should be introduced to pupils before they start to read on their own, so that these unknown words do not hold up their comprehension. However, once pupils have already decoded words successfully, the meaning of those that are new to them can be discussed with them, so contributing to developing their early skills of inference. (DfE 2014: 23)

In this approach to reading, there are overlaps with behaviourist pedagogy. In particular, that learning is an individual process and mind and brain are assumed to be the same. It is also assumed that a 'one-size-fits-all' approach to pedagogy is appropriate. For example, learning to read is viewed as a process of decoding symbols not meaning-making. This is evident in the separation in the policy guidance between the process of decoding (reading) and the process of developing vocabulary; words that children use with the 'correct' meaning or comprehension and acquire through discussions about the books that are read to them. Consequently, word-level work and comprehension can be taught independently. The behaviourist roots of the policy can be traced to the influence of specific evidence presented to the Select Committee enquiry into reading (2005). This evidence was based on research from within the psychological paradigm, a paradigm that assumes mind and brain are the same and that learning is an individual process. Positivist research approaches study psychological and social phenomena using methods from the scientific paradigm on the assumption that individuals can be analysed and studied in isolation from their social worlds. In this paradigm, human traits and behaviours are treated as variables to be manipulated and investigated to establish relationships between them. Using similar designs and approaches to science allows claims that psychological evidence has scientific objectivity. This reflects a commonly asserted dualism between objectivity and subjectivity. The former, because of its association with science, is described as 'hard', 'rigorous' and 'generalisable' in contrast to subjective or qualitative 'soft' evidence. The 'Simple Model' of reading proposed by the expert witness was based on such evidence which demonstrated that word reading and comprehension follow *'separate developmental paths and with separate knowledge bases'* which justified them being taught discretely (Ellis and Moss 2014: 245).

The phonics part of the model became the mandated approach to teaching reading; consequently, word-level work dominated language comprehension work in the curriculum (Elias and Moss 2014). This can be seen in the statutory requirements where children are expected to check *'that the text makes sense to them as they read'* (DfE 2014: 22). This suggests that making sense is relatively unproblematic and that decoded words have shared meaning. Yet findings from the educational research paradigm suggest that younger readers and those who struggle with reading do not recognise words when they do not understand their meaning. This makes sense, as research has shown that these readers understand reading as a decoding process rather than a meaning-making process; in other words, they view the point of reading as recollecting words rather than making sense of them (Wray and Lewis 1997; Smith et al. 2021).

The assumption that the process of making sense is the same for all learners is predicated on what Bredo (1999) refers to as 'task stability'. For tasks to be stable for all learners, symbols, such as letters or numbers, are assumed to carry the same meaning for all. So once the brain decodes the letters, it is assumed the individual has the meanings of the words. This policy view of reading relies on an epistemological belief in *representationalism*, that is, symbols like letters and numbers mirror or reflect a given reality and what we understand as 'knowledge' represents this reality. Therefore, once knowledge has been successfully transmitted, that is, students have the same words, sentences or statements in their head as the teacher or the textbook, then something has been learnt. The curriculum policy example, in arguing that learning to read requires the development of pre-requisite skills only after which can more complex meanings and understandings be acquired, aligns with a behaviourist view of knowledge. This assumes a 'biological' similarity about people that controls or determines learning. One of the criticisms of the phonics approach in English primary schools is the assumption that children start with the same level of preparedness for reading and any differences between them should not influence what teachers do (Connor et al. 2004). There is evidence that fluency in continuous reading only occurs for those students who come to school with good letter knowledge already and for whom the social practice of reading, as they have experienced it, corresponds with schooled literacy practices and purposes (Ellis and Moss 2014).

FROM BEHAVIOURISM TO INFORMATION PROCESSING

Views about knowledge that see it as building blocks that can be interrelated or combined into more complex structures have been resilient to change. It is one of the legacies of behaviourism that was taken up in *information-processing* theories of the mind in the 1960s and 1970s with the advent of the modern computer. These theories compare human mental processing to the algorithmic ways computers process information. Applied to education, children and young people are understood to be limited information processors. It is implied in behaviourism that mind and brain are similar because assumptions locate knowledge there. In information-processing theories, it is explicit: 'the human brain is an information-processing system' (Langley et al. 1987: 8). Underpinning many information-processing theories is the belief that human beings have *innate, biological, computational processes.*

Modelling the mind on a computer separates cognition and emotion. Thinking in this view, therefore, takes on a very particular quality emulating computer processing. Information-processing models, put very simply, can be represented in a series of stages of processing (Figure 2.1).

Figure 2.1 A Simple Representation of an Information-Processing Model

The stimulus or information from the environment is received by the sensory organs. An example provided by McLeod (2008: 1) describes how:

> the eye receives visual information and codes information into electric neural activity which is fed back to the brain where it is "stored" and "coded". This information can be used by other parts of the brain relating to mental activities such as memory, perception and attention [processing systems]......which alter the information in systematic ways.

The output response is in the form of behaviour, that is, action, for example, to be able to read a printed page. The storing, retrieval and transformation of the inputted information rely on 'mental programmes' in the brain. *Thinking* occurs in the serial processes outlined in the model. Thinking is therefore a stage that follows sensory input and, importantly, precedes activity. Thinking and activity are not enacted in parallel, one precedes the other, to generate the response, the output. Expressions such as 'make your mind up' and 'I am in two minds' suggest a similar view of mind to the computational and behaviourist view as the mind has to have processed *what to do before acting.*

Problem-solving in this view of mind is symbol manipulation. The brain receives a pre-given problem that is then related to existing stored symbol structures which have to be sought for correspondence and difference. The brain decodes the symbols, searches for similarities to recognise the problem and solves it by identifying and following the selected rules or algorithms that are retrieved for solving that kind of a problem. A computer does not know what the symbols it operates on represent. It is, therefore, worth considering if in practice students are provided with 'representations' without meaning, albeit unintentionally.

A common information-processing teaching approach provides instructions for students to follow in a step-by-step way. The algorithm (or method) they are given can then be applied to solve different types of problems. Consider perhaps your own experience of doing mathematics or calculations in physics. This approach is how one 15-year-old girl described why she could do physics even though she found it the *'least interesting'* of the sciences and where she put in the least effort:

> Physics you're given equations and I've got the sense to know how to use them to get the answer ... doesn't matter if the answer means nothing it's getting the answer that counts in the exams. (Sharp 2003: 195)

What students learn is to recognise the 'type' of problem that the algorithm or equation fits. Sadly, if they forget the algorithm, they can no longer solve these problems.

IMPLICATIONS FOR PRACTICE

Like behaviourism, information-processing approaches assume that students only need to employ mental activity to know how to *act on* the environment, through symbolically representing the problem situation. Bredo (1999) discusses how this perspective assumes a mind–body dualism because mind and body are treated as separate entities that do not interrelate, you can know one without understanding the other. This view of mind that locates it in the individual and is somehow separate from the world means that social influences are outside of people and have no beneficial impact on learning, other than to distract the learner. Consequently, there is little value in being with other people and learning with them as the world, and not people, are assumed to be the source of learning. Group work and discussion with others are not practices that are used in teaching that draws on these theoretical roots. Learning is assumed to be an individual affair.

This idea of learning being a specific kind of mental manipulation that occurs solely in the mind of individuals has a long history. Historically, to attain knowledge without the distraction of others required isolation or a removal from the everyday of life (Lave 2008). When people use images such as the 'scholars in their ivory towers' or the 'sage on the stage', they are reflecting this view. Both the tower and the mountain represent the removal from everyday life that learning is assumed to require. It is also why valued learning is typically understood only to occur in specialist institutions and why everyday learning is often not considered in theories of learning.

THEORIES ABOUT ABILITY

Traditional theories of intelligence which claim the existence of innate general reasoning processes, that is, ability, reflect similar assumptions to information-processing theories and behaviourist theories. These assumptions include the belief that if learners are passive receivers of 'knowledge', it follows that any problems with learning resides with them and within their brains.

An example would be if students fail to learn their times tables, this is explained as a 'problem' of 'dyscalculia'. There is no consideration of other explanations that might influence this. Yet, often it is not whether the answers are known, it's if they can be quickly recalled that determines whether a child is considered to have learnt their tables. This is how one student recalled her experience of mental arithmetic:

> I always hated it – having to answer out loud in maths. In the numeracy hour, we used to get numbered flash cards which were supposed to make it fun!
>
> The teacher would ask the question and you were supposed to hold up the answer, the whole class had to do this. So then you'd see who had the wrong answer. So if she asked 8x9 while I was trying to work it out everyone else would be putting up cards and I would just panic and put up the same card as the person next to me. I could do the mental maths just not as quickly as they wanted. But by the end I wasn't doing the maths just following other people. If you were wrong everyone looked at you.

For many students, it is the anxiety about the speed of response required that creates the problem not their inability to be able to learn.

Another assumption relates to the belief in the external nature of knowledge or representationalism, as it follows from this belief that everyone 'knows' in the same way. Hence, what is learnt does not vary in kind, only in quantity. If students have the same knowledge, then in either a learning or an assessment situation the same task should allow them to bring forth their knowledge. The 'knowledge' is in the brain waiting to be recalled; it is assumed that it is not tied to any other knowledge or to other experiences. So once the task is decoded, the knowledge, if it has been learnt (committed to memory), is available. In these theories, then mind is made up of innate abilities, which determine the capacity of the learner to learn.

McDermott (1996) discusses how learners for varied reasons learn more slowly or in different ways than others but that it only matters when school arrangements, such as organising learning by age and in ability groupings, make this problematic. So where did this view of mind and concern with rate of learning arise? In 1869, Francis Galton, a cousin of Charles Darwin, argued that human intelligence was largely a matter of genetic inheritance. His eugenic theory was that 'natural' or 'innate ability' such as height was normally distributed in the population (Figure 2.2).

It was assumed that those who were most successful in society were therefore those endowed with the greatest 'innate ability'. In 1905, Binet, a French psychologist who believed, in contrast to Galton, that intelligence evolved over time, published his first intelligence test. It was commissioned to develop techniques for identifying those children whose poor performance in school suggested a need for 'special' education. As Binet's concern was with learners' general potential, he separated out natural intelligence from instruction and included nothing that relied on reading and writing but tasks concerned

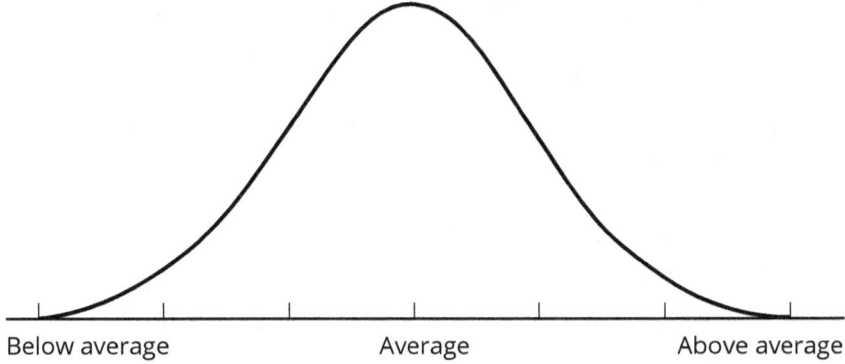

Figure 2.2 A Normal Distribution of Ability

with basic reasoning processes of ordering, comprehension, invention, etc. The scores on his tests were not given any meaning or theoretical interpretation but were used to distinguish between children in terms of mental age. For Binet, intelligence was too complex to be represented by a single score. So, the test was to serve a practical purpose to determine teaching provision for some children, to enable them to realise their potential rather than to label and constrain them (Gipps and Murphy 1994).

At this same point in time, there were others who believed in Galton's concept of innate (biological) general intelligence and for whom Binet's work offered a different possibility. William Stern, a German psychologist, further developed the scale of mental age by dividing it by chronological age and multiplying it by 100. This resulted in what was termed an intelligence quotient (IQ) and so a simple number became a measure of a learner's potential to learn. In America, Gould (1981) describes the way that psychologists who believed in hereditary views of intelligence 'hijacked' Binet's scores. Goddard, for example, used it (Zenderland 1998) to identify the 'feeble minded' to limit their reproduction and to monitor who could enter the United States. Although Goddard changed his views about the measure, it was taken up by many others in the United States, and later by English psychologists Burt and Spearman, for identifying children with different abilities.

Spearman was the first to argue in 1904 that human intelligence comprises specific abilities underlain by a general factor 'g'. He researched using statistical methods to try and isolate and measure 'g'. The development of these tests and the statistical methods convinced academics that intelligence could be measured and that this predicted future performance. A person's 'g' factor was the 'ceiling' or limit on their future achievements. These beliefs were challenged by research into the positive effects of coaching and practice on IQ test results. This evidence refuted the essential assumption behind eugenics that innate abilities were immutable. Although the use of IQ tests has declined, some of the concepts underpinning theories of ability remain embedded in educational practices. In particular, the notion of a normal population where the majority are within the average range and some are above average and some below average, with a minority at the two tails of the distribution, the gifted and the severely impaired, remains resistant to change.

Practices that Follow From Theories of Ability

Ability grouping or streaming in mainstream schooling are examples of school organisation that reflect a belief that biology determines the potential to learn. They are also practices that can unwittingly shape teachers' perceptions of learners. A telling anecdote from a highly successful composer demonstrates this:

> I hated school so much. The music sets were streamed with French for some reason, it was a stupid system. I was bad at French so I was in bottom set for music as well!
>
> I spent years trying to prove to my music teacher that I was worth taking some trouble with, but I never succeeded. I found things tough at that time.
>
> Despite that I was completely obsessed by music ... A temporary music teacher wrote 'below average but tries hard' on my end of year report for music. By this time I was a junior at the Royal College and composing a lot of music. My parents were livid and complained, so he crossed it out and wrote 'very good' instead! (Turnage 1998: 4)

Practices such as streaming or setting and how these are enacted and communicated by teachers can reflect to learners' views of themselves and their potential and become self-fulfilling. In Turnage's case, he had another 'view' from the Royal College of his competency, and with his parents' support, he could override the identity of a 'below average' learner, but this is not the case for most learners.

Questions for Consideration 2.8

Is learning determined by ability?
Do we judge what people do outside of educational institutions by their ability?

Task 2.5

Reflect for a moment on how you would describe yourself and your learning.
What would you say you were good at school and not so good at?
Is there a subject where you might have been considered very good? Is there a subject where you might have been considered poor? What evidence do you draw on in making those judgements?
Can you explain this in terms of your 'ability'? What other explanations might there be?

COMPARING FEATURES OF BEHAVIOURIST AND INFORMATION-PROCESSING THEORIES OF LEARNING

Figures 2.3 and 2.4 represent the key ideas discussed in the chapter in relation to what they suggest about views of learning, pedagogy and knowledge in behaviourist and information-processing theories of learning. Importantly, the figures show the relationships between learning, pedagogy and knowledge that can be useful in thinking about and analysing practice in classrooms and practices advocated in educational policy. It is often the case that what is intended by practitioners and what is stated in policy rhetoric is not what dominates the practice that emerges and how learners are positioned consequently. The figures are offered as a simple tool to consider ways of understanding where these potential conflicts might occur and, therefore, how they might also be addressed.

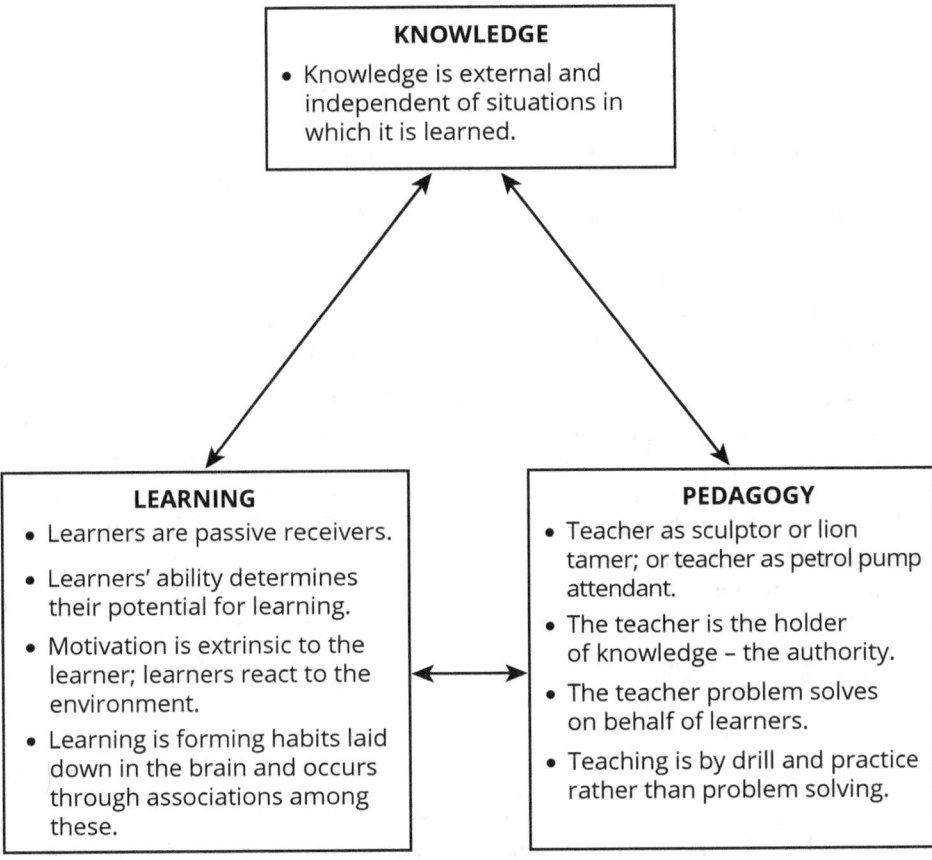

Figure 2.3 Features of a Behaviourist Theory of Learning

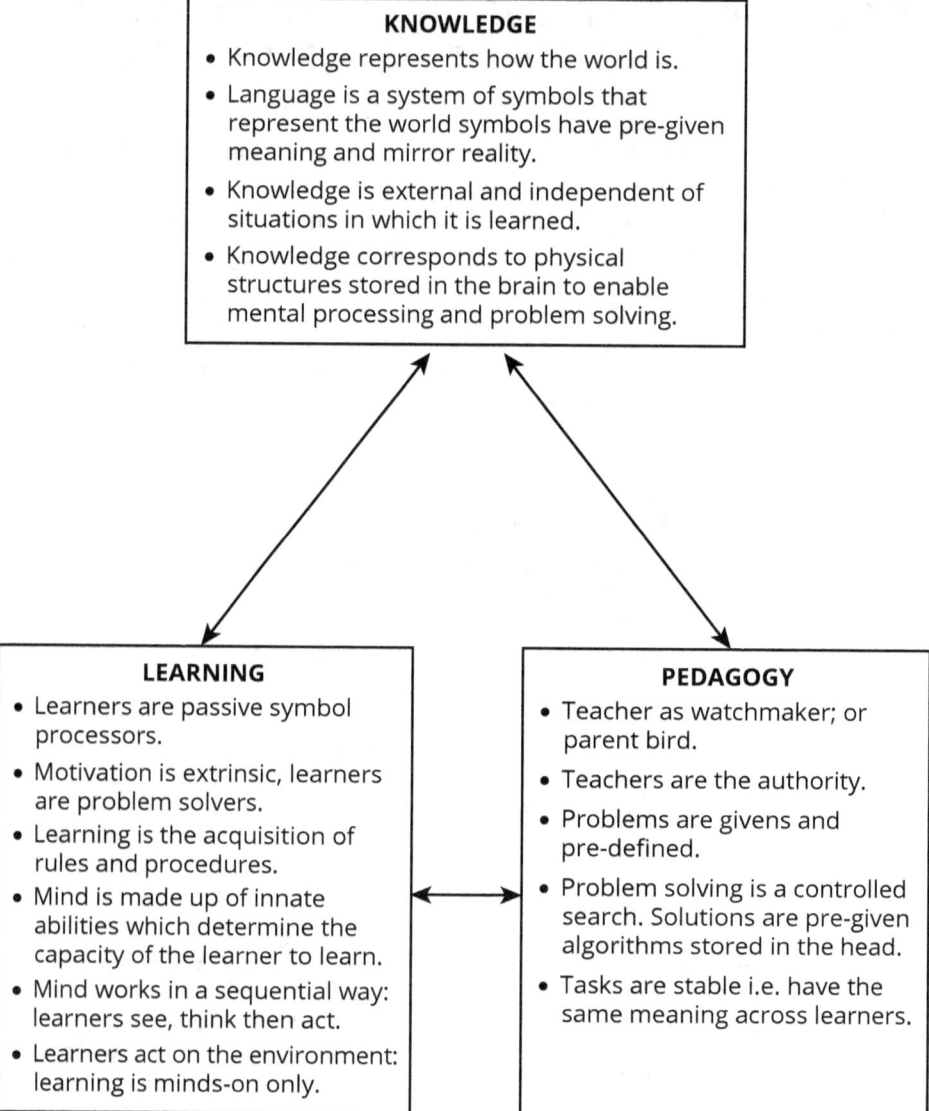

Figure 2.4 Features of an Information-Processing Theory of Learning

SUMMARY

The chapter has explored several related theoretical positions on learning, behaviourist, information-processing and ability that share a particular view of the nature of mind. Although behaviourist theories have declined in influence, some of the ideas about the brain and about learning and knowledge overlap with information-processing theories which continue to be influential. Both information-processing theories of learning and theories about ability assume the ontological view that innate processes and dispositions determine the potential to learn. They also share a similar view of the hierarchical relationship between teachers and students that is required for productive learning. In each theory, mind is an individual property and mind and brain are assumed to be the same. Many educationists recognise that learning is not a process of receiving knowledge or symbol decoding and processing. Yet, some of the ideas about what determines learning, that is, the potential of learners, that come from these theories remain as part of educational policy discourse and professional discourse about learning and learners. It is important, therefore, to bear these in mind when reflecting on your own theorising and beliefs and your encounters with policy and practice. In the next chapter, another theory of learning is considered and two questions are posed that challenge the assumptions about learning and learners discussed in this chapter:

- Is wanting to learn intrinsic to being human?
- What place does intention and meaning have in learning?

ADDITIONAL READING

Bruner, J. (1996) Culture, Mind and Education. In J. Bruner (1996) *The Culture of Education*, Cambridge, MA: Harvard University Press, pp. 1 - 43. Within this chapter, Bruner discusses and critiques two divergent views of mind. The first presents a computational view of mind and the associated features. The evidence for such a view is then considered in contrast with cultural influences on the development of mind.

Ellis, S. & Moss, G. (2014) Ethics, education policy and research: the phonics question reconsidered, *British Educational Research Journal*, 40 (2) pp. 241-60. This article uses the debate about phonics and reading to provide detailed insight into how educational policy is created and shaped by individuals and research. It provides a critique of how different research paradigms, that is, theoretical frameworks, construct and interpret data providing very different messages for practice.

Skinner, B. F. (1985) Cognitive Science and Behaviourism, *British Journal of Psychology*, 76, pp. 291-301. This paper presents a traditional view that human behaviour is initiated by an internal, autonomous mind.

REFERENCES

Askew, M., Brown, M., Rhodes, V., Wiliam, D. & Johnson, D. (1997) Effective teachers of numeracy: report of a study carried out for the teacher training agency. London: King's College, University of London. https://www.researchgate.net/publication/258423326_Effective_teachers_of_numeracy_final_report. Accessed 20/02/2025

Bredo, E. (1999) Reconstructing educational psychology. In P. Murphy (Ed) *Learners, Learning and Assessment*. London: Paul Chapman.

Bruner, J. (1996) *The Culture of Education*, Cambridge, MA: Harvard University Press.

Claxton, G. (1990) *Teaching to Learn a Direction for Education*, London: Cassell.

Connor, C. M., Morrison, F. J., & Katch, E. L. (2004) Beyond the reading wars: The effect of classroom instruction by child interactions on early reading, *Scientific Studies of Reading*, 8(4), 305-36.

De Abreu, G. & Cline, T. (2003) Schooled mathematics and cultural knowledge, *Pedagogy, Culture & Society*, 11(1), 11-30.

Department for Education (2013) *Learning to Read through Phonics Information for Parents*. Crown Copyright.

Department for Education (December 2014) *The National Curriculum in England Framework Document December 2014*. Crown Copyright. Available at https://assets.publishing.service.gov.uk/media/5a7db9e9e5274a5eaea65f58/Master_final_national_curriculum_28_Nov.pdf

Edovald, T. & Nevill, C. (2020) Working out what works: The case of the Education Endowment Foundation in England. *ECNU Review of Education*, 4(1), 46-64. https://doi.org/10.1177/2096531120913039

Ellis, S. & Moss, G. (2014) Ethics, education policy and research: The phonics question reconsidered. *British Educational Research Journal*, 40(2), 241-60.

Grady, J. R. Dolan, E. & Glasson, G.E. (2010) Agriscience student engagement in scientific inquiry: Representations of scientific processes and nature of science. *Journal of Agricultural Education*, 51(4), 10-19.

Gipps, C. & Murphy, P. (1994) *A Fair Test? Assessment, Achievement and Equity*. Buckingham: Open University Press.

Gould, S. J. (1981) *The Mismeasure of Man*. New York: W. W. Norton.

Halpern, D. F. (2000) *Sex differences in cognitive abilities* (3rd ed). Mahwah NJ: Lawrence Erlbaum Associates.

Hammersley, M. (2007) *Educational Research and Evidence – Based Practice*. Buckinghamshire: Open University Press.

Hodkinson, P. & Macleod, F. (2010) Contrasting concepts of learning and contrasting research methodologies: Affinities and biases. *British Educational Research Journal*, 36(2), 173-189.

Ivinson, G. & Murphy, P. (2007) *Rethinking Single-Sex Teaching Gender, School Subjects and Learning*. Buckingham: Open University Press.

Langley, P., Simon, H. A., Bradshaw, G. L. & Zytkow, J. M. (1987) *Scientific Discovery: Computational Explorations of the Creative Process*. Cambridge, MA: MIT Press.

Lave, J. (1988) *Cognition in Practice*. Cambridge: Cambridge University Press.

Lave, J. (2008) Everyday life and learning. In P. Murphy and R. McCormick (Eds) *Knowledge and Practice Representations and Identities*, London: SAGE.

McDermott, R. P. (1996) The acquisition of a child by a learning disability in S. Chaiklin & J. Lave (Eds) *Understanding Practice Perspectives on Activity and Context*, Cambridge: Cambridge University Press.

McLeod, S. A. (2008). *Information Processing*. Available at www.simplypsychology.org/information-processing.htm

Mercer, N. (1995) *The Guided Construction of Knowledge: Talk Amongst Teachers and Learners*. Clevedon: Multilingual Matters.

Murphy, P. & Ivinson, G. (2005) Gender, assessment and students' literacy learning: Implications for formative assessment. *Teacher Development*, 9(2), 185-200.

National Reading Panel (2000) *EU High Level Group of Experts on Literacy, 2012*. Available at https://www.nichd.nih.gov/sites/default/files/publicatio ns/pubs/nrp/Documents/report.pdf Accessed 04/01/25.

Richardson, K. (1998) *Models of Cognitive Development*, London: Psychology Press.

Sharp, G. D. (2003) *A Longitudinal Study Investigating Pupil Attitudes towards Their Science Learning Experiences from a Gender Perspective*, The Open University.

Skinner, B. F. (1968) *The Technology of Teaching*. New York: Appleton-Century-Crofts.

Smith, R., Snow, P., Serry, T. & Hammond, L. (2021). The role of background knowledge in reading comprehension: A critical review. *Reading Psychology*, 42(3), 214-240. https://doi.org/10.1080/02702711.2021.1888348

Spearman, C. (1904) General intelligence, objectively determined and measured. *American Journal of Psychology*, 15, 201-293.

Thomas, G. (2009) *How to Do Your Research Project*, London: SAGE.

Turnage, M. A. (1998) My inspiration. *Guardian Education*, March 31, 1998, 4.

Wertsch, J. V. (1991) *Voices of the Mind a Sociocultural Approach to Mediated Action*. Cambridge MA: Harvard University Press.

Wood, D. (1998) *How Children Think and Learn* Second Edition, London: Blackwell Publishers.

Wray, D. & Lewis, M. (1997) *Extending Literacy Children Reading and Writing Non-fiction*. London: Routledge.

Zenderland, L. (1998) *Measuring Minds: Henry Herbert Goddard and the Origins of American Intelligence Testing*. New York: Cambridge University Press.

3
INTRODUCING CONSTRUCTIVISM AND THE AGENTIVE MIND

CONTENTS

Challenges to Behaviourism: Motivation for Learning	46
Activity as Central to Learning	48
Learner Agency: A Cognitive View	55
Agency in Practice	56
Social Interaction in Piagetian Theorising	60
Teacher as *'Gardener'*: Dilemmas for Practice	61
Summary	66
Additional Reading	67
References	67

Chapter Aims

After reading Chapter 3, you will have considered:

- cognitivist challenges to behaviourist assumptions about learning and learners;
- how learners, mind and development are characterised within Piagetian theorising;
- the role of activity in learning and the curriculum implications;
- the Piagetian meaning of human agency and intersubjectivity;
- the metaphor of the teacher as *gardener*;
- dilemmas for teachers' practice.

Bruner (1996: 8) argues that for a theory of mind to be useful educationally it should contain some specification for 'how its functioning can be improved or altered in some significant way'. In the previous chapter, the theory of mind discussed that regarded mind and brain as the same began to lose its usefulness for educators in the latter part of the 20th century because it did not explain many observations about learners nor did it help them know how to act to improve learning. The 'drill-and-practice' approach of behaviourist pedagogy did not equip students well to solve problems or to tackle tasks in new situations. Learner's knowledge appeared inert if they were faced with tasks requiring similar solutions but involved different activities or contexts. This concern was raised in Chapter 1 around the transmission model of learning characterised in Kyriacou's (2009) three-phase view of learning. Pritchard described effective learning as that which is 'lasting and capable of being put to use in new and differing situations' (Pritchard 2009: ix). In this chapter, Piaget's theories are explored to consider how learning and cognitive development became more prominent in educational theorising.

In Chapter 2, it was explained how the ways that theory is taken up in practice depends on numerous factors: historical conditions; individual understandings and resources and societal pressures to name but a few. Piaget's theories were widely available before and throughout the period when behaviourism dominated research in psychology and practice in education. However, Piaget (1950; 1959a, b; 1973) was an epistemologist whose aim was to understand the nature, structure and evolution of human knowledge through studying the thinking and apparent understanding of children and adolescents. He based his framework for analysing young people's thinking on the assumption that the goal of human development was systems of mathematical and logical operations that enabled reality to be represented and the physical world to be understood. He did not write about the educational implications of his findings. Consequently, his theory lacked immediate relevance for policymakers and those who wished to develop their practice beyond behaviourist and information-processing approaches.

CHALLENGES TO BEHAVIOURISM: MOTIVATION FOR LEARNING

At the end of Chapter 2, it was considered whether wanting to learn was intrinsic to being human. Evidence about this emerged as research began to question behaviourism and whether external reinforcement was a necessary condition for learning. Behaviourism is predicated on the assumption that learners require extrinsic motivation to learn based on studies of how other animals 'learnt'. Wood (1998) describes Pribram's research with monkeys and quotes an example which appeared to undermine the view that motivation is extrinsic. The case involved a monkey being conditioned to pull a lever which intermittently delivered a peanut as a reinforcer. The monkey was observed to often store the peanut in its cheek pouch, and when no peanut appeared, after pulling the lever, it would sometimes eat a stored peanut. As Wood put it, the monkey reinforced itself after what was intended as a non-reinforcing trial. Indeed, the monkey continued to use the lever even when its pouch could hold no more peanuts. It was observed to throw the peanuts out of the cage whilst continuing to operate the lever to obtain even more peanuts. The question this raised was why did the monkey continue to press the lever when no nutritional gain was achieved? For Pribram it revealed the possibility that an activity itself might hold some intrinsic interest for the animal (Pribram cited in Wood 1998). This led researchers to begin to reconsider the possibility that students too were intrinsically motivated to learn. As evidence, such as this mounted, interest in the field began to turn towards Piaget's theory and ideas.

A Cognitive Perspective

At the same time as these issues around motivation to learn were being considered, questions were also being raised about the validity of extrapolating from animal learning to human learning. This practice assumed that there were commonalities between animals and humans in how they learn, with the former being merely a simpler form of the latter. Findings that showed that species of animals, and breeds within species, differed in their learning habits brought this assumption into doubt (Halpern 1992). These questions led to a focus on research into human cognition and educators and policymakers began to explore the potential of Piaget's theory about how children and young people think and understand the world around them.

> Questions for Consideration 3.1
>
> What makes me want to learn?
> What puts me off learning?
> What makes me keep going in these situations?

Task 3.1

Think of two experiences, they can be recent or from the past, where you have really:

- wanted to learn something?
- not wanted to engage and learn?

What was it about the experiences that you found motivating and/or demotivating? How would you describe your motivation in these instances?

Sometimes the motivation to learn is driven by a specific interest in something and there is a goal that the learner wishes to achieve such as being able to drive or wanting to do well in maths to become an accountant. So sometimes the activities themselves might not be engaging, they may even be frightening, for example, the first time a learner driver takes control of a car without instructions about where to go, but the goal is personally worth it. Sometimes the activity is of inherent interest, like putting on a school play or making your first polymer in science, quite amazing for some of us! One example a 13-year-old student gave was the thrill of exploring the Doomsday documents in her history lessons and finding links to local place names and imagining relatives from the past, as she analysed how King William divided up England. In both cases, a bit like Pribram's monkey, the activity itself was intrinsically motivating and enjoyable. There are several reasons why a person does not engage in an activity, for example, the activity does not make sense, the relevance is not clear or the goal to be achieved is not of interest to the person. In these instances, the lack of motivation can be understood to emerge between the interaction of the learner and the activity as they perceive it. Did any of these explanations fit your experiences?

At the end of Chapter 2, you were asked about the place 'intention' had in learning. In cognitive theorising, the learner is not a passive receiver of information but is active and focused on mastering or understanding the world around them. Learning occurs as the learner acts to understand their local environment. The learner is *self-directed* and motivation is *intrinsic*. Piaget, a key figure in the development of cognitive theorising, placed action and problem-solving at the centre of the learning process. Problems are not 'given' to Piagetian learners as they were with the behaviourist student. Problems for the Piagetian learner emerge as they try to organise, structure and rearrange meaning from experiences in the light of their existing knowledge and understanding. By acting on the world, Piaget's learner discovers how to control it. The notion of *discovery* is important in understanding how educators took up Piaget's theorising into practice. The move from understanding teaching as transmission to understanding learning as discovery has had profound implications for the way a teacher's role and relationship with learners can be characterised. The metaphor for the teacher in this view of teaching and learning is the *gardener*. However, depending on the ways that discovery is interpreted and valued as well as the ways that teachers enact practice to support it can promote significant differences in the way it emerges in classrooms.

ACTIVITY AS CENTRAL TO LEARNING

The view of the learner as the constructor of their own knowledge represents the child as an *agent* in the learning situation. The shift in views of the mind in this theorisation change from that of the passive receiver in behaviourism to the agentive, constructive mind of cognitive theorising. For the Piagetian learner, knowledge is actively acquired as a result of a life-long constructive process.

> **Task 3.2**
>
> What does it mean that activity is central to learning?
> Can you think of examples from practice that you use or have experienced which you consider to be activity based?

You will have perhaps heard of the expression 'learning by doing' and this is another phrase that is associated with Piaget's theory that reveals the emphasis that constructivist educators offer when interpreting what is meant by activity. Does this resonate with the examples you thought of? To understand what activity means it helps to consider how it is implicated in Piaget's theory of learning. In Piagetian theory and other cognitivist theories, the activity that is prioritised is the learner's, that is, the individual's sensory motor and conceptual activity (Cobb 1999).

Activity is considered to form the basis of thinking because as learners engage with the world and solve the problems that emerge in this involvement, they are acting on the world. It is through reflection on the consequences of those actions that students learn. In Piaget's theory of how students think and learn, the process of reflection or abstraction from interaction with the world around them (material experiences) facilitates abstract thinking to develop. Importantly, though, abstractions and generalisations could only develop if they are grounded in practical problem-solving.

Adolescents unlike younger learners are, according to Piaget, able to think abstractly by applying the conceptual models they have developed through this process of abstraction. They, therefore, do not necessarily need *concrete* material experiences, that is, physical interaction to substantiate an argument or a point of view. Nevertheless, they continue to need to understand the connections between their abstract mental models and the problem solutions their mental manipulations can enable. Relating abstractions to observations and experiences enable learners to deploy their mental constructions to achieve particular ends. It is through these connections that students extend their mental models and the repertoire of problems they can solve. This is both a much more functional, useable view of knowledge and, also importantly, a creative one. Creativity was absent from behaviourist accounts of learning. For Piaget, as learners develop their knowledge and reasoning abilities, *'there is a continual construction of novelty'* (Piaget cited by Richardson 1998: 95).

This notion of activity as the source of thinking rendered Piagetian theories attractive to those that found the view of thinking and problem-solving in behaviourist and information-processing views of mind problematic. In these theories if you recall, it was argued that thinking precedes activity, or in other words, the mind must process what to do before acting. Problem-solving in those views of the mind is rule-based. The brain receives a pre-given problem, decodes the symbols, searches for similarities to recognise the problem and solves it by identifying and following the selected rules or algorithms that are recalled for solving that kind of a problem. Critics of information-processing theories challenged the assumption that learning was rule-based and Garfinkel (1967) summed up the weakness perceived in the approach. In his view, if a learner followed sets of rules in the 'blind' way suggested by information-processing theories, then they would be a 'judgmental dope' (Garfinkel 1967 cited by Bredo 1999: 29). Problem-solving as a process of matching and selecting denies the significance of the learners' need to understand the connection between the rule and the solution and prohibits the potential for human judgement and creativity when learners are faced with new situations and problems. It also offers a possible explanation as to why 'drill and practice' alone was found not to help learners cope with new situations or problems.

The view of activity as forming the basis of thinking, in constructivism, changed how what was taught became understood and, therefore, what became specified in the school curriculum. Now *processes* and *procedures*, as well as ways of thinking and acting in school subjects, became as significant as the *concepts* and *generalisations* these procedures enabled learners to develop. It was no longer enough to provide rules or algorithms for solving equations without ensuring that students could reflect on and understand how those procedures related to the activity and the practical problem associated with it. Without these connections, students could not reflect on the consequences of their actions and therefore could only memorise and recall rather than understand and apply. This constructivist view of knowledge has had an extensive and long-lasting impact on how school curricula have developed.

Implications for Curricula

Curriculum policy documents are reifications of intentions for learning. They offer representations of knowledge which are not theoretically neutral. The following task and discussion exemplifies how a constructivist perspective on subject knowledge has shaped national subject curricula and how this might vary between subjects. By contrasting two specifications, you can consider how a theoretical perspective can be weakened and changed depending on the political and social context and the agents engaged in the policy development.

Task 3.3

Look at the three excerpts from the National Curriculum Level Descriptors for Subjects (QCDA 2010) for England. Levels 7 and 8 represent the level of achievement expected from pupils at age 16 at the end of their compulsory education. The maths and English excerpts are from one aspect of the subject content specification.

(Continued)

History

Level 7: Pupils show their knowledge and understanding of local, national and international history by analysing historical change and continuity, diversity and causation. They explain how and why different interpretations of the past have arisen or been constructed. They begin to explain how the significance of events, people and changes has varied according to different perspectives. They investigate historical problems and issues, asking and refining their own questions and beginning to reflect on the process undertaken. When establishing the evidence for a particular enquiry, pupils consider critically issues surrounding the origin, nature and purpose of sources. They select, organise and use relevant information and make appropriate use of historical terminology to produce well-structured work.

Level 8: Pupils show their knowledge and understanding of local, national and international history, constructing substantiated analyses about historical change and continuity, diversity and causation. They analyse and explain a range of historical interpretations and different judgements about historical significance. They suggest lines of enquiry into historical problems and issues, refining their methods of investigation. They evaluate critically a range of sources and reach substantiated conclusions independently. They use historical terminology confidently, reflecting on the way in which terms can change meaning according to context. They produce precise and coherent work.

Mathematics (Number and Algebra)

Level 7: When making estimates, pupils round to one significant figure and multiply and divide mentally. They understand the effects of multiplying and dividing by numbers between 0 and 1. They solve numerical problems involving multiplication and division with numbers of any size, using a calculator efficiently and appropriately. They understand and use proportional changes, calculating the result of any proportional change using only multiplicative methods. They find and describe in symbols the next term or nth term of a sequence where the rule is quadratic. They use algebraic and graphical methods to solve simultaneous linear equations in two variables.

Level 8: Pupils solve problems that involve calculating with powers, roots and numbers expressed in standard form. They choose to use fractions or percentages to solve problems involving repeated proportional changes or the calculation of the original quantity given the result of a proportional change. They evaluate algebraic formulae or calculate one variable, given the others, substituting fractions, decimals and negative numbers. They manipulate algebraic formulae, equations and expressions, finding common factors and multiplying two linear expressions. They solve inequalities in two variables. They sketch and interpret graphs of linear, quadratic, cubic and reciprocal functions, and graphs that model real situations.

English (Reading)

Level 7: Pupils show understanding of the ways in which meaning and information are conveyed in a range of texts. They articulate personal and critical responses to poems, plays and novels, showing awareness of their thematic, structural and

> linguistic features. They understand why some texts are particularly valued and influential. They select, synthesise and compare information from a variety of sources.
> **Level 8:** Pupils' responses show their appreciation of, and ability to comment on, a range of texts, and they evaluate how authors achieve their effects through the use of linguistic, structural and presentational devices. They select and analyse information and ideas and comment on how these are conveyed in different texts. They explore some of the ways in which texts from different times and cultures have influenced literature and society.
>
> Consider the extent to which these representations give value to understanding 'how' (process) as well as 'what' (concept) in subject learning. You could highlight where you see the two aspects and then any relationships between them.

In the first excerpt, for example, the *what* of history is clearly there in the references to historical terms and to concepts such as change and continuity, diversity and causality and historical terminology. The *how* (skills, processes and procedures of historical enquiry) is evident in the references to formulating questions, critically using sources as evidence, analysis, evaluation and investigation. The relationships are perhaps more implicit in, for example, the analysis of sources to form well-substantiated conclusions.

In the mathematics excerpt, the relationships between the *how* and the *what* are more explicit in the level 8 description. For example, students can choose to use processes to solve problems and in that choice, demonstrate understanding of the purpose and function of the process. The use of graphs that draw on mathematical concepts is another example of the relationship between *how* and *what* and here it is expected to be applied in new situations. The difference between the levels suggests that for some students (level 7), a more functional understanding of maths is expected with a prescriptive approach to the concepts and methods to be used. Although these learners are solving problems, there is less sense of them as problem solvers choosing to use their own particular mathematical processes and conceptual understanding as tools.

In the English excerpt, the reference to linguistics, structure and presentational devices and cultural and historical perspectives are examples of the *what* of the subject. The use of these to create effects and to convey ideas and information are examples of the way *how* can be connected to the *what*. The level 7 description reflects the same sense of the learner as the level 8 description but with less range and depth in both the *what* and the *how*.

The 2010 curriculum specification, like the versions before it, refers to levels. Levels define what students within an age range, described as a 'key stage', are expected to be able to do. Only some students are expected to attain the highest levels in a key stage suggesting that the concept of 'ability' influenced the structure of the specification. You will recall that this is a legacy of behaviourist theories of learning and knowledge discussed in Chapter 2.

The English national curriculum framework (DfE 2014) does not refer to levels, only to what is expected at a key stage. Key Stage 1 includes children aged 5-7 years; Key Stage 2 – students aged 7-11 years; Key Stage 3 – students aged 11-14 years; Key Stage 4 – students aged 14-16 years; and Key Stage 5 – students aged 16-19 years. This aligns in many respects with Piaget's concept of stage development.

Below is the 2014 curriculum specification for reading in the Key Stage 4 English curriculum.

Pupils should be taught to:

- read and appreciate the depth and power of the English literary heritage through:
    - reading a wide range of high-quality, challenging, classic literature and extended literary non-fiction, such as essays, reviews and journalism. This writing should include whole texts. The range will include:
        - at least one play by Shakespeare;
        - works from the 19th, 20th and 21st centuries;
        - poetry since 1789, including representative romantic poetry
    - re-reading literature and other writing as a basis for making comparisons
    - choosing and reading books independently for challenge, interest and enjoyment.
- Understand and critically evaluate texts through:
    - reading in different ways for different purposes, summarising and synthesising ideas and information and evaluating their usefulness for particular purposes
    - drawing on knowledge of the purpose, audience and context of the writing, including its social, historical and cultural context and the literary tradition to which it belongs, to inform evaluation
    - identifying and interpreting themes, ideas and information
    - exploring aspects of plot, characterisation, events and settings, as well as the relationships between them and their effects
    - seeking evidence in the text to support a point of view, including justifying inferences with evidence
    - distinguishing between statements that are supported by evidence and those that are not, and identifying bias and misuse of evidence
    - analysing a writer's choice of vocabulary, form and grammatical and structural features and evaluating their effectiveness and impact
    - making critical comparisons; referring to the contexts, themes, characterisation, style and literary quality of texts; and drawing on knowledge and skills from wider reading.
- make an informed personal response, recognising that other responses to a text are possible and evaluating these.

(DfE 2014: 81)

In the 2010 specifications, you can still discern aspects of constructivist epistemology. For example, *what* students are expected to read and *how* they are expected to engage with texts is detailed. Actions expected such as 'exploring', 'investigating', 'asking questions' and 'inquiring' suggest interaction, especially with historical texts, that is constructivist in nature. These kinds of actions are less prevalent in the mathematics and English specifications. However, independent activity, that is, individualised pupil interactions with texts and subject matter, is expected to some extent across all three areas.

In scrutinising curricular documents, what is emphasised and how it is phrased infer (as in Chapter 1) what the author/s assume. The order of the sentences and/or bullets can also matter, as does the ways in which similar words are repeatedly used and applied. Careful analysis of the specifications helps you begin to appreciate the assumptions that underlie curricular intentions.

In the 2014 specification excerpt, attention to the social and historical context of a text is to inform the process of evaluation but the purpose of that evaluation isn't emphasised. In the earlier specification for English, the purpose is to consider how selected texts from different times and cultures have shaped the field of literature and society. Is this significant? If this is linked to the shift between the specifications in what texts are valued, from which periods of history and cultures does it take on a new meaning? In the 2014 specification, the primary emphasis is that students read and appreciate the depth and power of an *English* literary heritage defined by high-quality classic literature. Implied is that both literary quality and what constitutes a classic are uncontested and unchanging. In the curriculum review before the development of the 2014 framework, it was stated that the new National Curriculum *'should embody our cultural and scientific inheritance, the best that our past and present generations have to pass on'* (DfE 2011, para. 10). The valorising of the past to be passed on to students is difficult to reconcile with constructivist pedagogy and the agentive, constructive mind of cognitive theorising. It suggests a tension in the specifications between how students are required to engage with texts, which texts and why. The tensions reflect different ontological positions where mind is a receptor and constructor and students are both passive and agentive. Theoretical tensions create dilemmas for practice. If students are to appreciate and accept a given literary heritage, what kind of criticality is anticipated as they engage with texts? Is there an external objective standard of quality defined by classic literature?

The detail about the use of evidence refers to the potential for bias and misuse, and, by implication, that objectivity in the creation and interpretation of data is both possible and desirable. This corresponds with a psychological positivist view of evidence that you considered in Chapter 2. Yet every judgement about what to measure and observe and how to do this involves the subjective judgements of the researcher. There is also explicit reference to the role of grammar in conveying meaning not stated in the earlier specification. There is in addition a nineteen-page glossary (the curriculum specification covers two pages) which details the technical aspects of language. This is described as including:

> ....all the technical grammatical terms used in the programmes of study for English, as well as others that might be useful. It is intended as an aid for teachers... (DfE 2014: 89)

This is a guide for teachers, yet such ways of representing this kind of knowledge is not theoretically neutral. The space made available to clarify the technical aspects of using English implies something about its significance that shapes how teachers 'read' the specification.

There was no specification for Key Stage 4 history in the framework document; however, if the Key Stage 3 history specification is considered, there is evidence of an epistemological shift. *What* is to be learnt is specified in seven content bullets each accompanied by details of example events, topics and issues (see DFE 2014: 249-251). The first three bullet points focus on periods of British history from 1066 to 1509; 1509 to 1745; and 1745 to 1901. This is followed by content looking at challenges to Britain, Europe and the wider world from 1901 to the present day. Then two further bullets refer to a local history study and a study of an aspect or theme in British history to consolidate and extend students' chronological knowledge from before 1066. The final bullet requires students to study a significant society or issue in world history. Like the English reading specification, the content and how it is structured indicate the importance of a British cultural heritage to be passed on to students. The emphasis placed on chronology suggests a move away from the practices of doing history towards the facts of history. The brief and general description of the *how* aspects of doing history supports this interpretation. The paragraph is replicated below. Explicit or implicit references to processes, procedures and skills are underlined for you to consider.

Pupils should extend and deepen their chronologically secure knowledge and understanding of British, local and world history, so that it provides a well-informed context for wider learning. Pupils should identify significant events, <u>make connections, draw contrasts and analyse trends</u> within periods and over long arcs of time. They should <u>use</u> historical terms and concepts <u>in increasingly sophisticated ways</u>. They should pursue <u>historically valid enquiries</u> including some they have framed themselves and create <u>relevant</u>, structured and <u>evidentially</u> supported accounts in response. They should understand how different types of historical sources are used rigorously to make historical claims and <u>discern how and why contrasting arguments and interpretations of the past have been constructed</u>.

(DFE 2014: 249)

You might ponder on the significance of these different ways of specifying subject curriculum. Does it suggest to you a shift in, and/or tension between, views of knowledge and/or learning?

Curriculum documents reveal how different theoretical perspectives, whether implicit or explicit, shape what is valued knowledge, how students are understood to learn and what being an school educated person means. Constructivist views have had, and continue to have, a significant influence on curriculum specifications and the notion of stages of development remains tenacious in the way they are structured. Yet behaviourist or information-processing views continue to exert an influence. These theoretical influences ebb and flow over time as different actors engage on the policy stage.

In the next section, you are invited to examine the distinction between *activity* and *agency* to clarify a key feature of Piaget's theory and how confusions about these meanings have often created problems for the ways Piaget's theory has been taken up in practice.

LEARNER AGENCY: A COGNITIVE VIEW

Questions for Consideration 3.2

How do I learn – is it just remembering?
Does what I know affect how I learn new things? In what ways does it affect my learning?
When I read something, do the words always make sense? How do I make sense?

Task 3.4

In Chapter 2, related to assumptions of behaviourism, examples were given to explain how individual learners cannot always be treated as though they understand in the same way.
Can you recall an experience of learning where you did not understand something when others seemed to? What helped you to make sense of that something?

When you think of the word agency in relation to people, what does it mean to you? For many people, it usually means acting or being active in everyday terms. Consequently, just by being engaged in activity, it is assumed that a person has *agency*, that *is, the capacity to act*. Because Piagetian theory argues that activity is the source of learning, it is often assumed that providing students with practical activities ensures that 'learning by doing' occurs. In your experience of things not making sense, did you feel you had the capacity to act? Piaget's theory refers to the process that involves both *being able to act and being able to construct meaning from the consequences of those actions*. It is in these circumstances that a learner's *experience of agency* emerges.

At the end of Chapter 2, you were asked what role 'meaning' has in learning as it seemed absent from behaviourist accounts. When the word passive is used, it implies not just sitting there but that the learner does not actively process messages that are being received after being transmitted by the teacher. The symbols enter the brain unchanged, and their meanings are stable across people, place and time. It was what Bredo (1999) referred to as the language – reality dualism, where language is understood to mirror an external reality. The idea that learners have agency rejects this view. Consider what you are reading now, particular understandings are being projected but those understandings cannot be achieved without you working out what the intended meaning is in the way the words are put together, the examples used and the experiences you are asked to recall. A key dimension or plane of learner agency is that knowledge is not given to people; rather, they must construct meaning and make connections between things to generate meanings. Hence, these theories are generally described as *constructivist* theories of learning and knowledge.

Agency is an *attribute of the learner* and how they are in the world. It is not a description of their actions in the teaching and learning process, though observing these can provide insights into students' expressions of agency. The absence of a capacity to act purposefully, the second dimension or plane of agency, for example, can arise because the activity or the task has no meaning for the learner or the meaning that the learners make of the words used to convey the task and the instructions do not correspond with what the teacher intended. So simply giving learners something to do does not necessarily mean that this enables them to be agentive.

Active learning is a commonly used term in writing about teaching both in policy documents and in educational literature. It is often used as a substitute for agency, but the *active* aspect often refers only to the nature of learning tasks rather than explaining how learners are understood to be agentive. The latter perspective not only requires that particular types of learning tasks are used but also dictates how a teacher relates to students and how students are encouraged, or not, to relate and engage in learning with others. So, teachers may describe their pedagogy in similar ways and share a concern for learners to play an *active* role but what that means can vary between them. These differences emerge in their practice.

AGENCY IN PRACTICE

Task 3.5

Think of a learning task that you have found to be effective either for your own learning or for those whose learning you support.
To what extent would you call it 'active' and what does this now mean to you?

Piagetian learning or active learning is often described as 'minds on' *and* 'hands on', but what does that mean? In Piagetian theorising, the individual and the environment are interdependent or *'an indissoluble entity'* (Piaget 1952: 16 cited by Rogoff 1990: 31). What that means is that the affordances or possibilities for human action exist in the environment and are perceived by individuals as they act to explore and investigate a situation seeking something. Cognitive processes are actions (remembering, thinking, perceiving) and not objects (memory, thought) possessed by the learner; their function is to guide *'intelligent purposeful activity'* (Rogoff 1990: 29). Thinking is not a separate activity that precedes action as in information-processing theories; knowing and doing co-construct each other and mind is not separable from the person-environment relationship. As Bredo (1999: 36) explains, *'mind is a property of the interaction between person and environment and not something possessed in the skull of an individual'*.

Various translations of this aspect of Piaget's theorising can be seen in teachers' practices. For example, the belief based on Piaget's stage model of development that young learners can only operate on concrete (or visible) feedback means that there is no expectation that they can deal with abstract phenomena until they are older. An example of an activity might be water play, where pouring water into different sized and shaped containers is a way of providing young learners with experiences that support them to think about the conservation of volume. For older learners between the ages of 7 and 11 who, in Piaget's stages of development, can begin to apply logic and make connections, 'hands-on' or active learning is used to motivate them to deal with abstract phenomena. An example of this was an activity where a teacher provided her students aged 9 and 10 with various colloids (an aerosol air freshener, toothpaste, 'slime' and shaving foam), powders and liquids to explore. This was to challenge their thinking about states of matter and their understanding of the conservation of 'shape'. For example, is a powder a solid or a liquid because it has flow? By making an activity intrinsically motivating, it is assumed that students' agency will be enabled allowing them to engage, and through their interactions with concrete experiences of phenomena, they will be able to abstract commonalities and begin to make connections. What is assumed, that might seem to undermine learner agency, is that teachers can give problems to students and that by careful selection of experiences students can both perceive the same problem and be prompted into new ways of thinking as they explore it.

However, another assumption within constructivist theories like Piaget's is that the sense learners make of new experiences is influenced by prior knowledge that is related to that experience. For these reasons, a constructivist teacher will be concerned not only to make learning 'active' providing sources of material experience but also to make available to students their prior thinking. This was expressed in James et al's (2007) description of learning (in Chapter 1).

Questions for Consideration 3.3

How does learners' prior knowledge affect the sense they make of classroom events? What can a teacher do to build on prior knowledge and experience in lessons?

An example of a way a teacher might deal with these challenges in science is when students are given the opportunity to observe phenomena and then use their observations as evidence to explain what is happening. Consider the example below. Collin was trying to develop his practice to become a constructivist teacher.

Collin, the teacher, was teaching his class of 8- to 9-year-olds about dissolving and evaporation. He started first by eliciting their ideas about dissolving following the belief that students' sensemaking depends on their prior experience. One child thought it meant '*if you're a cop and you dissolve your case*'. Other students tried to link it to science ideas that they were aware of. For example, one said, '*When something evaporates or disappears*'. Another, '*When something happens inside water*'. For another student, it was when food rots '*it dissolves in the air and then becomes air.*' These comments demonstrate that students start from very different positions in terms of their prior knowledge, some much closer than others to a 'scientific' understanding of the phenomenon of dissolving. Therefore, their view of what the problem might be will also vary. Collin appears to assume that understanding the phenomenon of dissolving was a problem students shared. He does not address the students' understandings but accepts them, which says something about how the process of reflection on experience is understood when teachers translate constructivist thinking into their practice. It is the individual, that is, the student, who must construct the meaning and move from prior understanding to new understanding. The teacher cannot do that for them but the teacher assumes that the motivation to do this is there.

To challenge the students' various ideas, Collin selected two experiences that he thought would provide observations that each child could use to develop their thinking about dissolving further. He asked the students to observe two solids, flour and sugar, to then add them to water, stir and write down their observations and to reconsider what they subsequently thought about dissolving.

Collin then discussed their observations:

Collin: What was the difference between the two solids [the flour and the sugar].

Student: The flour came up off the bottom.

Collin: OK ... but what's the main difference between the two?

Student: When you put the sugar in, it just went down to the bottom and stayed there, but when you put in flour, when it was going down it clumped all together.

Collin: OK so after you stirred it, what was the main difference?

Student: The flour's gone.

[For this student, the solid flour dispersed through the water as a suspension no longer existed. Ignoring this, Collin directed attention to the sugar.]

Collin: Look at the pot with the sugar. Someone over here said the sugar had disappeared. Put your hand up if you got the same result as that, if your sugar has disappeared, if you can't see it any longer. Ok some of you still have some sugar at the bottom ... is that the same amount you started with?

Student: No.

Collin: No. So, some of it seems to have disappeared somehow.

Collin assumes that the experience he offers will challenge his students to reconsider what they thought they knew about dissolving, but his approach assumes that the phenomenon of adding flour and sugar to water would be seen in the same way by all the children. Like the view of mind as an information processor, observations, if stable across observers, mirror an external reality. Therefore, in making this assumption, Collin's practice inadvertently positions the students as receivers of meaning rather than constructors of meaning, an important dimension of learner agency. What Collin did not consider was that what he observed was only significant or salient for him because he *knew* about dissolving. His prior knowledge made his interpretation make perfect sense. The students were supposed to be learning about this, so for them, the flour clouding the water was as significant a change as some of the sugar disappearing, whereas for others in the class, it was more significant. The experience did not provide all the children with evidence that some flour dissolved and some remained undissolved, so for some of the pupils they did not comprehend what Collin termed the 'main' difference between the observations of the two solids in water.

Eliciting Learners' Ideas

> Question for Consideration 3.4
>
> How can learners be helped to become reflective about learning?

Eliciting students' prior understanding is a practice intended to enable a change in students' perspective on a phenomenon or event. However, as the excerpt exemplifies, this depends on how those ideas are used and the quality of the evidence made available to challenge them. Many of the students in the process of reflection made sense of what they saw in terms of what they thought mattered; their prior perspective was consolidated. As one student in Collin's class wrote in his book, 'I was right the first time.'

Elicitation of learners' ideas and thinking is an important practice in constructivist pedagogy and any theory of learning that assumes mind is agentive. If each person constructs knowledge through their experience of the world, and that learning shapes how they engage with future experiences, teachers must consider both where a learner is coming from and where they are heading if they are to provide continuity in experience. Elicitation activities in constructivist teaching are also the means of making students' thinking explicit and available for them to reconsider, in the process of reflection on, new information gained from their actions or other learners' ideas. This is a key aspect of Piaget's theory about how people learn. 'Brain storming' or a 'thought shower' is often used to describe this process of elicitation. In some school subjects, it is common to use spider diagrams or concept maps to allow students to draw what they already 'know' about a topic they would be learning, that is, what they see as salient. Students are encouraged to identify concepts, terms, processes and relationships between them. This acts as a planning resource for teachers to select activities that challenge and progress students' understanding. For younger students, it is often drawings that are found to be helpful. Children can add descriptions as this 6-year-old did to her drawing in response to the question 'What happens to food and drink inside you?'

> When he swallows it, it goes into your tummy. It moves about in your tummy.
> It goes down into your legs or arm.

This 6-year-old's drawing depicts an outline of a body, within which she added a circle (representing the stomach) and some larger and smaller blobs of a round and rectangular shape that were scattered (or floating) in the main torso and not within the stomach or the pipework of the intestines. The drawing suggested how the young child appeared to think food and drink floated around inside her body and were not contained within a connected system of tubes and bags any kind (like a human digestive system).

Older students can annotate drawings or just write about what they know about a phenomenon or an event. Creating a new map or drawing after an activity allows students to construct and represent meaning in the information they gained from their actions.

A comparison of these representations provides teachers with assessment information about students' progress as well as supporting students' reflections on their own understandings, which can enable a change in perspective on a phenomenon.

In practice, elicitation activities (as discussed further in Chapter 8) can be enacted and used in very different ways by teachers. The usefulness of elicitations depends upon the extent to which it is assumed that what is represented is what is known by the learner and whether students' intended meanings are accurately communicated through these representations. The extent to which students' representations of their ideas become resources to support further discussions or are taken at face value will influence what activities teachers select to progress their students' learning. There is also the issue of who such resources are for. If they are for the students, what is the most effective way of supporting their reflection? Are they an individual or a collective resource? If the metaphor of the teacher as '*gardener*' is maintained, how is the tension between the concept of the self-regulated 'discovery' learner reconciled with the teachers' task to achieve common curriculum goals. To consider this, the Piagetian view of the influence of social interaction is discussed next.

SOCIAL INTERACTION IN PIAGETIAN THEORISING

Piaget focused his research on individual activity and how children make sense of the world through this activity. In Piaget's theory, learners amend their ways of thinking to better 'fit' reality when faced with conflicts or problems between their existing view of the world and new information. *Equilibrium* is the term Piaget used to represent the process of reaching a resolution, a justifiable understanding, achieved by a learner when faced with conflict or *cognitive dissonance*. Equilibration is a creative, solitary process of invention which has led to the notion of the student as the lone 'discoverer'. Piaget recognised, however, that social interaction could bring about cognitive conflict when students attempt to reconcile differing points of view about their experiences to re-establish equilibrium. To achieve this reconciliation in social interaction, a common frame of reference or intersubjectivity is required. For Piaget, the frame of reference that learners need to share is a '*common language and system of ideas*' (Rogoff 1990: 149), which depends on their stage of development. *Intersubjectivity* is a process by which learners make explicit their understanding of the same phenomenon, text or problem and how this might differ between them. It is not a process of co-construction but rather one of translation. Learning occurs as an individual thinks about or operates on other learners' ideas to advance their own thinking. The meanings created are individual and not shared. The locus or place of *intersubjectivity* and mind is therefore retained within the individual.

To achieve intersubjectivity, Piaget (Piaget 1977 cited in Rogoff 1990: 225) argued that co-operation was the ideal form of social interaction, and that this was only possible from age 7 onwards because of students' cognitive stage of development and the language (symbols and signs) they are able to use that are available to them to express and communicate their thinking. Younger children lacked the language skills to exchange ideas and the cognitive skills needed to de-centre and take account of others' perspectives. Co-operation depends on *reciprocity* between learners so that they grant each other's propositions *equal status* and share an interest to explore alternative perspectives. Piaget considered that difference in individuals cognitive stage of development altered the power relations between participants. This affected their ability to exercise agency, that is, to have the capacity to act and to experience reciprocity. He criticised teaching as direct instruction where the teacher as authoritarian and knowledge giver required learners to cede their ideas to those of the teacher. It was not until adolescence that Piaget considered it possible for students to discuss ideas as equals with teachers. To achieve inter-subjectivity, interactions must be between learners at a similar cognitive level because their status should be equivalent or *symmetrical* and issues of power differences that would undermine agency are obviated. The interaction with a teacher creates an *asymmetry* in the learning relationship, which can constrain possibilities of equality in discussion and co-operation.

For Piaget and constructivist teachers, other learners are significant as opportunities for dialogue, allowing individual learners to clarify and develop their own thinking. Elicitation techniques can enable the tracking and sharing of individual thinking. Below, secondary school students describe this approach to intersubjectivity:

> I think there is a lot of intelligence in the group work because you can't just say what you're feeling, you've got to think about saying it because you're saying it to about four to five people and it's got to make sense.
>
> In the small group, I think we learn more because that's ...say if you've got a big group [whole class] you've got more opinions. If you've got the teacher you've just got one, their opinion and nobody else's.... Because you've only got you know, the teacher's saying from her own experience but if you've got a group where you've got everybody else saying what they think so you gather more information. (Cowie and Rudduck 1988: 69)

Language does not play a primary role in generating thinking in a Piagetian view of learning. Piaget considered the role that language played in learning was a means to represent the world, that is, as labels to describe and remember objects and events in the social and physical world rather than being involved in the process of reasoning and making sense of the world. Co-operation with adults, teachers, parents and peers alike, in a constructivist perspective, has a secondary rather than a primary role in the development of knowledge and understanding. This aspect of Piaget's theorising is looked at in more detail in Chapter 4 where the differences between his theories and those of Vygotsky are further considered.

TEACHER AS 'GARDENER': DILEMMAS FOR PRACTICE

Piaget's learner is first and foremost a lone discoverer motivated to create and solve problems in his/her need to organise the world and his/her experience. Language and social interaction play a part in Piaget's theory of learning, but it is the learner's stage of development which determines their role. The teacher in the Piagetian perspective is a provider of appropriate materials and learning environment, guiding opportunities for students' interactions and individual reflection. As Jemberie (2021) suggests teachers perceive constructivist practices in varying ways. Interpretations and implementation of constructivist approaches, however, do suggest that individual work predominates.

The Piagetian view of knowledge is one of staged development or intellectual revolutions which chart learners' progression through different forms of logico-mathematical reasoning (for examples, see Chapter 8), leading eventually to abstract reasoning and reflection. Learners are only expected to be able to learn certain ways of thinking and reasoning when they are developmentally ready to do so. Stages of development are not the same as a view of innate ability, which assumes progression for some learners can only go so far, that is, a belief that innate, genetically determined ability places a ceiling on all potential learning. Rather, stages of development suggest that there is no point questioning or explaining things to learners before they are mentally ready. They may appear to learn but what they learn is arguably about procedures without knowing how, when or where to deploy them. The idea of stages of development has had a profound effect on the practice of teachers who have taken up this theory.

In a study into the teaching of mathematics, Askew et al. (1997) characterised how teachers, working in schools in England, who accept stages of development and the view of the learner and learning as represented in Piagetian theorising, understand how learners become numerate. Their assumptions are listed below.

> Pupils become numerate through individual activity based on actions on objects.
> Pupils need to be 'ready' before they can learn certain mathematical ideas.
> Pupils vary in the rate at which their numeracy develops.
> Pupils' own strategies are the most important: understanding is based on working things out for yourself.
> Pupils' misunderstandings are the result of pupils not being 'ready' to learn ideas.
> Learning is seen as separate from and has priority over teaching.
> Learning about mathematical concepts precedes the ability to apply these concepts.
> Mathematical ideas need to be introduced in discrete packages.
> Application is best approached through using practical equipment. (Askew et al. 1997: 31–32)

The influence of the concept of readiness to learn and the hierarchical nature of knowledge acquisition that is explicit in the stage model of development is evident in this characterisation of teaching and learning. The notion of learning having priority over teaching is a legacy that can be traced to influential curriculum development programmes in the 1960s. These were part of the progressive movement in education such as the Nuffield Mathematics Project which prioritised individual freedom for learners and argued that the focus of education should be on *'how to learn and not what to teach'* (Davis 1991: 21). To maintain this freedom and to address the Piagetian view that direct instruction was inimical to learning, it was incumbent on teachers to be *non-directive*. Murphy et al.'s (2001) study into primary science teaching found that teachers who embraced these ideas were anxious about leading students. As one teacher put it:

I haven't quite resolved that bit of the [science] investigation. How much are you leading them with what you put out [resources and equipment]? You are still influencing it in a certain way ... and I find that aspect quite hard in letting them choose completely about how they do it. (Murphy et al. 2001: 90)

The difficulties teachers experienced in enacting constructivist pedagogy were responded to by major curriculum developments based on detailed research into students thinking and learning. These curriculum developments occurred after criticism of the progressive movement in education had gained ground. A major concern was how the priority given to the self-directed discovery learner in progressive education limited teachers' ability to guide students' learning towards specified curriculum goals. To ensure continuity of experience for learners, it was considered essential to know where they were coming from and where they were going to. One example of such a curriculum programme (more is discussed in Chapter 8) was the Nuffield Primary Science, Science Processes and Concept Exploration (Nuffield SPACE). This was a major resource that provided teachers with activities and student books along with guidance about how to enact the approach with students.

SPACE guidance to teachers made clear that:

This approach is far from letting children discover for themselves. So-called discovery learning requires children to derive, on their own initiative, general ideas from a set of observations or experiences. This is not only impractical because it expects far too much from the unaided efforts of children, it is also unrealistic because it is not the way in which scientific knowledge is usually generated. (Nuffield-Chelsea Curriculum Trust 1993: 36)

The destination for learners was developing scientific ideas and skills. The teachers' role is to guide them along the path. The teacher's role was described in the following way:

- finding out what children's ideas are;
- reflecting on how children may have arrived at their existing ideas and on where they are in progression towards developing more scientific ideas;
- helping children to develop process skills so they can test out and apply their ideas scientifically;
- providing opportunities which test or challenge ideas, leading to possible changes;
- assessing the extent of any change in ideas and in process skills which may have resulted.

(Nuffield-Chelsea Curriculum Trust 1993: 35)

The belief that teachers could disrupt learning by being directive was explicit in the SPACE approach.

The key to the teacher's role . . .is to be responsive – accepting and exploring the children's ideas – above all to be non-directive. (Nuffield-Chelsea Curriculum Trust 1993: 36)

Yet teachers still had to be 'active' and 'be looking for opportunities to nudge, deflect or facilitate the course of development, to shape the outcomes' (Nuffield-Chelsea Curriculum Trust 1993: 25). It raises the question: when does guidance become instruction?

There are several dilemmas experienced by teachers depending on what they emphasise in Piaget's theory when it is applied to teaching and learning. This reflects the tensions between the metaphor of *gardener* and the extent to which guidance is supportive or undermining of individual learning. The concern not to influence the direction of learners' explorations means that teachers tend not to make available to students the learning outcomes anticipated as these are determined by the learner and not the teacher. Consequently, tasks are not framed in terms of what is to be learnt. This approach to teaching ensures that the connections between aspects of subject knowledge are understood by the teacher but not disclosed to students. It is up to the individual leaner to make the connections. However, as noted in the excerpt from Collin's classroom, this can lead to connections being made that run counter to subject learning where abstract models or concepts are valued for their power in explaining phenomena and informing how to solve subject-related problems. The intention of curriculum programmes is to deliver specified curriculum goals. Typically, teachers have dealt with this dilemma by relying on other students to offer the 'right' response and/or outcome believing that this maintains reciprocity and is more likely to be given consideration by students than if stated by the teacher. Collin provided an example of this when he referred to '*Someone over here said the sugar had disappeared*' as this was what he wanted to direct students to 'see' as a salient observation (Murphy et al. 2001).

The practice advocated in a constructivist pedagogy assumes that teachers can take responsibility for and 'know' what sense each individual learner makes and intends in what they say, do and represent. A pragmatic approach in the SPACE programme was to encourage teachers to elicit students' ideas to serve as a learning resource for others and in so doing make them aware of their peers' alternative views. To decide what ideas to explore the guidance suggested that activities might be '*pitched at the general level you would expect children to have achieved at this point in their development*' (Nuffield-Chelsea Curriculum Trust 1996: 29). This was based on the view that although children will differ in their learning encounters, they will have some common experiences and therefore some similar ideas. There is a tension within Piaget's theory that emerges in practice between the implications of individual's construction of meaning and unique construal of the world as an outcome of human agency and the normative approach embedded in the stage development model. The origins of the metaphor for the Piagetian teacher as the *gardener* should now be much clearer. As Claxton explains all the 'growing' is done by the learner (Claxton 1990: 31). Teachers make available the conditions for learning, that is, the learning tasks, access to peers and other resources, but their mediation of the process is necessarily constrained, otherwise contructivist learning is disrupted. To achieve this, a teacher must be able to analyse the cognitive demands of classroom activities (discussed further in Chapter 8) and to assess learners' cognitive development within a broad conceptualisation of a stage of development. Figure 3.1 represents the key features of learning, knowledge and pedagogy that are reflected in the practice of practitioners and educational policymakers influenced by aspects of Piagetian theorising.

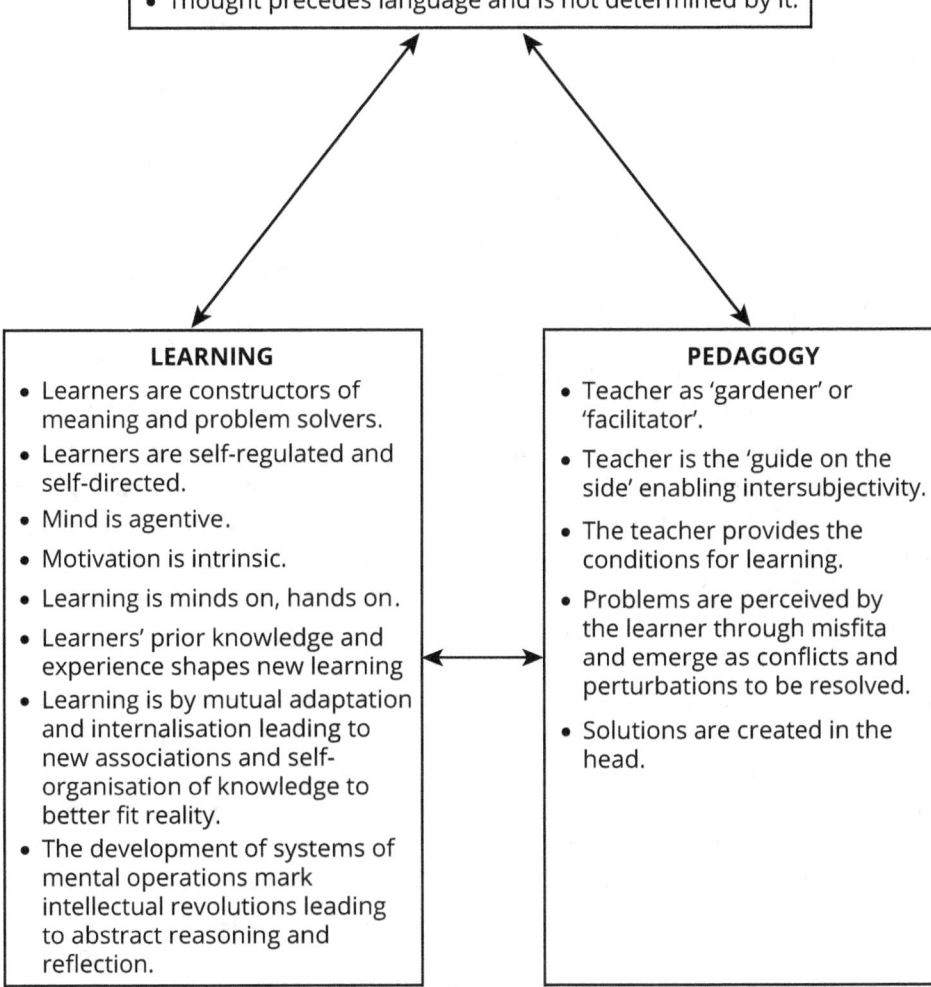

Figure 3.1 Features of a Constructivist Theory of Learning

SUMMARY

Piagetian theories have been and continue to be very influential in shaping educational policy and teachers' practice. Two important shifts occur in moving from behaviourist and information-processing views to cognitive, Piagetian theories of learning. The first is ontological. The mind remains individual but is no longer conceptualised as a passive receptor and processor of information requiring extrinsic motivation to learn but is understood to be *agentive*. An agentive mind is intrinsically motivated because in Bruner's (1996: 93) words, it is 'pro-active, problem-orientated, attentionally focused, selective, constructional and directed to ends'. Agency is both being able to act and being able to construct meaning from the consequences of those actions. It is in these circumstances that a learner's *experience of agency* emerges. However, despite interaction with others acknowledged as a source of information for the learner to consider, mind is still firmly located in the head of the individual. The locus of intersubjectivity is the individual. The second shift is epistemological, away from knowledge as rules and algorithms for routinised problem-solving towards knowledge as subject-specific processes and procedures related to activity and the practical problems associated with it. Consequently, the outcomes or goals of learning change from the capability to memorise and recall to the capability to understand and apply that understanding with judgement.

The major legacy of Piaget's theory is that of learner agency and the related belief in the fundamental role that prior knowledge and experience play in learning. These features are aspects of most educational theories of learning in current literature and to an extent in current policy recommendations about pedagogy. In both the theory and its take-up in practice, prior knowledge is typically only considered in terms of the subject concepts that are the focus of learning. The pedagogical shift implied by an agentive view of mind is in the movement from the teacher as an authoritarian controlling learning to a *gardener* or facilitator. However, this pedagogical shift is less clear if teachers and policymakers embrace the model of stage development. To be an effective '*gardener*', teachers have to analyse the cognitive demands of classroom activities and to assess learners' cognitive development within a broad conceptualisation of a stage of development. This aspect of Piaget's theorising has been widely challenged, and in Chapter 4, you will consider in more detail aspects of Piagetian theorising that suggest that the metaphor of the teacher as '*gardener*' misrepresents what Piagetian theorising implies for practice.

The tension between guidance and instruction remains and Chapter 4 examines this with reference to Vygotsky's theories. What remains contentious is the extent to which Piaget's theory represents any real shift in views of knowledge to that enshrined in behaviourist and information-processing theories of learning. This is because language can still be understood as reflecting an external reality even if what is valued in that reality has changed. Other contested aspects relate to how language is understood to be involved in the process of thinking and learning and the relationship between the individual and society – in other words, the extent to which individual learning relies on collective communication (Sfard 2008). In the next chapter, how these contestations and practice dilemmas have been addressed by the development of the educational implications of Piaget's theories and other theories are considered. The questions posed are:

- How do language and thinking relate?
- How are other people understood to support learning?

ADDITIONAL READING

Bruner, J. (2006) Chapter 9: How Mind Begins. In J. Bruner (Ed) *In Search of Pedagogy*. Volume II. London: Routledge. This chapter offers a narrative critique of various theorist's work (including Rountree, Piaget, Freud, Kroeber, Vygotsky, etc.).

Cobb, P. (1999) *Where Is the Mind*? In P. Murphy (Ed) *Learners, Learning and Assessment*, London: Paul Chapman. This chapter offers discussion about alternate perspectives and processes (constructivist and sociocultural) of learning in classrooms.

Driver, R., Asoko, H., Leach, J., Mortimer, E. & Scott, P. (1994) Constructing scientific knowledge in the classroom. *Educational Researcher, 23*(7), 5-12. This paper provides a clear theoretical discussion that straddles individual and social constructivism. It extends the discussion introduced in this chapter to include more social dimensions of constructivism.

REFERENCES

Askew, M., Brown, M., Rhodes, V., Johnson, D. & Wiliam, D. (1997) *Effective Teachers of Numeracy Final Report*. London: King's College.

Bredo, E. (1999) Reconstructing educational psychology. In P. Murphy (Ed) *Learners, Learning and Assessment*. London: Paul Chapman.

Bruner, J. (1996) *The Culture of Education*. Cambridge, MA: Harvard University Press.

Claxton, G. (1990) *Teaching to Learn a Direction for Education*. London: Cassell.

Cobb, P. (1999) Where is the mind? In P. Murphy (Ed) *Learners, Learning and Assessment*. London: Paul Chapman.

Cowie, H. & Rudduck, J. (1988) *Co-operative Group Work an Overview*, London: BP educational series.

Davis, A. (1991) Piaget, teachers and education: Into the 1990s. In P. Light, S. Sheldon & M. Woodhead (Eds) *Learning to Think*. London: Routledge.

DfE (2011) Review of the national Curriculum in England: Summary report of the call for evidence. Available at https://www.gov.uk/government/news/national-curriculum-review-launched. Accessed 25/02/25.

DfE (2014) *National Curriculum in England: English programmes of study*. Available at https://www.gov.uk/government/publications/national-curriculum-in-england-english-programmes-of-study. Accessed 25/02/25.

Galton, M., Simon, B. & Croll, P. (1980) *Inside the Primary Classroom*. London: Routledge and Kegan Paul.

Garfinkel, H. (1967) *Studies in Ethnomethodology*. Englewood Cliffs NJ: Prentice Hall.

Halpern, D. F (1992) *Sex Differences in Cognitive Abilities*. Hillsdale, NJ: Lawrence Erlbaum Associates.

James, M., McCormick, R., Black, P., Carmichael, P., Drummond, M-J., Fox, A., MacBeath, J., Marshall, B., Pedder, D., Procter, R., Swaffield, S., Swann, J., & William, D. (2007). *Learning How to Learn. Classrooms, schools and networks.* Abingdon: Routledge.

Jemberie, L. W. (2021). Teachers' perception and implementation of constructivist learning approaches: Focus on Ethiopian Institute of textile and fashion technology. *Bahir Dar. Cogent Education, 8*(1). https://doi.org/10.1080/2331186X.2021.1907955

Kyriacou, C. (2009) *Effective Teaching in Schools Theory and Practice.* Cheltenham: Nelson Thorne.

Murphy, P., Davidson, M., Qualter, A. Simon, S. & Watt, D. (2001) *Effective Practice in Primary Science; Research Report.* Buckinghamshire: Open University/Nuffield Foundation.

Nuffield-Chelsea Curriculum Trust (1993) *Nuffield Primary Science Science Processes and Concepts Exploration Teachers' Handbook.* London: Collins Educational.

Nuffield-Chelsea Curriculum Trust (1996) *Nuffield Primary Science Science Processes and Concepts Exploration Science Co-ordinators' Handbook.* London: Collins Educational.

Piaget, J. (1950) *The Psychology of Intelligence.* London: Routledge.

Piaget, J. (1959a) *The Language and Thought of the Child.* London: Routledge.

Piaget, J. (1959b) *The Child's Conception of the World.* St Albans, Herts: Paladin.

Piaget, J. (1973) *The Child's Conception of the World.* Bungay, Suffolk: Paladin.

Piaget, J. (1977) Les operations logiques et la vie sociale. In *Etudes Sociologiques.* Geneva: Librarie Droz.

Pritchard, A. (2009) *Ways of Learning.* Abingdon: Routledge.

Qualifications and Curriculum Authority (QCA) (2010) *The National Curriculum Level Descriptions.* London: DCSF/QCA.

Richardson, K. (1998) *Models of Cognitive Development.* Hove: Psychology Press.

Rogoff, B. (1990) *Apprenticeship in Thinking: Cognitive Development in Social Context.* New York: Oxford University Press.

Sfard, A. (2008) Participationist discourse on mathematics learning. In P. Murphy & K. Hall (Eds) *Learning and Practice: Agency and Identities.* London: SAGE.

Wood, D. (1998) *How Children Think and Learn* 2nd ed. Oxford: Blackwell Publishers.

4
THE IMPORTANCE OF LANGUAGE AND MEANING-MAKING

CONTENTS

A Radical Constructivist View of Knowledge and Communication	70
Stages of Development Reconsidered: Reflecting on the Legacy of the Stage Model	74
An Alternative View of Learning and Language?	80
Intersubjectivity Reconsidered	85
Assisted Learning – The Role of Instruction	89
The Zone of Proximal Development	90
Interpreting the ZPD	91
Summary	93
Additional Reading	94
References	94

Chapter Aims

After reading Chapter 4, you will have considered:

- knowledge and communication in radical constructivism;
- the metaphor of the teacher as *modeller* and *guide*;
- challenges to the Piagetian stage model of development;
- key aspects of Vygotsky's theory of social development;
- changing views of the role of instruction in learning and the teacher as *scaffolder*.

As explained in the previous chapter, this one considers further challenges to Piagetian theorising, particularly constructivist views of human agency, how knowledge and communication in teaching and learning are understood and the model of stage development. Interpretations of the evidence informing challenges to Piaget's model of stage development have led to different understandings about how learners' make sense of things. These understandings resonate with Vygotskian theories and those of Dewey and Bruner. The links between these theorists are highlighted by reference to Vygotsky's perspective on the relationship between language and thought and how it differs from that of Piaget. The chapter then concludes by looking at how the role of instruction in learning began to change around the turn of the century. These changes are then related to the Vygotskian proposition of the *zone of proximal development* (ZPD) and the metaphor of scaffolding in teaching.

A RADICAL CONSTRUCTIVIST VIEW OF KNOWLEDGE AND COMMUNICATION

> Question for Consideration 4.1
>
> What constrains teachers' capacity to understand what learners think and know?

Piaget did not elaborate on the educational implications (for teaching and teachers) of his theories as this was not his intent (see Chapter 3) but any theory of learning, as Wood (1998) notes, implies a particular view (or theory) of instruction. As the (constructivist) theory began to attract wider attention both in educational research and practice, Piaget's ideas were taken up and further developed by other researchers and educationalists. Ernst von Glasersfeld's theory of 'radical constructivism' is one example of this that influenced education in the United States, Europe and the United Kingdom. von Glasersfeld developed a theory of knowledge which, like Piaget, rejected a representationalist view of knowledge and communication. In Chapter 2, you will recall you were introduced to the idea that knowledge is assumed to represent how the world is in information processing views of learning. In this view, language is treated as though it mirrors reality (Bredo 1999) and knowledge is a commodity that can be transmitted, communicated and acrued. As Wertsch (1991) describes, it is a linear process involving what the teacher sends as a *signal* that remains unchanged and is received by the learner.

von Glasersfeld (1989) argued that knowledge does not correspond to, or mirror, an external objective reality but is constructed and derived from human reasoning informed by experience. Thus, the world is how we conceptualise it; there is no objective reality (common to everyone that is) mirrored in the mind.

Task 4.1

Think about how you 'see' colours. How would you explain what you 'see'?
Does your explanation suggest that 'colour' is part of an objective external reality?
Do you expect all people to 'see' colour in the same ways?

You probably know that different species physiologically 'see' the same colour differently, for example, some people are colour blind and cannot distinguish red and green; dogs can see red and blue, but confuse them; skate cannot 'see' any colours, and only detect black and white (contrasting greys). But when people say they see 'red', for example, what does that mean? In Newtonian theories of physics, the colour of something is defined by the colour of light that it reflects. There is an invariant relationship between the length of a light wave (wavelength) and the colour it transmits. Colour is therefore an objective reality. Oliver Sacks, an expert in the field of clinical neurology, argued for a different view based on Land's theory (the inventor of the Polaroid camera) who showed that colours are *'constructed by the brain'* through comparison with contrasting hues or other colours (Sacks 1995: 22). That is, the signals from the perceptual organs are not received unchanged as Wertsch (1991) suggests, but are reconstructed in the brain. Sacks described how an adult blind from birth regained the ability to see after an operation to remove cataracts. He argued this evidenced the process of reconstruction. After the operation, the man recovered his sight. The physical means to see became available to him (his lenses were receiving light and the retinas transmitting signals to the brain). Initially, when the bandages were removed, he could only 'see' the surgeon's face as a blur. As Sacks explained it:

> For we, born with a full complement of senses, and correlating these, one with the other, create a sight world from the start, a world of visual objects and concepts and meanings. When we open our eyes each morning, it is upon a world we have spent a lifetime *learning* to see. (Sacks 1995: 108)

The worlds that we construe are not only arbitrary as they are informed, but also constrained, by our experiences in the world. Roth describes the process of making sense from a radical constructivist perspective as a dialectic that exists between knowledge and reality:

> It takes the conceptions to perceive the experiential world, and the existence of the experiential world is necessary for any conceptions to be built. (Roth 1995: 14)

This understanding of making sense resonates with how we interpreted children's responses in Collin's class in Chapter 3. It was argued that what was salient to Collin was not salient in the same way to the children. That is, they lacked the conception that fits the reality as constructed by Collin from his understanding of science.

In a radical constructivist perspective, there are multiple conceptions or constructions that may 'fit' an experiential realm. Thankfully, we agree with most people that the traffic lights are indeed 'red' when we see the light at the top of the mast come on but what redness means can vary between us; what matters is that we know that different lights coming on at different positions signal what actions we should take. This book is a testimony to the existence of multiple constructions and alternate conceptions that inform theories of learning drawn on in education to describe and understand learners' experiences and teachers' practice.

von Glasersfeld used the concept of 'viable' knowledge to demonstrate the epistemological difference between constructivism and behaviourism. Viable knowledge, for von Glasersfeld, is knowledge that fits with experience and allows problems to be solved. How people come to know the world when knowledge cannot be compared with an external reality is through the notion of 'fit' in radical constructivism. von Glasersfeld applied a similar understanding of 'fit' to explain communication. He argued that words are not containers of meaning as assumed in a transmission view of communication. Rather, the meaning or concept attributed to a word is derived from the 'compound of abstractions' of an individual's experiences. Hence, meaning is subjective in origin and resides in the individual's head and not in the word itself. In von Glasersfeld's view, this posed the following communication problem for teachers:

> How could anyone be confident that the representations called up in the mind of the listener are at all like the representations the speaker had in mind when he or she uttered the particular words? (von Glasersfeld 1989: 9)

For von Glasersfeld, how people come to understand in the context of communication was analogous to the process of coming to know in the context of experience. Consequently, the representations associated with words do not have to be the same for all communicators but they must be 'compatible'. Compatibility is achieved if there is no perceived clash with the situational context or the speaker's intentions. Importantly, von Glasersfeld considered that for the listener to form expectations of the speaker about what has not yet been heard or read relied only on *'words and concepts, not actions or other experiential events'*.

[to] 'understand' the utterance, it is sufficient, therefore, that listeners have a conceptual structure that given their experience with words and the way they are combined 'fits'. (von Glasersfeld 1989: 11)

The absence of a conceptual structure to make a particular sense of words provides another way of thinking about the students in Collin's class. Colin wanted his students to gain a scientific understanding of dissolving, but his approach presumed that they had a shared and everyday understanding of the term (dissolving) that could be developed. He assumed that most students understood dissolving initially as something disappearing. But you will recall that for one student, it meant *'if you're a cop and you dissolve your case'*. For another student, it was when food rots *'it dissolves in the air and then becomes air'*. Collin expected the experiential event based on a shared grasp of 'disappearing' would offer a cognitive challenge to enable students to reflect, rethink and reconstruct their understanding. The students' knowledge of language and their expectations of what Collin intended did not correspond so compatibility was not achieved.

The Teacher as 'Modeller' and 'Guide'

von Glasersfeld argued that the ability to teach effectively relies on the teacher being a *modeller* of children's notions and operations and a *guide* for their learning. The teacher's role is to both construct a model of the learner's conceptions and operations and hypothesise pathways to adult competence. To do this, teachers must have an analytical model of schooled adult competence as it relates to each school subject. In a radical constructivist pedagogy, the goal is not achieving a 'match' between the learner and some external reality but between models constructed by teachers that allow them and their students to achieve a satisfactory organisation of knowledge, that is, a 'viable' way of dealing with experience. von Glasersfeld described the interaction between these two aspects of the teacher's role as a process of continuous testing by the teacher of his or her interpretation of learners' behaviours as they engage with tasks. The teacher 'tests' a learner's responses by modifying elements of the learner's experiential field and considers their rejoinders are compatible with their conjectures about the learner. von Glasersfeld made the important point that if we accept a view of mind as agentive, then it follows that:

> ...the teacher can never compare the model he or she has constructed of a child's conceptualisations with what actually goes on in the child's head. .. the best that can be achieved is a model that remains viable within the range of available experience. (von Glasersfeld 1989: 14)

What von Glasersfeld describes is assessment of the process of learning not of the outcomes of learning to inform both the teacher and the learner in the 'act of production' (Sadler 1989). In the SPACE programme referred to in Chapter 3 (and Chapter 8), assessment was a central part of the teacher's role and this formative view of assessment was described in the following way:

What this means in practice is that teachers consciously seek by listening, watching, open questioning or studying what has been produced, to gather information that helps them to understand a child's thinking whilst carrying out the normal interactions of teaching. (Nuffield-Chelsea Curriculum Trust 1993: 23)

It is difficult to imagine how this requirement for 'in the moment' testing is managed by teachers who typically work with whole classes of 30 or more students. Nevertheless, formative assessment has become an accepted aspect of teaching and learning globally. What it means and how it is enacted, however, varies. These variations reflect the different theoretical lenses that shape the construction and enactment of national and local educational assessment policies. For example, any assessment of the learning process relies on perceptions of what constitutes the goals of education and how those are achieved, that is, the learning trajectories anticipated for students. von Glasersfeld referred to this as the analytical model of schooled adult competence. As noted in Chapter 3, these differ between theoretical positions and for Piaget whose model of stage development continues to influence educational policy and practice even though its validity has been challenged by research evidence. In the next section, the legacy and some of the associated challenges of the stage model are considered further.

STAGES OF DEVELOPMENT RECONSIDERED: REFLECTING ON THE LEGACY OF THE STAGE MODEL

Teachers' practice is always mediated by policy which shapes what they can do and how they do it. The concept of students' 'readiness' to learn that underpinned Piaget's model of stage development was very influential in primary education from the 1960s onwards; this was particularly the case in the United States and to an extent in Europe (Brown et al. 1997). Across education, it legitimised policy approaches to curriculum specifications which have endured to this day. You can see this in national assessment systems and their fixed external frameworks of national standards which define the expected learning outcomes for students by age or stage. Examples of this from the National Curriculum for England were discussed in Chapter 3 and the 'phased' specifications of the approach to phonics. These age-related curriculum specifications make similar assumptions to the Piagetian model in that they purport to represent what students are capable of and, by implication, what they should achieve. Adey (2001) noted, for example, that in the National Curriculum for England descriptions of levels of achievement for each key stage showed '*a clear progression from early concrete operations through to mature formal*' (Adey 2001: 45). Examples of these in mathematics and science are presented for you to consider in Chapter 8.

Increasingly national standards are calibrated against other nations' performance on international assessments, such as the Programme for International Student Assessment (PISA) sponsored by the Organisation for Economic Co-operation and Development (OECD). PISA measures, classifies and ranks students, educators and school systems not against national educational goals but global standardised benchmarks. The PISA tests and their scales function as global representations of, for example, what being literate is, suggesting a model of knowledge that is cross-linguistic and trans-contextual, that is *universal*. Piaget's stages of development were imagined as universal too in that they offer a structure regarding everything a child perceives and thinks (Wood 1998). The assumption that generalisation is possible across diverse students, cultures and nations is widely accepted and this is evident in nations' responses to PISA results. The PISA 2022 results (Ingram et al. 2023) demonstrated England's scores for mathematics and reading had declined significantly since 2018 despite remaining above the OECD countries' average. Prior to the PISA tests, there had been curricular changes, for example, in the (current) 2015 specification that required adjustments in mathematics for primary children in England. The changes meant the pupils were expected to learn more at an earlier age than in previous specifications. Arguably an attempt to emulate the performance of high-scoring PISA countries included the following:

- Pupils were expected to be able to add, subtract, multiply and divide fractions in primary school so they can progress to more advanced topics like algebra when they go to secondary school. These four operations were not in the previous 2008 UK primary curriculum. The proposed changes were consistent with expectations in the high-performing education jurisdictions of Singapore and Hong Kong.
- By age 9, pupils should know their times tables up to 12×12. This is in line with expectations in the high-performing jurisdiction of Massachusetts. Currently, pupils only need to know up to 10×10 by the end of primary school.
- By age seven, pupils should know 'number bonds' up to 20. These are simple addition and subtraction facts that pupils should be able to recognise and use instantly (e.g. $9 + 9 = 18$ or $16 - 7 = 9$).

(DfE 2012, New primary curriculum will bring higher standards in English, maths and science, Press release 11 June 2012).

Currently, there are still ongoing national plans (DfE 2023) to improve maths attainment. International policymakers assumed that if the PISA measures represent 'universals', then what can be achieved by a child of a particular age can be achieved by other children of that age irrespective of their cultural context. This kind of expectation is reflected in the recent letter from Bridget Phillipson (the current Secretary of State for Education) inviting Becky Francis to carry out a 'Curriculum and Assessment Review' (DfE 2024) for England that supports high standards for 'all' in reading, writing and maths.

Challenges to the Stage Model

Piaget's theory of stage development remains contentious for several related reasons. One reason being the theoretical framework on which the model was based assumed that logical reasoning was the culmination of intellectual development. Children's development was analysed and interpreted in terms of logical operations that Piaget considered were the basis for understanding the physical world. Yet for many educationists, logic was an inadequate representation of mature thinking, one that neglected other ways of knowing and reasoning. Consequently, the logical capability that Piagetian teachers were required to nurture was challenged.

The concept of 'readiness' to learn was also considered problematic. Constraining what is made available to learn because pupils are not yet deemed ready limits what could be learnt. Restricted activity, particularly for early years and younger pupils, that only supports what they are believed to be capable of, rather than what they *potentially* could do can constrain learning. This perspective also limits the role of the teacher. For many educational researchers, the quandary about the role of instruction in learning reflected a theoretical misalignment between Piaget's constructivist learner who is self-directed and construes the world through the lens of personal experience and knowledge, a 'contextualist' (Bidell 1992), and the normative, individualistic view of the learner characterised in the stage development model. Bredo (1999) argued that modelling students' conceptualisations against a fixed framework for describing what is going on, that constitutes '*the unquestioned framework of an external observer*' (Bredo 1999: 32), assumes that what can be described is known, fixed and given from the 'outside'. Given the interrelated nature of theories of learning, knowledge and pedagogy, there is a potential pedagogical conflict between these two aspects of Piagetian theorising. The constructivist, self-directed agentive learner aligns with the metaphor of the teacher as '*gardener*', 'modeller' and 'guide'. Whereas the child in the stage model, as a limited thinker and reasoner, aligns more with metaphors of the teacher as '*parent bird*' or '*watchmaker*' discussed in Chapter 2. This denotes a pedagogical shift from a non-directive to a very directive role for teachers.

von Glasersfeld's elaboration of a Piagetian view of communication corresponds with the way language was used in the methodological approach to the studies that determined and corroborated the stages of development in Piaget's model. Researchers questioned the validity of this methodology. The concern was not with Piaget's data which were repeated across numerous research studies but how the research methods produced the data and how the findings were interpreted. To establish and document stages of development, researchers have used used experimental settings and specially designed tasks. Researchers, such as Donaldson (1978), observed pre-school and school-aged children's behaviour as they engaged with the tasks and questioned them about their behaviours. The tasks were 'given' in standardised formats, worded and resourced in the same way and communicated verbally to ensure that the same meaning and task was communicated to everyone. Assuming 'task stability' (Bredo 1999), the students' responses to Piagetian tasks were attributed to their cognitive abilities and their stage of development. Task stability is premised on children having the concepts associated with the words to achieve compatibility between the intended meaning and the constructed meaning. The methodology also assumes that it is through verbal language, and not through other means, that mutual understanding is achieved between the child and the researcher. You will recall that in Chapter 3, the agentive learner was characterised as the problem seeker and solver and yet in Piagetian methodology, the assumption that tasks are stable across learners suggests that problems can be given as opposed to being perceived and reformulated by the agentive learner. The weight given to linguistic form adopted in some Piagetian studies appears paradoxical when Piaget himself considered young children to have limited or different communicative abilities in comparison to adults.

Children as 'Contextualists'?

Questions for Consideration 4.2

> Do children make sense differently to adults?
> How do I interpret what another person says?

Task 4.2

Can you think back to an instance where you have struggled to understand or been uncertain about someone's expectations of you from what they said? Or the reverse where you have found that your expectations of your communication have not been understood?
Can you recall why that was?
How did you make sense of the experience?

Numerous research studies have subsequently explored Piaget's methodology to consider whether the interpretations of the data were valid. For example, one common procedure in a task about conservation that Margaret Donaldson (1978) reports involves two sticks of equal length. These are exactly aligned, and children are asked if they are the same length. If they agree, then the sticks are misaligned and the question repeated. If the children then state that the sticks are not the same length, they are judged to not be able to conserve length because they cannot de-centre and reason. This procedure of repeating questions was commonly used in conservation tasks and children under the age of 7 typically appear to be 'non-conservers'. Some argued that asking the repeated question implies to the child that their first response was incorrect and that children learnt this from their experience of interactions with adults, particularly in schools. When the first question was omitted, 6-year-olds were found to make far fewer errors. Donaldson and others saw this as evidence that making sense was not necessarily achieved through linguistic means alone as argued by constructivists and that children's expectations of the situation mattered. How does this explanation fit with your own experiences? Many researchers used modifications of Piagetian tasks whilst making sure that the task demands remained the same, that is, the cognitive capacity that was to be assessed. They found that whilst children may at times fail to consider other's points of view, there was evidence to challenge Piaget's claim that they were incapable of doing this; young children were found to be much less egocentric than previously claimed.

Other researchers examining the validity of Piaget's claim found that young children demonstrated little ability to reason correctly when the *purpose* of the task was not explained. For example, assessing children's ability to understand conservation often begins with two equal volumes of liquid in identical beakers. The fluid is then poured from one into a different shaped vessel, usually thinner and taller. Asked if the two containers contain the same amount, children often attend only to the height of the liquid, so the answer they give is incorrect. Light et al. (1979) modified the task so that one of the identical containers had a broken rim, and they then explained the reason for changing the container because the broken one was dangerous. This gave the task an everyday purpose that children could connect to their personal experience. When this explanation was given, children were more likely to say that the volume conserved between the two differently shaped containers was the same. The researchers argued that the task made better sense to the children, whereas an abstract problem of the same volume of liquid in different-sized containers was an adult-devised problem. For these reasons, it was argued that the child, in attempting to make sense of the task, was trying to figure out what the adult wanted them to say or do. Something that often occurs in schools. Children's responses were not the consequence of the absence of a conceptual structure related to words and how they fit together, as argued by von Glasersfeld. Rather, children needed to understand the *adult's intentions* and see value in the task if they were to appropriately engage with it. If children are trying to figure out what others mean and intend, then this suggests an ability to de-centre. Also, if children cannot make sense of a 'task' because it lacks authenticity, the extent of their reasoning is limited.

Margaret Donaldson (1978) investigated changing Piagetian tasks so that the same intellectual demands were set in situations children were familiar with. *Familiarity* was considered important in communicating tasks to children so they could connect prior experiences to the situation enabling them to make sense of what was being asked for. For the children, contextual clues mattered, indicating that meaning-making did not rely on 'sheer linguistic form' assumed in Piagetian methodology (Donaldson 1978: 65). Rather, children appeared to give priority to the meaning of the situation. Donaldson's findings suggested to her that children were more like adults than the stage development model suggested. In other words, by changing how tasks were communicated, children's performance exceeded what was expected of their theorised age-related stage of development. This raised the question about what, exactly, had the Piagetian tasks assessed. Was it the absence or presence of behaviour associated with a stage of development that determined the failure or success in communicating the task? Furthermore, was this a problem only for young children or a much wider problem?

An example from the national assessment of performance unit science project in England, Wales and Northern Ireland provides further insights into the way familiarity and purpose enable students to represent abstract variables and make sense of tasks (Murphy 1996). An investigation trialled with students aged 13 years asked them to carry out an investigation of the effect of the height of water in a container on the rate of flow of water from it. The assessors wanted to establish if students understood how to carry out a scientific investigation and what that entailed. Most students could not understand what to investigate; their difficulty was understanding the variables of height and rate of flow in an abstract way. That is, they struggled to develop a mental representation of them. To help the students, a revised task included a 'problem' set in a workplace canteen to find out why a queue of people waiting to serve themselves a drink steadily grew longer. A drawing of a large tea urn in a canteen gradually emptying and a queue of irritated people simultaneously growing was provided to help create the problem situation. Given this analogous example, more than 90% of students engaged with the investigation.

Task 4.3

Think of a recent new situation that you have had to cope with, for example, at work, in your studies or at home. It might be dealing with the latest software upgrade on your computer or phone. What did you pay attention to in dealing with this?
What helped you to know what mattered and what did not?
Donaldson refers to what matters or what is salient in a problem situation as 'contextual clues'. What does context mean to you?

In your response to Task 4.3, did familiarity between the new situation and one's you had prior experience of help you to know what to pay attention to? How learners interpret the meaning of words depends on many things including what they are familiar with because that influences what they pay attention to, that is, what they consider salient in particular learning and assessment situations. Evidence from neuroscience helps to understand this. Susan Greenfield (2000) explains how, from birth to adulthood, human brains undergo astonishing growth. She explains it is not so much that the number of neurons themselves increase, but more that the connections between them do. The thread like connections are conduits along which electric signals move and which push the main bodies of neurons further and further apart while remaining connected. It is through these connections that the neurons can communicate and 'interpret the world in the light of experience' (Greenfield 2000: 62). It is this experience of the world on which the mind acts. This view of how the brain functions aligns closely with a constructivist agentive view of mind. Neuroscience research, however, reveals that the brain functions on the 'use it or lose it' principle. The brain cells involved in activities that occur most frequently have the most extensive connections. Familiarity and its effects on meaning-making can be understood from this perspective as: 'With increasing frequency, previous associations start to dominate our interpretation and response to ongoing situations' (Greenfield 2000: 54). It is through these particular configurations of neural connections that the brain becomes personalised.

Donaldson's research findings about the context dependency of any particular intellectual performance of a child led her to challenge the epistemological basis of the stage development model and the universal nature of stages. Her findings also raised questions about how the individual and the social were related to explain evidence about how learners create meaning and make sense of things.

AN ALTERNATIVE VIEW OF LEARNING AND LANGUAGE?

> Question for Consideration 4.3
>
> Is language learning a process of labelling or about construing the world?

In his essay 'How we think', John Dewey (1991) listed three ways in which language was understood to relate to thought. The first aligned with representationalism that is they [language and thought] are identical as in information processing, the second aligns with constructivism including radical constructivism in that *'words are the garb or clothing of thought, not for thought but only for conveying it'* (Dewey 1991: 170). The third view, and the one he maintained, was that whilst language was not thought it was *'necessary for thinking as well as for its communication'*. He viewed language as much more than oral or written speech and included anything that was consciously used as a *sign*. He identified three functions of linguistic signs, as a *fence* in that they limit the meanings associated with them, as a *label* and as a *vehicle* for conveying meaning. Signs included images, gestures and much more. Dewey argued that as thought deals with *meanings*, to apprehend these meanings they must also be embodied in particular existences. The existences developed to convey meaning are the *intentional signs* of communication. They are important not in themselves but for what they have come to signify and represent. Classroom and assessment situations are examples of particular existences and provide another way of understanding what Donaldson referred to as the context dependency of children's response to Piagetian tasks. Dewey's view of communication in learning is distinguished from a constructivist view in that:

- Language can include intentional signs such as gestures, bodily movements, etc.;
- Existence (or context) is important in meaning-making;
- Language and thought are related to generate meaning.

Reconsidering intersubjectivity, Vygotsky's theory of the social origins of individual higher mental functioning offers a different view that helps to understand the fundamental human capacity Donaldson referred to as *'the grasp of meaning'* that enables children *'to make sense of what people do'* (Donaldson 1978: 38). It is the ability to interpret the context or the 'particular existences', the intentional signs, which allow children to learn language. A Vygotskian perspective therefore offers a different way of conceptualising the relationship between the individual and the social.

Vygotsky's Theory of Learning

As noted in Chapter 3, the take-up of Piagetian theorising in education tended to reflect particular emphases in the theory and not its scope (Mercer 1994). This is also the case with Vygotsky's theorising. The possibility of multiple constructions is to be expected, which is why this chapter looks at some core aspects of Vygotskian theorising and in later chapters how these are selected and interpreted in examples of influential educational theorising. In Chapter 3, it was noted how social, political and historical influences delayed the take-up of Piagetian theorising in education. Similar influences impacted on access to Vygotsky's work, and it was 60 years after his death before his work began to exert a widespread influence on Western educational thinking. Vygotsky (1896-1934) was a Soviet psychologist and a Marxist. With the rise of Stalinism, his work was banned and erased in the Soviet Union until his rehabilitation in 1956. Even when his work become available, what penetrated the West was highly selected, translated and heavily edited (Daniels 1996).

Vygotsky and his colleagues in their early work were concerned to explain the origin of human higher mental functions or psychological processes such as voluntary attention and memory as well as rational, self-directed, goal-orientated thought. This intellectual development distinguishing humans from other animals informs Vygotsky's view of the cultural line of development. Vygotsky did not research the development of lower mental functions, referred to as the natural line of development. As Rogoff (1990) puts it, he assumed *'the availability of natural development as a substrate on which cultural development is built'* (Rogoff 1990: 36). Wertsch (1991) describes the relationship between the two: *'both planes of development, the natural and the cultural, coincide and mingle with one another'* (1991: 22). Vygotsky was critical of Piaget's theory as it placed the learner outside of the social whole. His learning theory represents a reorientation from an individualistic to a sociocultural perspective on the basis that to understand the individual, you must understand the social relations in which that individual exists, their social milieu. In his theory of learning, the development of higher mental functions depends on *human and symbolic mediation*. To explain this human mediation, Vygotsky (1981) argued that:

> Any function in the child's cultural development appears twice, or on two planes. First it appears on the social plane, and then on the psychological plane. First it appears between people as an interpsychological category, and then within the child as an intrapsychological category. (Vygotsky 1981: 163)

For Piaget, the meeting of minds involves individuals and the understanding constructed is individual and the view of mind remains local. For Vygotsky, what is developed between people in social interaction is shared understanding that is then appropriated by individuals. In Vygotsky's theory of learning, *intermental processes*, that is, the *joint cognitive processes* that emerge in interactions between people, are *primary*. *Intramental processes*, that is, an individual learner's cognitive processes as they make sense of, and appropriate the meanings emerging from these social processes, are *secondary*.

Another distinctive aspect of Vygotsky's theory of learning is that all human action on both the social and individual planes is mediated by tools, that is, the technical/physical and the symbolic/psychological. The latter includes signs (gestures, images, language, symbols, texts) and sign systems (such as the human spoken language or the language of mathematics which involves numeric symbols, for example). It is in social interaction that signs function as psychological cognitive tools in behaviour. When people act, they employ these mediational means which shape and make possible certain actions. The forms of behaviours encountered through social interaction are eventually internalised by the individual, structured and organised according to social goals. Specific contexts within which social goals are achieved are what Dewey refers to as 'particular existences'. Imagine, for example, young children using counters in school to understand numerical symbols (numbers and the quantities they represent). As they begin to develop relations between the symbols through engaging in ways of communicating, they pay attention to what is valued in their culture. The relations and how they are expressed, and for what purposes, will depend on these cultural values. This understanding can then progress as learners manipulate numeric symbols and specific relationships between them to achieve social purposes such as buying or bartering for goods. In the process of buying goods, there will be specific speech forms that are involved and payment practices that will vary between different cultural contexts and situations. These will also evolve over time. Human action and agency in Vygotskian theorising cannot be understood independently of the sociohistorical and cultural context in which they arise.

For example, imagine yourself in a bartering situation that is not familiar to you. Do you engage or feel unable to act? How comfortable are you with the increased use of self-service checkouts in shops? Some people will avoid situations that require understanding of the way new technology works, opting to queue for checkouts that are staffed. They lack familiarity with, and mastery of, the mediational means involved in paying for goods. This requires understanding about; how to align the bar code on an item to be purchased, with the reader of the digital code; how to categorise (and input) items that are not coded; choosing, manipulating and reading a loyalty card or a phone app; knowing what option to select to complete the cash or card purchase; and if using a card, subsequently following instructions on a different machine designed to read credit or debit cards, contactless or pin-coded payment. The entirety of this process requires a user to understand numerical symbols (of amounts and prices of goods) as well as social literacy practices and linguistic syntax that utilise letters (linguistic symbols) to provide a set of instructions to be followed to complete automated payment. As Roth notes, '*Changes in tools…bring about changes in thinking. These changes are associated with changes in culture*' (Roth 1995: 15).

Importantly, in Vygotsky's theory of learning, unlike Piagetian theorising, for students to gain understanding of symbolic relationships requires guided and directed experience. Furthermore, if symbolic mediators are to become cognitive tools for cultural use, the human mediation or guidance must emphasise their instrumental nature, their 'particular existences', as Kozulin explains:

> Symbolic tools …..have no meaning whatsoever outside of the cultural convention that infuses them with meaning and purpose. If this purpose is poorly mediated to learners, the proper understanding of the tool's instrumental function can be missing. (Kozulin et al. 2003: 26)

Cultural development involves gaining mastery of the mediational means for thinking required in society through engagement with others more experienced with such tools. Vygotsky's view of development helped explain findings that showed cultural differences in performance on tests such as Piagetian tasks. For example, in a study that examined children's competence in the reproduction of patterns (Serpell 1979 cited by Rogoff 2003), Zambian children performed well when modelling patterns with strips of wire, a common cultural practice in their community. English children did well with paper and pencil but much less well when using strips of wire. Both groups performed equally well when modelling patterns with clay, a practice common to both cultural communities. These differences in cultural experiences, particularly notable at the formal operational stage when learners engage in abstract mental modelling, led Piaget, at a much later stage in his life, to revise his claim of universal stages, arguing instead that stages were 'contextually variable'.

A Vygotskian Perspective on Speech and Thought

Vygotsky focused specifically on tools and systems (semiotics) used in communication because of his assumption that individual mental functioning has its origins in social processes. He argued that an individual's higher mental functions emerged as a result of social processes that were 'interpsychological' (Wertsch 1985: 60) in nature. He was particularly interested in the relationship between speech and thought. His primary emphasis was discerning how different forms of speaking were related to different forms of thinking (Wertsch 1991). He assumed that verbal mediation of learning was both widespread and frequent, which it is. However, this is not the case across all cultural contexts. Kearins (cited in Wertsch 1991: 31), for example, demonstrated cultural differences in reasoning by using tasks that did not rely on verbal mediation (visual spatial memory tasks like having to remember and recreate an arrangement of coloured objects on a board). The study with Australian children from 6 to 17 years of age found that aboriginal children of desert origin consistently outperformed European Australian children on these tasks. The aboriginal children used visual strategies that Kearins suggested were common in their cultural practices, whereas the European children relied on verbal mediation using lists and labels to memorise. Findings like these were seen to limit the application of Vygotsky's theories but not to invalidate them (Wertsch 1991).

Vygotsky, in contrast to Piaget, argued that the development of thinking was determined by language, that is, the linguistic tools of thought, and the sociocultural experiences of the learner. Vygotsky's theorising reverses the Piagetian argument of individual language development. Rather than individual egocentric speech becoming socialised through talk with others as discussed in Chapter 3, Vygotsky theorised that the *primary* function of speech in both adults and children is *communication*. He described language development as a process that moves from the 'outermost plane' to the 'innermost plane'. Earliest speech is, therefore, social not individual in nature.

> ... egocentric speech. . ... grows out of its social foundations by means of transferring social, collaborative forms of behaviour to the sphere of the individual's psychological functioning. (Vygotsky 1934: 45 cited in Wertsch 1991: 34)

For Vygotsky, there is a reciprocal relationship between thought and language. He referred to thought as inner speech, which can be construed and uttered in words. In external verbal speech, thought is embodied in words, whereas in inner speech as Vygotsky describes, it is not so stable:

> 'words die as they bring forth thought' and 'thought is pure meaning'. (Vygotsky 1962 in Stierer and Maybin, 1994: 48)

Vygotsky characterises inner speech which organises thought as dynamic, unstable '*fluttering between word and thought*' (p. 48). This view resonates with Dewey's view of how language and thought relate.

Task 4.4

Think of a situation where your thinking has 'fluttered between word and thought' and you have not been able to express it fully in words?
What kind of a situation was it? How did you feel about your lack of words?

What Vygotsky refers to is the difference between thought and words in their structure and development. As Dewey put it:

> Some meaning seems almost within reach but is elusive; it refuses to condense into definite form; the attaching of a word[s] somehow puts limits around the meaning, draws it out from the void, makes it stand out as an entity on its own account. (Dewey 1991: 173)

When we say 'it's at the back of my mind', this often signals something we appear to be trying to recall but it is often something we are thinking about but cannot express. This can be because the situation and the dialogue it entails have cued some ongoing thinking searching for meanings in words that express the thought. It is very difficult to articulate or 'put into words' what we are thinking. As Bruner observed when thinking about something new or unfamiliar:

> When we are thinking at the far reach of our capacities, we are engaged with words, even led forward by them. . . . .
>
> . . . . . .the power of words is the power of thought. (Bruner 1966: 104)

Language for Vygotsky is the social means of thought. He argues that communication through words can enact meanings and thought:

> 'thought does not express itself in words but rather realizes itself in them'...'Thought must first pass through meanings and openly then through words'. (Vygotsky 1962 in Stierer and Maybin, 1994: 462)

The following quotation suggests how, for Vygotsky, thought, speech and meaning are related:

> Thought, unlike speech, does not consist of separate units. When I wish to communicate the thought that today I saw a barefoot boy in a blue shirt running down the street, I do not see every item separately: the boy, the shirt, its blue colour, his running, and the absence of shoes. I conceive of all this in one thought, but I put it into separate words. A speaker often takes several minutes to disclose one thought. In his mind the whole thought is present at once, but in speech it has to be developed successively. A thought may be compared to a cloud shedding a shower of words. Precisely because thought does not have its automatic counterpart in words, the transition from thought to word leads through meaning. (Vygotsky 1986: 251)

Vygotsky argued how word meaning could only be understood if both the *communicative* function of speech and its *intellectual* function were considered. To understand the development of word meaning requires an analysis of the function of words in mediating specific types of social interaction and communication. As Minick puts it, 'The characteristics of the word meaning reflect the characteristics of the communicative activity in which it develops' (Minick 1996a: 42).

INTERSUBJECTIVITY RECONSIDERED

> Question for Consideration 4.4
>
> How do we come to understand each other?

Bakhtin, a linguist and a contemporary of Vygotsky, offers insights about the social factors necessary to understand speech and writing that go beyond Vygotskian theorising. His view of how understanding emerges between people connects with the Vygotskian premise (Emerson 1996) in that *intermental processes*, that is, the *joint cognitive processes* that emerge in interactions between people, are *primary* in understanding learning and what is made available to learn. It recasts how we might think about individualised human agency.

For Bakhtin, words cannot be understood apart from the voices who speak them. He, therefore, focused his analysis not on word meaning but on 'utterance' which he described as the 'real unit of speech communication' (Bakhtin, cited in Wertsch 1991: 50). An utterance, as Bakhtin argues, only exists by being produced by a 'voice'. 'Voice' he described as the 'speaking consciousness' and consequently, an 'utterance' always expresses a 'point of view'. Therefore, to understand another person's utterance, the listener must 'orientate oneself with respect to it, to find the proper place for it in the corresponding context' (cited in Wertsch 1991: 54). This distinguished his work from linguistic analysis which focused on language (only the words and sentences for example). For Bakhtin, *meaning* only comes into existence when two or more voices come in contact – where the listener responds to the speaker. He referred to this 'turning to someone else' as 'addressivity'. An utterance reflects the voice producing it and the audience or voices it addresses. As we make sense of what someone says, we, at the same time, are considering the words of our response. Understanding emerges *between people* in this *dialogic* process. This aligns with Vygotsky's view that mind shifts beyond the individual to being *between people* in society. Mind is no longer local in an individual. *Dialogicality* is a fundamental Bakhtinian concept. Dialogue can be direct face to face, but Bakhtin also saw it as a way of understanding inner speech, that is as, 'alternating lines of dialogue' (Wertsch 1991: 54).

Question for Consideration 4.5

If I develop my thinking through meanings generated with others and express my sense of it in words, is it my thinking?

You will recall that in a constructivist view of intersubjectivity, its locus, like mind, is in the individual. In Vygotsky's theory of learning, human guidance is directed to developing shared understanding through a negotiated or 'dialogic' process that promotes mutual contingency. Mutual contingency relies on a 'common focus of attention and some shared presuppositions that form the ground for communication' (Rogoff 1990: 71) to achieve intersubjectivity and shared meaning. For Bruner (1966), *reciprocity* with others is an attribute of all people whatever age, and status. In contrast to the Piagetian view of the egocentric, self-centred child, he describes how people come together within a shared human endeavour which 'sweeps' the learner into a competence valued by the social group. He later described the human ability to 'grasp meaning' as the 'astonishing well-developed talent for "intersubjectivity", the human ability to understand the minds of others, whether through language, gesture, or other means' (Bruner 1996: 20). This aligns closely with Vygotsky's view of cultural development. In Vygotskian theorising, the *locus of intersubjectivity* is *between people* and mind emerges between people *in society*. What this might mean and how it might influence teaching depends on how 'between people' and 'in society' are understood. It nevertheless allows for the possibility of a *non-local mind*.

> **Task 4.5**
>
> The concept of a non-local mind runs counter to common-sense references of mind that you considered in Chapter 2. To help think about this, Wertsch uses an example from Tharp and Gallimore (1988) of a child who has lost a toy and with her father's help (he doesn't know where it is), they 'remember' where it could be. Wertsch asks who does the remembering?
> Can you recall a situation where through interaction with others a problem was solved, assuming that the problem was shared, or an object like spectacles, a book or a car in a car park is retrieved? Think of the kind of dialogue it involved and the sharing of possibilities this entailed.
> Ask yourself who solved the problem or who remembered where the car was or the keys were?

Rather than language limiting the possibility of intersubjectivity as Piaget argued, the human capacity for making sense of situations verbally is what can enable children to learn language.

A cross-cultural phenomenon is the dramatic improvement in children's performance on reading tests used in schools to assess cognitive development after 2–3 years of schooling (Rogoff 1981). Given the research evidence that familiarity and situational cues support learners to make sense of school assessment and learning tasks, how might this finding be explained?

Do children get better at reading the situational cues in assessment tasks or do they develop a better understanding of the intended meanings in 'words' in such contexts or genres? Norris Minick and James Wertsch researched how this phenomenon might be related to children's experiences in the classroom. From their observations in elementary classrooms, they found that teachers put a great deal of effort into training their learners to interpret their directions/instructions by helping them focus attention on what is being said and what their words 'represent', that is, their 'literal' meaning. This practice suggests to students that words have precise and unique meanings – meanings which are 'fully encoded in language forms' (Minick 1996b: 355). If students grasp the representational meaning intended by the teacher, then it follows that they will understand how they are expected to act. A failure to grasp that meaning or to perceive other meanings is then a failure of the learner.

In the study, children's understandings were evident through their actions that were based on their attempts to orientate themselves towards teachers to find meaning from their directions in the context of the classroom activity. For example, when told to put their 'pencils down' when they completed an activity, the teacher explained that this action was to signal that they had finished and were ready to go on to the next activity. The teacher intended, but did not say, they should keep their pencils out on the desk in readiness for the next activity. One child returned his pencil to the pencil pot on his table (a common early years classroom practice when you put your pencil down). However, in the teacher's view, he had put the pencil away. She consequently changed her next utterance to elaborate the situation asking the children to 'keep your pencil' contradicting the first utterance. When this failed to help the children understand the situation and her intentions, the teacher started to use representational directives. 'Just put it down.... Next to ... next to your paper'. The child in response moved the pot next to his worksheet. The teacher responded to this by asking the child 'Where did I say? Didn't I just say put it DOWN ... by your paper? Put it down not back in your mug' (Minick 1996b: 353-354). Teachers, in the study, resorted to representational directives to guide students through tasks when they failed to communicate the situational sense of a task to them. It was a distinguishable speech genre used across all classrooms observed.

> ### Task 4.5
>
> Think of your experience of trying to teach something for the first time to someone, like a younger sibling or relative. It could be driving or baking a sponge cake for the first time.
> How common is it for instructions to assume that words carry meaning? Do you rely on situational sense to help others and/or yourself make sense of what is intended? Recall if you can, an experience where you were learning in school. Did you experience having to follow instructions without understanding the task? How did this make you feel? Was it an effective way to learn in your experience?

As Minick notes, this strategy sends a message to children that they must do only what they are told to do. A message which was reinforced in observations when teachers reprimanded those children who, having developed a situational sense of a task, took equally appropriate, but different actions to those sanctioned. You will recall how in Piagetian tasks children were trying to figure out the task by guessing what was going on in the adult's head, something that children often do in school. Wood (1988) observes how in the home children are used to people making what they say and do *contingent* upon their activities. In school, that is reversed with students having to make what they think and do *contingent upon* the teacher's thinking and intentions (Wood 1988: 204). Does this resonate with your experience? In contrast, von Glasersfeld's constructivist teacher, the *modeller* and *guide*, has a responsibility to ensure that the guidance they provide is contingent upon the learners' actions and thinking.

When students participate in representational speech practices, they must learn how and when to put aside situational sense-making and consider the meanings of words embedded in schooled communicative practices. At the same time, through their participation in these practices, they are encultured into a social reality that conceptualises the world as a representation. To be successful at school, students must accept this (represented) reality and recognise the contexts where representational speech practices are used. External assessment in most forms is a prime example of such a context. Students are even further distanced from the thinking and intentions of people who write test and examination items than they are from their teachers and it is essential that they interpret the assessor's intentions and meanings in the words used. This might explain why several years of school experience of representational speech practices lead to the enhanced performance results that puzzled Minick and Wertsch. School 'failure', in turn, might be explained for some students not as an absence of the knowledge being assessed but rather an absence of understanding of, and familiarity with, representational speech practices along with a lack of commitment to making situational sense. Margaret Donaldson's concern with the educational value placed on disembedded modes of thought was precisely for those learners whose enculturation into the social reality of a represented world was problematic. As she notes:

> the pursuit of education.... [is] a difficult enterprise for the human mind – one which many minds refuse at an early stage. (Donaldson 1978: 81)

ASSISTED LEARNING – THE ROLE OF INSTRUCTION

von Glasersfeld argued a role for the teacher as 'modeller' and 'guide' but not 'instructor'. You will recall from Chapter 3 that the idea of the non-directive teacher emerged with progressive education and continued to be upheld in major curriculum developments in the 1980s and 1990s. The resistance to instruction or teacher direction reflects Piaget's concern that learners had to experience reciprocity in social interaction, which he considered relied on learners' ideas being accorded equal status to those they co-operate with. Instruction implies that children's and adults' ideas do not have equal status. Instruction was also seen to impose on students a teaching agenda irrespective of their readiness to learn.

Dewey (1938) in his essay 'Experience and Education' looked at the differences claimed between traditional transmission education and progressive education. He argued that it was not enough for the progressive education movement to reject traditional ideas and practices without reflecting on the assumptions behind their own principles (Dewey 1938). Whilst supportive of key tenets of progressive education, Dewey was critical of the polarisation of ideas that followed from the emphasis placed on learner freedom. For example, the assumption that to reject external authority meant that no form of direction and guidance by adults was of value. On the contrary, Dewey argued that progressive education should be based upon personal experience, which:

> may mean more multiplied and more intimate contacts between the mature and the immature than ever existed in the traditional school, and consequently more, rather than less, guidance by others. (Dewey 1938: 21)

Jerome Bruner (1966), like Vygotsky, considered the direction of intellectual growth to be from the outside in and that it occurs through 'contingent' dialogue in social interaction with agents of the culture, that is, parents, teachers and siblings. Bruner's commitment to instruction is central to his ontological position, and like Dewey, he saw contingent guidance as crucial to learning. In his view, what distinguishes humans as a species was not only the capacity to learn but also the capacity to teach. His view of teaching, like von Glasersfeld's, requires that guidance or instruction is translated into, and contingent upon, the learner's way of attempting to solve a problem. The aim of teaching was to lead learners towards self-sufficiency, that is, stand-alone competence. At this time in his theorising, Bruner drew on Vygotsky briefly. His arguments aligned with central aspects of Vygotskian theorising. For example, he argued, the teacher must:

> become part of the student's internal dialogue...It is like becoming a speaker of a language one shares with somebody. The language of that interaction becomes part of oneself. (Bruner 1966: 124)

Question for Consideration 4.6

Is learning constrained by children's cognitive readiness?

Bruner's view of the significance of instruction led him to challenge how Piagetian theorising was understood and taken up in schools. For example, he theorised that intellectual growth was not easily linked to age and rejected the concept of readiness to learn arguing that:

> ...one *teaches* readiness or provides opportunities for its nurture one does not simply wait for it. (Bruner 1966: 29)

Bruner's theory of instruction was based on the premise that anything could be taught at any time in an appropriate version of any skill or knowledge. He envisaged the school curriculum as a spiral; as children progress through schooling, they revisit, deepen and enrich their earlier understandings. He also argued for multiple pathways for learners to achieve the same learning, rejecting a pedagogy that leads all children through the same steps. A fundamental part of Bruner's view about how to support learning was to look forward and not back, to consider the pathway a learner was on, both on a task and in the wider educational process. The view that instruction should focus on learners' potential resonates with Vygotsky's approach to instruction and his conceptualisation of the ZPD.

THE ZONE OF PROXIMAL DEVELOPMENT

Vygotsky focused his research on higher mental functions that are closely linked with formal instructional contexts such as school. In theorising that individual cognitive processes were social in origin and internalised from joint intellectual processes, he was concerned to understand the relationship between the inter (between people) and intra (within the person) planes of mental functioning and the role of human mediation within this. His theory, in contrast to Piaget's, foregrounded a role for guidance and instruction in the learning process because of the difference between the theories in how *reciprocity* is understood and what has primacy in learning, the individual or the social.

In Vygotsky's theorising, inequality between participants is essential rather than problematic as in a Piagetian perspective, but inequality is understood not in terms of power but in the knowledge of what assistance is needed to enable a child's development (between ages 5 and 16). Asymmetry in knowledge relations between the learner and the more expert other is crucial. The goal of interaction is not co-operation but collaboration in joint problem-solving. Cultural development was theorised by Vygotsky as occurring in given periods of time within which a child's learning progresses to moments of structural reorganisation of psychological functions. These periods of time are not fixed by age, and the structural reorganisations are not universal in the way that Piaget's stages of development were conceptualised, but culturally determined. That is, developmental reorganisation is structured and organised according to the social goals and ways of acting of a given culture resulting in 'the development of mediated, voluntary, historically developed mental functions' (Minick 1996a: 33).

Vygotsky argued that it is in the ZPD where assessment of a learners' holistic maturing functions informs teachers about the state of students' development (their *actual* development determined by independent problem-solving and their *potential* development with support in joint problem-solving). The ZPD is the distance between these two levels of development. Vygotsky gave an example of two children who perform at the same level on a test unaided and then with aid: 'one of them easily solves test items taken from two years above the child's level of [actual] development. The other solves test items that are only a half-year above his or her level of [actual] development' (Vygotsky 1956, cited in Wertsch and Tulviste 1996: 56). He questioned whether this meant that the mental development of these children was the same; for Vygotsky, it was not. The measurement of potential development was seen to be essential as it directs teachers' attention to those mental 'processes that are now in the state of coming into being, that are only ripening, or only developing' (Vygotsky cited in Wertsch and Tulviste 1996: 57). The ZPD is the zone of proximal development and not learning. However, working within the zone is where learning occurs.

INTERPRETING THE ZPD

In the book, three general interpretations of the ZPD are considered (here, in Chapter 5 and then Chapter 6). Each depends on the interpretation and understanding of 'social'. In the narrowest sense of the ZPD, the focus is on the problem-solving abilities of a learner working alone on a task. The *actual zone*, and the problem-solving that is achieved with mediation provided by a more expert, knowledgeable other, is the *proximal zone*. The goal is the achievement of the task and the social is between the learner and the more expert other in their interaction. This view is exemplified in a research study by Wood et al. (1976) who explored the impact of different forms of aid or instruction on 3- to 5-year-olds' ability to solve problems. The study demonstrated that young children could be taught to successfully *'carry out a task or achieve a goal which would be beyond his unassisted efforts'* (Wood et al. 1976: 91). The authors described the teaching that achieved this using the metaphor of *'scaffolding'*. Scaffolds are the pedagogic moves within the ZPD to enable learning.

For scaffolding to work, children must have a sense of the task and its solution. The teacher provides some effective feedback but not regarding all the competences to achieve the task. These competences are the focus for the child's learning. Wood et al. (1976) explain that to enable learners to gain a sense of the task involves scaffolding that encourages children to engage first in 'trying out behaviours'. 'Trying out behaviours' recruits children to engage with tasks on their level of understanding and provide both learners and their teachers with important information to 'scaffold' learning central to maintaining mutual contingency. At the same time, 'trying out' confronts learners with puzzles to be addressed with support. This is quite different from Piaget's view that it is cognitive dissonance alone that facilitates an individual's eventual accommodation of something newly encountered in the learning environment.

Wood et al. (1976) describe the adult tutor's role and the instructional intent of different scaffolds to achieve different pedagogic functions.

> to recruit attention, reduce degrees of freedom in the task to manageable limits, maintain 'direction' in the problem solving, mark critical features control frustration and demonstrate solutions when the learner can recognise them. (Wood et al. 1976: 104)

Wood (1988) expanded this view of teaching of young children which he referred to as 'contingent' teaching:

> Contingent teaching helps children to construct local expertise – expertise connected with that particular task or group of tasks – by focusing their attention on relevant and timely aspects of the task, and by highlighting things they need to take account of...We have used the metaphor of 'scaffolding' to describe this aspect of the teaching process. Built well such scaffolds help children to learn how to achieve heights that they cannot scale alone. (Wood 1988: 80)

The more expert other provides instructional support and guidance (scaffolds) as learners solve problems until they achieve stand-alone competence, or in assessment terms their 'best performance'. Part of the aid provided is in the negotiation of meaning between students' understanding of the task and the teacher's view of where their learning is progressing to achieve the solution of the task. What is learnt is internalised or acquired from the shared cognitive processes and the sense the learner makes in this joint problem-solving activity. In this view of the ZPD, acquisition of culturally valued knowledge remains an individual process and the social relations and social milieu central to Vygotsky's view of how human action is understood are not considered. The nature of knowledge within this interpretation does not change from that of other theories discussed so far.

SUMMARY

In this chapter, you have considered briefly how post-Piagetian theories have been developed and how this changes the metaphor for the teacher away from the *gardener* to the *modeller* of learners' ways of knowing and the *guide* towards adult competence. The evidence that challenged the stage model of development extended ontological understanding of how students make sense and construe the world. Importantly, it introduced the idea of the learner as a *contextualist*, seeking to make situational sense. This opened up the possibility of thinking differently about communication and the relationship between language and thought from Vygotsky's theorising and briefly how Bakhtin's theory extends this. Vygotsky argued that to understand meanings of words used in verbal exchanges requires an analysis of the function of those words, particularly in the ways they mediate specific types of social interaction and communication. Although constructivists, and those taking up aspects of Vygotsky's theories, reject a representationalist view of knowledge and communication, research shows how representational speech practices are drawn on in schools and enculture learners into a social reality of a represented world. This offers insights into how school 'failure' might be understood for some students.

Vygotsky's view of learning suggests a quite different role for instruction than that recognised by Piaget. Asymmetry in expertise is the source of social learning as learners engage with the tools and agents of their culture to achieve stand-alone competence in socially productive practices and activities. The metaphor of the teacher as *scaffolder* was related to one interpretation of Vygotsky's concept of the ZPD. This interpretation took little account of the social character of learning central to Vygotsky's theorising. You were introduced to pedagogic practices, referred to as scaffolds, that emerged from research to find out what forms of guidance enabled young children's learning. This research was carried out in experimental rather than naturalistic conditions and Wood (1988) had reservations about the possibility of extending the metaphor of scaffolding to classrooms where groups of students are taught simultaneously. Chapter 5 discusses how addressing this dilemma led to the development of a social constructivist view of learning. What was clear from the teacher metaphors of *modeller*, *guide* and *scaffolder* was the importance of instruction or teaching being *contingent* upon the learners' actions and thinking. In the interpretation of the ZPD discussed, the nature of knowledge has not changed nor the educational goals for learning; learning has remained a process of internalisation and acquisition. This indicates how different theories about learners, and about teachers, can still share similar views about knowledge (as organised sets of externally determined mental structures and procedures). In Chapter 5, the following questions are addressed:

- How is context understood in social constructivist and sociocultural theories of learning?
- How does this influence how learners are positioned in classrooms and how diversity between students is understood?

ADDITIONAL READING

Donaldson, M. (1978/2006 edition) *Children's Minds*, London: Harper Perennial. This provides examples of research which challenged Piaget's stage model of development, Including Donaldson's theorising about learning that developed from tensions with the staged development model.

Bruner, J. (2008) *Celebrating Divergence*. Piaget and Vygotsky. This chapter provides an informative discussion about fundamental differences between the theories that these two developmental psychologists offered.

Dewey, J. (1938) *Experience and Education*, New York: Free Press. This essay demonstrates the influence of Dewey's ideas and how they correspond with theorising about learning that take a different view of the individual–social relationship to Piaget.

REFERENCES

Adey, P. (2001) 160 years of science education: An uncertain link between theory and practice. *School Science Review*, March, 2001, 41-48.

Bidell, T. (1992) Beyond interactionism in contextualist models of development. *Human Development*, 35, 306-15.

Bredo, E. (1999) Reconstructing educational psychology. In P. Murphy (Ed) *Learners, Learning & Assessment*, London: Paul Chapman Publishing.

Bruner, J. S. (1966) *Towards a Theory of Instruction*. Cambridge, MA: Harvard University Press.

Bruner, J. (1996) *The Culture of Education*. Cambridge, MA: Harvard University Press.

Brown, A. L., Campione, J. C., Metz, K. E. & Ash, D. B. (1997) The development of science learning abilities in children. In K. Harnquist & A. Burgen (Eds) *Growing up with Science, Developing Early Understanding of Science*. London: Jessica Kingsley Publishers.

Daniels, H. (1996) Introduction: Psychology in a social world. In H. Daniels (Ed) *An Introduction to Vygotsky*. London: Routledge.

Dewey, J. (1938) *Experience and Education*. New York: Free Press.

Dewey, J. (1991) *How We Think*. Amherst, NY: Promethueus Books.

DfE (2012) *New primary curriculum to bring higher standards in English, maths and science*. Available at https://www.gov.uk/government/news/new-primary-curriculum-to-bring-higher-standards-in-english-maths-and-science#:~:text=By%20age%20seven%2C%20pupils%20should,16%2D7%3D9. Accessed 27/02/25.

DfE (2023) *'Maths to 18' England*. Available at https://commonslibrary.parliament.uk/research-briefings/cbp-9780/ Accessed 05/01/25.

DfE (2024) *Letter from Secretary of State to Becky Francis*. Available at: https://assets.publishing. service.gov.uk/media/6699755dfc8e12ac3edaffda/Letter_from_Secretary_of_State_to_Becky_ Francis.pdf Accessed 19/08/24.

Donaldson, M. (1978/2006 edition) *Children's Minds*. London: Harper Perennial.

Emerson, C. (1996) The outer word and inner speech: Bakhtin, Vygotsky, and the internalization of language. In H. Daniels (Ed) *An Introduction to Vygotsky*. London: Routledge.

Greenfield, S. (2000) *The Private Life of the Brain*, London: Penguin.

Ingram, J., Stiff, J., Cadwallader, S., Lee, G. & Kayton, H. (2023) *PISA 2022: National Report for England*. Available at https://assets.publishing.service.gov.uk/media/656dc3321104cf0013f a742f/PISA_2022_England_National_Report.pdf Accessed 19/08/24.

Kozulin, A., Gindis, B., Ageyev, V. S. & Miller, S. M. (Eds.) (2003) *Vygotsky's Educational Theory in Cultural Context*. New York: Cambridge University Press.

Mercer, N. (1994) Neo-Vygotskian theory and classroom education. In B. Stierer & J. Maybin (Eds) *Language, Literacy and Learning in Educational Practice*. Clevedon: Multilingual Matters.

Minick, N. J. (1996a) The development of Vygotsky's thought. In H. Daniels (Ed) *An Introduction to Vygotsky*. London: Routledge.

Minick, N. J. (1996b) Teachers' directives: The social construction of 'literal meanings' and 'real worlds' in classroom discourse. In S. Chaiklin & J. Lave (Eds) *Understanding Practice Perspectives on Activity and Context*. New York: Cambridge University Press.

Murphy, P. (1996) Integrating learning and assessment – The role of learning theories? In P. Woods (Ed), *Contemporary Issues in Teaching and Learning*. London: Routledge.

Nuffield-Chelsea Curriculum Trust (1993) *Nuffield Primary Science Science Processes and Concepts Exploration Teachers' Handbook*. London: Collins Educational.

Light, P., Buckingham, N. & Roberts, A. H. (1979) The conservation task as an interactional setting. *British Journal of Educational Psychology*, 49, 304-310.

Rogoff, B. (1981) Schooling and the development of cognitive skills. In H. C. Triandis & A. Heron (Eds) *Handbook of Cross-Cultural Psychology: Vol 4. Developmental Psychology*. Boston, MA: Allyn and Bacon.

Rogoff, B. (1990) *Apprenticeship in Thinking, Cognitive Development in Social Context*. Oxford: Oxford University Press.

Rogoff, B. (2003) *The Cultural Nature of Human Development*. Oxford: Oxford University Press.

Roth, M. W. (1995) *Authentic School Science, Knowing and Learning in Open-Inquiry Science Laboratories*. Dordrecht: Kluwer Academic Publishers.

Sacks, O. (1995) *An Anthropologist on Mars*. London. Picador.

Sadler, D. R. (1989) Formative assessment and the design of instructional systems. *Instructional Science*, 18(2), 119-44.

Tharp, R. G. & Gallimore, R. (1988) *Rousing Minds to Life: Teaching, Learning, and Schooling in Social Context*. Cambridge University Press.

Von Glasersfeld, E. (1989) Learning as a constructive activity. In P. Murphy & B. Moon (Eds) *Developments in Learning and Assessment*. London: Hodder and Stoughton, pp. 5-18.

Vygotsky, L. S. (1962) Thought and language. In B. Stierer & J. Maybin (Eds) *Language, Literacy and Learning in Educational Practice*. Clevedon: Multilingual Matters.

Vygotsky, L. S. (1981) The genesis of higher mental functions. In J. V. Wertsch (Ed) *The Concept of Activity in Soviet Psychology*. Armonk, NY: Sharpe.

Wertsch, J. V. (1985) *Vygotsky and the Social Formation of Mind*. Cambridge, MA: Harvard University Press.

Wertsch, J. V. (1991) *Voices of the Mind. A Sociocultural Approach to Mediated Action*, Cambridge, MA: Harvard University Press.

Wertsch, J. V. & Tulviste, P. (1996) Contemporary developmental psychology. In H. Daniels (Ed), *An Introduction to Vygotsky*. London: Routledge.

Wood, D. (1988) *How Children Think and Learn* 1st ed. Oxford: Blackwell Publishers.

Wood, D, (1998) *How Children Think and Learn* 2nd ed. Oxford: Blackwell Publishers.

Wood, D., Bruner, J. S. & Ross, G. (1976) The role of tutoring in problem solving. *Journal of Child Psychology and Child Psychiatry*, 17, 89-100.

5
INTRODUCING SOCIAL CONSTRUCTIVISM AND SOCIOCULTURALISM

CONTENTS

Complementary or Irreconcilable Theories of Learning	99
Understanding Learning in the Classroom Microculture	106
Context Beyond the Classroom	113
The Social Constructivist Teacher: *'Tourist Guide'* or *'Sherpa'*	115
Nature of Knowledge and Knowing	119
Summary	121
Additional Reading	122
References	122

Chapter Aims

After reading Chapter 5, you will have considered:

- versions of social constructivist theorising and how they interpret and represent the social dimension of teaching and learning;
- the view of the ZPD implied;
- the metaphor of the teacher as *tourist guide or sherpa*;
- the impact of social constructivism on curriculum specifications and educational goals;
- tensions between relativist and realist ontological and epistemological perspectives.

The theories discussed in Chapters 3-6 all assume individual human agency and an agentive mind. In this chapter and in Chapter 6, you will consider theories that present different perspectives on social dimensions of learning. Within these theories, the individual and the social are seen to influence each other, though they are not necessarily considered to be interdependent or mutually constitutive. We will also continue to consider how policy, practice and these more socially oriented perspectives of learning are related. The beginning of the chapter considers perspectives that are labelled as social constructivism or align closely with it. Later in the chapter cultural influences are brought to the fore to introduce socioculturalisim. This introduction is necessarily a partial consideration of a complex and evolving field. Chapter 6 extends consideration of social perspectives of learning beyond social constructivism. To remind you of the meaning attributed to agency in Chapter 3, two dimensions or planes were highlighted. Piaget's theory refers to the process that involves both *being able to act* and *being able to construct meaning from the consequences of those actions*. It is in these circumstances that a learner's *experience of agency* emerges. Biesta et al. (2015) refer to this as an actor-situation transaction. So agency is described as an emergent phenomenon, an experience of agency or its absence. There is potential to define agency in different ways (see for example Edwards 2015) and to emphasise different aspects of it and this will be considered later in this chapter and Chapter 6. Chapter 5 examines to what extent these selected versions of social theories differ from and/or elaborate Piagetian views which place the learner outside of, or apart from, the social whole and treat the individual and social as a dualism, and Vygotskian theorising where meaning emerges between people through social interaction in joint cognitive processes. As in previous chapters, you will be invited to examine the views of learning, knowledge and pedagogy embedded in the practice advocated.

Particular labels concerning theories of learning are umbrella terms which encompass differences as well as similarities between people's perspectives. For example, you have seen in earlier chapters how the practice advocated in curriculum initiatives that claimed constructivist perspectives varied in the emphasis given to learner freedom and, consequently, in how the teachers' role and guidance were understood. In Chapter 4, one interpretation of Vygotsky's concept of the zone of proximal development (ZPD) was considered that highlighted what it meant for who was involved in social interaction to achieve particular learning outcomes. In this chapter, a further interpretation of the ZPD is discussed and the influence of Vygotsky's theorising about the distinction between 'genuine' or 'scientific' concepts and spontaneous everyday concepts and how they develop (Wertsch 1991). The chapter offers a way of 'reading' (i.e. interpreting and understanding) social constructivist perspectives drawing on the theories discussed so far in the book. It is open to you to judge the extent to which the 'reading' resonates with your view and how it enables you to position yourself and adopt or not the practice you value in relation to it.

Question for Consideration 5.1

How do terms such as

'inter-thinking'; 'shared thinking'; 'exchanging thinking'; 'joint thinking'; 'explaining thinking'; justifying thinking; 'critiquing others' thinking'

convey contrasting epistemic ways of learning under a social constructivist umbrella?

COMPLEMENTARY OR IRRECONCILABLE THEORIES OF LEARNING

As Vygotsky's socio-historical theory of development became more widely available and the role of 'teaching' or expertise in enabling learning became firmly re-established, there was an evolution in educational theorising. For some, Vygotskian views were irreconcilable with constructivist views of mind and knowledge. This led to a divide between constructivist, social constructivist and sociocultural perspectives on learning and knowledge. For others, rapprochement was possible and pragmatically desirable as the views were considered partially complementary with the potential to illuminate different educational issues (Cobb and Yackel 1996; Smith et al. 1999; McPhail 2017). These educationists focused on the possible relationships between constructivist and social constructivist theories of learning and mind and how they might inform and guide practice. In the debates that ensued, social constructivism in various forms was elaborated. It is also a label that became less widely used over time as people increasingly referred to their use of Vygotskian theories, for example, as sociocultural, cultural, socio-historical or cultural historical. This has led to recent confusion because there are educationalists who refer to sociocultural learning, but only consider a very limited perspective or aspect of it. This chapter, consequently, seeks to clarify for the reader why there remains a widespread range of interpretations about this theory of learning.

Views of Context

Brown et al. (1997: 19) note that towards the end of his career Piaget considered that his model of stage development, particularly formal operations, was flawed as it failed to take account of the role of the situation in *'influencing and constraining the direction and form of children's thinking'*. Piaget observed in a speech that:

> one cannot think of the child without asking whether logic is a social thing and in what sense. I have been bothered by this question; I have sought to put it aside; it has always returned. (Piaget, 1977 cited by Rogoff 1990: 33-4)

Piaget argued that the individual and the environment are inseparable, as we noted in Chapter 4. His research, however, did not investigate social influences.

Questions for Consideration 5.2

What is 'context'?
Are there different ways of understanding context?

Task 5.1

You thought about the nature of context in Task 4.3. How would you understand context now?

In Chapter 4, you were introduced to one interpretation of the ZPD. What constitutes context in a more social view of learning do you think?

A common, everyday use of the word *context* is to imply a specific situation, but what constitutes a situation varies. In behaviourist and cognitive constructivist theorising, it was noted that little or no attention is paid to context in a situational sense. In school activities, context can be used very specifically in relation to a learning or assessment task. However, it is quite vaguely applied in a 'real life' context which typically means outside of school. Curriculum specifications of expected learning outcomes in policy documents have for many years given value to the application of knowledge across contexts. That is, as part of their learning, students are expected to acquire abstract concepts and skills *and* an understanding of how and when to apply them to new situations to solve problems and make progress in learning. Many assessment items test for achievement by setting tasks in real-life contexts to measure whether students can re-situate their knowledge in answering a particular question. This assumes two aspects of context: both knowledge transfer and the item or problem content are the only relevant contexts (Lave 1988: 39). Assuming this view, each new learning or assessment situation represents an isolated context which positions school as a decontextualised site of learning (Lave 1988). The interpretation of the ZPD discussed in Chapter 4 similarly focuses on the problem or task content as the context. Learning and teaching occur in the distance between the problem-solving abilities of a learner working alone, the *actual zone* and the problem-solving that they can achieve with human mediation provided by a more expert, knowledgeable other, that is, the *proximal zone*. The goal in this view of the ZPD is the stand-alone achievement of the task; the social is in the interaction between the learner and the more expert other. In the next section, you are introduced to another view of the social dimension of teaching and learning.

Context as the Classroom Microculture

One version of social constructivist theorising is based on a social interactionist perspective of constructivism. The social sciences as well as psychology inform this perspective. As Bauersfeld notes:

> In the human sciences different actions and different concerns often produce different theories, and different theories in turn produce different realities. (Bauersfeld 1980: 25)

Social interactionists, like constructivists, reject a representationalist view of knowledge; they share the view that people actively construct their understanding of the world. Those educationists who adopt this perspective focus on the ways that individuals come to know how to act and make sense of things through engaging in common activities, that is, how they achieve intersubjectivity. You were introduced to the Vygotskian view of this in Chapter 4. Roth and Hsu (2010) explain the ethnomethodological view that underpins social interactionism using the example of a queue. For ethnomethodologists, queues can only be understood if the researcher understands how queuing works and can function as a member of a queue, that is, from within practice. Can you recall experiences of queuing? Typically, you work out where the queue starts and that varies between situations and how people interpret queuing instructions such as 'Queue here'. Then you might have to decide if a person who appears to not follow the queuing protocol is pushing in or has just failed to work out the situated meaning of 'Queue here'. A further consideration is whether your view is shared by other queue members. If so, how does that inform your next actions? Do you just shrug or do you tell the person appearing not to understand like you do what the problem is, reinforcing what 'being' in a queue means? According to interactionists, 'We learn to behave in social settings through the reflected participation and action in social settings' (Bauersfeld 1980: 38). Consequently, a social interactionist researcher in this case would focus on understanding the knowledge and actions that make queues possible in specific situations and cultures. Applied to classrooms, the interactionist researcher seeks to understand how teachers and students constitute social norms and practices in classroom interactions.

For example, children from a young age must learn what being in a subject classroom means and part of that includes understanding what is expected of them. Learners need to 'get it right'; 'Getting it right means practising the culture in an identifiable individual way and to do this students have to know the ways in which cultural practices can be varied' (Davies 2003: 9–10).

> **Question for Consideration 5.3**
>
> How are learning opportunities created between teachers and students if a classroom is a social context?

> **Task 5.2**
>
> Think of your experience of schooling and some of the social norms and conventions. Wearing school uniform, which kinds of trousers or skirts were accepted or not. Practices such as how you were expected to move along corridors or stairs and sit in assemblies and ways that access to equipment in science laboratories or sports halls were organised.
> Think back to experiences of your own or of learners you have supported.
> Can you remember when you struggled to 'get it right'? What was it about the routine ways of being in school that helped you understand what was expected of you?

Negotiating Meanings

Did you find that you looked to other learners and what they were doing to help you understand the teacher's intentions? Did you ask them for help or did they ask you? Do you recall if 'getting it right' was more difficult for some students than for others? Was it more difficult for you or for them in some subjects than others? Why was this? Heinrich Bauersfeld's (1980) interactionist version of constructivism, which he labelled *social constructivism*, developed through his research in mathematics classrooms and is grounded in practice. He describes his research concern as both pragmatic (action) and highly theoretical (reflection) and sees both as being 'deeply interwoven' (Bauersfeld 1980: 25). He drew on radical constructivism discussed in Chapter 4, which he considered compatible with his argument for a social dimension in the individual processes of the construction of meaning.

In discussing the 'so-called reality of a mathematics classroom', Bauersfeld argued that teaching and learning are realised through human interaction as people negotiate meaning through a process of *mutual adaptation*. In this view, social situations in classrooms are dynamic and emergent. They are created, adapted and re-created as teachers and students *reflect* on the actual and perceived moves of others in the classroom. Internal reflective activity is informed by an individuals' experience of a classroom situation and their role within it. This kind of internal reflective activity informs how teachers might modify their intentions for their learners and enact them in ongoing classroom activity. Students' interpretations also change as they 'guess ahead' about the teacher's intentions. Consequently, task stability is not assumed either across participants or for any one student over the period of an interactive classroom episode. The task is a function of the evolving situation and something students continue to try and make sense of. It is through reflective activity that teachers' and students' versions of classroom reality are constructed. Reality emerges through reflexive activity (Bauersfeld 1980: 30). Does this description of working out what is going on and what you are supposed to do resonate with your memories of making sense of schooling and the different ways you learnt in different subject classes?

Language in this process of social negotiation is also understood to be situated. You will recall from Chapter 4 how Bakhtin argued that words cannot be understood apart from the voices that speak them. To understand another person's utterance, the listener must orientate oneself with respect to it and the speaker to be able to appropriately respond. Bauersfeld, in describing interaction within a mathematics classroom, expresses a similar view:

> While speaking, each participant anticipates the understanding and interests of the specific addressee [the person being spoken to]. The speech gets organized through the expectation of what the addressed person already knows. Each speaker uses his [or her] interpretation of the given situation and of the addressee as an index from which he forms his utterances. (Bauersfeld 1980: 34)

The process of negotiation of individual meaning in this version of social constructivism differs from a constructivist view where negotiation is explicit and occurs when perturbations signal a breakdown in communication which cues cognitive conflict (see Chapter 3). For Bauersfeld, negotiation is both an explicit and implicit process as teachers with their students mutually adapt to *'establish expectations for other's activity and obligations for their own activity'* (Cobb 1999: 139).

> The student's reconstruction of mathematical meaning is a construction via social negotiation about what is meant and about which performance of meaning gets the teacher's (or the peers') sanction. (Bauersfeld 1980: 35)

Bauersfeld argued that it is within the local microculture that students learn *when to do what* and *how to do it* within a subject. He describes this as enculturation into a subject which comes into effect at a meta level, beyond the level of individual consciousness (Bauersfeld 1995 cited by Cobb 1999).

Questions for Consideration 5.4

If there is a social dimension to teaching and learning, does that alter what students are expected to learn?

Does a social perspective on learning mean that different tasks are appropriate for different learners?

Learning Tasks and the Nature of Understanding

The focus of learning in social constructivism is primarily the constructive processes through which meaning is achieved, and secondly the quality of the outcome. It is through critical enquiry and reflection on the processes of construction that students learn to evaluate the effectiveness of their solutions and search for more effective ones. This aligns with Dewey's view:

> Were all instructors to realise that the quality of mental processes, not the production of correct answers, is the measure of educative growth something hardly less that a revolution in teaching would be worked. (Dewey, 1926: 206–207 cited in Hiebert et al. 1996)

In contrast to Dewey, however, Bauersfeld argued that any task can be re-orientated with a change in pedagogy away from a product-orientated approach, that is, a focus on the correct solution, to a construction-orientated approach, focusing on achieving and searching for different (mathematical) solutions. Consequently, tasks that support students' learning can be abstract or decontextualised; that is the context could be doing mathematics in school or linked to everyday life through content and setting, what is often referred to as real-life or realistic settings. An example of a 'realistic' setting from Bauersfeld (1992) involves a lumber merchant's shop which has a small range and number of fixed-length timber planks (unlikely in most lumber merchants!) and customers with varying requirements. The task for the third-grade students was to discuss and construct possible solutions with the finite number of planks available to meet different customers' needs. The children had to choose mathematical methods that were effective in achieving a solution. Initially, the students addressed each customer's needs without consideration of the cost of 'waste'. Once this variable was introduced, the problem was reformulated and the students rethought their initial solutions. In a construction-orientated approach, the teacher's primary focus is individual students and how they construct and attribute mathematical meaning. However, in a social constructivist perspective, the goal is to develop students' flexibility in mathematising so they become competent in reformulating problems, constructing solutions and judging their own adequacy. So how is transfer to new situations understood? This is clearer if you consider problem-solving approaches to subject learning. These share similarities with social constructivist theories of teaching and learning although they are often not expressed explicitly.

Problem-solving approaches focus on making subject matter 'problematic' and position students as problematisers by engaging them in critical, reflective enquiry. Hiebert et al. (1996), a mathematics education reformist in the United States, advocated this approach and considered it had application across school subjects. The similarities with an interactionist social constructivist perspective include:

- the focus for teaching and learning is the process and methods of constructing solutions, and the search for more effective ones rather than the product or solution itself;
- teachers and students together create a social and intellectual classroom community;

- students share the responsibility for developing and maintaining the community or classroom culture through sharing their thinking and findings and explaining and justifying their methods;
- students recognise the inventiveness of their own practice (Lave et al. 1988: 69 cited by Hiebert et al. 1996);
- probematising and reflective enquiry *'rely more on the student* [their prior mathematical knowledge] *and the culture of the classroom than on the task'* (Hiebert et al. 1996: 16).

Mathematical understanding is defined as both *functional* in terms of *'the ways in which students contribute to and share in collective activity in the here and now'* (Hiebert et al. 1996: 16) and *structural*. Structural understanding is the knowledge students take away from the classroom, the 'residue' of participation in problem-solving activity. Hiebert et al identified three kinds of residue:

- knowledge of the structure of the subject;
- strategies for solving problems and the procedures associated with these strategies;
- positive dispositions towards the subject.

It is in the construction of problem solving strategies that mathematical procedures (how) and concepts (what) are drawn on, developed and importantly, related. The way the problem is perceived by the learners depends upon the students' prior mathematical knowledge and experience. Strategic mathematical understanding, like Bauersfeld's enculturation into the subject, is understood to be at the meta level and, in that sense, is abstracted. It is the generalised nature of this strategic understanding that enables new problems to be tackled and new strategies to be developed. There is no separation between acquisition and application as the knowledge acquired is instrumental.

There are alignments here with constructivist epistemology. That prior mathematical knowledge matters and shapes the problems perceived and, therefore, the learning opportunities and that knowledge is an individual construction not tied to the situations in which it is acquired. Lave (1988) would argue that this latter point assumes that there is 'no interaction between tool and situation' (Lave 1988: 41). Bauersfeld recognises this interaction. He argues that there are no universal objective meanings in subjects like mathematics as each symbolic form has meaning attributed via contextual interpretation (situational sensemaking). Consequently, each concept 'gets infiltrated with contextual information' (Bauersfeld 1980: 35).

Task 5.3

How does the teacher's role differ from that of von Glasersfeld's (1989) *modeller* and *guide* in this interactionist social constructivist perspective of learning?
Does the learner's role differ in your view?
Do learners appear to have more or less freedom than the constructivist learner?

In von Glasersfeld's view, the onus is on the teacher to understand and model the child's thinking. The guidance is translated into, and contingent upon, the learner's way of attempting to solve a problem. The teacher has responsibility for maintaining mutual contingency. The learner you will recall is self-directed, which suggests considerable freedom for the learner yet the absence of direct instruction can constrain students in what they recognise as opportunities for learning and in their ability to engage with them. In Wood's example of contingent teaching (Chapter 4), the learner is carefully supported via scaffolding in one-to-one teaching situations. Social constructivist theorising applies to the classroom and how the teacher with her students manage the teaching and learning process. For the social constructivist teacher, the responsibility for maintaining intersubjectivity is a joint one; both the teacher and students must adapt to achieve mutual contingency. The student must pay attention to the teachers' ways of making sense, their own expectations of this and how they 'read' and create meaning in classroom interactions 'in the moment'. To understand a teacher's expectations and intentions, students must understand what 'doing' a subject means. In a social constructivist approach, learners have increased responsibility for learning *and* for the learning of others. There is a shift from Piagetian co-operation to collaboration between students. Learners also have freedom and responsibility to determine what is problematic, to develop their own methods of solution and to validate them.

In both interactionist and problem-solving approaches, there is wider recognition of the 'social' than in constructivism or Wood's contingent teaching; it extends across a class but not beyond classroom 'walls'. Teachers and students co-create a culture that enables reflective enquiry where willingness to share, to discuss and to listen is crucial. The teacher's role is to co-ordinate meanings, provide information and offer feedback from the perspective of the structure and logic of the subject. The teacher is the subject authority and a key feature of their role is the selection of tasks that are potentially productive within that subject's logic.

UNDERSTANDING LEARNING IN THE CLASSROOM MICROCULTURE

Cobb and Yackel (1996), as part of a classroom-based research project, developed an interactionist view of teaching and learning with reference to Bauersfeld with whom they collaborated. They described their interactionist perspective as an *emergent* or *social constructivist* approach which they considered augmented rather than replaced a psychological constructivist perspective. For Cobb and Yackel (1996), like Bauersfeld, theory and practice are reflexive. Theory grows out of practice and feeds back and informs practice. In arguing for the usefulness of an interactionist perspective, they were careful to make connections and distinctions between it and constructivist and sociocultural theoretical positions. For example, they argued that both interactionist and Vygotskian perspectives view learning as inherently social and conceptual development is mediated by symbols and artefacts. However, in the interactionist perspective, social refers to the local practices within the classroom microculture which differs from the Vygotskian concern with the wider system of mathematical practices. Importantly too the 'link between collective and individual processes is indirect' (Cobb and Yackel 1996: 185). In an interactionist view, meanings evolve in the process of *mutual adaption* as teachers' and students' individually co-ordinate activities. Meanings are social products but thinking is an individual construction rather than directly derived from joint cognitive processes as is assumed in a Vygotskian perspective.

Question for Consideration 5.5

How is social interaction understood in different perspectives of learning?

Cobb and Yackel specify three dimensions of the social and intellectual community that need to be in place to support learning from an emergent social constructivist perspective (see Figure 5.1). *Social norms* are negotiated between teachers and their students to delineate the ways students and their teachers relate and work together in a subject classroom. There is mutual responsibility for creating and maintaining these social norms, for example, always raising a hand before answering a question, but the teacher has authority. The teacher also has responsibility for guiding students in understanding *socio-mathematical* norms, for example, what constitutes a mathematical solution or explanation, and the basis for determining the mathematical quality of solutions and explanations. Learner autonomy develops as students engage in the process of validating their claims using *mathematical practices* such as argumentation as they negotiate these socio-mathematical norms. As the community develops and students become more adept at knowing when and how to act mathematically, *mathematical practices* become part of the taken-for-granted repertoire of the collective and no longer need explicit validation. Can you imagine how this might play out in practice?

Interactionist Social Constructivist Perspective

Classroom Microculture
Classroom social norms
Socio-mathematical norms
Classroom mathematical practices

Figure 5.1 Social and Intellectual Dimensions of the Mathematics Classroom Microculture

In Task 5.3, you considered what the teachers' and students' roles might be like in a social constructivist classroom. Consider these excerpts from practice and reflect on your response. Magdalene Lampert (2001), an experienced teacher, published her research into her practice through a case study of teaching 10-year-olds mathematics over a year in an American public school. She does not offer a theoretical label for her practice but describes herself as '*teaching with problems*' and in line with interactionist and emergent versions of social constructivism considers her actions in teaching to be '*simultaneously social and intellectual*' (Lampert 2001: 35).

She describes through her practice how she established a classroom culture making explicit to students the social norms of *'how we do school'* and mathematical practices of *'how we do math'*. The norms refer to action and interaction. In this excerpt from when she first starts to teach her new class of students, she refers to notebooks and pens placed on each child's desk. The desks she has grouped in fours encourage children to think and work *collaboratively*.

> That's going to be your math notebook... The purpose of this notebook is for you to write down your thinking.
>
> Now as Mr Dye said on Thursday, [a teacher she collaborates with who teaches the class in the morning] sometimes when you write down your thinking the idea is to keep track of it for yourself and sometimes when you write down your thinking the idea is to communicate what you're thinking to other people. And we're going to use the notebooks for both of those kinds of recordkeeping. (Lampert 2001: 59)

In addition to these norms of action, she wanted students to use their notebooks to support them in the process of revising their mathematical thinking. She involved the children in negotiating what revision meant and in the process introduced further *social norms* of interaction for the class.

> I'd like to hear all those ideas [about revision], but it's not only me that you're talking to. It's everybody in the class. And if you haven't raised your hand with an idea, I want you to listen to the people who have an idea and see if you agree or disagree and if you have something to add. (Lampert 2001: 61)

To support her students, Lampert modelled her approach to discussion to teach aspects of the practices of mathematics. These included soliciting contributions across the class; responding to each student's contribution in a way that communicated her understanding of what the student was saying; and asking students to 're-voice' the contributions of other students. In these ways, she provided opportunities for reflection and adaptation of meaning. In her response to students, Lampert highlights when a view is productive mathematically, for example:

> Charlotte: That you write down what one idea that you think and then you decide that maybe that's not the right, you don't think that that's the right idea and that you want to change it. And you use revision by writing your other answer instead of erasing your first idea and then using it again, just it's a second answer.
>
> Lampert: OK that's a good way of explaining revision . . . ..
>
> Karim: Like thinking twice over an answer. Like the first time you thought it was the answer then you thought of it again and it was right.
>
> Lampert: Okay. Thinking twice. That's a good way to think about it and sometimes I think when something is important you might even want to think about it three times or more and go over it a couple times and then revise it. (Lampert 2001: 62-63)

Lampert (2001: 66) taught her class over the first few weeks three new activities or 'routines of interaction' so that they could learn both mathematical content (socio-mathematical norms) and mathematical practices. She describes how these must be deliberately taught as they represent the 'essence' of mathematical activity. These activities were regular features of her teaching across the year and the three terms 'conjectures', 'conditions' and 'revisions' became part of the discursive practices of the classroom. These included:

- *finding* and *stating* the *conditions* or assumptions in problem situations so that solution strategies can be evaluated and judged;
- *producing conjectures* about aspects of the problem situation and solution to make them available for reasoned argument;
- *revising* conjectures based on mathematical evidence and the identification of conditions.

Lampert's goals for her practice were to develop students mathematical reasoning and problem-solving abilities; they were not to prepare children '*to be mathematicians or to teach them to mimic the way mathematicians talk*' (Lampert 2001: 66). This echoes Hiebert et al.'s (1996) view that children are not being asked to think like mathematicians but to think like children about problems that are mathematically productive.

Central to an interactionist social constructivist view is that individual students' activity and the classroom microculture are reflexively related; neither can be understood without reference to the other. For Cobb and Yackel (1996), this means that any analysis (psychological) of students' learning must take account of the specific situation that is interactively constituted within the classroom microculture. This serves as the interpretive background. This represents an important step in relocating mind moving from the learner as an isolated individual to the learner reflexively related to others within the classroom microculture. However, Cobb and Yackel (1996) continue to refer to individual minds. As individuals now contribute to the classroom microculture, what is made available to learn can both enable and constrain individual learners' agency and teachers' agency.

Task 5.4

Consider the following excerpt from a classroom interaction.
Use Cobb and Yackel's perspective to make sense of where the problem for learning might arise.
You might also think about agency and whose was enabled or not.
What do you see as the purpose of the task content?
What else would you need to know about the situation and the participants to understand the students' scientific capability?

A class of 8- and 9-year-olds are working in groups with a worksheet for their science lesson provided by their teacher (Murphy 2000). The worksheet begins with a domestic situation which frames the task and implies its purpose. The situation is that Megan's father can't get his sugar to dissolve in his tea. Megan, his young daughter, suggests this is because he leaves it too long, five minutes later, before adding the sugar. The task highlighted in a box is to 'Find out how the time taken for sugar to dissolve depends on the temperature of the liquid'. The intention is that the students would establish a simple graph of time for dissolving against temperature of the water and look at the relationship demonstrated between the variables. It would involve them in small groups planning and carrying out their investigation. The excerpt is from interactions between one group of two boys and a girl.

In the initial planning:

> Girl: *We're going to have two tests. One, putting the sugar in straight away, and then five minutes later.*
>
> Boy: *Rubbish, not just straight, five minutes. Not just two tests. I think we should have at least three, and one where you put it in after 10 minutes.*
>
> Girl: *No, we're not asked to do that.*
>
> Boy: *Two tests won't give us the proper answer.*

The other boy agreed with the need for three readings.

> Girl: *It will just be colder and it won't dissolve so much.*

In researching the instructional sequences over time in this classroom, it was evident that scientific practices such as the minimum number of readings (three) required to see a relationship between two variables had become part of the collective repertoire. These understood ways of doing science investigations and what students can expect from each other in complying with these practices were part of the classroom microculture. Hence, the boy's rather uncharitable comments about the girl's suggestions. The students were quite exasperated with each other and neither would change their views, so the teacher joined the group.

The teacher knew from past situations that the three students were knowledgeable and competent at doing science. His intent was to enable them to develop conceptual understanding of the phenomenon of dissolving and his starting point was to check if the scientific practices were understood.

> Teacher: *Why did he suggest another reading after ten minutes?*
>
> Girl: *But nobody puts their sugar in ten minutes later do they?*
>
> Teacher: *I know, but what are you trying to find out?*
>
> Girl: *How much the sugar will dissolve...*
>
> Boy: *How much the sugar will dissolve in water at different temperatures.*
>
> Teacher: *So what's the thing you are changing each time?*
>
> Boy and Girl: *The temperature of the water*
>
> Teacher: *Right that's the thing you're interested in?*
>
> Girl: *I know but ... but nobody drinks cold tea*

Here the students demonstrate that they know what the independent and dependent variables are. What seems to differ between them and between the girl and the teacher is the purpose of the investigation and therefore what constitutes a solution. For the girl, if the problem is to help demonstrate why it's best to put your sugar in your tea when it's hot, she doesn't need a third reading when the tea is cold – even Megan's father is not that daft.

> Teacher: *I'm not sure why you don't want to do it.* You haven't given him a good reason why not.
> Boy: *You're just thick.*
> Girl: [Referring to the worksheet] *[sugar] dissolves quicker if the tea's not left five minutes?*

The girl continues to feel that her idea has not been considered.

> Teacher: *... I can't understand your reason for not doing it.*
> Girl: *Right, the situation is that someone wants their sugar to dissolve quicker in their tea right? So we, so nobody, but they still want warm tea or hot tea but they don't want it cold.*
> Teacher: *You're too hung up on this rather than what it is you're trying to find out.*

There are questions that could be asked here about the *social norms* of the classroom as one child appears not to be treating the other child with respect. Later in the interaction, the teacher comments directly to the boys about the norms of discussion, '*No. No that's not the right way to do it*'. However, from the teacher's interaction, it is apparent that it is not only the boys but the teacher who cannot understand the girl's reasoning about what constitutes the problem and, therefore, the solution. She is '*hung up*' in the teacher's words on the situation, which he treats separately from the task. For the girl, the situation and the problem determine the task and the appropriate solution. What she hasn't established is that the teacher's purpose for the task is to understand the phenomenon of dissolving scientifically to acquire understanding of a socio-scientific norm or concept. If the girl does only two tests, then the boys' learning about science and her own is constrained. The teacher understands that she knows '*how to do science*' and is limiting what she can learn from the investigation. After spending time with her and asking her to explain her thinking, and by this he means her scientific reasoning, the teacher gives up asking 'Would it be a big hardship if you did it [three readings]?' The girl replies 'Be more to write up but you'd find out more yeah.' In other words, she knows how to carry out a science investigation.

Lampert (2001) argues that any instance of teaching and learning must be understood in the ongoing stream of action and interaction over time that captures the practice of a teacher and the experiences of learners. Without knowledge of the instructional sequence over time in this classroom, the girl's scientific competence on this task could be misunderstood. The teacher's knowledge of the children could also be underestimated. The girl abandons her view of the 'problem' and the teacher recognises how this disempowers her, which in turn he experiences as a lack of agency as he is unable to work out what is going on. As he left the group, the girl placed her head on the table in defeat, an expression of her experience of the absence of agency because although she could act, it was not purposeful in relation to her understanding of the situation. This raises several questions. Why did the 'situational sense' discussed in Chapter 4 have salience and importance for the girl and not for the teacher or the boys? Does it matter in your view? The teacher does attempt to negotiate meanings with the girl but is unsuccessful. What might the excerpt suggest about the social constructivist assumption of transfer across situations by applying strategic knowledge? Is it the girl who is failing to transfer her science understanding or is it that the problem situation doesn't allow a task that is scientifically productive? Is the domestic setting a motivational hook that implies that science is useful to know? If so, wouldn't problem situations matter? And what relates them as a focus for teaching and learning?

Microcultures and the Constitution of Students

Question for Consideration 5.6

How do students experience different microcultures within schools?

Bauersfeld (1980) makes the point that learning mathematics or any other subject depends on learners' social and historical conditions but does not offer insights into how this relationship is understood. McDermott (1996) in his discussion of 8- to 9-year-olds that he observed across different subjects and learning situations offers a view of context that is consistent with the social interactionist view that individual students' activity and the classroom microculture are reflexively related. Based on his observations he describes, how context is not a fixed entity 'for it shifts with the interactional winds' (McDermott 1996: 290). He describes context not as something: 'into which someone is put, but an order of behaviour of which one is part' (McDermott 1996: 290).

Different orders of behaviour or classroom microcultures can bring forth different versions of the ways the same student interacts with others.

Task 5.5

In Task 5.1, you considered the notion of 'getting it right' in school. In your reflections, did you recall different versions of yourself being called forth in the *'interactional winds'* of different subject classrooms?
Which subjects allowed you versions of yourself that you were comfortable with? What characterised your experience of these microcultures?

Ivinson and Murphy (2007) in their research were interested in how students experienced different classroom microcultures. Myra, a 14-year-old girl, said art was her favourite space. 'Enjoy, fun, comfortable' were the words she used to express her feelings when she participated in art. In the Sports Hall, which was her second favourite space, the words that came to mind were 'cold, happy, know what to do'. History got seventh place and was 'hard', with 'long words [and about] war and death'. Her least favourite space was examinations in the hall, where students sit in isolation from each other. She described it as 'horrible'; her feelings were of 'hate' and being 'worried'. From an interactionist perspective, understanding what it is to get it right and conversely to get it wrong emerges in social interaction. Myra's words 'know what to do' reflect her understanding of what doing sports means and her ability to do it in ways that get the teacher's and her peers' sanction; in this space, she experiences herself as agentive. Getting it wrong is therefore not something an individual does in isolation, it is constituted in social interaction as an individual's behaviours are interpreted within the order of behaviour of the classroom microculture. Learners cannot get it wrong on their own. In an exam situation, the social interaction is between Myra and the test and the expectations of the assessor. There are right and wrong answers and no possibility of negotiation and mutual adaptation to work out what they might be. McDermott (1996) describes how children 'hide' in classroom contexts where the possibility of them not 'getting it right' is likely to be made visible; this defensive strategy is understandable, but it is a strategy that compounds their marginalisation and undermines their opportunity to learn.

An interactionist social constructivist perspective (McGregor 2008) takes context beyond tasks as it is dependent on the sense the learner makes of how tasks are communicated and the expectations of others, and of themselves, in subject classrooms. This seems to locate context within school although interactionists argue these expectations are determined by students' social experience. The teacher's reality is also reflexively created as you saw in the excerpt of the group in science. How the social experiences of students mediate their interactions in classrooms and the meanings they construct and attribute is not addressed as part of the emergent social constructivist framework. Nor is attention paid to how the teacher's practice might be mediated by school policies or practices. School practice demands placed on teachers can enable or undermine the ways they could agentively create productive microcultures.

CONTEXT BEYOND THE CLASSROOM

Driver et al. (1994) in their social constructivist approach to science education reject the constructivist notion that learners' prior naïve or everyday knowledge schemes are *replaced* with new schemes through a process of successive equilibrations wherein they are elaborated and refined. They argue instead that people develop 'plural conceptual schemes' (p. 7) or parallel ways of knowing that are applicable to different social contexts and knowledge domains. They distinguish between everyday concepts, or commonsense ways of explaining the world and scientific ways of knowing and explaining. The latter relies on ontological entities such as atoms, electrons, waves, genes and chromosomes; organising concepts such as evolution; and procedures of experimentation and measurement which make up the symbolic world of the science community. It is humans that theorise about phenomena and generate theories.

These theories are then scrutinised by the scientific community and if accepted become part of the taken-for-granted ways of understanding the world. Bruner describes this socially constructed world:

> That world is a *symbolic world* in the sense that it consists of conceptually organized, rule bound belief systems about *what exists*, about how to get to goals, about what to be valued. (Bruner 1985: 32 cited in Driver et al. 1994: 7)

For Driver et al., '*A social constructivist perspective recognizes that learning involves being introduced to a symbolic world*' (Driver et al. 1994: 7). This view of the goals of education can be related to Vygotsky's distinction between 'genuine' or 'scientific' and spontaneous everyday concepts and his early views about how they develop (Round and McPhail 2019). Everyday concepts are said to result from generalisations from everyday personal concrete experience and not instruction. Scientific concepts (which includes for Vygotsky the natural sciences, the social sciences and the humanities) represent the generalisations of the culture and involve direct instruction. The distinction between scientific and everyday concepts offers insights into how transfer is understood in this social constructivist view of learning. Scientific concepts are decontextualised mediational means in that they are *treated* as abstract objects of reflection in particular discourse modes, scientific in the case of Driver and her colleagues, rather than embedded in an everyday context. The acquisition of scientific concepts mediates children's thinking and problem-solving as Vygotsky argued 'reflective consciousness comes to the child through the portals of scientific concepts' (Vygotsky 1986: 171). Karpov (2003: 66) explains how, as a result, students' thinking becomes much more independent of their personal experience. They become 'theorists' rather than 'practitioners'. The teacher's role is not to guide students in making direct sense of the world as in constructivism but in mediating these socially constructed ways of knowing and acting (sociosubject norms). Whilst there is a place for empirical enquiry as in constructivist pedagogy, on its own, it is insufficient. Learners need access to the concepts and models of 'conventional' science that have generality and scope and are not, it is argued, situation specific. Driver et al. (1994) refer to these as the *cultural tools of science*. In this version of social constructivism, students are theorists able to construct and make sense of models of the world. What students must learn is understanding of these socioscientific cultural tools *and* their domains of application.

Like interactionists, understanding is constructed as students engage with each other through talk and activity in shared problems or tasks. Driver et al. (1994) specifically identify meaning making as a dialogic process and what constitutes effective dialogue is determined by the discursive practices associated with the scientific community. It is recognised that there is a disjunction between the classroom microculture and the practices and discursive discourses of communities of professional scientists. What is made available to students are versions of these discursive practices, scientific argumentation being a key one (considered further in Chapter 9). It is through scientific argumentation that students with their teachers are said to co-construct scientific knowledge. You will recall that Cobb and Yackel identified argumentation as one of the practices students needed to engage with to validate their mathematical claims For Driver et al., in line with other versions of social constructivism, it is through participating in these discursive practices that students are encultured into a community of knowledge (not of practice) 'in the context of relevant tasks' (Driver et al. 1994: 9). To be encultured into a community of knowledge, student must develop a 'critical perspective on scientific culture' (p. 11), that is, they come to understand the epistemic values, methods and institutional practices of a scientific community. As future citizens they can be invited to engage in community tasks concerned with scientific contemporary issues (Calabrese Barton and Tan 2010).

There is close alignment between this version of social constructivism and interactionist social constructivism in the educational goals and the three dimensions that make up the classroom microculture. Driver et al. do not emphasise the reflexive nature of the social interactions, so there is less insight into what might emerge within the classroom culture that could mediate collective and individual learning and teachers' practice. Nor is it clear that this reflexivity is recognised.

Question for Consideration 5.7

How is the teacher's role different in this social view of learning?

Task 5.6

Do you consider that the concern for students to gain a *'critical perspective on scientific culture'* extends the meaning of context beyond the 'walls' of the classroom? You considered the teacher's role and the student's role in Task 5.3. Does the Driver et al. view alter how you understood it?
What metaphor seems to fit?

THE SOCIAL CONSTRUCTIVIST TEACHER: 'TOURIST GUIDE' OR 'SHERPA'

Driver et al. (1994) use several terms and descriptions that demonstrate the influence of Vygotsky's theories on their view of the social constructivist teacher's role. For example, there is reference to learning being a process by which individuals are introduced to the culture by more skilled members. The more experienced member structures tasks so that the less-experienced person can perform them. It is within dialogic exchanges between peers and between students and their teachers that support to construct new meanings is given and is referred to as 'scaffolding', which was central to contingent teaching and the *first interpretation* of the ZPD that you were introduced to at the end of Chapter 4. The social constructivist teacher's aim for students is to achieve stand-alone competency within the ZPD. However, rather than competency in the performance of a task, it is competency in achieving and using the accepted scientific explanation to interpret observed phenomena. Karpov (2003) describes how it is the acquisition of scientific concepts (in the Vygotskian interpretation) that creates the ZPD of learners' everyday understanding as it relates to the subject. There is no direct reference to the ZPD, but it is implied. The ZPD in this *second interpretation* is the distance between the cultural knowledge made available *through instruction and participation* in classroom subject learning and the individual's everyday understanding. McPhail (2016: 308) refers to the teacher as the 'activator' rather than the facilitator who brings subject content to life.

The construction of personal meanings relies on intervention and negotiation with an 'authority', the teacher. This differs from the constructivist teacher as *gardener* and *guide*. Social constructivist teachers must manage the dialogic process and ensure too that students understand their responsibilities to co-create and maintain the social norms and microculture of the classroom. Teachers manage the dialogic process by introducing new ideas or cultural tools, for example, conventions and ways of representing phenomena involving symbolic representations like numbers, formulae, equations and terms such as rays to describe paths of light, and by providing scaffolded support to the whole group and to individuals within the group to enable students to make sense of them for themselves. Re-voicing as part of this scaffolding connects students' contributions to the argument structures and practices of the subject discipline which they must also learn. The teacher needs to listen to students and diagnose how instructional activities are being interpreted as meanings, subject content and the use of language are negotiated and evolved.

In both constructivist and social constructivist perspectives, the teacher is a strategist but what they must be strategic about differs. The social constructivist teacher orchestrates and manages subject narratives to create coherence across subject content and has responsibility for maintaining intersubjectivity across the class. Driver et al. (1994) use the metaphor of the teacher as a 'tour guide' mediating between learners' everyday worlds and the world of science. Claxton's notion of the teacher as '*Sherpa*' acting as a knowledgeable guide (cited in Price et al. 2017) also seems apposite. He describes the teacher as a 'knowledgeable local guide' to the students who are exploring the unfamiliar terrain of subject domains (Claxton 1990: 31). Lampert (2001: 423-448) in her models to represent her practice also includes how she maps the subject terrain and relates it to the whole class group and individuals within it. These metaphors cast the student as a person who chooses to engage in the adventure of learning and who is proactive in what they consider problematic and how they chose to construct problem solutions. Yet they do not seem to have the same choice as a tourist in deciding what their destination is.

Question for Consideration 5.8

Does the curriculum change if a more social perspective on knowledge construction is taken?

Social Constructivism and Policy

Pupils in schools are assumed to learn in social situations with each other. National policy (DfE 2014) requires they develop both intellectually and socially. Inherent assumptions about learning collaboratively through social constructivism have previously influenced curriculum specifications and views of pedagogy.

For example, in the National Curriculum for England prior to 2004, scientific enquiry involved planning experimental and investigative procedures and obtaining, analysing and evaluating evidence (Erduran and Jimenez-Aleixandre 2007). In the 2004 version for students aged 11-14 (Key Stage 3), scientific enquiry changed and one dimension of enquiry, 'ideas and evidence in science', included the statement that students should be taught:

> About the ways in which scientists work today and how they worked in the past, including the role of experimentation, evidence and creative thought in the development of scientific ideas. (DfE 2004: 72)

The view that meaning-making is dialogic and subjects should be taught in ways that equip students to make informed future judgements and decisions was reflected in the expectation that students would question and discuss the effects of scientific and technological developments on the environment and in other contexts and consider their impact on the direction of society and the future of the world. For older students aged 14-16 (Key Stage 4), the social dimension of knowledge construction was more explicit. Scientific enquiry was relabelled as 'How science works' and one dimension, 'Applications and implications of science', specified that students should be taught:

> About the use of contemporary scientific and technological developments and their benefits, drawbacks and risks
>
> To consider how and why decisions about science and technology are made, including those that raise ethical issues, and about the social, economic and environmental effects of such decisions
>
> How uncertainties about scientific knowledge and scientific ideas change over time and about the role of the scientific community in validating those changes. (DfE 2004: 184)

In the 2007 version of the science national curriculum, the specification for 11- to 14-year-olds was amended to map onto the Key Stage 4 specification so that 'How science works' became common to both. Teachers had the responsibility to ensure that students developed understanding of the content and concepts of science through the medium of the knowledge, skills and understanding of 'how science works', integrating practices, procedures and concepts. This new model of science required students to engage in the critical reasoning and enquiry advocated generally by social constructivists and those who argue for a problem-solving approach to pedagogy.

In mathematics, the influence of social constructivism on the curriculum was less clear. In the 2004 specification, the contribution of different cultures to the subject is emphasised and mathematics is described as equipping students with a 'uniquely powerful set of tools to understand and change the world' (DfE 2004: 151). In the 2007 version, the emphasis on the historical and cultural roots of mathematics and the relevance of mathematical tools to various employment fields and personal life remained. Students were also to consider the limitations and scope of the application of mathematics which aligns with Driver et al.'s view that students need to learn disciplinary cultural tools *and* their domains of application. Maths was described in the specification as universally important for solving problems, transcending cultural boundaries. This suggests that mathematical practices and ways of knowing were viewed as more fixed than scientific ideas and theories whose provisional nature was emphasised in the specifications. Whilst students were to engage in mathematical reasoning and adopt a questioning approach, there was no explicit reference to communities of mathematicians and their role in mathematical knowledge construction.

The social dimension of knowledge construction was taken up in policy across many countries at a time when there was concern about the suitability of the science curriculum on two counts. First that it failed to provide students with an education that enabled them to keep abreast of rapid scientific and technological change. Second that it misrepresented the nature of science, that is, its epistemic basis (McGregor and Frodsham 2019). This concern was exacerbated by research findings that established the international phenomenon that as children progressed through schooling, there was a gradual decline in their interest in the sciences (Osborne et al. 2003). The social model of science was seen to more faithfully represent the nature of science and have the potential to equip students for tertiary education in the sciences whilst ensuring that all students developed the skills of scientific reasoning that could be 'extended to everyday life for an informed citizenship' (Erduran and Jimenez-Aleixandre 2007). The argument put forward was that the social constructivist model of science would halt the decline in students' interest and ensure 'a citizenry that was scientifically literate as opposed to scientifically alienated' (Murphy et al. 2006: 230).

More recently, the DfE has offered guidance for all those 'supporting the future generation of teachers' (DfE 2019: 3). The Initial Teacher Education Core Content Framework reflects government's expectations regarding classroom practice.

Task 5.6

How far do you think the following standards taken from the DfE's 2019 guidance on 'planning and teaching well-structured lessons' appear to support social constructivism?

The DfE (2019) guidance provides support in five core areas, behaviour management, pedagogy, curriculum and assessment and professional behaviours. These offer congruence with the eight teacher's standards (DfE 2021). Extracts from advice about teaching well-structured lessons include practices of modelling, questioning and using homework as well as the following specific guidance:

i   Guides, scaffolds and worked examples can help pupils apply new ideas, but should be gradually removed as pupils expertise increases;
ii   High-quality classroom talk can support pupils to articulate key ideas, consolidate understanding and extend their vocabulary;
iii Paired and group activities can increase pupil success, but to work together effectively, pupils need guidance, support and practice (DfE 2019: 17-18).

Obviously, the guidance above does not specify how these practices might be applied in particular subject-related contexts. You will also have undoubtably realised reading this chapter that practice supporting social constructivism can vary. Although this teaching advice could be broadly interpreted to be supportive of social constructivism, it will depend on the ways that teacher interpret and enact such guidance. How teachers enculturate peers to collaborate within different contexts; extend opportunities for agentive action, collectively enact sharing what is valued within each different discipline and mediate curricular demands are examples of ways that learning may be characterised to a greater or lesser extent as social constructivism.

NATURE OF KNOWLEDGE AND KNOWING

Central to constructivist and social constructivist perspectives on learning is the rejection of a representationalist view of the world; human knowledge does not represent an objective reflection of an externally given world. A representationalist view, you will recall, underpins behaviourism and symbol-processing approaches to learning. In social constructivism, the knowledge that emerges within subject communities is typically referred to as *relativist* or *anti-realist*, a term often invoked as part of an epistemological critique of the perspective, on the grounds, that there is no way of judging whether knowledge reflects what is 'true' or real about the world. This epistemological relativist view of knowledge is highly contentious.

For example, McPhail (2016) working in the New Zealand context is critical of how constructivism and social constructivism have shaped policy and teachers' discourse, creating a hegemonic educational perspective which locates the knower rather than knowledge at the centre of educational thinking. For McPhail, this hybrid view of constructivism is 'confused'. In explaining the confusions, he attributes particular characteristics to social constructivist positions. For example, he describes how social constructivism along with constructivism 'draws on an anti-realist ontology and a subjectivist-relativist epistemology'. The latter, he defines as 'knowers construct their own knowledge of the world from their experiences' (McPhail 2016: 298). This conflates constructivism and social constructivism in ways that you will recall social constructivists like Bauersfeld challenge. What McPhail claims on behalf of social constructivists, as do many others, is that knowledge construction is restricted to learners' experiences and interests, which is not a position argued across social constructivist perspectives. You will recall that what is advocated are experiences which are relevant, productive and valued within subject domains. McPhail further suggests that knowledge construction is interpreted by teachers as knowledge creation, highlighting how human agency is understood. He argues instead that what students construct is understanding of existing knowledge which closely reflects social constructivist theorising. McPhail argues for a Popperian *realist* view of knowledge:

as collectively evolved products of the human mind that gain a level of autonomy and warranted objectivity through critical scrutiny in public arenas. (McPhail 2016: 308)

Do you consider this to conflict with a social constructivist view of knowledge such as that advanced by Driver et al. (1994)?

Social constructivism is recognised by McPhail as being concerned with collective knowledge production. He argues extreme relativism, as an epistemological position within a social constructivist perspective, is a misrepresentation. It is this relativism which McPhail considers supports a 'pluralistic epistemological democracy' (Desautels et al. 1998: 259 cited in McPhail 2016: 298) that has allowed academic and non-academic subjects to be treated as equivalent in external assessments and examinations. Young (2014) is critical of an interpretation of knowledge as a social construct if it denies the boundaries between subject disciplines, between vocational and academic curricula and between school and the everyday. These are not distinct epistemological realities, however, because they represent historically arbitrary selections and distinctions which are expressions of power and privilege. This interpretation, and concern with subject domains as privileging particular ways of knowing, is more likely to be argued from a sociocultural view of learning (see below and Chapter 6). Young refers to this epistemology as the knowledge of the powerful, whereas he argues for the curriculum to be based on 'powerful' disciplinary knowledge. As Dupré (2004) points out, there is nothing that social constructivists argue that suggests the former is a position they support.

Driver et al. (1994) clearly value and assume boundaries between disciplinary knowledge as they want learners to develop a critical understanding of subject cultures and their epistemic values, methods and institutional practices. They reject the dichotomy of knowledge as either absolute or relative and argue that a socially constructed view of knowledge does not logically imply relativism (Driver et al. 1994: 6). They refer to Harré's (1986, cited by Driver et al. 1994) *realist* ontology in defence of this claim. A *realist* ontology considers that knowledge even if socially constructed and validated is constrained by how the world is and that scientific progress is judged by its empirical basis. In mathematics, Rav (1999: 36 cited by Schwarz and Hershkow, 2010: 106) argues similarly that the social process do not make mathematics less objective or true. Rather, it enhances the reliability of mathematics through the process of validation and the application of 'objective' criteria to evaluate and judge arguments. These criteria are socially constructed but 'objectified' through the practices of communities and treated by them as abstract objects (see the earlier discussion about 'scientific' concepts in Vygotsky's theorising). Young (2014) makes a similar claim for 'social objectivity'. For Young, social objectivity is fallible and always open to change, which resonates with social constructivist views and why they argue for a curriculum that is *'future orientated'*.

Social realist arguments about the curriculum and pedagogy which have current influence do not necessarily differ from a social constructivist perspective but overlap in terms of the understanding of social objectivity and their support for the value of disciplinary knowledge (Figure 5.2).

Introducing Social Constructivism and Socioculturalism

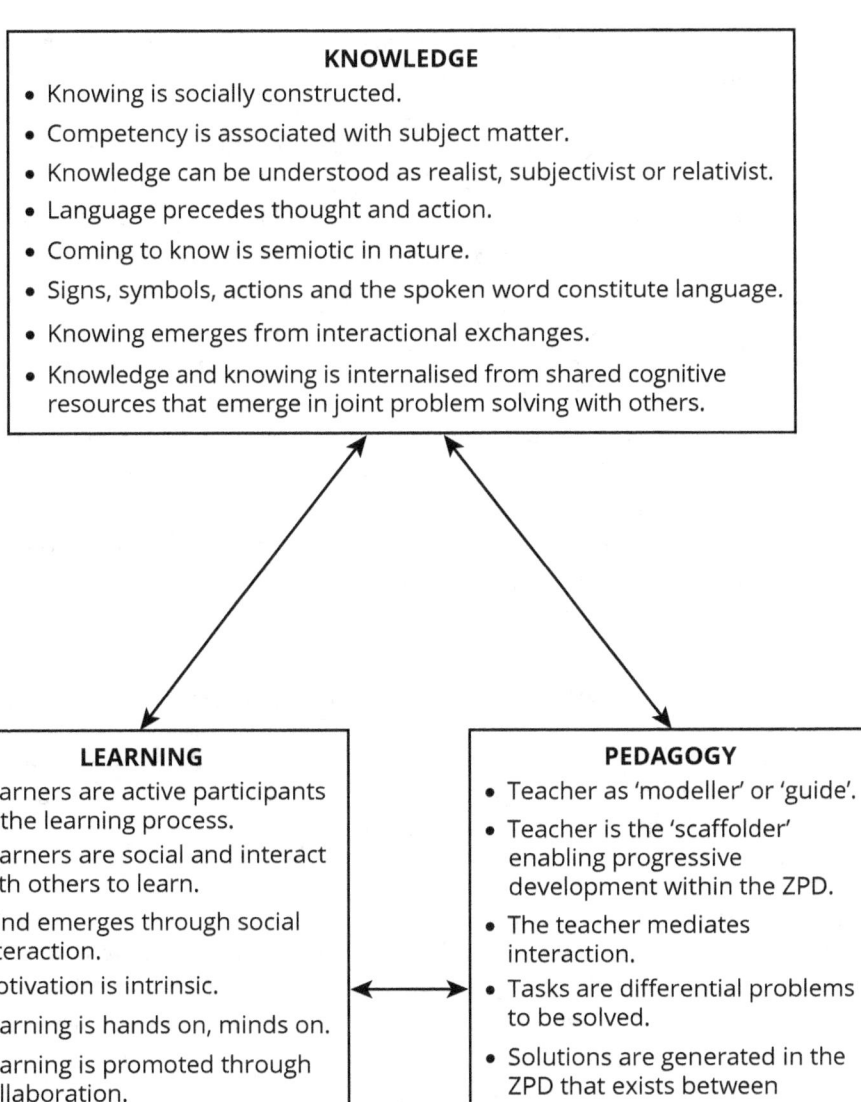

Figure 5.2 Features of a Social Constructivist Theory of Learning

SUMMARY

This chapter has introduced the various ways that social constructivism is interpreted and understood. It has been explained how different activities and ways of interacting influence the social dimension of teaching and learning and consequently reflect ways of interpreting and understanding the ZPD. You were introduced to thinking about different dimensions of context and considered how they each related to views of the ZPD. These varied perspectives of context included how teachers and learners might interpret learning tasks differently and consequently relate to the ZPD differently too. You were also introduced to various classroom studies that drew on dialectical and observational illustrations to demonstrate how different ways of pupils socially interacting (at small group and whole class levels) can influence learning processes and achievements. The ways that microcultures in classrooms provided interactional spaces were also discussed. Reflections on the school studies are recounted through the application of the teacher metaphors, particularly the *tourist guide* and *sherpa*. The challenges of social constructivism were also considered including the ways that strategically mis-managed approaches to learning might result in learner marginalisation. The ways that policy has been influenced by social constructivism were also considered. Finally, the ways that ontological tensions (regarding relativism and realism) emerge in alternate understandings of social constructivism are discussed. Perspectives of relativist and realist views of knowledge highlight where and how learning is understood to arise differently.

ADDITIONAL READING

Rannikmäe, M., Holbrook, J., & Soobard, R. (2020). Social Constructivism—Jerome Bruner. In B. Akpan & T. J. Kennedy (Eds) *Science Education in Theory and Practice*. Springer Texts in Education. Springer, Cham. https://doi.org/10.1007/978-3-030-43620-9_18. This chapter considers how collaboration, nature of learning and the social context are related within science education contexts.

Round, R. & McPhail, G. (2019). Using music: From spontaneous to scientific concepts in the primary school writing classroom. *International Journal of Education & the Arts*, 20 (5). http://doi.org/10.18113/P8ijea20n5. This article discusses how a teacher employed Vygotskian principles, beyond the subject contexts discussed, to teach through music.

REFERENCES

Bauersfeld, H. (1980) Hidden dimensions in the so-called reality of a Mathematics Classroom. *Educational Studies in Mathematics*, *11*(1), 23-41.

Bauersfeld, H. (1992) Structuring the structures. In L. P. Steffe (Ed) *Constructivism and Education*: Hillsdale, NJ: Lawrence Erlbaum.

Biesta, G., Priestley, M. & Robinson, M. (2015) The role of beliefs in teacher agency. *Teachers and Teaching*, *21*(6), 624-640.

Brown, A., Metz, K. E. & Campione, J. (1997) Social interaction and individual understanding in a community of learners: The influence of Piaget and Vygotsky. In A. Tryphon & J. Vonèche (Eds) *Piaget Vygotsky. The Social Genesis of Thought*. London: Psychology Press.

Bruner, J. (1985) Vygotsky: Ahistorical and concsptual perspective. In J. Wertsch (Ed) *Culture, Communication and Cognition: Vygotskian Perspectives*. Cambridge: Cambridge University Press, pp. 21-34.

Calabrese Barton, A. & Tan, E. (2010) We be burnin! agency, identity and science learning.. *Journal of the Learning Sciences*, *19*(304), 187-229.

Claxton, G. (1990) *Teaching to Learn: A Direction for Education*. London: Cassell.

Cobb, P. (1999) Where is the mind? In P. Murphy (Ed) *Learners, Learning and Assessment*. London: SAGE.

Cobb, P. & Yackel, E. (1996) Constructivist, emergent, and sociocultural perspectives in the context of developmental research. *Educational Psychologist*, *31*(304), 175-190.

Davies, B. (2003) *Shards of Glass: Children Reading and Writing beyong Gendered Identities*. Cresskill, NJ: Hampton Press.

Desautels, J., Garrison, J. & Fleury, S. (1998) Critical-constructivism and the sociopolitical agenda. In M. Larochelle, N. Bednarz & J. Garrison, *Constructivism and Education*. Cambridge: Cambridge University Press, pp. 253-270.

DfE (2014) *National Curriculum*. Available at https://www.gov.uk/government/collections/national-curriculum. Accessed 02/03/2.

DfE (2004) *The National Curriculum. Handbook for Secondary Teachers in England*. Available at https://www.education-uk.org/documents/pdfs/2004-nc-secondary-handbook.pdf Accessed 02/03/25.

DfE (2019) *Initial Teacher Training (ITT): Core Content Framework*. Available at: https://www.gov.uk/government/publications/initial-teacher-training-itt-core-content-framework. Accessed 03/06/24.

DfE (2021) *Teacher's Standards*. Available at https://www.gov.uk/government/publications/teachers-standards. Accessed 03/06/24.

Driver, R. Asoko, H., Leach, J., Mortimer, E. & Scott, P. (1994) Constructing scientific knowledge in the classroom. *Educational Researcher 23*(7), 5-12.

Dupré, J. (2004) What's the fuss about social constructivism? *Episteme*, 73.

Edwards, A. (2015) Recognising and realising teachers' professional agency. Teachers and teaching. *Theory into Practice 21*(6) 779-784.

Erduran, S. & Jimenez-Aleixandre, M. P. (2007) *Argumentation in Science Education: Perspective from Classroom-Based Research*. Springer Science.

Harré, R. (1986) *Varieties of Realism*. Oxford: Blackwell.

Hiebert, J., Carpenter, T.P., Fennema, E., Fuson, K., Human, P., Murray, H., Olivier, A. & Wearne, D. (1996) Problem solving as a basis for reform in curriculum and instruction: The case of mathematics. *Educational Researcher*, *25*(4), 12-21.

Price, D., Claxton, G., Stevenson, M., Robinson, L., Kidd, D., Hannon, V., Waters, M., Roberts, H., McGill, R.M., Barwell, C. & Holt, M., (2017) *Education Forward: Moving Schools into the Future*. Crux Publishing Ltd.

Ivinson, G. & Murphy, P. (2007) *Rethinking Single Sex Teaching*. Maidenhead: Open University Press.

Karpov, Y. (2003). Vygotsky's doctrine of scientific concepts: Its role for contemporary education. In A. Kozulin, B. Gindis, V. Ageyev & S. Miller (Eds) *Vygotsky's Educational Theory in Cultural Context* (pp. 65-82). Cambridge: Cambridge University Press.

Lampert, M. (2001) *Teaching Problems and the Problems of Teaching*. New Haven, CT: Yale University Press.

Lave, J. (1988) *Cognition in Practice: Mind, Mathematics and Culture in Everyday Life*. New York: Cambridge University Press.

Lave, J., Smith, S. & Butler, M. (1988). Problem solving as an everyday practice. In R. I. Charles & E. A. Silver (Eds) *The Teaching and Assessing of Mathematical Problem Solving* (pp. 61-81). Reston, VA: National Council of Teachers of Mathematics.

McDermott, R. P. (1996) The acquisition of a child by a learning disability. In S. Chaiklin & J. Lave (Eds) *Understanding Practice: Perspectives on Activity and Context.* Cambridge: Cambridge University Press.

McPhail, G. (2016) The fault lines of recontextualisation: The limits of constructivism in education *British Educational Research Journal, 42*(2), April 2016, 294-313.

McPhail, G. (2017) Constructivism: Clearing up the confusion between a theory of learning and 'constructing' knowledge. *Set: Research Information for Teachers*, 2, 30-22. https://doi.org/10.18296/set.0081

McGregor, D. (2008) The influence of task structure on students' learning processes: Observations from case studies in secondary school science. *Journal of Curriculum Studies, 40*(4), 509-540.

McGregor, D. & Frodsham, S. (2019) Epistemic insights: Contemplating tensions between policy influences and creativity in school science. *JBritish Educational Journal of Research, 45*(4), 770-790.

Murphy, P. (2000). Are gender differences in achievement avoidable? In J. Sears & P. Sorensen (Eds). *Issues in Science Teaching.* pp. (165-174). London: Routledge.

Murphy, P., Lunn, S. & Jones, H. (2006) The impact of authentic learning on students' engagement with physics. *The Curriculum Journal, 17*(3), 229-246.

Osborne, J., Simon, S. & Collins, S. (2003) Attitudes towards science: A review of the literature and its implications. *International Journal of Science Education.* 25(9), 1049-1079 https://doi.org/10.1080/0950069032000032199

Rogoff, B. (1990) *Apprenticeship in Thinking: Cognitive Development in Social Context.* Oxford: Oxford University Press.

Roth, W. M. & Hsu, P. L. (2010). Discursive psychology and ethnomethodology. In *Analyzing Communication*. Brill, pp. 295-327.

Round, R. & McPhail, G. (2019). Using music: From spontaneous to scientific concepts in the primary school writing classroom. *International Journal of Education and the Arts, 20*(5). Retrieved from http://doi.org/10.18113/P8ijea20n5

Schwarz, B.B. & Hershkow, R. (2010) Argumentation and mathematics. In K. Littleton & C. Howe (Eds) *Educational Dialogues.* London: Routledge.

Smith, Dockerell & Tomlinson (1999) *Piaget, Vygotsky and beyond.* London: Routledge.

von Glasersfeld, E. (1989) Learning as a constructive activity. In P. Murphy & B. Moon (Eds) *Developments in Learning and Assessment.* London: Hodder and Stoughton.

Vygotsky, L. (1986) *Thought and Language.* Cambridge, MA: MIT Press.

Wertsch, J. V. (1991) *Voices of the Mind: A Sociocultural Approach to Mediated Activity.* Cambridge, MA: Harvard University Press.

Young, M. (2014) *The Curriculum and the Entitlement to Knowledge.* Available at https://www.cambridgeassessment.org.uk/Images/166279-the-curriculum-and-the-entitlement-to-knowledge-prof-michael-young.pdf Accessed 03/06/24.

6

THINKING FURTHER ABOUT THE SOCIAL AND CULTURAL ASPECTS OF LEARNING

CONTENTS

Contextual Matters	127
Activity and Another View of the ZPD	135
Agency and Being Agentive	140
Position, Agency and Becoming	142
Summary	147
Additional Reading	147
References	147

Chapter Aims

After reading Chapter 6, you will have considered:

- that there are a wide range of concepts associated with the sociocultural movement;
- how different forms of knowledge and knowing are developed through interaction with others;
- the ways that participation and activity in learning matter;
- how affordance and agency are related;
- that multiple dimensions of identity can manifest;
- how context, culture and history matter;
- the metaphor of the teacher as *tourist guide*, *sherpa* and *co-adventurer*;
- tensions between educational goals and epistemic goals in socioculturalism.

As explained earlier, Chapters 3-6 discuss theories that assume humans can be agentive, that is, they can determine what they *do* as well as what they *think*. This chapter extends what was introduced to you in Chapter 5 about the extent to which varied social dimensions can affect affordances or opportunities made available for development of agency and consequently learning. Although there has been a significant increase in the ways that sociocultural processes are talked about in education, as many (Lave and Wenger 1991; Holland et al. 1998; Rogoff 2003, 2008a; Sfard 2006) demonstrate there remains much confusion. Sfard elaborates on and contrasts how those who believe that 'individual minds are the principle source of their own development' pay attention primarily to a person's increasing acquisition of concepts, knowledge, skills and mental schemas (Sfard 2006: 2-5), whilst those who acknowledge the profound influence of social, historical and cultural processes recognise that learning originates from collective activity with others which can lead to performing single-handedly. This theoretical perspective suggests how human thinking, therefore, originates in and from interpersonal exchanges. What is important is the way that the social world, the agentive individual within it and practice are interconnected. As will become clearer by the end of this chapter, learning from a sociocultural perspective is theorised to emerge through 'social practice that emphasises the relational interdependency of agent and world, activity, meaning, cognition [...] and knowing' (Lave and Wenger 1991: 51). The extent of the zone of proximal development (ZPD), introduced in Chapter 3 and elaborated upon in Chapters 4 and 5, introduces how social aspects can constrain or extend it. The teacher as metaphor in the chapter shifts a little to the previous one. Here the teacher as *co-adventurer* participates with others who all have a particular purpose in mind. In doing so, everyone (new and old timers) experience new practices. The activity can involve traversing unfamiliar terrain, but everyone is working collectively, achieving singular, joint or multiple goals.

As introduced to you at the beginning of Chapter 5, both the individual and their social world influence each other. The different kinds of social worlds individuals find themselves in shape and influence how they act and are, that is, their very *being*. How individuals relate to each other through dialogic exchanges and the activities they engage in influence, in turn, the culture of the community within which they play a part. Therefore, the context or community within which an individual exists comprises the culture within which they engage in activity with others and in so doing become who they are. In this chapter, although many aspects of sociocultural theorising could be considered, there is a limit to the space and word count. As Murphy and Hall (2006: ix) explain, 'sociocultural approaches to learning transcend typical boundaries' and emphasise the 'socially negotiated and embedded nature of meaning-making' and the ways that 'learners learn to use the cognitive tools of their cultural community through participation in social activity'. For pragmatic reasons, therefore *context*, *activity*, *agency* and *identity* and the relational connections between them are the main foci of discussion here. Consideration of these entities offers a range of opportunities to think more specifically about the ways these dimensions are important in sociocultural theorising but overlooked, under-acknowledged or even mis-understood (Lave 1993) in behaviourist, information processing or constructivist perspectives. Additional complexities of the relational nature and differential forms of context, activity, agency and identity, key in sociocultural perspectives, beyond the scope of this chapter, are considered further in the recommended reading at the end of the chapter.

CONTEXTUAL MATTERS

In Chapter 5, you were invited to think about context. You were reminded that in behaviourist and cognitive constructivist theorising, little or no attention is paid to context in a situational sense. However, in social constructivism, you were introduced to considering how the classroom microculture (i.e. groups of learners interacting with each other whilst engaged in collaborative tasks) can come to generate their own cultural ways of working.

You have already been introduced to Lave's view (Chapter 5) that context and culture matter in studies of human thinking or cognition. To consider in more depth how culture and cognition are related, it is useful to think further about Lave's studies.

Jean Lave (1988), widely recognised for her work on social and cultural impacts on learning, initiated investigations on human cognition beyond the research laboratory. She began by looking at arithmetic problem-solving within the domain of everyday life. An early study focused on individuals' arithmetic practices in everyday life situations such as shopping, cooking and dieting. An ethnographic and anthropological approach involving interviews and observations of participants in the study enabled her to explore mathematical adult learning in 'life after school' (Lave 1988: 45). The findings of this study did not test a theory, but rather supported the development of a 'new way of understanding human thought processes and offered a view of cognition as a dialectic between persons-acting and the setting in which their activity is constituted' (Lave 1988). In other words, understanding human thinking (as the process of learning) requires acknowledgement of the activity and context within which the thought processes were initiated.

Studying the use of arithmetic *in situ* led her to theorise analytically about context. To recognise 'experience in the lived-in world', she conceived of two interrelated layers, 'arena' and 'settings'. For Lave, the arena may be a 'physically, economically, politically and socially organised space-in-time', for example, a supermarket, a school or tailor's shop within which activity takes place. Arena offers a 'higher order institutional framework within which the setting is constituted' (Lave 1988: 150). People interacting in certain ways within the arena constitute the 'setting'. That is, a setting is a 'relation between acting persons and the arenas in relation with which they act' (Lave 1988).

Looking further at arithmetic practices among Vai and Gola apprentice tailors in West Africa (1973-1978), she realised that 'routine calculations in the tailor shops were quite different to those evoked in experiments, whether or not the tailors had attended school' (Lave 1988: xiv). She argued that this evidence raised doubts about 'learning transfer as a source of knowledge and skill across situations' (Lave 1988). In seeking to understand more about situated learning (Lave and Wenger 1991), she and Etienne Wenger examined the ways that apprentices learned in several different work contexts. They compared and contrasted the nature of apprenticeships of Yucatec midwives; Vai and Gola tailors; naval quartermasters; butchers; and non-drinking alcoholics, which provided historical and culturally specific examples of learning within work situations. Arguably, these studies reify the diversity of the social nature and character of learning, which is dialectically influenced by the situation in which it emerges.

Question for Consideration 6.1

Why does the character of learning in schools limit what can be researched about the social, cultural and historical nature of cognitive development?

Lave and Wenger (1991) argue why researching the social, cultural and historical nature of learning is limited in school contexts. Despite providing much empirical evidence on cognitive research, they suggest how school research is often underpinned by constrained views of the ZPD (see Chapters 4 and 5) and as such is conceptually tied to school curriculums and pedagogic intentions of teachers. The historical roots of school learning are 'inescapably specialised' (Lave and Wenger (1991: 61) and unlikely to afford a wide historical and cultural breadth.

To investigate 'being' and 'becoming', Lave and Wenger (1991: 32) argued that apprenticeships offered a way of looking at social, historical and cultural influences on learning. From the outlines below, can you appreciate how the character of knowledge and learning, the ways that meanings are negotiated and the nature of learning activity are each integrated to the situation they are enacted within? The apprentices do not 'receive' a body of factual knowledge about the world. It is through activity 'in and with the world, and on the view that agent, activity and world mutually constitute each other' (Lave and Wenger 1991: 33); thus, learning is 'situated' in specific circumstances.

West African Tailors

The first example offers evidence that would-be-tailors (all men, usually unrelated) came to know what to *do* without being formally taught. Anthropologically observing how they learnt their trade, they realised that apprentices working with more experienced master tailors, over the period of several years, became expert craftsmen themselves. The apprentices began as novices working in 'wooden, dirt-floored, tin-roofed tailor shops' on the edge of commercial districts (Lave and Wenger 1991: 71). The 5-year apprenticeship 'involved a sustained, rich structure of opportunities to observe maters, journeymen, and other apprentices at work'. This meant that the novice tailors were able to witness the full process of producing different garments. They only require simple technology, scissors, measuring tape, thread, needle and treadle sewing machines. Interestingly, 'apprentices first learn[ed] to make hats and drawers, informal and intimate garments for children. They [then] move[d] onto more external, formal garments, ending with the Higher heights suit' (Lave and Wenger 1991).

Yucatec Midwives

The midwives (all women, mothers and daughters) provide services for would-be mothers that include various rituals, use of herbal remedies, massages and medical interventions preventing breech births. Specialised knowledge and practice are passed down (Lave and Wenger 1991: 70) through families. Apprenticeship is integrated into daily life, but is only recognised once mastery is achieved, usually in mid-life. Teaching is not explicitly recognised. Girls absorb the essence of midwifery because they live with their grandmother or mother and witness what they practice. After giving birth themselves, the daughters may be asked to do massages or help collect herbs and then assist as the mother ages. In doing so, she gradually takes on more and more of the workload, eventually becoming culturally accepted as a midwife.

These examples of apprenticeship, that is, novices coming to learn or appropriating knowing and practice that is salient to be deemed a tailor or midwife in their respective communities, suggest how cultural ways of working are taken up by individuals. As Rogoff describes, though, in sociocultural theory, the individuals themselves also affect how culture develops,

> individual development that constitutes and is constituted by social and cultural-historical activities and practices [...] culture is not an entity that influences individuals. Instead, people contribute to the creation of cultural processes and cultural processes contribute to the creatin of people. Thus, individual and cultural processes are mutually constituting rather than defined separately from each other. (Rogoff 2003: 51)

It can be that, as Lave and Wenger (1991: 116) themselves acknowledge, the conflict that emerges as power relations change between the novice and the more expert other shifts the nature of the cultural way of working. Rogoff (2003) argues that,

> Rather than individual development being influenced by (and influencing) culture [...] people develop as they participate in and contribute to cultural activities that themselves develop with the involvement of people in successive generations. People of each generation, as they engage in sociocultural endeavours with other people, make use of and extend cultural tools and practices inherited from previous generations. As people develop through their shared use of cultural tools and practices, they simultaneously contribute to the transformation of cultural tools, practices and institutions. (Rogoff 2003: 52)

Cultural Ways of Working

In the reflective considerations related to Task 5.3, you are introduced to Lampert (2001) who describes how her practice enables or *affords* opportunities for her students to work differently to 'existing action patterns in classrooms' (p. 65). She structured activities for her 10-year-old students that introduced them to study mathematical content through adopting mathematical ways of working. This new cultural way of working involved the students adopting three particular new *routines of interaction*. They were *finding* and *articulating* assumptions in problem situations; producing *conjectures* regarding the problems to be discussed; and *revising conjectures* depending evidence and subsequent consideration.

This is what is possible in a school classroom. However, in the 'real-world' beyond school, mathematics, for example, is intuitively thought about quite differently in a Brazilian street market context (Nunes et al. 1985). Nunes et al. studied how children working on street corners worked out costs (and change needed) in *cruzeiros* (Brazilian currency) for customers buying the goods they were selling. The school-aged children working in the markets were 'informally tested' through the researchers naturalistically purchasing coconuts, lemons, watermelons or fish, for example, from them. The children calculated (usually out loud) the price the researchers paid and were able to note. They (the children) were then later (within a week) invited to complete similar mathematical tasks (the formal test) in the same place or at home. The formal tests involved similar problems to those the interviewers posed when buying goods from the children at the market. These tests utilised the same numbers without context, that is, only abstract numbers, not amounts of coconuts, lemons, watermelons or fish, and pencil and paper were offered to reflect a schooling situation. Their results showed that problem-solving within the situational context of selling, that is, the children working in the market, led to significantly superior resolutions compared to the same mathematical processes undertaken as an abstract worded task with pencil and paper that more closely resembled school mathematics.

The following is provided as an illustrative example:

Informal test (researcher as customer)

Customer: I'm going to take four coconuts. How much is that?

Child [as street seller]: Three will be 105, plus 30, that's 135 ... one coconut is 35 ... that is ... 140!

Formal test (same child asked about 35 × 4)

Child [in formal context]: 4 times 5 is 20, carry the 2; 2 plus 3 is 5, times 4 is 20 [Answer written is '200'].

In line with Lave et al. (1984), the findings suggest that 'context-embedded problems' were much more easily solved than those that were more abstract, without a context.

Arenas and Settings

Supermarket as an 'arena' is a durable space (physically, economically, politically and socially). It is not negotiable by an individual. A supermarket as an 'arena' is a physical entity that transcends the experience of the individual, exists prior to them and is entirely beyond their control (Lave et al. 1984: 71). However, for individuals regularly shopping in the supermarket arena, they may not visit particular aisles because they have no need for those items or they may pursue others in seeking certain genres of products (such as baby-related commodities or 'free from' foodstuffs). These are arguably (Lave et al. 1984: 71) a different unit of analysis to 'arena' and referred to as 'setting', that is, an aspect of the environment that can be selected or determined by individuals when responding to their context.

Task 6.1

Reflecting back on your time in school and then at work or at home, when and where do you carry out similar mathematical calculations?
Consider the different 'arenas' of home and work, what other aspects of 'context' influence and effect the arithmetic processing to work out solutions for the following:

- How early do I need to get up to arrive at work on time?
- How much does travelling to work cost?
- How much does the weekly shopping cost?
- How much money is left each month to save (for a holiday, a meal out or a birthday celebration)?

In the case of the Brazilian children carrying out mathematical problem-solving above, how would you define the 'arenas' and 'settings' as part of the context in which they solve arithmetic problems? Are there any other aspects of context that might affect their working out what customers should pay for a kilo of fish; 30 watermelons; 7 lemons or 40 coconuts?

In the case of your own problem-solving, deciding how early to get up to arrive at work on time is likely to arise within your home arena. However, depending upon the when, where and how the routinised ritual of setting the alarm occurs to wake you the following morning, you may need to think about many other aspects of the setting. These might include local weather and implications of preparing to drive the car to work in snowy or wet conditions, the children needing to be ushered to the bus stop earlier or the possibility of a medical appointment before travelling to work. Each of these factors influence how you engage in particular activities within the early morning setting in your home arena. In the case of the Brazilian street children within the arena of the street market, the formal and informal testing took place within a 'buying and selling setting' and a more 'educational setting'.

The World of School and Beyond

Investigating further the experience of children in street and school situations, Hatt (2007) examines how the urban youth understand being smart in different cultural settings. She draws on Holland et al.'s (1998) view of figured worlds, where people are 'formed in collectively realized "as if" realms' (Holland et al. 1998: 49). This resonates to some extent with Lave and Wenger's (1991) views about communities discussed later in this chapter. Holland et al. suggest how figured worlds are groups or collectives of individuals that people can choose to be participants of, whereas Lave and Wenger suggest that communities are situated and comprise those who share common interests, desires and purposes. Cultural realms (Holland et al. 1998 p. 51) are 'peopled by characters from collective imaginings' such as academia, factories or even Alcoholics Anonymous. Holland et al. (1998) describe how figured worlds 'take shape within and grant shape to the coproduction of activities, discourse, performances and artifacts'. They clarify that participants within a figured world have particular ways of interacting with others, and that they hold distinct perspectives and orientations towards it. Interviewing students about their views of 'book smart' and 'street smart', it became clear that the cultures in high school and on the street result in different emergent identities of youths. 'Smart' is a term habitually used and associated with education. Hatt (2007) demonstrates how different groups of students develop different academic identities, that is, their perceptions about their own efficacy, ability and success in studying shapes who they believe they are and how they think others 'see' them. Students who were not successful in school were able to clearly distinguish between 'book smart' and 'street smart'. Unsurprisingly, they valued being street smart rather than being book smart. Being street smart meant they could successfully navigate street culture, abusive 'others', poverty and even the police. Within sociocultural theorising, these students were able to agentively counter social structures, which represented school and education such as achieving a high school diploma, honours or high standardised test scores. Jeremy, for example, stated,

> [A]nybody can be book smart. You can sit down and read a book and say, *Oh I know this and that* ... You got to get that experience. You have to have had a hungry mouth to be street smart. (Hatt 2007: 146)

Sheena and Ardelia distinguish other aspects of street smart. Sheena suggests that,

> "A street smart person would know not to let a cop search their car without probable cause. Someone without that knowledge, may be someone with school smarts because they don't know about the law. . . .. The police can get over on, and its just not going to happen to someone that has street smarts". Ardelia adds, "Gang bangers. You have to know what area to go in and not go in. How to wear your clothes and that type of knowledge." (Hatt 2007: 154)

These perspectives indicate how people in different figured worlds act, speak, think and even dress differently because different social structures (e.g. culture, power and status) exist in the world that they live in. Activity, therefore, for these street smart youths involves being agentive in different ways to their counterparts in school. Directly related to the 'book smart' and 'street smart' students' different ways of being agentive are their emergent and distinct identities.

Contextualising Activity in a Community of Practice

In endeavouring to further consider how context, activity, agency and identity relate, Lave and Wenger's (1991) perspective of situated cognition emphasises how learning and identity are linked within communities and offer possibilities for those within them. The view of communities of participants engaging in collective activities by including Wenger's (1998) model suggests ways that participants can interact and learn from, and with, each other (see Figure 6.1).

	Facets of the community of practice	The nature of interactional processes that contribute to emergent learning in the community of practice
LEARNING	Practice	Learning as doing
	Meaning	Learning as experience
	Identity	Learning as becoming
	Community	Learning as belonging

Figure 6.1 Key Facets and Processes Related to Learning in a Community of Practice (after Wenger 1998, p.6)

Wenger (1998: 6) discusses how we each belong to multiple communities, such as at home, at work, at school or where we engage in our leisure activities. He describes how families can develop routines, practices, rituals, conventions, artefacts and stories, suggesting that these emerge through interaction and a joint focus on survival. He also discusses how communities of practice are an integral part of our lives, but can be informal and pervasive such that they may not come into explicit focus (Wenger 1998: 6). He also argues how communities are purposely collated, with specific aims in mind which afford a means to learn (both from and with each other). In thinking about learning, it is useful to consider Wenger's (1998: 6) features of a community of practice because he argues how they are all centred on learning (see below Box). Within a community of practice, like for example that of a school or a classroom, the nature of the culture that emerges takes shape through the activities engaged in, linguistic exchanges that emerge and the use of artefacts that those people in the group regularly utilise. In other words, how the inhabitants of a community interact and collectively engage in shared endeavours generates their social and cultural ways of *being*. It is not only the ways they interact with other but also how artefacts that matter are adopted or generated and used that shape their cultural world and reify the values they hold.

Within each community which might be a social group within school, a whole class or even just a small trio of pupils working together on a project, there are assumptions about interactions that emerge through collective activity of participants. In each community, there are interactional opportunities to learn as 'doing'; 'experiencing'; 'belonging' and 'becoming'. These processes contributing to learning (as recognised by Wenger 1998) are outlined in below Box and considered further at different points in the chapter.

Practice: Learning as Doing

A way of talking about shared historical and social resources, frameworks and perspectives that can sustain mutual engagement in action. (Wenger 1998: 5)

Meaning: Learning as Experienc(ing)

a way of talking about our (changing) ability – individually and collectively – to experience our life and the world as meaningful. (Wenger 1998: 5)

Identity: Learning as Becoming

a way of talking about how learning changes who we are and creates personal histories of becoming in the context of our communities. (Wenger 1998: 5)

Community: Learning as Belonging

a way of talking about the social configurations in which our enterprises are defined as worth pursuing, and our participation is recognizable as competence. (Wenger 1998: 5)

This Figure 6.1 suggests how different processes at play in a community of practice contribute to different dimensions of learning in a sociocultural view.

ACTIVITY AND ANOTHER VIEW OF THE ZPD

The ZPD (discussed in Chapter 4) is typically characterised for an individual as the distance between a learner's abilities exhibited when working collaboratively with more experienced others and their ability to problem solve or achieve alone without that assistance. Teachers providing support for a learner working initially on a task they could not perform alone and then removing that assistance has been widely recognised metaphorically as scaffolding. As explained in Chapter 4, the nature and extent of scaffolding as well as context can be understood differently in distinct perspectives of learning.

The nature of learning activity in schools is usually framed by teacher-set goals. These are not normally negotiated by students. This is in tension with a more sociocultural view of learning. Pupils have little or no control over the tasks they are expected to engage with. National curricular policies, examination specifications and the resources available are factors that inform teachers' decisions about the tasks they expect their students to work on. It is usually expected that students will complete the tasks and consequently achieve 'knowing' what the teacher intended. The nature of support provided by teachers in this context is likely to be directed towards ensuring the learners 'know' what is prescribed on the curriculum. This kind of support could take the form of scaffolding provided for individual students. As you were reminded in Chapter 4, Wood's (1988) example of contingent teaching shows how the learner was carefully supported via scaffolding in one-to-one teaching situations, such as learning to drive mentioned earlier. In Chapter 5, you were introduced to a second, more cultural interpretation of the ZPD. This was construed as the distance between the everyday and scientific concepts which Hedegaard (1988, cited in Lave and Wenger 1998: 48) describes as the 'distance between understood knowledge, as provided by instruction, and active knowledge, as owned by individuals'. This characterises a more social view of learning as the ZPD explained to you in Chapter 5. The 'aura' of cultural socialness evident when small numbers of people or learners collaborate (e.g. in a classroom) extends the collective ZPD.

Vygotsky generated the notion of mediation by arguing how the response of a subject in achieving an act may be mediated by an artefact (from their culture). That is, he recognised,

> by being included in the process of behaviour, the psychological tool alters the entire flow and structure of mental functions. It does this by determining the structure of a new instrumental act, just as a technical tool alters the process of a natural adaptation by determining the form of labour operations. (Vygotsky 1981: 137)

He continues,

> the following can serve as examples of psychological tools and their complex systems: language, various systems for counting; mnemonic techniques, algebraic symbol systems; works of art; writing; schemes, diagrams, maps and mechanical drawings; all sorts of conventional signs and so on. (Vygotsky 1981: 137)

Sfard (2006) illustrates how within a mathematics discipline mediators can include concrete objects, such as boxes, batteries and marbles. She also demonstrates how symbolic tools or artefacts can mediate interaction in learning. In mathematics, these may be 'bar diagrams', 'dot plots' or even algebraic functions, like g(x) (Sfard 2002). These artefacts mediate the discursive communication between learners when problem-solving. Sfard argues how artefacts can be 'aids to thought', that is, they are 'thought enablers and generators and are inseparable from the thought just like our physical actions are inseparable from our own body and the tools we use' (Sfard 2002: 37). As she also suggests ... 'the nature and quality of thought is a function of the nature and quality of the mediating artifacts, just like the nature and quality of our physical action is a function of the nature and quality of the materials tools we use' (Sfard 2002: 37).

Question for Consideration 6.2

What range of factors do you now understand can mediate 'activity' in different perspectives of learning?

The third view of the ZPD views the mind as distributed and extends learning trajectories beyond the immediate learning environment. This sociocultural perspective of the zone where developing know-how and knowing happens involves a more complex relationship between (a group or community of) learners and the ways that members of their culture use many forms of tools and signs to convey meanings over time. This more 'collectivist' or 'societal' view of the ZPD is defined by Engestrom as the 'distance between the everyday actions of individuals and the historically new form of the societal activity that can be collectively generated as a solution to the double bind potentially embedded in ... everyday actions' (Engestrom 1987: 174). In this account, the changing relations between newcomers and old-timers emerge through the development of social or cultural transformation, that is, the process of a changing shared practice. Investigating further the nature of social transformation that constitutes this third form of ZPD, Engestrom expands on cultural-historical activity theory (CHAT) that was informed by Vygotsky (1978) theorising and further developed by Leont'ev (1978). Vygotsky first suggested how artefacts can mediate a per'on's actions and thinking. He proposed that neither artefacts nor actions can exist in isolation. He offered a triangular model (Vygotsky 1978: 40) that demonstrates a relational view of 'stimulus', 'mediating artifact' and 'response'. Vygotsky's (1978) recognition of the ways that symbolic artefacts can influence the nature of higher mental functions is arguably tied to the nature of Russian society he lived in at the beginning of the 20th century when he was developing his theories about social, historical and cultural influences on the mind (Wertsch 1985). At this time, the theory and practice of Russian symbolism appeared strikingly in the forms of poetry, painting, theatre and film, influencing his socio-historic theory of development introduced in Chapter 5. At that time, recognising the significance of cultural artefacts influencing human actions was 'revolutionary' (Engestrom 1987: 134) and led to a divergence between the cartesian or dualistic ways that an individ'al's thinking and learning were understood and the processes by which culture shapes individu'ls' minds. This meant that an individ'al's learning and development could no longer be understood without paying attention to their cultural world. It also meant that society could no longer be understood without paying attention to individual's agency, their production and use of concrete and symbolic artefacts. This divergence in understanding human development meant that objects were no longer seen as 'things' to be simply observed or manipulated as Piaget assumed when formulating his constructivist ideas about logical thinking (explained in Chapter 3). Instead, this Vygotsky perspective assumes objects are artefacts of cultural significance and that the 'object orientedness of action became key to understanding human psyche' (Engestrom 1987: 134). What remains central to Vygotsky's theory of mind is the mechanism by which there is transition from inter-individual activity to intra-individual activity. This view of the cultural-historical development of higher mental functions led to the evolution of activity theory. Leont'ev (1981) recognised the difficulty of integrating the multifaceted influences in the kind of activity that involves a collective group of individuals. As outlined earlier and mentioned in previous chapters (Chapters 4 and 6), the differential extent to which the ZPD is developed (for an individual, with others or collectively) reflects the extent to which various people are involved in learning activity. Activity, then, is understood differently across theories of learning. Engestrom (1987) concretises the complexity and relational nature of activity in activity theory through explaining his study on a hospital setting in Finland. Diagrammatically representing how the nature of human activity is mediated by artefacts and culture, Engestrom offers a representation (Engestrom 1987: 134) that focuses on the 'object', that is, what is being made sense of, to make explicit the complex interrelations between individual subjects and their community. In this socio-historical theorising about the nature of human development, there are six basic entities: human subjects, objects, tools, rules, community and division of labour. In this kind of model, activities involve more than one person as the 'system' represents a whole community.

Task 6.2

Consider communities of people, for example, in a school or a collective of schools, working towards a common objective or a particular learning outcome. What kinds of tensions might emerge?

Lund (2008) researched the ways that members of two school communities keen to adopt Wikis, a networked website developed collaboratively by a community of users for teaching and learning English as a second language (ESL), implemented the project.

The *learning* challenge was for the school communities to work collaboratively to develop a new flexible resource to teach and promote independent and collective learning of ESL. The aspiration was to engage and enable teachers to use new tools, new infrastructures and new settings and develop fresh learning and dynamic learning activities. The Wikis afforded extensive collaborative development in language learning across the school communities. The intention was to develop new practices in teaching and learning ESL, but there were challenges in involving teachers, researchers and designers (and learners) in the dialogic exchanges required to jointly agree pedagogic, communication and technological principles. In the school societies where collective problem-solving and knowledge production were valued, there was an expansion of teacher's and learners' repertoires. More sophisticated individual actions were required to contribute to the collective expertise that promoted varied working modes in an offline and online sense (Lund 2008), resulting in a case of polycontextuality (Engeström et al. 1995). The process of establishing the Wikis in the school communities demanded dynamic conformation and reformation of not only the roles and practices of the human actors (teachers, researchers, learners, technologists, etc.) but also the mediating artefacts (the network arrangements, the software design, ways of accessing the Wiki, etc.). Students, for example, had access to laptops with wireless connections at all times; however, sometimes they worked individually, in base groups, or cross-curricular groups or even peer assessment groups. Learning tasks differed during the school day and also as the year progressed. As learning activities were engaged in, the new features of the Wiki were tested and refined (co-designed) so that collective knowledge informed the advancement in practices. That is, the interplay between the actors in the community, their cultural tools and contextual affordances represented Engestrom's 1999 activity theory framework.

Proponents of this theoretical model suggest how it simplifies the complexity of learning and enables some analysis of the conditions in which it occurs. Arguably it offers a cultural perspective that takes account of some ways that the context (situation, arena, setting etc.) extend affordances that influence action. It also allows for consideration of both material and conceptual tools and which aspects of tasks are prioritised. As noted in the schools illustration above, there is an obvious interactional dialectic between the collective mind of the actors and the culture within which they are working (Fenwick et al. 2011). Initially, it seems activity theory offers a useful and insightful framework through which to consider researching sociocultural learning. However, as Murphy (2022) suggests, there remain some concerns about the clarity or exact nature of the relationship between some of the six entities, the subject and the outcome, the nature of 'object' and objective or purpose of the activity, for example.

Activity theory has informed a range of subsequent theoretical models, including the third generation or CHAT and social network theory (Daniels et al. 2010). However, the collective activity theory does not pay particular attention to the impact on individuals. Although social interaction, linguistic tools and a collective ZPD are emphasised in CHAT, critique suggests that individual agency and identity are somewhat overlooked. As Lund et al. (2008) note, the Wiki 'rests on a collective epistemology' and is not devised for individuals alone. Concerns about identity and agency are considered further below.

Sociocultural Activity on Three Planes

In contrast to Engestrom and his activity theory that assumes 'collective activity' as the main focus, Rogoff (2008b) offers an alternate perspective to the sociocultural theory of learning. Her (2008a: 49) perspective of a sociocultural approach involves 'cognitive, social, perceptual, motivational, physical, emotional and other processes' that are regarded as aspects of activity rather than 'free-standing capabilities or faculties as has been traditional in psychology'. In focusing on developmental processes, she considers three planes of analysis: the personal, the interpersonal and community processes. These are inseparable, mutually constituting planes, each of which becomes a focus at different times when thinking about apprenticeship, guided participation and participatory appropriation. These interrelated and interdependent planes can be considered a little like the organ systems that work inside human bodies. Their structures and functions are interlinked, but at different moments, different systems will come into play. Consider, for example, when feeding the digestive system is placed at the forefront of bodily functioning. However, engaging in exercise, the skeletal–muscular system is significant, but later after exercising, the functioning of the skin (another organ) becomes more important in cooling down the body. This simplistic analogy is intended to serve as a way of making the complexity of the different entities and their relational connections more obvious. To elaborate further, the metaphor of apprenticeship models the plane of community activity. Newcomers to a community of practice (Wenger 1998) advance their skill and understanding through participation with others in culturally organised activities (Rogoff 1990). Vygotsky (1978) emphasised the importance of interaction with others in society who are conversant with scholarly practices and tools (especially language) for mediating intellectual activity. Dewey (1991) also advocates that others who are familiar with educative methods and subject matter are significant in social interactions with those who are less experienced. Rogoff's (2008b) perspective of *apprenticeship* conceives of small groups of people, each with varying levels of experience serving as resources and challenges for each other as they explore an activity together. These activities could be situated in school or at work. Her view of *guided participation* refers to processes and systems people engage with as they communicate and co-ordinate their efforts in a collaborative endeavour. The guidance emerges from the social and cultural values the participants collectively hold and enact. *Participatory appropriation* refers to how individuals change (in a cognitive, social, perceptual, motivational, physical, emotional sense, etc.) in activities, whilst in the process of becoming prepared for subsequent involvement in related activities. As Rogoff (2008a: 60) explains,

> With guided participation as the interpersonal process through which people are involved in sociocultural activity, participatory appropriation is the personal process by which, through engagement in an activity, individuals change and handle a later situation in ways prepared by their own participation in the previous situation. This is a process of becoming, rather than acquisition.

For a more detailed explanation of these concepts and the ways that they can be applied to an everyday context, Rogoff applies the personal, interpersonal and community processes through the activity of Girl Scout cookie sales and delivery (Rogoff 2008a: 61-72). The application of Rogoff's theorisation regarding sociocultural activity on three planes is adopted by Bird (2012) also analyses the activity of his year 7 history class (discussed further in Chapter 10) and ways they participate and appropriate different understandings of mediaeval England through collectively studying Domesday book data. Calabrese-Barton and Tan (2010: 2) also investigate informal learning and describe how in adopting sociocultural framing, learning is seen as a cultural process that involves guided participation (Rogoff 2003) and apprenticeship (Lave and Wenger 1991). Explaining Rogoff's three planes of analysis is intended to demonstrate how a sociocultural perspective contrasts with 'conventional explanations [that] view learning as a process by which a learner internalizes knowledge, whether "discovered", "transmitted" from others or "experienced in interaction" with others' (Lave and Wenger 1991: 47). Learning is too easily conceived as an unproblematic process of 'absorbing the given, as a matter of transmission and assimilation' (Lave and Wenger 1991: 47).

AGENCY AND BEING AGENTIVE

In Chapter 3, you were introduced to the ways that Piagetian theory recognised two dimensions or planes of agency. They were *being able to act* and *being able to construct meaning from the consequences of those actions*. It was explained to you how *agency* is an *attribute of the learner* and how they are in the world. Agency is not a description of learners' actions in the teaching and learning process, though observing these can provide insights into students' expressions of agency. In Chapter 4, you were introduced to social constructivism and how understanding emerges between people. This social view of learning recasts how we might think about human agency. Human action and agency in Vygotsky theorising cannot, therefore, be understood independently of sociohistorical mediational means. As Biesta and Tedder (2007) confirm, agency does not reside within an individual; it is 'achieved' through active engagement within a particular context rather than reified. Figure 6.2 offers a diagrammatic representation of the situational influences that may influence development of a learner's agency and identity. In Chapter 5, the concept and complexity of agency was reconsidered. Although the concept has become much more widely used, it still remains a somewhat ambiguously understood concept (Prestley et al. 2015), and this is because within social contexts, agency can be understood in different ways (Edwards 2015).

Depending on the paradigmatic assumptions adopted, for example, Adie et al. (2018) discuss how it concerns acknowledging the choices that can be made by students in a performative culture. They discuss how individuals' decisions inform subsequent actions they engage in. They specifically connect how within particular learning contexts the expected criteria and examination standards of the institution influence the 'actors' (the students and teachers) deciding upon particular 'actions' that demonstrate their choices in learning situations. This resonates with Bruner's view that agency is 'proactive, problem-oriented and attentionally focused' (Bruner 1996: 92).

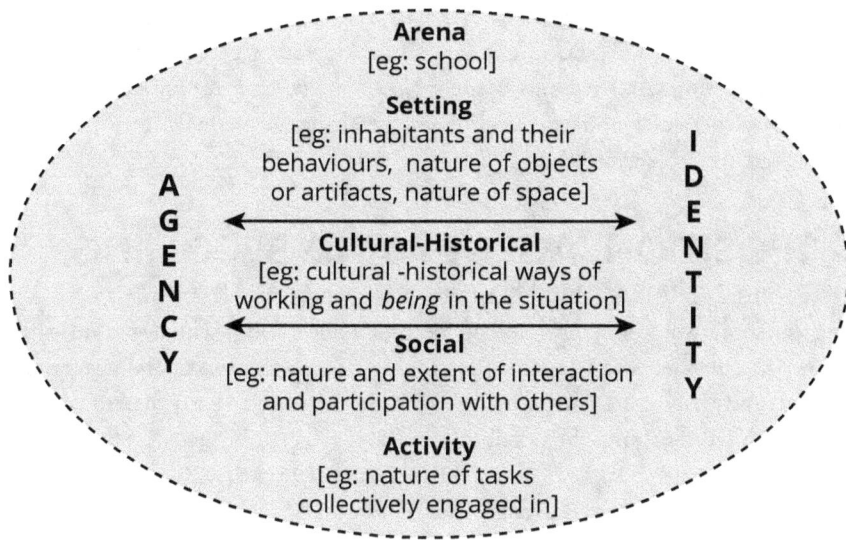

Figure 6.2 Situational Influences on Emergence of a Person's Agency and Identity Within a Particular Arena

---

Question for Consideration 6.3

Why do different individuals act differently in apparently similar situations?

The extent to which agentive actions enacted by individuals emerge as a result of social interaction is not always clearly explained in studies on learning. Consider Wenger's (1998) perspective that focuses attention in varied settings, practice and the affordances made available for students to enable them to negotiate (with others in that setting) ways of being a person in that particular context. Within different settings, more experienced others (like teachers) can make available more or less possibilities or opportunities for students to *think*, *act* or *be* such that agentive actions (cognitive, dialogic and affective) can emerge. So, as Murphy (2008: 162) suggests, 'agency is a situated, negotiated experience'. She also elaborates how 'identities emerge in the interaction between students' experiences and their social interpretations over time', indicating how agency and identity are interrelated or 'intertwined' as Edwards (2015: 780) suggests. Within a sociocultural theorising, agency emerges 'within a dialectic of person and practice' (Edwards, 2015). Her study examining the nature and extent of teacher agency in classrooms revealed how they, [teachers] as actors, recognised, interpreted and responded to different phenomena in their schools. In various international situations she argues how professional agency [of teachers] involves the capacity to make strong evaluations, interpret complex problems and utilise effectively available resources to address the challenges. Interestingly, though, Biesta et al. (2015) noticed that teacher agency was often limited, lacked vision, was short term and did not embrace broader notions of the purpose of education. As Lave and Wenger (1991) attest, educational contexts that are constrained by curricular policies and historical routines and rituals limit the extent to which teachers can act agentively.

POSITION, AGENCY AND BECOMING

Calabrese-Barton and Tan (2010) illustrate how young people in an urban context, working collaboratively on a project, can become collectively agentive within a figured world (or particular setting) related to developing others' environmental awareness. The students were initially concerned with the lack of knowledge that other inhabitants of their city exhibited regarding the possibilities of green energy in their locality. Positioned initially as low-income youths who knew little about science, they became confident and informed about science. They 'asserted their community science expertise in ways that made science talk accessible to others by situating scientific talk and thinking within the workaday lives of ordinary people' (Calabrese-Barton and Tan 2010: 221). Interestingly this project demonstrated how the learning youth could not always determine how they were positioned, but that they could respond to where they found themselves.

Hatt's (2007) work introduced earlier identified how the dominant discourse in schools of smartness relates to book smart. However, to the students of low socioeconomic status, repositioning themselves within an everyday life context and recognising what it means to be street smart enabled them to navigate the street culture outside school. This distinction is significant because street smart youths emphasised agency in countering social structures, whereas book smarts represented those structures. In other words, different positions may be afforded to pupils by teachers' actions and words, but it is possible for learners to subvert their 'given' identity, exercise agency and re-position themselves through their interactive negotiations with others in the 'figured world'.

Task 6.3

Can you think back to a learning situation where you were 'given' or 'designated' a particular identity? Perhaps this was in a class in school where you were notably 'able' or 'good' or perhaps 'struggling'. This often happens in PE classes where nominated captains are asked to select their team players and the 'sporty' students are picked first and those less athletic are left until last. Can you recollect how the label made you feel. Do you think you behaved in a way that fulfilled this designated identity or did you assert yourself and behave differently to your given label? Did you notice how others might have been 'labelled' too? Did they thwart their designated identity or embrace it?

Identity

Lave and Wenger (1991: 35) describe learning ontologically as 'an integral part of generative social practice in the lived-in world'. Adopting a view of learning that acknowledges the social dimensions of developing capabilities of different kinds, it is easy to perceive of learners in a new situation defined as 'legitimate peripheral participants'. Locating learners or novices on the periphery of a particular community (such as a new school, new class, new working group) situates or positions them as someone who does not yet know the 'rules, rituals or practices' of that community. A new child entering a classroom part way through the academic year, for example, is likely to be quietly watching, tentatively engaging with others and incrementally figuring out how to behave and appropriately respond to the teacher and peers in the class. Their identity as the new member of the school community will initially place them on the periphery in terms of their significance and extent to which they can contribute to the social interactions of the various classes they are part of. It may take some time for them to become enculturated into their new classes and for their actions within the school to be regarded as relevant and significant.

Question for Consideration 6.4

How and why might a new pupils identity change throughout a school year?

How are position and identity related?

As a new pupil in school, especially if you have moved region or even country, you may experience something of a culture shock as you find yourself immersed in an unfamiliar school community. As Lave and Wenger (1991/2011) discuss although schools are predicated on claims that knowledge can be decontextualised, they remain social institutions within which exist multiple social practices. As a place of learning, a school constitutes 'a very specific context'; however, learning does not arise naturalistically. Schools are places where teaching is a 'special mode of inculcation' (Lave and Wenger 1991/2011: 40). Therefore, in a sociocultural sense, applying the perspective of 'legitimate peripheral participation' regarding learning within school is contentious. As Lave and Wenger explain, novices positioned as legitimate peripheral participants in a community of practice offer an analytical view of the progress of learning rather than suggesting a pedagogical strategy. Their focus shifts from the individual as a learner to learning as participation in the social world. This perspective of learning, also, shifts from that of cognitive processing to one of acknowledging the importance of social practice(s). Adopting this view, the individual is understood as a person-in-the-world, that is, they are recognised as a member of the school community. In thinking about a new student entering a school, the concept of legitimate peripheral participation suggests how their membership of that community is an evolving one and that learning implies becoming able to be involved in new activities, performing new tasks and roles and mastering new understandings. However, these activities, tasks, roles and understandings do not exist in isolation. They are relational. The person-in-the-world is defined by them. Learning, therefore, involves becoming a different person whose identity is defined by their relational connections with activities, tasks, roles and understandings (Lave and Wenger 1991/2011: 52). A new entrant to the social world of the school can be understood as a person-in-the-world who can agentively contribute to the reproduction and transformation of the community through participating in collective activities. Communities of practice in school, for example, are formed by people who engage in a process of collective learning in a shared domain of human endeavour. This could involve a clique of pupils defining their identity in the school (Wenger 2015); an art class developing a group sculpture for a competition; or the netball team practising ready to represent the school.

Over time, their knowledgeably skilled identities-in-practice will emerge as they become more expert in particular community practices of the school. Some things may be learnt, too, that are not directly intended, like the street smart kids (Hatt 2007) described earlier who subverted the positions afforded them to become book smart.

As novices (or new students) become more familiar, skilful and knowledgeable in school, class or group practices, they are likely to re-position themselves (as do others and themselves in relation to others) to a more central position within that particular community. This may be because they demonstrate more investment in school life, become part of the history of the institution, develop insights into how it works and know what is expected of them as a pupil or student. As learners, therefore, over time, they might become more agentive and competent in certain areas, for example, practising the use of English language or working with mathematical practices, but they may stutter in the development of their identity in other dimensions of their schooling, for example, musical performance and practices. They can also become marginalised and disaffected if they can find no space to be the person they are and/or the person they are expected to become. Their position, therefore, within the evolving nature of their learning trajectories is reflected in the discursive ways that they and other participants interact and relate themselves to each other and what is to be learnt.

Question for Consideration 6.5

How can identity reflect learning?

Whilst conversations involving comments such as these can illustrate how a learner sees themselves or others, they can also be interpreted to appreciate how individuals perceive their place in the world (school or classroom) and indicate how they wish to be known or wish to become (Holland et al. 1998; Urrieta 2007). As Holland et al. (1998: 3) explain,

People tell others who they are, but even more importantly, they tell themselves and they try to act as though they are who they say they are. These self-understandings, especially those with strong emotional resonance for the teller, as what we refer to as identities.

Sfard and Prusak (2005: 14) in their study of 17-year-old immigrant Russian mathematics students arriving in Israel followed their learning journeys by analysing newcomers' and old-timers' narratives about who they thought they were. In their study, they argue how identity can be defined as 'a set of reifying, significant endorsable stories about a person'. They demonstrate how learning can be thought of as closing the gap between actual identity and designated identity. They found that mathematical fluency constituted a key element of the newcomers' designated identity, but not the old-timers'. The newcomers regarded mathematics as important in becoming 'a fully fledged human being' (Sfard and Prusak 2005: 20). The apparent acknowledgement of parents' influence and their role in their offsprings' stories was also more prominent in the newcomers' narratives. Identity is significant to any view of learning within sociocultural theory, and as Sfard and Prusak demonstrate, they are shaped by cultural and societal influences. As Wenger (1998) describes identity as more than just a label, a role, a self-image or how others consider you, it is an individual's on-going negotiation of their place within a community, such as a particular class or group within a school. The ways that pupils participate and exercise agency in different school communities shape their identity. In schools, this is complex because pupils, developing their participation within and between different groups of others, are evolving competencies in a range of different practices (both inside and outside of classroom arenas) and across subject disciplines. This 'nexus of multi-membership' of different communities or groupings that are constituted within schools for various purposes such as form groups, sporting, dramatic or other artistic endeavours as well as specific disciplinary lessons in particular classrooms presents a multitude of participatory experiences. Pupils participating in various school-based activities will undoubtedly involve resolving emergent conflicting identities (Murphy 1999; Ivinson and Murphy 2003). As Wenger (1998) suggests, the nexus of multi-membership does not mean an individual develops fragmented identities, but rather they need to effortfully reconcile different forms of membership. This is because:

- different ways of engaging in practice may reflect different forms of individuality;
- different forms of accountability may call for different responses to the same circumstances;
- elements of one repertoire may be quite inappropriate, incomprehensible or even offensive in another community (Wenger 1998: 160).

As Culver and Trudel (2008) demonstrate, for example, the concept of communities of practice can potentially be applied to many different sporting and social contexts, promoting the emergence of a range of activities, varying the ways that individuals interact agentively with others to develop their identities both within and beyond the classroom (Figure 6.3).

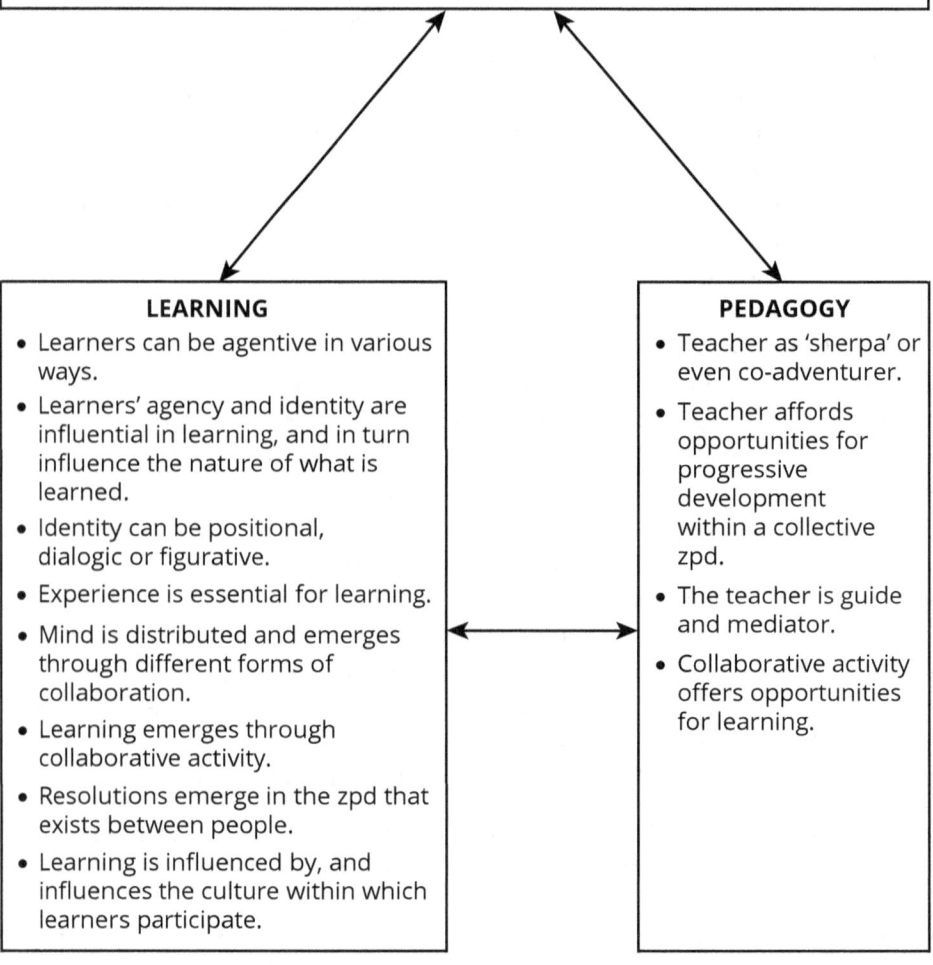

Figure 6.3 Features in Theorising Further About the Social Aspects of Learning

SUMMARY

This chapter discusses some of the concepts in sociocultural theorising further than those introduced in Chapter 5. Theorising a sociocultural perspective of learning is more than just paying attention to the multiple component parts or dimensions of learning, for example, the cognitive, the social, the physical, the emotional, etc. To wholly appreciate and understand this view of learning, it is the relational connections and links between all of the contextual, human and social factors that have to be borne in mind. As Rogoff highlights, it involves multiple planes (including the psychological and physical) that connect the personal, the interpersonal and community processes. Each aspect cannot be considered alone, because in a sociocultural view context, activity, agency and identity, each of which can be studied from multiple perspectives themselves, are all inter-related.

The view of the teacher in this theorising extends from the metaphor of *tourist guide* or *sherpa*, guiding novices, to one of *co-adventurer* working collaboratively on unfamiliar terrain with others to seek resolutions.

ADDITIONAL READING

Holland, D., Lachicotte, W., Skinner, D. & Cain, C. (1998) *Identity and Agency in Cultural Worlds*. Cambridge, MA: Harvard University Press.
This book introduces and explains the notion of the culturally figured worlds. The ways that identity and agency emerge in different cultural settings are explained in-depth. There is also a useful historical section explaining how this work has emerged from that of others including Caughey, Weiner, Vygotsky and Cain.

Christensen, T. S. (2016) Student notes as a mediating tool for learning in school subjects. In Ane Qvorrup, Merete Wiberg, Gerd Christensen & Mikala Hansbol (Eds) *On the Definition of Learning*.
This chapter provides an insightful application of an aspect of Vygotsky and Luria's concept of symbolic tools. The chapter discusses how students note-taking mediates their learning in a Danish secondary school.

Bruner, J. (1996) *The culture of Education*. This book provides an incredibly informative chronological narrative that argues and substantiates how we now come to see educational processes as rooted in cultural practices.

REFERENCES

Adie, L. E., Willis, J. & Van der Kleij, F. M. (2018) Diverse perspectives on student agency in classroom assessment. *Australian Educational Researcher, 45*, 1-12.

Biesta, G. Priestley, M. & Robinson, S. (2015) The role of beliefs in teacher agency. *Teachers and Teaching, 21*(6), 624-640. https://doi.org/10.1080/13540602.2015.1044325

Biesta, G. J. J. & Tedder, M. (2007) Agency and learning in the life course: Towards an ecological perspective. *Studies in the Education of Adults, 39*, 132-149.

Bird, M. (2012) *Rethinking Formative Assessment from a Sociocultural Perspective: A Practitioner Investigation in a History Classroom*. Unpublished EdD thesis. The Open University.

Bruner, J. (1996) *The Culture of Education*. Cambridge, MA: Harvard University Press.

Calabrese Barton, A. & Tan, E. (2010) We be Burnin! Agency, identity and science learning. *The Journal of the Learning Sciences, 19,* 187-229.

Culver, D. & Trudel, P. (2008) Clarifying the concept of communities of practice in Sport. *International Journal of Sports Science & Coaching, 3*(1), 2-11.

Dewey, J. (1991) *How we Think*. Amherst, NY: Promethueus Books.

Daniels, H., Edwards, A., Engestrom, Y., Gallagher, T. & Ludvigsen, S. R. (2010) *Activity Theory in Practice. Promoting Learning across Boundaries and Agencies*. London: Routledge.

Engeström, Y. (1987) *Learning by Expanding*. Helsinki: Orientakonsultit Oy.

Engeström, Y., Engeström, R. & Kärkkäinen, M. (1995) Polycontextuality and boundary crossing in expert cognition: Learning and problem solving in complex work activities. *Learning and Instruction, 5,* 319-336.

Engeström, Y. (1999) Activity theory and individual and social transformation. In Y. Engestrom, R. Miettinen & R. L. Punamäki (Eds) *Perspectives on Activity Theory*. Cambridge, MA: Cambridge University Press.

Edwards, A. (2015) Recognising and realising teachers' professional agency. *Teachers and Teaching. Theory and Practice, 21*(6), 779-784.

Fenwick, T., Edwards, R. & Sawchuk, P. (2011) Cultural historical activity theory in educational research. In *Emerging Approaches to Educational Research: Tracing the Socio-Material*. Abingdon: Routledge.

Hatt, B. (2007) Street smarts vs book smarts: The figured world of smartness in the lives of marginalized, urban youth. *The Urban Review, 39*(2), 145-166.

Holland, D., Skinner, D., Lachicotte, W. & Cain, C. (1998) *Identity and Agency in Cultural Worlds*. Cambridge, MA: Harvard University Press.

Ivinson, G. & Murphy, P. (Eds) (2003) *Boys Don't Write Romance: The Construction of Knowledge and Social Gender Identities in English Classrooms. Pedagogy, Culture and Society, vol. 11,* no. 1, pp. 89-109. Maidenhead, Berks: Open University Press/McGraw-Hill.

Lave, J. (1993). Situating learning in communities of practice. In L. B. Resnick, J. M. Levine & S. D. Teasley (Eds) *Perspectives on Socially Shared Cognition* (pp. 17-36). Washington, DC: American Psychological Association.

Lave, J. (1988) *Cognition in practice: Mind, mathematics and culture in everyday life*. Cambridge: Cambridge University Press.

Lave, J., Murtaugh, M. & de la Rocha, O. (1984) The dialectic of arithmetic in grocery shopping. In B. Rogoff & J. Lave (Eds) *Everyday Cognition: Its Development in Social Context*. Cambridge, MA: Harvard University Press.

Lave, J. & Wenger, E. (1991) *Situated Learning: Legitimate Peripheral Participation*. Cambridge: Cambridge University Press.

Leont'ev, A. N. (1978). *Activity, Consciousness, and Personality*. Englewood Cliffs, NJ: Prentice Hall.

Lund, A. (2008). *ReCALL, 20, Issue 1, January 2008,* pp. 35-54. https://doi.org/10.1017/S0958344008000414

Murphy, P. (1999) Supporting collaborative learning: A gender dimension. In P. Murphy (Ed) *Learners, Learning & Assessment*. London: SAGE.

Murphy, P. (2008) Gender and subject cultures in practice. In P. Murphy & K. Hall (Eds) *Learning and Practice. Agency and Identities*. Milton Keynes: The Open University/Sage.

Murphy, T. (2022) Exposing the uncomfortable: Activity Theory and the limitations of the academic in the world of TEL and programme development. *Studies in Technology Enhanced Learning, 3*(1), 1-12.

Nunes, T., Carraher, D. & Schiemann, A. (1985) Mathematics in teh streets and in Schools. *British Journal of Developmental Psychology*. https://doi.org/10.1111/j.2044-835X.1985.tb00951.x

Prestley, M., Biesta, G. J. J. & Robinson, S. (2015) Teacher agency: What is it and why does it matter? In R. Kneyber & J. Evers (Eds) *Flip the System: Changing Education from the Bottom up*, London: Routledge, pp. 134-148.

Rogoff, B. (1990) *Apprenticeship in Thinking: Cognitive Development in Social Context*. New York: Oxford University Press.

Rogoff, B. (2003) *The Cultural Nature of Human Development*. Oxford: Oxford University Press.

Rogoff, B. (2008a) Observing sociocultural activity on three planes: Participatory appropriation, guided participation and apprenticeship. In K. Hall, P. Murphy, J. Soler (Eds) *Pedagogy and Practice. Culture and Identities*. London: Open University Press/Sage.

Rogoff, B. (2008b) Thinking with the tools and institutions of culture. In P. Murphy & K. Hall (Eds) *Learning and Practice. Agency and Identities*. London: Open University Press/Sage.

Sfard, A. (2002) The interplay of intimations and implementations: Generating new discourse with new symbolic tools. *The Journal of the Learning Sciences, 11*(2 - 3), 319-357. https://doi.org/10.1080/10508406.2002.9672142

Sfard, A. (2006) Participationist discourse on mathematics learning. In J. Maasz & W. Schloeglmann (Eds) *New Mathematics Education Research and Practice*. Sense Publishers, pp. 153-170.

Sfard and Prusak (2005) Telling identities: In search of an analytic tool for investigating learning in mathematics. *Educational Researcher, 34*(4), 14-22.

Urrieta, L. (2007) Figured worlds and education: An introduction to the special issue. *The Urban Review*, 39(2). https://doi.org/10.1007/s11256-007-0051-0

Vygotsky, L. (1978) *Mind in Society. The Development of Higher Psychological Processes*. Cambridge, MA: Harvard University Press.

Vygotsky, L. (1981) The instrumental method in psychology. In J. Wertsch (Ed) *The Concept of Activity in Societ Psychology*. Armonk, NY: Sharpe, pp. 3-35.

Wenger, E. (1998) *Communities of Practice: Learning, Meaning and Identity*, Cambridge, Cambridge University Press.

Wenger, E. (2015) Communities of practice. A brief introduction. *Communities of Practice*. Available at: http://www.ewenger.com/theory/ Accessed 21/08/24.

Wertsch, J. (1985) *Vygotsky and the Social Formation of Mind*. Cambridge, MA: Harvard University Press.

Wood, D. (1988) *How Children Think and Learn* 1st ed. Oxford: Blackwell Publishers.

PART 2
APPLYING THEORY TO MAKE SENSE OF PRACTICE

INTRODUCTION

This part refers to excerpts from practice that are presented as narrative construals (Bruner, 1996). They serve to illustrate moments of action in learning contexts. These illustrations offer examples of ways concepts within selected theoretical movements are enacted in classrooms. They make available for reflection, for you the reader, the ways that pedagogy shapes and extends opportunities for learners to learn. The narratives also include consideration of what is made available to learn as well as how it is made available.

To better understand the nature of learning that unfolds as it does in classrooms, and make sense of the 'messy reality' of school life (Ball et al. 2012: 43), Stephen Ball and his colleagues highlight how teachers are 'policy actors'. That is, they are involved in both the *interpretation* and *translation* of educational policy which in turn informs what they think and do. As Law (2008) suggests, 'theory is embedded and extended in empirical practice' (p. 141) through the ways that 'actors', in this case teachers, enact their practice in the professional workplace. He also proposes that by considering empirical cases and the ways teachers work in practice, the relational nature of the material and social world can be told as a story. He does warn, however, about over simplifying and objectifying relational influences through recounting case studies as stories. However, like Stenhouse and other case-study researchers, he suggests that empirical cases 'tell particular stories about particular relations' (Law 2008: 142). As Rule and John (2011) describe, researchers can present in-depth case studies that enable critical engagement with key issues. This is extended by Thomas (2016) who suggests 'cases' can be analysed theoretically to present characterisations of events or social phenomena. Bassey (1999) highlights, too, how cases can allow focus on interesting and significant features of events or happenings enabling 'story telling' and 'theory testing' (p. 12). He goes on to explain how this kind of research relates to theoretical frameworks and can underpin both 'educational practice and policy' (p. 13). Each of the classroom cases presented over the next few chapters, offer illustrations of the ways that 'policy enactments' that is, for example, how teachers in schools action a set of 'embodied practices' that are translated and transformed through their interpretations of educational policies that incorporate 'standards, assessment and discipline' (Ball et al. 2012: 121).

So, in generating narratives from illustrative cases, the following four chapters present ways that you as the reader can 'make meaning' (Bruner, 1996: 41) from detailed descriptions of classroom happenings and theorise about learning from observable practice.

There are tasks, for you as reader, to consider and engage with the discussion about the ways that policies and practices influence learning. This approach recognises that narratives evolve, and more importantly, no excerpt from practice has only one construal. The nature of meaning–making, as argued in this book, is that there is no one definitive account of moments in classrooms. The intention instead being to construct something that is convincing and useful to develop understanding about practice and how it shapes learning from different theoretical perspectives. These narrative construals are ultimately intended to inform and enable practitioners or teachers to appreciate potential directions for their professional development. Analysing teachers' practices and the ways that learning arises from classroom activity, makes available material to think about, consequently this book provides 'tools' for thinking about the ways that learners are oriented and supported and by practitioners (working as policy actors) to learn. Using theories as tools for thinking about classroom education will enable practitioners or teachers to make choices about the direction they wish to take their practice and engage with supporting their learners and their learning. It is recognised, too, that these narrative construals are informed by personal theoretical beliefs. That is what teachers pay attention to because of their values and beliefs about learners, learning, pedagogy and practice, as well as those of others, for example, policy makers, head teachers, heads of departments, line managers, curricular developers etc. As part of this process of meaning-making [from the narrative construals] I attempt to highlight the consequences of different practice directions for learners and what is made available for them to learn.

REFERENCES

Ball, S., Maguire, M. & Braun, A. (2012) *How Schools do Policy. Policy enactments in Secondary Schools*. London: Routledge.

Bassey, M. (1999) *Case Study Research in Educational Settings*. Buckingham: Open University Press.

Bruner, J. (1996) *The Culture of Education*. Cambridge, MA: Harvard University Press.

Law, J. (2008) Actor network theory and material semiotics. In B. S. Turner (Ed) *The New Blackwell Companion to Social Theory* (pp. 141-158). Blackwell.

Rule, P. & John, V. (2011). *Your Guide to Case Study Research*. Pretoria: Van Schaik.

7

CLASSROOM CASES FEATURING ASPECTS OF BEHAVIOURISM AND INFORMATION PROCESSING

CONTENTS

Introduction	156
Teaching Phonics	157
Reflecting on the Way the Teacher Positioned the Learners and How She Presented What was to be Learnt	164
Developing Fluency in Arithmetic Processes in a Primary Classroom	166
Later in the Afternoon: More Mathematics	173
Teaching About Grammar with Older Students	174
Learning About Commas with Mr Thomas	175
Contrasting Features of Teachers' Practices	178
Summary	178
Additional Reading	179
References	179

Chapter Aims

After reading Chapter 7, you will have considered:

- how behaviourist and information-processing theories of learning can be used as 'tools' to think about the ways that policy and practice influence learning;
- that the nature of learning that unfolds in classrooms is influenced by a range of factors;
- that what teachers pay attention to, value and believe informs their pedagogy and practice;
- how teachers' enactments of practice position learners to experience ways of learning that can reflect policy;
- the extent to which teachers' enactments in classroom episodes illustrate how contemporary practice reflects characteristics that have similarities with behaviourist and information-processing theories of learning;
- how theories can be used as 'tools' to think about policy, practice and learning;
- extrinsic motivations, imitative behaviours, a lack of learner agency, limited dialogue and unilateral communication characterise behaviourist and information-processing theories of learning;
- how applications of the metaphors of a *lion tamer* and sculptor highlight features of teachers' practices supporting learning that is behaviourist in nature;
- how applications of the metaphors of the *watchmaker* and *parent bird* highlight features of teachers' practices that support information processing.

INTRODUCTION

In Chapter 2, you will recollect that you were introduced to the ways that behaviourism and information processing were discussed in terms of generalised theories (Mercer 1995) that have been developed over time through research into human behaviour and activities. You were also introduced to the ways that learning is talked about in an everyday way by 'ordinary folks' (Scott et al. 2007). Introduction of intuitive or folk theories (Bruner 1996) included drawing on metaphors of the teacher (Claxton 1990) as a *lion tamer*, sculptor, *watchmaker* and *parent bird* that illustrated different features of behaviourism and information processing. This chapter, then, invites you to think further about the characterisations of hegemonic (or prevailing) practices and beliefs in relation to learning that demonstrates behaviourism or information processing within contemporary classrooms.

As outlined in Chapter 2, the tasks in this book invite you to think beyond 'folk theories' (Bruner 1996) and consider how long held assumptions, customs and practices require further consideration to make a better theorised sense of learning.

The ways that policy shapes and influences pedagogy (the teacher's beliefs and intentions) are challenging to observe in reality. However, the following descriptions of

Classroom Cases Featuring Aspects of Behaviourism and Information Processing

moments of action in learning that are determined by the teacher, are presented to help demonstrate concepts related to the behaviourist or information processing movement. You are invited to think about details of aspects of practice enactments that influence learners' responses and participation in various learning activities. For some of these moments in action, limited details are available regarding the context (e.g. school policy and teacher materials) and the teacher's intentions for the learners. Teacher and learner actions and dialogue, that emerge within the classroom environment though, are presented for you to think about. You will be invited to consider what it is possible to infer about teaching and the ways that learning has been supported, for whom and how. By drawing on a range of current practices across disciplines and phases in education, this chapter aims to highlight features of behaviourist practices and information processing that exists in contemporary classrooms.

The episodes considered include:

- Teaching phonics to five- and six-year-old children;
- Teaching for fluency in arithmetic processes in a primary classroom;
- Teaching to improve recall and application of grammatical rules in secondary education.

In reading the following transcripts, you will be invited to consider whether the motivation for pupils to learn appears to be intrinsic or extrinsic; which teaching metaphor characterises the practice enacted; who controls and holds responsibility for learning; what kinds of exchanges unfold in the episode; the nature of dialogue that emerges between teacher and learners and peers and the nature of knowledge that is valued by both teacher and learners.

TEACHING PHONICS

The National Curriculum Policy, for England, regarding teaching reading, introduced in Chapter 2, from the 2014 Programme of Study was presented. You were guided to consider how the ways that learners' experience reading letters and words phonically overlapped with behaviourist pedagogy. In England, schools are inspected to judge how well teachers are delivering the National Curriculum to their pupils. The re-focus on processes of learning announced by the Chief Inspector of Education, Children's Services and Skills, in October 2018 (DfE 2018a) highlighted how the new 2019 framework included 'prioritising phonics and the transition into early reading' (p. 7) in primary schools. Performance of each individual student in phonics screening tests at the beginning of primary school (at age five and six years) is collated for each school and entered into a national database. This kind of data, along with many other examination and test results (DfE 2024c), provides information that is archived and made available for public scrutiny (https://www.gov.uk). The DfE draws from Ofsted (school inspection) data and mandatory test data that are presented for all state schools on their website. Annual performance of schools is archived, and general trends and patterns are reviewed by various organisations including the DfE. In primary education, there is particular focus on phonics, spelling, punctuation and grammar for 5 to 7-year-olds, seen by policymakers as appropriate preparation for reading and writing. Of 634 teachers responding to a recent survey (Wyse and Bradbury 2022), 66% indicated that they taught 'synthetic phonics first and foremost'. The percentage of pupils in each school achieving the government's 'expected standards' (DfE 2019) is reported through the Inspection Data Summary Report. The proportion of pupils achieving above and below the national standards, reported as percentages, is compared annually to assess each individual school's progress. Pupil performance above and below expected standards is also compared across schools nationally. These data inform the national performance league tables (DfE 2024a) comparing all schools' demographic, academic and financial information. Interestingly, of the 634 teachers questioned in the recent survey (Wyse and Bradbury 2022), 71% indicated that the phonics screening check affected how they choose to enact their practice.

> **Task 7.1**
>
> As a teacher aware of the various annual national tests (like phonics screening), the results of which are reported publicly for anyone (pupils, teachers, head teachers, parents, governors, politicians, etc.) to scrutinise, how would you enact practice? If you were responsible for year 1 in a primary school and you knew they would be tested at the end of the year for their competency in reading and speaking phonically (as outlined below), what would you do?

In England, young children, in year 1, for example (as demonstrated in the classroom episode later in this chapter), are expected to understand that written letters, words and grapheme–phoneme correspondence (GPCs) represent sounds in spoken words; this understanding should underpin reading and spelling. The phonics screening test, undertaken annually in the summer term of school by all five- and six-year-olds in England, assesses the proportion of children who can successfully de-code letters and words (some of which they may never have seen previously and are referred to as pseudo-words) using phonics. It is also expected that each child will have a good knowledge of 85 GPCs and will be expected to perform to a particular standard to 'pass' (usually a score of 32 out of 40 questions). Any child failing to achieve the pass mark will be expected to re-sit the test the following June. External pressure exerted by national policy frameworks of this kind is exacerbated by scrutiny of pupils' performances, not only as part of regular Ofsted inspections (that take account of learner's progress in academic performance) but also through reviews by the head teacher, governors, parents and even the Local Authorities review of improvement in performance in national academic tests.

Consider, then, a teacher who has been teaching for several years and is a year 1 teacher of 5 and 6-year-olds. A recent Ofsted inspection had indicated that there was a need for 'accelerating progress' and 'lifting attainment' at the end of year 6 (for the 10- and 11-year-olds).

Knowing that the head teacher held a long-term view about improving attainment and encouraged staff to raise expectations with the younger children in the school to ensure progress was steadily improved. The school policy indicated that 15 minutes a day should be spent on whole class phonics teaching.

> **Task 7.2**
>
> A school inspection is coming up. You need to 'perform' well. Previously inspectors noted that 'Reading skills were not taught well in Key Stage 1' and that learning needed 'speeding up' and recommendations included the adoption of 'phonics teaching'. Your senior leadership team decides that Key Stage 1 teachers should develop their phonics teaching to accelerate progress in reading and that they will be closely monitoring progress. How could you develop your practice with your five- and six-year-olds to ensure they become more rapid readers.

Below are a number of practitioner beliefs that are a kind of folklore that you might choose from:

- *Practice makes perfect*
- *Giving clues to get the right answer helps*
- *Seeing letters and saying them out loud is effective*
- *Seeing is believing*
- *Routine is the backbone of an effective classroom*
- *Copy the expert*
- *Modelling how to sound letters makes things clearer*

The testing of spelling, punctuation and grammar, seen as prerequisite skills for reading in England, is reported on nationally (DfE 2024d). There are therefore significant stakes riding on pupils' performances in those tests, the impact of which Ball et al. (2012: 36) have investigated in schools. As one interviewed head teacher explained, 'the combination of the national curriculum and an inspection structure to hold you accountable, and publication of their league tables of course has completely changed the way people think about their work' (cited in Ball et al. 2012: 36).

Perryman et al. (2011) also describes the powerful 'pressure cooker' effects in schools that result in a preoccupation with polices of achievement. Carter (2020) illustrates how this is continuing to be a powerful policy influencing the practice of teachers in England. The experience of learning to read for young children has consequently been noted to contrast to that intended by policymakers (Carter 2020: 52). They 'see' phonics separately to learning to read. Carter (2020: 52) reports from transcripts that children think phonics is about 'learning sounds', 'to get brains brainer' and 'learning diagraphs'.

> **Task 7.3**
>
> In the classroom episode outlined below (inspired by Knowles 2012), Ms Jones could be from a school like that described in Task 7.2. Consider how various classroom materials and enactment of practice might be adopted to improve pupil achievement.
> After reading the transcript, and thinking about the questions for consideration, how would you describe the practice adopted by the teacher?
> Which teacher metaphors introduced in Chapter 2 relate to this approach?
> What assumptions appear to be made about the learners and learning?
> How would you characterise the way the children appear to experience learning?

The year one classroom provides a colourful display of the letters of the English alphabet, each presented on a separate A4-sized poster, above the whiteboard. The 26 letters are displayed in sequence from left to right, from A through to Z. On other walls in the classroom are brightly presented collages or pictures providing clear and unequivocal examples of the different ways a letter might be written in capital or lowercase form, with accompanying illustrations that represent an object or animal whose name begins with a particular associated letter.

> **Question for Consideration 7.1**
>
> Will learning be more effective if what is to be learnt is explicitly displayed?

The large, centrally positioned, white notice board is surrounded by speech bubbles upon which are written 'Learning Objectives' or 'Success Criteria' that provide clues about the lesson focus for the day.

The 5- and 6-year-old children are all sat, crossed legged on the carpeted floor, facing the whiteboard.

> **Questions for Consideration 7.2**
>
> Is what is to be learnt external to the knower?
> Is what is to be learnt independent of the situation and classroom context?

The teacher, Ms Jones, activates the whiteboard and the letters of the alphabet appear in turn in the centre of the screen. As each symbol materialises, she rapidly verbalises the sound of the letters and the children mimic reciting 'a, b, c, d, e [. . .] z'. At the end of sounding all the alphabet letters, they all recount together, 'Now I know my abcs, won't you sing along with me'.

> **Question for Consideration 7.3**
>
> To what extent does learning, as enacted here, appear to be assumed to be recitation, involving given rules and focused on de-coding letters?

Ms Jones proceeds to question individual children (selected randomly from her classroom list).

Ms Jones: [pressing the whiteboard keyboard]: Jacob, are you ready? [she presses the button and 'e' appears] Can you sound the letter?
Jacob: e [rhymes with tea]
Ms Jones: Fantastic [tapping the whiteboard keyboard again]: Ted, can you tell me how this letter sounds? [she presses the button and 'i' appears]
Ted: i [sounds like eye]

Ms Jones then challenges Joe, Olivia and other children in the group. She points to a number of different letters and they each, in turn, reply with the correct sound the teacher is looking for.

> **Question for Consideration 7.4**
>
> The children appear to know exactly what to say in response to the teacher. Why do you think that is the case?

Ms Jones then goes on to a different activity that she describes as 'sounds and their actions'. She tells the children to watch the screen and she proceeds to tap the keyboard to initiate the diagraphs (a pair of letters that signify a single sound) appearing on the screen. The dialogue is indicated in the transcript below.

Ms Jones: [taps the keyboard to initiate 'ch' appearing on the whiteboard] ch [pumping her arms back and forth like the movement of the wheels of a steam train]
Children: Ch
Ms Jones: Move your arms like the wheels on a steam train and create a sound the train makes.
Children: ch ch ch, ch ch ch [whilst moving their arms back and forth]

Ms Jones: Good. Now these letters make another sound [taps the keyboard to initiate 'sh' appearing on the whiteboard] sh [places her index finger to her pursed lips]

Children: [mimic the teacher] shhhhhhhh [moving an index finger to their lips]

Ms Jones: Great. Now how do these letters sound? [taps the keyboard to initiate 'qu' appearing on the screen] 'qu' [sounding like the first part of quack. She then moves her fingers and thumb to mime how a bird might open and close their beak]

Children: [mimicking the teacher] qu [they sound the first part of quack whilst moving their fingers and thumb on one hand, up and down to indicate a bird's beak opening and closing]

Questions for Consideration 7.5

In leaning the digraphs, what does the teacher do?

To what extent does she invite suggestions or demonstrate how to make the sounds?

Ms Jones goes on to present 'zz' and 'ss' and the sounds they represent for the children to practice.

Ms Jones: [taps the keyboard to initiate 'zz' appearing on the whiteboard] zz [she holds her arms up at her side and flaps her hands as if a buzzing bee]

Children: [mimic the teacher] zz [flapping their hands]

Ms Jones: Good. Now sound this [taps the keyboard to initiate 'ss' appearing on the whiteboard] ss [she makes a 'ss' sound with her lips curled back, flattening her hands together and creates a weaving movement representing a snake]

Children: [mimic the teacher] ss [flattening their hands together and creating a weaving movement].

Questions for Consideration 7.6

How far is learning demonstrated here about forming habits?

To what extent does the teacher encourage thinking about the context and application of what is being learnt?

Ms Jones: [taps the keyboard to initiate 'ck' appearing on the screen and turns her upper body and points to her back and says aloud] ck
Children: [copy turning upper body, pointing to their back and sounding] ck
Ms Jones: [taps the keyboard to initiate 'ai' on it] Noel, what sound is it?
Noel: Eye
Ms Jones: Close. Watch what I am doing [placing her hand behind her ear]
Noel: Ear

Question for Consideration 7.7

To what extent are the children invited to problem-solve?

Ms Jones: No Noel, that's still not correct, try again

She looks around the room to see if anyone else knows what it is. She points to another child.

Charlie: ai [as in rain or pain].
Teacher: Good. Well remembered everybody.

Question for Consideration 7.8

What has the teacher valued about the children's responses in this part of the lesson?

The teacher then progresses onto three-lettered words:

Ms Jones: [taps the keyboard to initiate 'air' appearing on the screen] This is a tricky one Leon
Leon: Eye
Ms Jones: Watch me [moving her hands in a circular motion around her and mouthing the word 'air']
Ms Jones: Everyone, Say with me 'air'
Children: [the whole class chorus] air [as they move their hands around in a similar circular fashion]
Teacher: When a, i and r come together, they join up to make 'air'

> **Questions for Consideration 7.9**
>
> To what extent does the teacher ask the children to piece together what they know when three letters are combined to make a word?

Teacher: [Presses the keyboard to produce 'ear'] Grace?
Grace: Not sure
Teacher: Tugs her ear lob
Children: [Chorus] ear.

REFLECTING ON THE WAY THE TEACHER POSITIONED THE LEARNERS AND HOW SHE PRESENTED WHAT WAS TO BE LEARNT

The teacher was the 'controller' of the learning process and retained responsibility for what was learnt and how each child engaged with what was to be learnt. The teacher determined the order and sequence of the learning activities, introducing letters, digraphs and then graphemes. There was no opportunity for the learners to offer how they thought the letters, digraphs, graphemes or trigraphs might sound. There was no discussion about what they may have read before or mention of words or stories they may be familiar with to discuss the context of grapheme use. Pupils were not encouraged to work things out for themselves or problem-solve. The process of learning involved the children passively absorbing what the teacher bestows. Presenting phonics knowledge in this way resonates with the teacher as *petrol pump attendant*, illustrating that what is to be learnt is 'external' to the learners and that the teacher is the expert 'holder' of information to be learnt. The children's previous phonics exercises and reading experiences are not drawn from or taken account of, the learners were each deemed equally 'unskilled'. The teacher expected speedy recognition of the sounds of letters, decoding of digraphs and then the blending of three letters (a, i, r) to form a trigraph (or word). Ms Jones modelled the sounds and controlled turn-taking for the children to imitatively (Bruner 1996: 53) recite how the letters and digraphs sound. This resonates with the teacher as a *lion tamer*, managing behaviours without the need for explanatory dialogue. As explained in Chapter 2, behaviourist views of learning do not involve learner agency, and there is no apparent cognitive processing, only routinised drills that practice imitative oration. There is no encouragement of peer–peer interaction, learning activity appears to be an individualised process and the nature of verbal communication is directive, from the teacher to the pupils.

Epistemologically, this approach assumes a one-size-fits-all approach and that all learners (although unique) will essentially learn in a similar way, at a similar pace, echoing assumptions of the *lion tamer* metaphor. All the learners are deemed subjects of teaching and the teacher assumes that once one pupil has decoded, others in the class have too. Successful learning appears to be understood as being able to 'store' the phonemes, that is, acquiring the information presented for accurate recall at a later time. Repeated practice and recitation appears to be assumed to embed reflexes, which will enable rapid retrieval of this 'stored' information in future. As Ms Jones indicates with her comment, 'well remembered everyone', she values the pupils memorising how to sound the letters and graphemes.

Applying the metaphors of a *lion tamer* and *petrol pump attendant* also suggest a uni-directional flow of information, with no dialogic or interactional exchanges between the learners. Pupils are all expected to respond uniformly to external stimuli. No account is taken of their cultural background and previous experiences and the uniqueness of each learner is overlooked. The sculptor metaphor, also demonstrated by the teacher, assumes learners are similar raw material to be moulded into shape.

The Teacher as a Policy Actor Enacting Assumptions About Learning

What was learnt in this classroom episode was made available to the children through the ways that the teacher presented letters on the white board (via the computer) and actioned her interpretation of the ways that the letters and graphemes needed to be de-coded. Neither the children's interpretations or previous experiences of letters and similar sounds were sought. The teacher assumed decoding 'z' was unproblematic for the children and a straight forward matter of recollecting what she had told them. There was no discussion or consideration of the way that 'z' might be decoded 'zed' when verbalising the letter in the English alphabet, or 'zee' if talking about it in an American context, or that the 'z' pronunciation might be represented as an 's' in other languages (like Portuguese). The 's' in 'hens' also sounds like a 'z' in 'buzz'. Decrypting a single letter 'z', in a particular way to logically progress to 'zz', does not consider alternate pronunciations and the various contexts in which they would be appropriate. The unilateral decoding of a 'z', without consideration of 'zed', or 'zee' or 's' will present problems for pronunciation in future for the children. Applying the systematic phonics rules as presented in this lesson would not be helpful for children learning how to pronounce words such as 'Ibiza' or 'wise', which do not adhere to the decoding routines demonstrated.

This narrative construal serves to demonstrate how an early years teacher is attempting to 'do' phonics policy (Ball et al. 2012). Her practice directs routinised behaviour of learners to be able to recite letters and sounds through 'habitual' learning.

Characterising the Way the Activities Are Designed for the Pupils to Experience Learning

In the routinised sequences in which the teacher directs the recitations the children are positioned as imitative (Bruner 1996: 53) passive receivers of what is to be learnt. They are positioned by the teacher (the knowledgeable controller) as raw material, metaphorically to be tamed and disciplined. They *perform* as directed by the lion-taming teacher reciting aloud the alphabet and sounds of combinations of letters. Chorus responses to commands obviate mis-pronunciations, hesitations or lack of confidence by more timid members of the group. The class 'performances' are led by louder, more confident pupils. What is experienced by the children is a presentation of 'patterns and sounds of language through songs and rhymes' as indicated in the National Curriculum (DfE 2014: 253). The pupils are recipients of 'informed prescription' (Whitty 2014: 9) and are expected to repetitively and passively *imitate* how to decode symbols. Each learner is assumed to 'build' their knowledge, like 'bricks' being placed one on another as they first encounter single letters and then common phonemes (as pairs of letters written on cards). Recitation and recall of abstract letters and graphemes without considering context are likely to contribute to a more problematic way children make sense of extended texts. The material presented for learning is not negotiated or discussed. The teacher tightly controls the lesson, beginning with the easy recitation of single letters, then progressing to pairs of letters (and actioning a particular depiction of these phonemes). A child who does not respond correctly, Noel, is not given feedback. Instead an alternate responder is sought to correctly imitate 'ai', sounded as 'air'. No questions are asked other than those to reinforce what the teacher has determined should be learnt, that is, all the letters, phonemes and three-lettered words, to be remembered, recalled and uttered as prescribed and demonstrated by Ms Jones.

There is no teaching involving discussion to negotiate understanding of meanings and the use of words in different contexts, like a story, poem or other piece of literature. The whole class engages in the same learning activity; there is no account taken of slower or faster learners; and the brisk pace of the lesson, to ensure speedy responses (DfE 2014: 21), is maintained.

DEVELOPING FLUENCY IN ARITHMETIC PROCESSES IN A PRIMARY CLASSROOM

In the previous classroom episode, learning was focused on decoding letters and digraphs through a systematic phonics approach. National screening tests administered for five- and six-year-olds during the first formal year at school are used to determine the proportion of children who have achieved an appropriate benchmarked standard (DfE 2018b); this country-wide approach is now used to compare the fluency (multiplication tables check) of nine-year-old children's application of arithmetic processes (DfE 2024b).

Task 7.4

Consider the following extracts from the National Curriculum related to mathematics.

i As in Chapter 2, how do these policy statements suggest learners should experience learning mathematics?
ii How closely does the following classroom episode demonstrate enactment of these policy statements?

The aims of the National Curriculum for mathematics include:

- become fluent in the fundamentals of mathematics, including through varied and frequent practice with increasingly complex problems over time, so that pupils develop conceptual understanding and the ability to recall and apply knowledge rapidly and accurately.
- can solve problems by applying their mathematics to a variety of routine and non-routine problems with increasing sophistication, including breaking down problems into a series of simpler steps and persevering in seeking solutions.

(DfE 2014: 108)

What do these statements convey to you? How would you intend your pupils should learn? Can you see the threads of information processing as introduced in Chapter 2.

In mathematics, as a core subject, it is expected that pupils will become competent in mastering multiplication tasks accurately and at speed. As Gallagher (2006) explains, fluency in component skills (somewhat akin to discrete phonics decoding in preparation for reading) can prepare pupils to progress and tackle more advanced curricular tasks later in school. He argues that students who are dysfluent in basic skills find complex tasks strenuous and laborious (Gallagher 2006: 305). McGeown (2017) compares research evidence from five studies, where she 'maps the field' and illustrates how, through quasi-experimental approaches, the impact of precision teaching (PT), that is, rapidity in recall and fluency, has been measured. PT is a highly structured interventional approach that provides very specific timed activities that can be applied for both literacy and numeracy teaching (Solity 1991; Gallagher et al. 2006). Key features of the PT approaches included regular (usually daily, sometimes three times a day), short, rapid timed activities that are teacher directed, and through repetitive practice, learners are encouraged to become quicker at processing numerical information involving basic arithmetic processes, such as addition, subtraction, multiplication and division. The goal of PT is to enable learners to develop accuracy and fluency in specific targeted skills (McGeown 2017) and the 'desired pupil performance should be precisely defined in observable and measurable terms' (Solity and Bull 1987). In endeavouring to put aspects of the above mathematics National Curriculum into practice, adhere to government guidance and improve children's performance in numeracy tests, an increasing number of schools in the United States, the United Kingdom and Ireland have adopted practice similar to the PT (Gallagher 2006; Gallagher et al. 2006; McGeown 2017) approach. The approach is designed to develop learners' competency in numeracy in particular kinds of ways (a little like the systematic phonics approach), building basic fluency in recognising the written form of whole numbers, counting, place value and simple arithmetic operations of addition, subtraction, multiplication and division before working on more abstract and complex problems. The following transcript of an episode of PT as an enactment of practice takes place in a primary teacher's classroom. The senior leadership team of the school was convinced by the research evidence (Gallagher 2006; McGeown 2017) that argues how the approach can result in significant increases in children's basic numeracy strategies. The teacher, as a policy actor, interprets and enacts the PT approach for her class of 5- and 6-year-olds.

A Morning Episode of Teaching Numeracy With a Year One Class

The children are all sat cross-legged in rows on the carpet, attentively focused on the front white screen. The teacher, Ms Ramen, reminds the children it is their usual morning mathematics lesson.

Ms Ramen:	Today we are doing number sets. Say the numbers as they appear on the white board [the first set is 68–75].
Children [loudly in chorus]:	Sixty-eight, sixty-nine, seventy, seventy-one, seventy-two, seventy-three, seventy-four, seventy-five.
Ms Ramen:	The second set of numbers [15–32 appear one at a time in quick succession on the board].
Children [loudly recount the numbers as they appear on the whiteboard]:	Fifteen, sixteen, seventeen, eighteen, nineteen [. . .] thirty-two.

After the children in the class have practised reading and recounting loudly several other number sets presented on the whiteboard, Ms Ramen changes the arithmetic tasks to be done.

Ms Ramen:	Good. Now we are doing skip counting. As the numbers appear say them out loud. Each time we reach a ten hold up a finger like this [she shows how raise first their index a finger, then another each time they recite a multiple of ten]. Ready [she presses the button on the computer and the numbers from 0, 2, 4, 6, 8, 10 [. . .] 20 in twos appear on the white board].
Children [in chorus]:	Zero, two, four, six, eight, ten [most children elevate a hand with one finger raised], twelve, fourteen, sixteen, eighteen, twenty [most children raise a second finger].
Ms Ramen:	Good, now skip count in fives. Raise a finger each time we count a five.
Children:	Zero, five, ten, fifteen, twenty, twenty-five, thirty, thirty-five, forty [. . .] 100. Ms Ramen: Great! now in tens backwards.
Children [rapidly responding]:	One hundred, ninety, eighty, seventy, sixty, fifty, forty, thirty, twenty, ten, zero.

Once several skip counting practices are completed, the teacher shares how the next task is the one-minute challenge.

Ms Ramen: Great! Now we are doing the one minute challenge. The one minute challenge today is to skip count in threes ten times. We need to beat our previous record of skip counting in threes up to thirty, five times within a minute. Are you ready? Go! [she starts the timer that counts down from 60 seconds on the white board].

Children [shouting]: Zero, three, six, nine, twelve, fifteen, eighteen, twenty one, twenty four, twenty seven, thirty [this is repeated rapidly seven times within a minute].

Ms Ramen: Well done! You have beaten your previous record of repeating the three times table (to thirty on six occasions) more than seven times in one minute!

We are now going to do set building, thinking about how many tens and ones there are in a number. [She writes the number 35 on the board] How many tens?

Children: Three.

Ms Ramen: How many ones?

Children: Five.

Ms Ramen: Let's check [she draws a tally of five straight lines under the five of 35 on the board and three oblique circles under the three of 35].

The teacher shows how to represent the number of tens and ones of other numbers by the simple symbols of tally lines and oblique circles.

Ms Ramen: [Writes 75 on the board] How many tens?

Children: Seven [Ms Ramen points to the seven]

Ms Ramen: How many ones?

Children: Five [Ms Ramen points to the five]

Ms Ramen: [Writes 92 on the board] How many tens?

Children: Nine [Ms Ramen points to the nine]

Ms Ramen: How many ones?

Children: Two [Ms Ramen points to the two]

Question for Consideration 7.10

What similarities can you see in the practice demonstrated by this mathematics teacher with those described in the phonics class?

Ms Ramen:	Now we are going to use set building to help solve simple equations. What is the problem? [She writes $23 + 5 = \square$ on the board].
Children:	[Reading aloud] Twenty-three plus five equals how many box.
Ms Ramen:	What do we need to do?
Children:	Show the calculations on the board.
Ms Ramen:	What is the equality rule?
Children:	We must have the same amount on both sides of the equals sign.
Ms Ramen:	[Writes $28 = \square$]
Children:	Twenty-eight equals box.

After the recitation practice is extended into problem-solving, the teacher then introduces another problem to be solved that is more directly related to everyday life.

Ms Ramen:	Okay, our last problem. Ollie has six chocolate cakes and two lemon cakes. How many does he have altogether? [the problem is written out in text on the board]. Let's read it together.
Children:	[Reading aloud] Ollie has six chocolate cakes and two lemon cakes. How many does he have altogether?
Ms Ramen:	What are the important numbers in this equation?
Children:	[several hands are raised] Six. Two.
Ms Ramen:	What equation do we need to write for this word problem? You can use your fingers to work it out.
Ryleigh:	Six plus two.
Ms Ramen:	Equals how many? [writing the equation '$6 + 2 = \square$' on the board].
Ella:	Eight.

Task 7.5

Consider the description of the morning episode of teaching of year 1 mathematics.
What features of practice are evident in this episode?
What are the assumptions the teacher is making about the ways her children will learn about number bonds?
Who is in control of what is being learnt?
What does the teacher assume is learnt?
What kind of teacher–pupil and peer–peer interactions are evident?
Which teacher metaphor introduced in Chapter 2 relates to this episode of teaching?

Reflecting on the Teacher's Practice

In the episode described above, there are a number of similarities and differences in the practice of Ms Jones and Ms Ramen. The mathematics teacher controlled what was learnt, when and how. She presented the material, at a fast moving pace for her pupils. She initially intended the children should rapidly recall sequences of numeric symbols (as each appeared on the screen). Recollecting and reciting numbers in this way deemed the learners passive receivers. This was followed by skip counting (a way of reciting times tables) an approach to acquiring some basic mathematical rules and procedures. The children then rehearsed set building (looking at number bonds), another particular mathematical method. Recalling successions of numbers, simple multiple counts and then number bonds enabled the children to practice and apply particular mathematical rules and procedures and then apply them to solve a real-life problem (how many cakes Ollie has). The problem the children solved was devised by the teacher and she controlled the way they reached the solution (which was the answer she held in her head). The learners were not offered an opportunity to reflect back on what they had done in the lesson and consider how they might work out for themselves how many cakes Ollie had. This is a significantly different to Lampert's practice described in Chapters 4 and 10 that demonstrate a sociocultural approach to problem-solving. The language used in the lesson involved signs and symbols that represented mathematical objects and processes. However, in this lesson, the mathematics teacher constructed a learning experience that was arranged and connected in a progressive order.

> Question for Consideration 7.11
>
> From the transcription of the episode, what appears to be the teacher's assumptions about the learners and their mathematical learning?

Gradually increasing the complexity of the mathematical tasks, the recalling of numbers, their bonds, sets and finally finding a solution to a problem were presented incrementally, step-by-step. This provided the opportunity for the pupils to practice the mathematical rules they had been introduced to before progressing to the next step (each determined by the teacher). This resonates with metaphor of *parent bird*. Ms Ramen broke down the final problem to be solved into a more manageable form for the five- and six-year-old children. Initially she began began with simple counting, incrementally adding challenge and finishing with a complex addition problem that involved cakes and not just abstract numerical entities.

There was evident enthusiasm from the pupils in the mathematics class. They strongly vocalised numbers (represented as words and symbols), the problem equations and responded with (mostly accurate) replies to the questions posed. It appeared, judging by the volume of the verbal responses, that many in the class confidently knew the numbers from 68–75 and 15–32. They indicated they could count in several multiples of skip counting, including 2s, 5s and 10s backwards. The teacher timing them challenged them to beat their previous speedy record of completing more skip counting in 3s within a minute than the previous day. Many pupils (evidenced by the chorus replies) provided the correct answers to how many 10s and 1s are in 35 and several other challenges. Many also provided the correct solution to the abstract equation (23 + 5 = □) and were able to translate it to verbalised words. However, despite the teacher's expectations for the whole class too engage at pace for the whole lesson, it is not clear whether or how many children did not utter the correct responses to each task. Finally, when the teacher presented the cake problem and asked the children to translate it to an abstract mathematical equation, a smaller number of pupils uttered the correct answer. The sequential tasks made available opportunities for the children to practice recalling numbers and more rapidly carryout simple additions (DfE 2014: 108) suggest how a teacher like Ms Ramen assumed that incrementally complex tasks were achievable for the pupils. The nature of the tasks also demonstrated how a primary teacher could engage with National Curriculum directives as a policy actor (Ball et al. 2012).

Questions for Consideration 7.12

Adopting this kind of practice, how can teachers know what each individual pupil is capable of?

What assumptions might be made about each of the pupils in this class?

The teacher appears to be aiming to ensure *all* children are able to learn similar material at the same pace, can recognise numbers in both numerical and word format, can represent numbers using their digits (fingers) and can verbalise the method and answers to the mathematical tasks. Implicitly, teachers might theorise that if the children are actively occupied in verbalising the arithmetic processes and rehearse these repeatedly to illustrate increasing fluency and accuracy, they are approaching mastery (Solity and Bull 1987; Coles and Helme 2022). This episode could arguably serve to illustrate how a teacher has attempted to 'do' policy (Ball et al. 2012) related to arithmetic learning. Draw on existing research (Archer and Hughes 2011) that suggested models of practice involving long-held assumptions about controlling the routinised behaviour of learners to eventually come to recite skipped counts (or times tables) through 'habitual' learning. The routinised approach to teaching mathematical fluency appeared to adopt the *lion tamer* metaphor.

Reflecting further on this learning episode and drawing on the ways that information processing is described in Chapter 2, there are some features that relate to the teacher as a *watchmaker* and *parent bird*. However, it is not clear to what extent each individual has participated in the mathematical tasks, nor is it clear what was learnt by each child in the class. It is impossible to know how far individual learning differed (and why). During the morning session, although the children were positioned as information processors manipulating numerical information in the cake problem, for example, each was regarded as being essentially similar in ability. The teacher as a *watchmaker* has assumed learning to mathematically solve problems is like doing a jigsaw. Providing the pupils with mathematical knowledge (in the form of rules and processes), it appears the teacher interprets the earlier, simpler processes (like the *parent bird* teacher) as building blocks for the later more complex problem-solving tasks.

LATER IN THE AFTERNOON: MORE MATHEMATICS

The precise teaching approach introduced earlier suggests three short mathematical learning episodes in a day. The first to re-iterate the previous day's work and extend into 'new' or previously un-encountered concepts, a second to 'apply' the notions rehearsed at the beginning of the day and a final third episode to 'revise' what has been 'learnt' during the day.

The second episode of mathematics learning takes quite a different approach. The children work silently, writing answers in booklets to questions that re-iterate and consolidate the mathematical work presented earlier. They are organised to sit at particular tables in the classroom. There is a spread of abilities on each table. Differing abilities work through differentiated booklets, so that copying is minimised as no two children next to each other have the same workbook.

Each child, however, has a 'new' learning arithmetic task to complete first before moving onto the second task, labelled 'old' learning (that revises previous work) and then there is 'interleaved' work and finally 'generalising and applying' which is usually a final problem to solve which rounds off the workbook activity. The children have a 'timed' opportunity to work at the problems in their books.

The teacher marks (correct or wrong) the responses each of the children write in the neatly presented answer boxes. The problems are given, and the answers are pre-determined.

This approach to learning involves the children processing given information rather than responding through behavioural or sensory means. In this episode of mathematics, there is only interaction with the teacher and the task. If an individual is stuck they refer to the teacher. Learning is expected to happen quietly for each individual through reading and manipulating mathematical symbols to solve problems presented in their booklets. The nature of mathematical processing required has been introduced earlier in the day or in the previous lesson. The problems and solutions are sometimes abstract. Later problems are often written in words, so linguistic translation is required to interpret what is needed numerically to work out a resolution.

The learning processes involved in the afternoon session could be theorised as illustrated in Figure 7.1.

In contrast to later Chapters 9 and 10, it is clear that the nature of talk and discussion in these kinds of behaviourist and information-processing learning episodes is very limited and focus only on recall, reinforcement and reiteration of mathematical terms and notions that the teacher introduces and anticipates the pupils will learn. The metaphor of teacher as a *parent bird*, ensuring that information is presented in an accessible form, reworking known parameters or familiar numbers and numerical relationships for the learners is a key feature throughout the latter part of the morning session and the afternoon mathematics class.

The presentation of the mathematical problems to be individually resolved, using personal mental processing, conveys a belief that social interaction and sharing collective resources are not valued. There is a privileging of individuals practising particular types of cognitive processing or algorithms presented by the teacher.

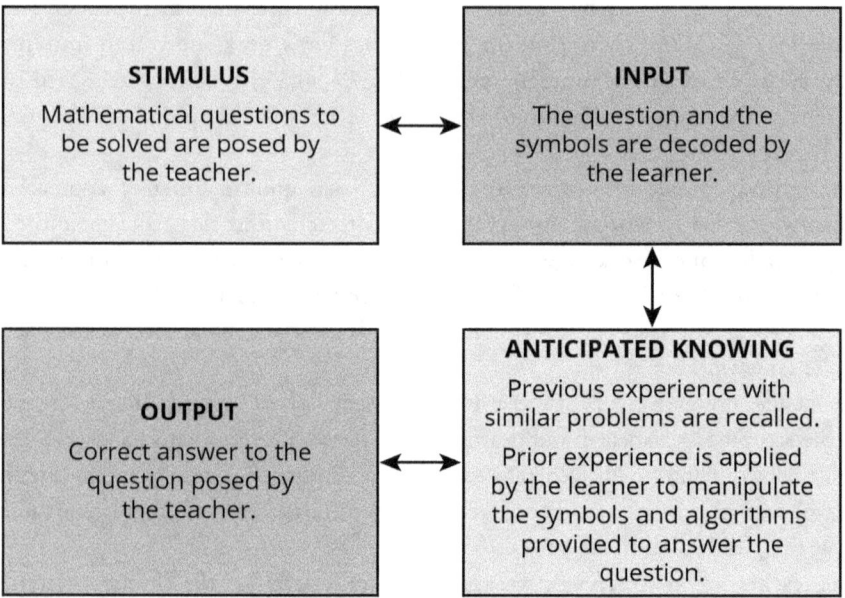

Figure 7.1 Highlighting the Features of the Information-Processing Episode of Learning in the Afternoon Mathematics Lesson

TEACHING ABOUT GRAMMAR WITH OLDER STUDENTS

At Key Stages 3 and 4 (for students in secondary schools), the following is prescribed from the National Curriculum:

> Pupils should continue to develop their knowledge of and skills in writing, refining their drafting skills and developing resilience to write at length. They should be taught to write formal and academic essays as well as writing imaginatively, They should be taught to write for a variety of purposes and audiences across a range of contexts. This requires an increasingly wide knowledge of vocabulary and grammar.
>
> Opportunities for teachers to enhance pupils' vocabulary will arise naturally from their reading and writing. Teachers should show pupils how to understand the

relationships between words, how to understand nuances in meaning, and how to develop their understanding of, and ability to use, figurative language.

[. . .]

It is important that pupils learn the correct grammatical terms in English and these terms are integrated within teaching (DfE 2014: 81).

This aspect of the National Curriculum Policy directs how teachers should show learners how to use grammar to develop their writing skills. What follows is an outline of a teacher's approach to teaching about the use of commas for writing.

> **Task 7.6**
>
> How does the teacher's practice to encourage learning with this class differ to the Y1 phonics and mathematics episodes?
> How would you describe Mr Thomas's practice?
> What does he appear to do as a policy actor, interpreting and translating the National Curriculum requirements for learning grammar?
> What teacher metaphors are applicable in this episode?
> How would you describe the relational way that learning, knowledge and pedagogy are assumed to be related by Mr Thomas?

LEARNING ABOUT COMMAS WITH MR THOMAS

This episode (informed by Teachers TV n.d.) involves 14- and 15-year-old students and their teacher, Mr Thomas, in a large room that resembles a drama studio. There are benches, large cushions and chairs to sit on. There is also a large central space to move around in too, if needed. Mr Thomas is concerned with ensuring the year 10 class are clear about the different use of apostrophes for their writing in English.

Mr Thomas begins by explaining how the lesson is focused on learning five different ways to use a comma. He often asks rhetorical questions that he expects the students to rapidly answer. Immediately after telling them they are going to learn about five uses of commas, he asks them 'How many ways can you use a comma?', and he expects them to respond with 'five'. He also reiterates the focus of five uses of commas by punching his right fist in the air and then splaying his five fingers. He expects the students to copy him by also raising their arm in the air and spreading out their hands too.

Mr Thomas then explains to the secondary students how a former English teacher of his used to talk about the 'music of language' and that he did not understand what it was about. He shares with the students how he thought language was not music and that he disagreed with his teacher. However, after several years, he did understand what the teacher was talking about. He came to realise that there is a musical link to language. He explained further how music has both rhythm and melody. In English, in writing, he argued the melody could be the words and the rhythm can be created by the punctuation. He then tells the students they are going to listen to a piece of music and he wants them to tap their right foot along to the beat of the music. To demonstrate what he expects, he begins tapping his foot to the beat of the music being played.

Mr Thomas plays three contrasting pieces of contemporary music.

The first is jarring, staccato and is difficult to listen to. The second is smoother and relaxing. The third piece of music has lyrics, but is slower in tempo. For each, he explains how the rhythm differs by having the students tap their feet to the differing beats of the music. To immerse them in appreciating the beat of the three different pieces of music, Mr Thomas demonstrates to the students how slapping their thighs, tapping their knees and shoulders can contribute to recognising the rhythm differences.

After experiencing the differences in musical rhythms, Mr Thomas asks the students what provides the rhythm in writing. One student, Jack, provides the correct answer, 'punctuation'. He then goes on to explain how the first piece of music sounded like 'bosh, bosh, bosh', which he aligned with writing that only has full stops in. The second piece of music was more sophisticated, he explains, it had both full stops and commas in it. He then describes how the third piece had different syncopated rhythms going on in it and that it parallels with a full piece of writing employing a full range of punctuation.

Mr Thomas then has the students depict different comma usage by having them copy him in moving his arms, hands and legs in ways that represent the different ways they are used. He provides them with a series of actions that depict a pause comma, speech marks, conjunction of two sentences and an embedded clause.

Questions for Consideration 7.13

To what extent does the teacher control what and how grammar is learnt about?

What assumptions does Mr Thomas appear to be make about the pupils' achievements as the lesson progresses?

After practising (by copying the teacher) how to move and bodily represent a pause comma, speech marks, conjunction of two sentences and an embedded clause, Mr Thomas changes what he wishes the students to do.

Mr Thomas: I'm going to give you variety of words, can you moan at me these ways? …..reluctantly, unrepeatedly, roughly, rudely, sadly, seriously, smoothly, softly, successfully, suddenly, tenderly, violently.….

As Mr Thomas utters each of the words, the students collectively moan with a different kind of emphasis. He goes onto explain how two commas are used to enclose this type of descriptive word in a sentence and that the way the comma is used can change the meaning of the sentence.

He then demonstrates, with the help of the students, the structure of a sentence using the movement of a football to represent commas and full stops.

At the end of the lesson, Mr Thomas reiterates the different ways that commas can be used and reinforces that if they use embedded clause well they should become an A-grade writer. As a conclusion to the lesson, he encourages the students to respond to a final question.

Mr Thomas:	In order to make sure you are [at least an] a C-grade writer, which one of the rules must you use?
Students [collectively]:	Commas before connectives.

> Question for Consideration 7.14
>
> To what extent does this episode of learning about grammar echo features of the phonics and mathematics lesson portrayals?

This brief episode outlines quite a different learning context to the phonics and mathematics lessons. Although the students are older, what is learnt is controlled by the teacher and the learners also respond imitatively (verbally and actionally) to the teacher's directives. Mr Thomas's directions and occasional rhetorical questions suggest how his intention was to demonstrate and ensure the students could recall how and why punctuation should be used in writing. He also wanted them to know that commas can grammatically change meanings in sentences. Features in common with the previous cases include the rapidity of recounting, recalling and imitating behaviours expected by the teacher. The teacher retains authority throughout the episode as in information-processing theorising. Mr Thomas is the holder of the 'knowledge' to be learnt, that is, knowing what the rules are to be learnt about where to insert commas to adhere to grammatical protocols in sentences. Learning, therefore, is characterised by processing symbols and applying rules and procedures. The learners see, think and then (re)act. Solving how to correctly insert commas for particular purposes is provided for the students as an algorithm that Mr Thomas assumes they can store in their heads. Pedagogically, the teacher metaphor that this practice appears to resonate with is that of a *watchmaker* or *parent bird*. As the narrative construal suggests, Mr Thomas provides pieces of information (like a *watchmaker*) to be gradually acquired by the learner. As a *parent bird* teacher, he has simplified how to learn about commas and provides step-by-step tasks that incrementally demand more as the learning activity progresses.

CONTRASTING FEATURES OF TEACHERS' PRACTICES

To demonstrate how the three cases of practice (phonics, mathematics and grammar) differ, but are still in some ways similar, and illustrate aspects of behaviourist or information-processing theories, it is useful to consider features that are prominent in each (see Table 7.1).

Table 7.1 Behaviourist and Information-Processing Characteristics From the Three Cases

	Phonics	Mathematics	Grammar
Prominent features of teachers' practice (as policy actors)	Controls the words and phonemes to be learnt like the *petrol pump attendant*.	Controls the arithmetic material to be learnt like the *petrol pump attendant*.	Controls what is made available to the learner.
	Paces and practices activity like a *lion tamer*.	The pace of repeating times tables is maintained like a *lion tamer*.	Knowledge is external to the knower.
	Frames incremental learning processes like a sculptor.	Provides problems to be solved with pieces of information like the *watchmaker*.	Provides (and models) symbolic actions, expects imitative repetition.
		Graduates tasks to become more complex like a *parent bird*.	Provides simple problems to be solved.
			Demonstrates how rules and routines can be applied to solve problems by connecting pieces of information like the *watchmaker*.
Inferences about learning and learners	Learners are essentially similar.	Learners are essentially similar.	Learners are essentially similar.
	Motivation is external to the learner.	Learning is about forming habits.	They are also passive receivers, imitators and symbol processors.
	Learning involves passive imitation that leads to recognising sounds, letters and words.	Learning involves passive imitation that leads to becoming symbol processors.	Learning is about recalling the rules of comma use.

SUMMARY

This chapter has considered the theories presented in Chapter 2 to provide narrative construals of practice that have been applied in contemporary classrooms.

Practice that demonstrates features of behaviourist and information processing has been considered in different areas of the curriculum and with differently aged pupils to illustrate the nature of learning in those theoretical movements. Teachers, their pedagogy and what they indicate they value in particular circumstances are inferred from the classroom episodes narrated. Epistemologically, learners' individuality is ignored, knowledge is given and practice values recitation, recollection and recapitulation of teacher determined material to be learnt.

ADDITIONAL READING

Bruner, J. (2006) The functions of teaching. In Bruner (Ed) *In search of Pedagogy I*. London: Routledge.

The section in this chapter, entitled 'Teaching can never be just the presentation of material', is a thought-provoking discussion that considers the role of the teacher in learning.

Coles, A., & Helme, R. (2022) Teaching for mastery in primary mathematics: A study of translating research into policy and practice. *Review of Education.* https://doi-org.oxfordbrookes.idm.oclc.org/10.1002/rev3.3326.

This paper discusses the response of teachers to curricular (policy) reform that requires them to adopt new classroom practices to teach about numbers. What is interesting to note is that through adopting new practices, they implicitly revise their mathematical beliefs about the concept of number.

Fisher, H. (2011) Inside the primary classroom: Examples of dissatisfaction behind a veil of compliance. *British Journal of Educational Studies, 59*(2), 121-141, https://doi.org/10.1080/00071005.2011.567969.

This paper discusses challenges related to prescribed teacher practices and associated learning constraints and learner dissatisfaction.

REFERENCES

Archer, A. & Hughes, C. (2001) *Effective and Efficient Teaching*. The Guilford Press.

Ball, S., Maguire, M. and Braun, A. (2012) *How Schools Do Policy. Policy Enactments in Secondary Schools*. London: Routledge.

Bruner, J. (1996) *The Culture of Education*. Cambridge, MA: Harvard University Press.

Carter, J. (2020) The assessment has become the curriculum: Teachers' views on the phonics screening check in England. *British Educational Research Journal 46*(3), 593-609.

Claxton, G. (1990) *Teaching to Learn*. London: Cassell.

Coles, A. & Helme, R. (2022) Teaching for mastery in primary mathematics: A study of translating research into policy and practice. *The Review of Education.* https://doi-org.oxfordbrookes.idm.oclc.org/10.1002/rev3.3326

DfE (2014) *National Curriculum in England: Framework for Key Stages 1 to 4*. Available at https://www.gov.uk Accessed 6/3/17.

DfE (2018a) *National Curriculum Assessments at Key Stage 1 and Phonics Screening Checks in England, 2018*. https://assets.publishing.service.gov.uk/government/uploads/system/uploads/attachment_data/file/743499/Phonics_KS1_Text_1.2.pdf

DfE (2018b) *Key Stage 2 Tests. Mathematical Assessments*. Available at https://www.gov.uk/government/publications/key-stage-2-tests-2018-mathematics-test-materials

DfE (2019) *Inspection Data Summary Report*. Available at https://www.gov.uk/guidance/school-inspection-data-summary-report-idsr-guide#full-publication-update-history Accessed 12/6/24.

DfE (2024a) *National Performance League Tables*. Available at https://www.gov.uk/school-performance-tables Accessed 12/6/24.

DfE (2024b) *Multiplication Tables Check*. Available at https://www.gov.uk/government/collections/multiplication-tables-check

DfE (2024c) *Phonics Screening Checks Guidance*. Available at https://www.gov.uk/government/publications/key-stage-1-phonics-screening-check-administration-guidance/2024-phonics-screening-check-administration-guidance#:~:text=Schools%20should%20administer%20the%20check,administration%20arrangements%20within%20their%20school. Accessed 02/03/25.

DfE (2024d) *KS2 Attainment - National Headlines*. Available at https://explore-education-statistics.service.gov.uk/find-statistics/key-stage-2-attainment-national-headlines. Accessed 02/03/25.

Gallagher, E. (2006) Improving a mathematical key skill using precision teaching and education. *Irish Educational Studies*, 25(3), 303-319.

Gallagher, E., Bones, R. & Lambe, J. (2006) Precision teaching and education: Is fluency the missing link between success and failure? *Irish Educational Studies*, 25(1), 93-105.

Knowles, S. (2012) *Phonics in Year One*. Available at https://www.youtube.com/watch?v5x9Cd-CRbH6s. Accessed 25/7/24.

McGeown, R. (2017) *An Evidence-Based Practice Review Report. How Effective Is Precision Teaching in Teaching Numeracy Skills to School-Age Pupils with Maths Difficulties*. Available at https://www.ucl.ac.uk/educational-psychology/resources/CS1McGeown17-20.pdf Accessed 24/2/19.

Mercer, N. (1995) *The Guided Construction of Knowledge. Talk amongst Teachers and Learners*. Clevedon: Multilingual Matters Ltd.

Perryman, J., Ball, S., Maguire, M. & Braun, A. (2011) Life in the pressure cooker – School league tables and English and mathematics teachers' responses to accountability in a results-driven Era. *British Journal of Educational Studies*, 59(2), 179-195. https://doi.org/10.1080/00071005.2011.578568

Scott, P., Asoko, H. & Leach, J. (2007) Student conceptions and conceptual learning in science. In S. Abell & N. Lederman (Eds) *Handbook of Research on Science Education*. London: Routledge.

Solity, J. E. (1991) An overview of behavioural approaches to teaching children with learning difficulties and the national curriculum. *Educational Psychology*, 11(2), 151-167.

Solity, J.E. & Bull, S. (1987) *Special Needs: Bridging the Curriculum Gap*. Milton Keynes: Open University Press.

Whitty, G. (2014) Recent developments in teacher training and their consequences for the 'University Project' in education. Available at https://discovery.ucl.ac.uk/id/eprint/1475992/3/Whitty_ORETeacherEd.pdf. Accessed 03/03/25.

Wyse, D. & Bradbury, A. (2022) Reading wars or reading reconciliation? A critical examination of robust research evidence, curriculum policy and teachers' practices for teaching phonics and reading. *The Review of Education*. https://doi-org.oxfordbrookes.idm.oclc.org/10.1002/rev3.3314

8
CLASSROOM CASES FEATURING ASPECTS OF CONSTRUCTIVISM

CONTENTS

Introduction	182
Exploring Ideas in Science	184
Concept Cartoons	187
Problem-Solving in Mathematics	192
Writing Poetry	197
Summary	205
Additional Reading	207
References	207

Chapter Aims

After reading Chapter 8, you will have considered:

- how the constructivist theory of learning and associated concepts can be used as 'tools' to think about the ways that policy and practice influence learning;
- how examples of teachers' enactments in learning contexts demonstrate moments of action that can illustrate concepts related to the constructivist movement;
- how the nature of activity in learning that is constructivist can be influenced in multiple ways;
- how extrinsic motivation, resources made available and the ways that tasks are presented for the learner can influence the nature of constructivist learning;
- how social interaction reflected through dialogue relates more closely to 'translation' rather than 'co-construction';
- how the nature of activity engaged with influences opportunity for agency;
- how applications of the metaphor of a *gardener* highlight features of teachers' practices supporting constructivism.

INTRODUCTION

Many different interpretations of constructivist learning exist (Richardson 2003; McPhail 2016) that have been construed and re-construed over time, by practitioners and academics adopting aspects of the theory without necessarily revisiting the intellectual origins of Piaget's work, as detailed in Chapters 3 and 4. As already explained, the metaphor of teacher as *gardener* depends on the ways that 'discovery is interpreted and valued'. How teachers enact their practice to enable learners to work things out in a 'free' and 'unfettered' manner for themselves varies.

Over time, translation, hearsay and misinterpretation have resulted in sometimes quite a distorted emphasis of different features or concepts within constructivism. Richardson (2003: 1624) cites Matthews (2000) who identifies 18 different forms of constructivism offering variations in the ways it is methodologically, dialectically, psychologically and socially understood. Building directly on from the introduction and discussion of Piagetian constructivism earlier in the book, this chapter presents moments of action in learning that are determined by the teacher, demonstrating concepts related to the constructivist movement. The pivotal relationship between the teacher and learner is considered and particular aspects are highlighted for readers to emphasise which key concepts of the constructivist movement are evident.

As Hendry (1996) suggests, constructivism within educational practice is 'useful, notably in science and mathematics [...] education'. Naturalistically, practice within these disciplines is assumed to extend opportunities for learners to interact with immediately available resources, problem-solve and make sense independently. These are three key concepts clearly associated with the constructivist movement. In mathematics and science, Cobb (1994: 4) discusses how the oft-accepted mantra of 'students construct their own knowledge' is a simplified view of constructivism that is limited, but frequently considered indubitable. When considering actual practice with real students in authentic classrooms, it may become clearer how, as McPhail (2016: 294) suggests, it can even become romanticised! He highlights how we need to heed the idealistic notion of constructivism as a natural way for learners to come to understand the world around them but recognise that it is in tension with the demands of curricular policy designed for particular ontological outcomes that schools instrumentally 'deliver'. He argues that classrooms as sites of constructivism are where students' individual constructions of multiple realities emerge epistemologically and that the process of 'knowers constructing their own knowledge from experiences' (McPhail 2016: 298) needs to be considered carefully alongside curricular demands of disciplinary knowledge. In offering the following observations and narrative construals of moments in practice for reflection, you, the reader, are invited to consider features relating to the constructivist movement. The intention is to illuminate how teacher's enactments shape and influence the process of learning. The recounts of practice are intended to make available for consideration the ways that constructivism in learning can be thought about.

Constructivism and Practice

In Chapter 3, it was explained how within the constructivism movement a key concept is that of intrinsic motivation, that is, the desire or curiosity of learners to 'find out' and make sense for themselves. This means that learning is deemed an active rather than passive process. In school contexts, the kinds of subject disciplines where learners act (through interaction with their environment) to understand something and generate their own personalised knowledge commonly arise through activities where individuals are self-directed. In subject disciplines where individual originality and uniqueness are valued, constructivist learning may naturalistically arise. This is arguably more likely in contexts such as music, art and design, dance and drama lessons. However, there are tensions even in these more creative areas of the curriculum (Round and McPhail 2019). Creativity and innovation (McGregor et al. 2022) arguably can also become evident where learners pursue their own lines of enquiry, such as problem-solving in mathematics, investigations in science or imaginative writing in literacy.

The following narrative construals are offered to engage you, the reader, in considering the nature of practice that supports aspects of constructivism in learning:

- Exploring ideas in science
- Concept cartoons
- Problem-solving in mathematics
- Writing poetry

EXPLORING IDEAS IN SCIENCE

The longevity and extent of influence of the constructivist movement informing practice can be traced back to the early 1990s and the SPACE project as introduced in Chapter 3. Scientific concepts such as materials and their properties underpinned by 'particle schema about the nature of matter' (Russell et al. 1991: 20) can be taught in such a way that the child comes to believe in conservation during transformations of form (e.g. flattening, stretching, cutting) and state (e.g. melting, evaporating). Russell et al. (1991) also describe how Piaget's work on conservation of matter (reported in Inhelder and Piaget 1958) and other scientific concepts such as density and dissolution could inform practice that firstly elicited what children knew about science and subsequently offered active opportunities for individual construction of ideas and understandings.

Question for Consideration 8.1

How open does a task need to be to offer constructivist opportunities?

Five activities detailed below carried out by teachers involved in the SPACE project focused on finding out what pupils thought about materials and their properties and subsequently provided tasks to further their thinking.

Task 8.1

Can you 'see' how the design of the activities (in Table 8.1) are related to different concepts (particularly the nature of interaction with, and examination of, the materials and the extent of agentive action and thought) of the constructivist movement? Can you also identify where teachers may have been challenged to ensure each individual child developed meaning from their interactions with the resources in the classroom environment.

Table 8.1 Activities Designed to Elicit and Explore Children's Ideas About Materials (after Russell et al. 1991)

Title of Activity	Nature of Learner Activity
1. Comments on display materials	Looking carefully at everyday materials such as 'food stuffs and other items found in a kitchen, plastic and metal objects, cloth, building materials and other household items such as paint, oil and polish' (Russell et al. 1991 p. 9).
	Encouraged to record observations and whatever they could say about each item of choice.
2. Finding out about materials	Encouraged to 'test' and interact with the materials using implements made available by teachers 'including water, containers, magnet, torch, sandpaper, sieve, pestle and mortar, scissors, hammer and nail, magnifying glass and moulds' (Russell et al. 1991 p.11).
	Children to make records of what was done and found out.

Table 8.1 Activities Designed to Elicit and Explore Children's Ideas About Materials (after Russell et al. 1991) *(Continued)*

Title of Activity	Nature of Learner Activity
3. Where does it come from?	For three contrasting materials (a metal spoon, coloured cotton fabric and flour), annotate drawings to show how they thought objects were made.
4. Comparing materials	Five containers each with either a small steel rod, piece of cotton wool, treacle, talcum powder and malt (coloured) vinegar in were provided. Pupils to choose two to compare and record ideas on similarities and differences.
5. Ideas about solids, liquids and gases	Pupils were asked to draw what they thought solids, liquids and gases were like (inside).

For activity one, the use of familiar materials that children may have previously encountered is an effective way to initiate learner's thinking about what is in their immediate surroundings both at home and in school. However, especially, in today's multi-cultural society, the nature of objects that teachers select may limit the extent to which some ethnic groups or children from poorer or more diverse backgrounds are able to relate to the materials made available to look at. Reflecting on the teacher as a *gardener* metaphor, eliciting each pupil's unique construals about the world around them, may have been further extended by inviting them to bring in items that were salient to them from their own home environment.

For activity two, where learners could choose which implements to use and examine the nature of provided substances further, this approach offered extended opportunities for meaning-making through interaction with the materials. Pupils in this activity were able to act and think agentively, they could determine not only what they wished to look at but also how.

For activity three, it was expected that pupils would be able to explain to the teacher or sketch how three contrasting materials were made. This extended exploration of pupil's ideas about different materials so that teachers were able to unravel further what children knew about contrasting production processes (of metal, cloth and flour). However, this sketching mode of elicitation may not suit all children, some individuals might not have encountered the materials previously and having the ability and lexicon to articulate production processes may have been challenging for some pupils.

For activity four, the children were able to act and think more agentively, choosing how they physically examined and interactively compared the three given materials. The provided resources though meant they were constrained in their exploration of avenues of enquiry that interested them. The implements available could influence what they might decide to do. As with activity three, the opportunity to decide or select any materials they are interested in is not made available for the children.

For activity five, each child was expected to generate a personalised mental model of the inside of solids, liquids and gases and be able to draw what they thought. Explaining the abstract particulate nature of solids, liquids and gases in their own words echoes the constructivist approach. Building on learners' prior knowledge, engaging in the previous four activities affords reflection on personal experiences that a teacher can support to encourage progressive development of each individuals' ideas about solids liquids and gases.

Each of these kinds of constructivist activities, where teachers minimised their intervention, but provided appropriate resources as a *gardener*, might elicit a fascinating range of learners' ideas (Russell et al. 1991). This kind of practice nurturing learner's interactions with the world around them and not directing or practising in a more didactic way 'telling' students what the 'correct' answer is challenged the dominant practice at the time. Previously teachers, ontologically, accepted the undisputed and factual nature of science and believed it should be directly 'transmitted' to the pupils (examples of which have been discussed in Chapter 2) via more didactic approaches. Previously, the incorrect ideas that children conveyed would have been deemed misconceptions; however, through the constructivist approach, in this project teachers accepted whatever ideas the children came up with as 'interim' and continued to provide additional opportunities for the children to actively explore these further and make further sense of things for themselves. A surprising outcome from the work underpinning the research that informed the subsequent development of several curricular resources (e.g. Nuffield primary science, Nuffield (lower) secondary and advanced level biology, chemistry and physics) was that young children held well-defined (albeit contrary to established scientific views) explanations for scientific phenomena. The views of students regarding different phenomena have been researched by Ros Driver (1983; 1989; 1994; 1998: 385) who suggests that learners' perceptions that differ to the 'correct' scientific beliefs have also been thought of as preconceptions, misconceptions, intuitions, alternative conceptions or naïve theories.

Questions for Consideration 8.2

How would you define the ideas, responses or even answers that children, students or other adults came up with that differ to your ideas?

How would you decide whether they were preconceptions, misconceptions, intuitions, alternative conceptions or naïve theories?

What does this indicate about the way that you understand the nature of knowledge or what is important to know?

Research into learners' ideas (Driver and Scanlon 1989; Driver et al. 1994, 1996) before teaching them indicates the nature of their personal constructions, or preconceptions prior to being taught. Eliciting personal constructions can inform the ways that pupils come to understand academic concepts such as number (Piaget 1965), movement and speed (Piaget 1970) time (Piaget 1969) and cultivate logical thinking (Inhelder and Piaget 1958). A culmination of studies recognising the importance of eliciting secondary students' conceptions (Driver 2015), including the range of alternate understandings they hold across many scientific topics, reflects acknowledgement of learner's prior knowledge and experience. Driver's work presents the range and depth of 'alternate' understandings students hold, that are not in agreement with well-established scientific concepts. She argues how these may be 'partially' correct, echoing aspects of the widely agreed views about science, or that they might be based on 'intuition' or 'naivety' through lack of appropriate experience. Understandings that resonate with Piagetian perspectives regarding the chronological age at which children appear to grasp particular concepts of a concrete or more sophisticated abstract nature (introduced in Chapter 3) may also be referred to as cognitive levels (see Table 8.2). Having been introduced to the approaches applied in the SPACE project, consider how you might teach in a constructivist way (applying the nomenclature summarised in the below box). Building on Driver's research into students' ideas, a constructivist approach for older secondary students was promoted through the Children's Learning in Science work (Driver et al. 1994) summarised in the Figure 8.1. Elicitation of learners' ideas and subsequent consideration and comparison of others' understandings that might result in an individual changing their view underpins many teaching approaches that have subsequently been developed in various disciplinary areas (Shayer and Adey 2002) including mathematics, literacy (Adey 2008), drama and music (Gouge and Yates 2002), for early years, primary and secondary students, each drawing on Piagetian staged development theory (see Table 8.2). Although developed and researched many decades ago, many are still used today (e.g. Seleznyov et al. 2021).

Elicitation of Ideas
(what children think about different concepts are explored through explaining their ideas)

↓

Restructuring of Ideas
(the following processes, i, ii, iii, iv, should be encouraged by the teacher through questioning and providing an appropriate task to work on collaboratively)

i. Clarification and exchange (of the range of ideas the children hold)
ii. Exposure to conflict situations (considering what the contrasting notions or suggestions others mean)
iii. Construction of new ideas (reviewing personal ideas in light of others' views)
iv. Evaluation (what has been achieved)

Figure 8.1 The Processes That Contribute to Re-structuring Learners' Ideas in the Constructivist Teaching Sequence (adapted from Driver et al. 1994)

CONCEPT CARTOONS

Keogh and Naylor (1999) also drew on aspects of Piaget's work, to offer a different way to apply a constructivist approach by providing pupils with cartoons presenting various alternate ways to interpret something to think about.

> **Task 8.2**
>
> Consider the following description of such a concept cartoon. Which aspects of constructivism, that perhaps resonate with the earlier approaches outlined, do you recognise?
>
> Small groups, usually three or four primary school pupils, around eight or nine years of age, are sat looking a picture of a snowman and three children. One child on the picture is holding a coat. On the drawing, each child has a speech bubble emerging from their mouths. They each offer different ideas. The question posed, as the heading of the cartoon, is 'Will a snowman melt faster if he is wrapped in a coat?' One child says, 'Don't put the coat on the snow man. It will warm and melt him'; another says, 'It will keep him cold and stop him melting'; and the third says, 'I don't think the coat will make any difference'.

Keogh and Naylor (1999) designed a range of these kinds of cartoons for teachers that focused on different topics of science. The intention was to provide contrasting learners' ideas for the children to think about and discuss. It was intended that the groups of learners were each encouraged to exchange views about the distinctly different perspectives and finally decide which was the most accurate. This approach, presenting learners with examples of different ways the same thing can be thought about (usually including what the teacher deemed a correct answer), echoed the constructivist concept of relativism. These cartoons pre-empted prominent interpretations that could exist in learners' minds (as Driver's 2015 work illustrated). Interestingly, this concept cartoon approach has been developed across other subject disciplines too, such as mathematics and English. Cartoon-like pictures of characters appearing to think about something, with additional thought or speech bubbles, offer utterances to be thought about that could be plausible and offer alternate, partially correct explanations related to the issues being considered. These kinds of different perspectives that are teacher-generated resonate with Piagetian perturbations.

> **Question for Consideration 8.3**
>
> Is the Piagetian staged model of cognitive development still relevant today?

Another adaptation of the stages of development that Piagetian constructivism offers is the way that activities might be designed to comprise an intervention designed to progress thinking and learning (as in Table 8.1). In Table 8.2, there is an example of the ways that Shayer and Adey (1981) adopted Piagetian notions about conceptual progress (Piaget 1950). Their focus on cognitive demands offers a framework that identifies levels 1 (pre-operational) to 3B (abstract or late formal) of thinking. Table 8.2 presents how Adey and Shayer drew on Piagetian stages of development to inform teaching the topic of floating and sinking, for example.

Task 8.3

Consider how an instrument such as this which is an adaptation of an aspect of a Curricular Assessment Taxonomy (Shayer and Adey 1981) devised across the primary and secondary science curriculum that could be used across the disciplines by teachers to inform cognitive progression. Can you 'see' how this resonates with the National Curriculum we use today?

Table 8.2 Adaption of Piagetian Development Theory by Shayer and Adey (1981: 88-89, adapted)

Cognitive Level	General Descriptor of Cognitive Ability Demonstrated by Pupils	Curricular Application of the Cognitive Level (from Exploration of Floating and Sinking)
1 (pre-operational)	Makes observations, but doesn't use rules or patterns	Pupils think the objects themselves can determine whether they float or sink.
2A (early concrete)	Can make simple descriptions using one variable with a number of values	Pupils think that an object's heaviness determines whether it sinks or floats, however, 'heaviness' in their minds is related to either 'size' or 'weight'.
2B (late concrete)	Can use concrete patterns/rules using two variables	Pupils recognise that 'size' is related to 'volume'. They also recognise that 'weight' is related to 'mass'. They realise that there is a pattern or connection between volume and mass that determines whether something floats or sinks; however, they do not yet appreciate how the mass-to-volume ratio determines density and whether something floats or sinks.
3A (early formal)	Can derive and use simple models, abstracting qualitatively, can consider several variables simultaneously	Pupils recognise that the mass-to-volume ratio (mass/volume) determines an objects density and whether it sinks or floats. If the density is higher, the object sinks, and if it is lower, it floats.
3B (late formal)	Can derive and use sophisticated model(s) (often) quantitatively if appropriate with 3 or more relevant variables and recognises the relative importance of the factors and can manipulate both absolute and relative values in an algebraic fashion, able to analyse and handle multivariant relationships.	Pupils recognise that the density of an object and the density of the medium (e.g. water or brine) in which it is placed can also affect whether it floats or sinks.

This kind of curricular framework, informed by Piagetian development stages, offers a way of providing teachers with starting points that could guide and scaffold what is made available to learn about in successive lessons. Activities can be designed to offer challenge and problem-solving opportunities (Adey et al., 2001) focused around the conceptual levels summarised in Table 8.2. Activities devised in this way have offered the potential for learners to progress through the levels enabling cognitive development for students in science, mathematics, technology and the performing arts (Adey 2008; Adey and Shayer 1981; Gouge and Yates 2002; Hamaker and Blackwell 2003; Shayer and Adhami 2010; Seleznyov et al. 2021).

> **Task 8.4**
>
> In the following classroom discussion, how might the information provided in Table 8.2 help you determine the cognitive level that the following pupil appears to be (mentally) operating at?

A significant proportion of adolescents hold alternate conceptions about plants (Driver et al. 1994). There are some that think that all plants have roots growing into the ground and through these they obtain their (ready-made) food. Some also believe leaves are green to make plants look attractive and do not appreciate the photon-stimulated chemical processes taking place within them.

The teacher and student dialogue below is an extract from a lesson designed to promote cognitive challenge by considering different kinds of plants (a house plant with purple leaves, an Asian air plant and a floating aquatic plant) and the ways they manufacture their food. The teacher is focused on the floating water soldier plant that has a diurnal pattern of movement, floating during the day and sinking at night.

Ms Rosen:	This plant floats at the top of the water during daylight and sinks lower at night. How does it make its food?
Paulo:	Photosynthesis
Ms Rosen:	Okay. It doesn't have roots in the soil, so how does it make it's food?
Paulo:	Uses sunlight
Ms Rosen:	How?
Paulo:	Absorbs it through the leaves
Ms Rosen:	Okay. So how does that help the plant float on water?
Paulo:	Air around the plant is taken in.
Ms Rosen:	Are you sure it is just air? What happens in photosynthesis?
Paulo:	Oh, carbon dioxide is absorbed and oxygen is given out!
Ms Rosen:	Okay. So can that explain how the plant floats during the day, but sinks at night?
Paulo:	Ummm. Not sure…

Ms Rosen: Well during the day, there is sunlight, so photosynthesis occurs. At night it is dark so photosynthesis stops. How might the gaseous exchange and carbohydrate production affect the daily movement of the plant?

Paulo: Dunno, will have to think about it.

Questions for Consideration 8.4

How far do you think this student was the constructor of their own knowledge?

What was the teacher doing to support, like a *gardener*, their personal understanding?

How far was the learner agentive?

How does determination of an individual's cognitive level inform teaching?

Construing one's ideas about something through interaction with the environment around them (as theorised by Piaget) is a process engaged in to reach cognitive equilibrium. The excerpt above does not provide sufficient detail to indicate whether or not the pupil has or will be able to engage in some activity (or experimentation) to find out for themselves why a floating aquatic plant behaves as it does. The teacher avoids telling the pupil the complete answer(s) and instead asks a series of questions to support their consideration and development of the conceptual understanding of the connections between plant behaviour, light source, photosynthesis, etc. The conversation did indicate that the pupil understood aspects of the relationship between light, leaves, different gases and photosynthesis, a complex abstract concept. In Piagetian terms, applying the nomenclature (in Table 8.2), Paulo appears to be operating at the 3A early formal level as he can recollect how several variables are related (correctly we assume) in the photosynthetic process. However, the extent to which he was unable to connect these related variables and build a mental model that explained how the many factors involved in photosynthesis affected an aquatic plant's behaviour would suggest that he is not operating yet at the 3B or late formal level. This level of cognitive operation requires abstract thought that involves manipulating several variables simultaneously to model alternate outcomes if input variables are altered. Although we can conjecture about the level of knowledge the pupil demonstrates, we do not know what prior experience may have informed his understandings of aquatic plants, photosynthesis and their behaviour. Paulo, it seems from the excerpt provided, did not engage in dialogic exchanges with others in the class. In other words, the development of intersubjectivity (outlined in Chapter 4) was not demonstrated to arise between pupils in this excerpt. Although Ms Rosen initially asks open scaffolding questions of Paulo, after some toing and froing, she finally provides the answer she is looking for from him. This demonstrates a common perspective that asking questions rather than 'telling' pupils what they need to know is constructivist practice. However, as explained in Chapters 3 and 4, this demonstrates only one concept within the constructivist movement.

PROBLEM-SOLVING IN MATHEMATICS

As introduced earlier, Hendry (1996) suggested that offering problems for students to solve so that they generate a unique way to resolve a mathematical conundrum is a concept that demonstrates another aspect of constructivism. In considering the extent to which it is of current concern to schools and teachers, consider this excerpt from the English National Curriculum for Mathematics (DfE 2021). The policy document states that:

Purpose of Study

Mathematics is a creative and highly interconnected discipline that has been developed over centuries, proving the solution to some of history's most intriguing problems, It is essential to everyday life, critical to science, technology and engineering, and necessary for financial literacy and most forms of employment. A high-quality mathematics education therefore provides a foundation for understanding the world, the ability to reason mathematically, an appreciation of the beauty and power of mathematics, and a sense of enjoyment and curiosity about the subject.

Aims

The national curriculum aims to ensure that all pupils.

- become fluent in the fundamentals of mathematics, including through varied and frequent practice with increasingly complex problems over time, so that pupils develop conceptual understanding and the ability to recall and apply knowledge rapidly and accurately
- reason mathematically by following a line of enquiry, conjecturing relationships and generalisations, and developing an argument, justification or proof using mathematical language
- can solve problems by applying their mathematics to a variety of routine and non-routine problems with increasing sophistication, including breaking down problems into a series of simpler steps and persevering in seeking solutions

(DfE 2021)

Task 8.5

In reflecting on the *Purpose* of the mathematics programme of study, to what extent can you see resonance with aspects of the constructivist movement?
What does the statement convey about the epistemic nature of mathematics education that should be included in English schools?
How do the *aims* also indicate learning should or should not be constructivist?

In Chapter 2, creativity was acknowledged as a concept within the constructivist movement. It is related to novel and even abstract ways of thinking. Development of (new) mental models that could be deployed to achieve particular ends is also recognised within constructivism. The National Curriculum Policy goes on to indicate how mathematics education can provide a foundation for understanding the world. This infers an assumption that mathematics could provide a way of pupils relating (potentially through interaction with the environment) to the world around them in a constructivist manner. Paying attention to reasoning within everyday and STEM (Science, Technology, Engineering, Mathematical) contexts, including future employment beyond school, suggests how learning in school should be active rather than passive.

Table 8.3 Mathematics – A Curriculum Analysis and Constructivist Taxonomy

Piagetian Level	National Curriculum Level	Properties of Numbers
2A, 2A/B: Early/Mid Concrete	1, 2	Pupils can add and subtract a small number of objects. They can solve whole number problems, order integers and count to a hundred.
		Pupils can work out simple sequences of numbers and count backwards or forwards. They can add or subtract two single-digit numbers in their heads. They can count in 10s backwards and forwards.
2B: Mature Concrete Operations	3	Pupils know where 1,000 comes in number sequences. They can work out and give change from shopping with £1 coins. They can use addition and subtraction to find the differences between numbers up to 1,000. They can manipulate numbers in units of 10s and 100s.
2B*: Concrete Generalisation	4, 5 (5 spans 2B* and 3A)	Pupils can understand the use of negative numbers in everyday contexts. They can add and subtract two-digit numbers in their heads. They can write how to add or subtract whole numbers. They can enter money in £/p on a calculator.
3: Formal Operations	5, 6+	Pupils can use and manipulate negative numbers in multiplication. They can make estimates in their calculations.

Source: Adapted from Adey (2008: 123).

In also applying the constructivist view of staged development that could underpin teaching programmes in mathematics, how far does the following curriculum analysis (Table 8.3) provide a structure that can inform development and conceptual progress for pupils?

Von Glaserfeld (1995: 4) describes from 15 years of research on reasoning at the University of Massachusetts how first-year physics students can be well trained to provide the *right* answer to standard questions. However, when faced with problems to solve that differ to those they are familiar with in textbooks, 'they reveal that they have no understanding of the conceptual relationships indicated by the symbols in the formulas they have learnt by heart'. How far does this suggest that the constructivist approaches applied in primary mathematics may not be sustained into higher education contexts?

In primary mathematics, lessons that present children with problems to solve in their own unique and different ways are still celebrated (Ofsted 2011: 22).

The national curriculum for mathematics aims to ensure that all pupils [...]

...can solve problems by applying their mathematics to a variety of routine and non-routine problems with increasing sophistication, including breaking down problems into a series of simpler steps and persevering in seeking solutions.

Question for Consideration 8.5

What does the Mathematics National Curriculum summarising Key Stage 1 – year 2 suggest about the nature of constructivist learning that is currently required in schools?

Mathematics National Curriculum: Measurement

Pupils should be taught to:

- recognise and use symbols for pounds (£) and pence (p) and combine amounts to make a particular value
- find different combinations of coins that equal the same amounts of money
- solve simple problems in a practical context involving addition and subtraction of money of the same unit, including giving change (DfE 2021: 14).

Consider also how the 2021 curricular policy relates to the practice of a teacher, the activities he supports, the resources he provides and the way in which he expects students to make available for others their thinking processes in the following mathematics lesson.

Task 8.6

Consider the lesson overview below. It is Mr Edwards' mathematics lesson (informed by Teachers TV (n.d.)). Are there any moments where you think learning about the value of coins, addition and subtraction might be experienced by the learners in a constructivist way?

Problem-Solving with Money

The learning objectives of the lesson included understanding the value of different coins, adding and subtracting different amounts of money to solve different problems. Mr Edwards had planned that there should be a combination of whole class and independent tasks within the lesson.

Overview

Introduction: whole class [10 minutes]

Recall of coins and their value through presenting visual representations of the English currency [coins and notes].

Practicing adding the total value of different combinations of coins.

Game: Whole class [5 minutes]

Applying the 'greater than' > or 'smaller than' < rule to varied sums of money to work out which total has the biggest value. The game involves choosing the commensurate side of the classroom that represents which coins represent the largest amount [ie: which is greater than the other sum].

Independent task: In pairs [10 minutes]

Working in pairs to calculate total costs of several items, on a worksheet provided by the teacher that frames the column method of addition, a little like a shop receipt.

Independent tasks: In small groups [15 minutes]

Working in table groups on differentiated tasks. One group are allocated forty pounds to spend on food and drink for two days for two people. Deciding what combination of foods are affordable for breakfast, lunch and dinner are documented to share with the rest of the group. Another group have to select from given foods what could be afforded for lunch for two people for ten pounds. The third group were given a handful of coins and had to work out which coins they would need to pay for differently priced foods.

Final task: Whole class [10 minutes]

Interactive activity on whiteboard at the front of the classroom. Purchasing food for lunch with a five pound note, calculating the total cost and subtracting the change required.

In reviewing the lesson from the summary provided, it is challenging to 'see' exactly where constructivism could have arisen. However, the teacher's intention of having the students work independently on tasks suggests he may be thinking that individual activity is important for students to construct their own knowledge. Even observing the lesson, it would be difficult to tell whether each or just a handful of students were able to generate personalised mental models relating to the value of food items, what is possible to afford with limited amounts of money or even managing the cost of meals for two people. Elements of this lesson could resonate more closely with the information-processing movement discussed in Chapters 2 and 7 depending on the way that the teacher engages individuals or groups in thinking about money to solve problems.

Returning to constructivism, consider the 'game' that emerges in the lesson excerpt below. The teacher expects the students to think, then act by moving to the side of the classroom indicating their understanding. This is a narrative construal of that episode in the lesson:

Mr Edwards: I'm going to show you some coins [on the interactive white board]. I would like you to think about which side of the board is the biggest value of coins. If you think this side [left of the screen] has the greater value I want you to move to this side of the classroom [he points to the left]. If the other side is greater I want you to move to the right [he points to the right of the classroom].

Students: [All stand up]

Mr Edwards: I will press the keyboard in a moment to show you the coins. I don't want you to speak. I just want you to move to the side of the room that echoes which side of the screen you think is the biggest value. Don't follow anyone else. Think for yourself. Okay. Are you ready. Look carefully [there are 2 coins 50p and 5p on the left and 20p, 20p, 5p on the right of the whiteboard screen].

Students: [Some begin moving]

Mr Edwards: Think first then move to the side that you think is the biggest.

Students: [Eventually they are all stood on the left side of the classroom]

Mr Edwards: Okay. So it seems we all think that the side with two coins is greater than the side with three coins. Are you sure? [he gives them a few more minutes to change their minds. Several students move closer to the screen to look more carefully at the coins to re-check their decision but remain on the left side.]. So the 50p and 5p are greater than [he draws the greater than '>' symbol indicating the 2 coins on the left are a higher value than the 3 coins, 20p, 20, 5p on the IWB screen].

How far are the students able to discover something for themselves? To what extent, do you think, they are problem-solving and/or developing a 'rule-based model' in their heads to then decide how to move within the classroom? Are they all able to do so independently?

Consider now, this next excerpt. Does this demonstrate any additional features or concepts within the constructivist movement?

Mr Edwards:	Here's another one. Five coins [10p, 10p, 10p, 5p, 5p] that side [right] and one [20p] this side [left]. Do we need to move? Have a look. Work it out. [Zaman immediately moves across to the other side of the room]. Zaman why are you over there?
Students:	[Several move closer to look carefully at the screen. Many then move to the right side of classroom. The teacher waits until everyone appears to have decided where to be.]
Zaman:	I worked it out. I knew there was 20p on one side and then added the others. I added ten and ten and ten is thirty. I added five and five is ten. Thirty and ten is forty. The right-hand side is bigger than the left-hand side because, um, the right-hand side has forty and the left-hand side [. . ..] has only twenty.
Mr Edwards:	Thank you. Forty is greater than twenty. Good working out.

Reflecting on Zaman's response to Mr Edwards, can you 'see' how he has generated his own method or process by which to work out what the answer is to the problem the teacher presented. In other words, he has not recalled or recounted a strategy previously provided by the teacher. He has illustrated how he, as a primary student, actively expressed his thinking to explain how he worked out a solution. However, consider the extent to which Mr Edwards has positioned Zaman to elaborate on the cognitive strategy he developed and applied to figure out which side of the whiteboard presented the highest value of money. How do you know whether all the other students solved the problem the same way or differently?

Mr Edwards only asks Zaman for his 'workings out'. This is an important concept within constructivism. Social interaction is limited (as explained in Chapter 3), but extends individuals an opportunity to learn from each other through explaining and making explicit their cognitive strategies. Shared reflections on each other's cognitive processing required to find resolutions (Seleznyov et al. 2021: 2) promotes intersubjectivity. This limited kind of intersubjectivity (explained in Chapters 3 and 4) enables learners to advance their own thinking through reflecting on the ways that others' might solve similar problems differently or even more effectively.

WRITING POETRY

Within the English National Curriculum, some extracts from the statutory policy (DfE 2012: 21) that apply to the teaching of poetry in primary schools state that:

Pupils should be taught to:
Develop pleasure in reading, motivation to read, vocabulary and understanding by:

- listening to, discussing and expressing views about a wide range of contemporary and classic poetry, stories and non-fiction at a level beyond that at which they can read independently;
- recognising simple recurring literary language in stories and poetry.

Develop positive attitudes towards, and stamina for, writing by:

- writing poetry;
- recognising some different forms of poetry (e.g. free verse, narrative poetry).

Pupils' knowledge of language, gained from stories, plays, poetry, non-fiction and textbooks, will support their increasing fluency as readers, their facility as writers and their comprehension.

From the scrutiny of policy in Chapters 2 and 7, it was demonstrated to you how interpretation of national directives can indicate how behaviourism or information processing is expected in classrooms. From a constructivist perspective, the kind of learning opportunities that a policy document suggests would involve learners creating their own original outcomes, actively solving problems, being able to be agentive and draw on experience to develop concrete and subsequently, after reflection, abstract reasoning.

Task 8.8

Reviewing the policy extracts above, can you discern whether a constructivist approach is implied in any aspects of learning about poetry?

The statement that pupils should develop a pleasure of reading by listening, discussing and expressing views about different kinds of poetry could potentially be orchestrated as very socially interactive (see Chapters 4 and 5). The learning opportunities and development of the Zone of Proximal Development (ZPD) (Chapters 4 and 6) could be extended if pupils read different poems, present them to their peers and then engage in discussion about alternate meanings and interpretations. However, if a teacher chooses to read out the poems (particularly those which a pupil could not read independently) and subsequently 'tell' the pupils how they might interpret them, then possibilities for constructivist learning are very limited. Learning to recognise simple recurring literary language or different forms of poetry requires the more knowledgeable teacher to present (or make available) contrasting texts, support the reading by the pupils and subsequently scaffold or mediate (Chapters 4 and 5) in some way reflectively enabling the learners to 'see' how they are similar or different. Can you also 'see' how there is an assumption that learners 'will' develop pleasure in reading, be motivated to read and increase their vocabulary and understanding because they have been introduced to 'contemporary and classic poetry, stories and non-fiction' texts that are more challenging than they can read by themselves. Exposing learners to texts they cannot read independently suggests an application of the staged theory of development (discussed in Chapter 4) whereby the ZPD is developed through individuals working with more capable others.

Consider the following narrative construal of practice (Frodsham and McGregor 2021). Can you identify whether any concepts within the constructivist movement were evident?

Mrs Potts is teaching a class of eight- and nine-year-olds in a state primary school, rated 'Good' by Ofsted. It is a small school located on the edge of a medium-sized city.

Mrs Potts often creates her own stories for the pupils to read in her lessons. In the lesson presented here, she shares some of her methods for generating a creative piece of writing. She begins by telling the pupils a story entitled 'The bat that learned to click'.

Mrs Potts:	Going to tell you a story. All about a bat. Are you ready?
Pupils:	[chorus] Yes!
Mrs Potts:	Once, long ago, in the time of ancients, there lived a colony of cave dwellers. They were almost like shrews [indicating with her hands how small they were], very tiny and they lived on the ground and they hardly had any eyesight [with her eyes scrunched closed]. They couldn't see hardly anything at all and more than anything they longed to eat the flies that skittered and buzzed across [her hands and fingers indicating a skittering movement], in front of them. Even though they reached out with their fingers [her hands fully stretched as if to catch flies] but they just couldn't catch them. So they had to eat the creepers and crawlers that lived on the ground. Time passed and one day one of the long fingered shrew-like creatures [extending and widening her digits] was born with webbing between its fingers and it could fly. It was a bat! [and so the story carries on ...explaining how young flying bats were born but they also had terrible eyesight. However, one bat had a cold and the sneezing became a way of communicating, echo location, to locate flies or other prey]. So that's how they all find their prey. Did you like my story?
Class:	[Chorus] Yes!
Mrs Potts:	I have made my story into a map. We've done mapping before. So I am going to talk you through my map. Then we are going to work with the story. Is that okay?
Class:	[Chorus] Yes!
Mrs Potts:	[renarrates the story as depicted by each pictorial moment illustrated in sequential circles, all captured on a huge poster. She points to the first picture]. So here are my cave dwellers with their long ....
Class:	[chorus] Fingers
Mrs Potts:	And their terrible ....
Class:	[chorus] Eyesight
Mrs Potts:	Their long shrew like noes and they can only eat ...
Class:	[chorus] Creepy crawlies

The whole story is re-narrated with the pupils in the class adding key words at the end of each sentence the teacher provides.

Mrs Potts: Now we are going to do speedy art. In teams, I'm giving you bits of the story to draw. Think about who [with your own bat character] is in that bit of the story. What are they thinking? What are they feeling? Are they smiling? Are they grumpy? Are they feeling sick? What might the animals look like?

The pupils are then given a blank booklet each to draw a picture illustrating their bit of the story (with own particular bat in it) on the front cover.

Once the pupils have generated their front covers, Mrs Potts encourages them to think further about their particular bats in the story. To help them engage more deeply with the content of their own particular piece of expressive writing, Mrs Potts directs the class again.

Questions for Consideration 8.6

To be constructivist, should pupils work entirely on their own throughout the whole lesson?

Mrs Potts: Now that you have had a little think about that little bit of the story I want you to think about what [your bat] feels like. Are the creatures happy? Are they frustrated? Are they worried? Are they annoyed? So, open up your booklets and in the writing box, write for me how it feels [your bat] at that particular bit of the story. Can you write some descriptive words? To describe how they feel and what they are doing. Who has an idea?

Aaron: My bat hasn't eaten anything.

Mrs Potts: Hungry, can you think of anything else? What's really hungry?

Ryan: Starving!

Mrs Potts: Yes, Starving. Anyone got another one?

Lana: Extremely hungry.

Mrs Potts: Another word, Dermot?

Declan: Famished!

Mrs Potts: That's a good word! What were you going to say Toby?

Troy: Ravenous.

Mrs Potts: That's a good word!

A range of words including 'Nibbling, Chomping, Gobbling, etc' are also suggested by the children.

Mrs Potts then asks the children about how their bats might be feeling, they offer further words including, sad, miserable, depressed, angry, hopeless, grumpy, determined, curious, inquisitive and strange.

Mrs Potts:	Everyone have at least two words for how their bat is feeling?
Class:	[chorus] Yes. [They write their descriptive words that apply to their bat in their booklet].
Mrs Potts:	Now look at the surroundings your creature [bat] is in. Look at the cave, the sky, the ground, the lake. Who has got a good describing word for the surroundings of their creature?
Class:	[several hands go up]
Ryan:	Its autumn-ey.
Mrs Potts:	Autumnal. A great adjective. Who has another word?
Class:	[several hands go up]
Mrs Potts:	Eva?
Eva:	Grey skies.
Mrs Potts:	Love it!

Other suggestions are elicited through teacher questioning, pupils putting hands in the air and then them sharing their suggestions. Many words that could describe the nature of the surroundings of the creature [bat] as well as words that could describe what the bat is doing are verbalised first by pupils and then reiterated by the teacher. The pupils then add these words in the box on the inside of their booklet cover.

Questions for Consideration 8.7

To what extent is the creation of an original class poem social and/or constructivist?

To what extent do you think intersubjectivity is engaged in?

Mrs Potts then introduces the poetry and explains that they are going to work in teams to produce one involving the whole class.

Mrs Potts:	I love a poem. So, here's how its gonna work [writes dashed lines on it on the white board – these indicate the number of words needed for the four lines of the poem]. We are going to choose some necessary words for our part of the story. Not unnecessary words like 'the', 'of', 'at' and 'is'. I am going to model [writing a poem about] when all the bats went out and tried a new way of catching flies and it worked really well. I need words that indicate excited and happy [points to Sophie].
Sophie:	[hand up] Joyful
Mrs Potts:	Good [points to Simon].
Simon:	[hand up] Overjoyed.
Mrs Potts:	Good [points to Layla].

Lana [hand up]:	Jolly.
Mrs Potts:	Good [points to Nathan].
Nicholas:	Enthusiastic.
Mrs Potts:	Good [she writes 'overjoyed', 'enthusiastic', 'jolly' and 'bats' on the first line of four dashed lines].

Mrs Potts then asks for words that describe the actions the bats might engage in to try out catching flies. The pupils share their ideas, hands-up first, of course. Words that were elicited included flying, catching, gobbling, coughing, capturing. She then writes three descriptive words for the second line of the poem.

Mrs Potts:	For the third line of the poem we need four words [so they fit the number of dashed lines on the white board].
Sean:	Bats never starve again.
Mrs Potts:	Brilliant [Rama].
Rafael:	[hand up] Capturing scrumptious yummy flies.
Mrs Potts:	[counting the four words on fingers of hand as she repeats them] Capturing scrumptious yummy flies. Yes! Layla.
Lana:	[hand up] Getting their bellies full.
Mrs Potts:	I love it! [and adds the line to the poem on the white board] I am going to correct the grammar a little [and writes 'getting their bellies filled'].

The pupils continue to offer original four word lines that could be added to the poem. She then asks them to think about and discuss how the bats will now be feeling.

Mrs Potts:	What three words tell us how the bats are feeling for the final line of the poem? Brielle tell me your idea.
Brielle:	Hurrah, hurrah, hurrah.
Mrs Potts:	I love it. Wesley?
Wesley:	[Hand up] Now we're happy.
Mrs Potts:	I love it. Declan.
Declan:	[hand up] Gimme some flies.
Mrs Potts:	I love it [points to Ella].
Ella:	Yummy, delicious, stuffed.
Mrs Potts:	Lovely.

Mrs Potts then asks the pupils to work in their teams to write their poem in their booklets. Ella, Eva and Nicholas produce this:

Confused, curious, soaring bat.
Thinking, flying, hoping.

As black as black.
Flies by lake.

The whole class then take turns to read out what they have written for each stage in the story and 'perform' their collective poem about bats.

Pupil 1:	Unhappy, famished, bored, shrews.
Pupil 2:	Sleeping, munching, grumbling.
Pupil 3:	Extremely, extremely, extremely hungry.
Pupil 4:	Need more food.
Wesley:	As dark as soot
Brielle:	Sleeping and dreaming.
Lana:	About lots of flies.
Wesley, Briella and Lana:	Zzzzzzzzz.
Pupil 5:	New, special, surprise different.
Pupil 6:	Soaring, showing off.
Pupil 7:	Looking at himself enthusiastically.
Pupil 8:	Feeling happy, joyful.
Gael:	Move away other bats.
Gael and Troy:	I am dying.
Ed:	Poorly, hopeless left-out bat.
Zander:	Sitting, crying, sniffing.
Ryan:	Getting his belly emptied.
Ed:	Let.
Zander:	Me.
Ryan and Ed:	Die.
Pupil 9:	Annoyed, grumpy, famished bat.
Pupil 10:	Sitting feeling hungry.
Pupil 11:	Thinking about delicious food.
Pupil 12:	Let me eat.
Aaron, Eleanor and James:	Starving upset sick bat. Coughing, flying dreaming. Hears cough coming back. Thinks something new.
Ella:	Confused, curious soaring bat. Thinking flying hoping.
Eva:	As black as black. Flies by lake.
Zaylee, Amy, and Ivan:	Starving, tried, determined bat. Sad, sigh, cough. Listening for an echo. Eat until night.
Pupils 13 and 14:	Amazing, enthusiastic, overjoyed bat. Stuffing gorgeous stuff. Merrily eating hundred flies. End of starvation.
Pupil 15:	Excited, joyful, enthusiastic bat.
Pupil 16:	Chatting, listening, learning.
Pupil 17:	Telling the others how.
Pupil 18:	Trying it out.
Mrs Potts:	Overjoyed, enthusiastic, jolly bats. Coughing, listening, gobbling. Getting their bellies filled. Hooray, hooray, hooray.

> **Task 8.9**
>
> In the classroom episode outlined above, Mrs Potts enacts her practice quite differently to Ms Jones, Ms Ramen or, indeed, Mr Thomas in Chapter 7.
> After reading the narrative construal, how would you describe the practice adopted by Mrs Potts?
> Which of the teacher metaphors mentioned previously relate to this approach?
> What assumptions does she appear to be make about the learners and learning?
> How would you characterise the way the children appear to experience learning? Is this the same throughout the lesson?

As already explained in Chapter 3, and reiterated by Richardson (1998), the constructivist movement involves individuals creating their own understandings, based upon what they already know and believe, and the phenomena or ideas with which they come into contact. As Kosnik et al. (2018) discuss, constructivism potentially offers the 'best way' (p. 105) to improve literacy. This is supported by Ugwuozor (2020) who investigated the impact of a 'constructivist' approach (p. 1) to learning through poetry. As evidenced in the narrative construal of Mrs Potts' practice with her eight- and nine-year-olds, there were opportunities for her pupils to be constructive in the lesson; however, to begin with, she was authoritative in her practice. Her pupils were expected to listen. She recounted for the pupils a story she had written, and she then mapped her story through a series of connected encircled diagrams and invited the pupils to create a pictorial image of a bat that they imagined from a particular point in the fiction they had listened to. The drawing activity (Mrs Potts called speedy art) was a little more constructivist in nature, offering the pupils the agentive opportunity to decide what kind of bat they wanted their character to be. Their teacher, though, controlled much of the material to be thought about despite a seemingly interactive approach to eliciting original ideas and words (adjectives in this case) to describe the bat characters in the poem. The descriptive words that emerged through interaction of pupils with each other and the teacher are evidenced in the poem. Despite a seemingly constructivist approach involving the whole class contributing to a unique poem, initially the more experienced other (the teacher) is more like a modeller and guide supporting the processing of information in the bat story from one form to another. Mrs Potts, models, guides and scaffolds poem writing opportunities for the pupils. However, as the social interaction becomes more important, there are some opportunities for individual pupils to offer unique perspectives through their proposed images and adjectives contributing to the collectively constructed whole class poem. As both Kosnik et al. (2018) and Ugwuozor (2020) point out, often transforming a theory of learning into classroom practice can be difficult. To devise opportunities that offer learners experiential opportunities to build their own knowledge and retain the integrity of individualism is challenging.

Berninger et al. (2009) identified several contrasting ways that teachers can support the development of writing: transcription, focusing on spelling (including phonics discussed in Chapters 2 and 7), handwriting and punctuation; executive functions, involving planning, reviewing and revising ideas; and text generation, that is, producing written texts that are more concerned with meanings of words and semantics. These types of writing (Dockrell et al. 2016, p. 409) may overlap, but the model offers a theorised way of appreciating educational intentions that can resonate with behaviourism and information processing, social constructivism and constructivism, respectively. Fisher et al. (2011), McLachlan (2020), Dockrell et al. (2016), Rosário et al. (2017) and Rosario et al. (2019) offer a range of teaching strategies to develop literacy that support various aspects of constructivism. One good example is providing an empty exercise book that becomes a student's journal. Weekly entries are written into it so that the document becomes a personalised narrative (Rosario et al. 2019) recounting their experiences. It provides an opportunity to reflectively think back on their encounters over the last few days before they action generating their original accounts.

Writing regularly in this genre has been show to improve writing quality and adopt more self-regulation strategies (Rosário et al., 2017). The self-regulation strategies that emerge include planning ahead about what to write, as well as structuring the journal entry to include an introduction to the context of the experience, description of the event, participants and even evaluation of the happening.

SUMMARY

Constructivism involves learners constructing personalised meanings through interaction with their environment. It involves solving problems in original ways by following personal volitions without being constantly directed by teachers. It can also involve consideration of others' views and subsequent adjustments of an individuals' ideas. Pupils develop and regulate their learning as a result of their own intrinsic motivations. They learn through activity that involves thinking and doing. These are interrelated and not separate (as in information processing explained in Chapter 2). It is not a matter of just action, as in behaviourism, nor is it a matter of thinking first, and then acting as a result of that contemplation as in cognitivism. In this theory of learning, the mind is agentive, that is, learners are pro-active, rather than reactively responding to a teacher's instruction or direction. They learn instead from their interactions with their surroundings and consolidate their understanding through reflection and (to a lesser extent) contrasting their ideas in discussion with peers engaged in similar activity. Prior knowledge and previous experience shape an individual's learning, but not necessarily in the way that a teacher might specifically wish for. Pedagogically, teachers may hope that after engaging in an activity (interaction with the immediate environment), subsequent reflection about that exchange (and perhaps through discussion with individuals which may present further perturbations from others' contrasting views) allows the individual to accommodate the experience and abstractly internalise knowledge. This subjective knowledge or coming to know [something] is assumed to be actively accrued by an individual and becomes part of their personalised reality.

McPhail (2016) suggests that constructivism has much to offer in developing approaches to pedagogy. He suggests, however, that there are serious limitations when applied to matters of epistemology and ontology. He warns that it is particularly important to clarify the limitations of constructivism before it becomes a new 21st-century pedagogy that is not clearly defined with universal agreement so that it becomes pragmatically feasible in institutions like schools. In considering the narrative construals of practice presented, you have hopefully come to realise yourself how naturalistically there are more or less appropriate moments in classrooms where learners can be supported to develop [ontologically] their own personal view, understanding or construction of reality, but this may not be feasible to maintain in an educational culture where regular measurement of attainment matters and performance indicators determine the future (or not) of successful schools (Table 8.4).

Table 8.4 Summary of Different Concepts Within the Constructivist Movement That Are Evident in the Narrative Construals

Narrative Construals	Nature of Constructivist Practice	Nature of Knowing	Process of Learning
Exploring ideas in science	Providing a range of everyday materials, resources and tools which could be examined and/or tested/manipulated by pupils.	Exploring in a somewhat unfettered way to find out whatever they can about different materials and processes.	Interacting with resources (everyday stuff) provided within learner's environment and thinking/reflecting on the experience to make sense.
Concept cartoons	Presenting a range of alternate perspectives for individuals to think about.	Recognising there are a range of possible, plausible and more accurate explanations of observations.	Contrasting personalised understandings with those of others.
Problem-solving with money in mathematics	Providing a range of resources and scaffolded activities to engage pupils in offering problem solutions.	Solving mathematical problems posed by the teacher.	Independent activity, offering propositions and reflecting on process to reach solution.
Writing poetry	Supporting a range of strategies that promote ways of students generating unique poetry or fictional narratives.	Generating original image, words and poetry.	Thinking, discussion and then writing.

Constructivism in schools is still evident today, but the ways that teachers understand it and enact practice to support it differ. There are many different kinds of *gardeners* out there nurturing aspects of the constructivist movement in a variety of ways.

ADDITIONAL READING

McPhail, G. (2016) the fault lines of recontextualisation: The limits of constructivism in education. This article discusses how the lack of clarity in ways that policymakers and teachers understand constructivism generates tensions.

O'Toole, J., Stinson, M. and Moore, T. (Eds.), *Drama and Curriculum. A Giant at the Door*. Dordrecht: Springer. This book offers much insightful discussion about the nature of drama and learning. Drama is an obvious area of the school curriculum where unique and original opportunities for pupils to engage in learning constructively are presented.

Coates, J. and Pimlott-Wilson, H. (2019) Learning while playing: Children's Forest School experiences in the UK. *British Educational Research Journal*, 45(1), 21-40. This paper offers discussion about a core principle of forest schools, constructivism, and describes many ways that the children demonstrate their originality.

REFERENCES

Adey, P. (2008) *Let's Think Handbook. A Guide to Cognitive Acceleration in the Primary School*. London: GL Assessment.

Adey, P., Shayer, M. & Yates, C. (2001) *Thinking Science: Materials of the CASE Approach*. London: Nelson Thornes.

Berninger, V., Garcia, N. & Abbott, R. (2009). Multiple processes that matter in the writing instruction and assessment. In G. Troia (Ed) *Instruction and Assessment for Struggling Writers: Evidence Based Practices*. New York, NY: The Guildford Press, pp. 15-50.

Cobb, P. (1994) An exchange: Constructivism in mathematics and science education. *Educational Researcher*, 23(7), 4.

DfE (2012) *What Is the Research Evidence on Writing? Education Standards Research Team*. London: Department for Education.

DfE (2021) *National Curriculum in England: Mathematics Programme of Study*. Available at https://www.gov.uk/government/publications/national-curriculum-in-england-mathematics-programmes-of-study/national-curriculum-in-england-mathematics-programmes-of-study. Accessed 14.08.22.

Dockrell, J., Mershall, C. & Wyse, D. (2016) Teachers' reported practices for teaching writing in England. *Reading and Writing*, 29, 409-434. https://doi.org/10.1007/s11145-015-9605-9

Driver, R. (1983) *The Pupil as Scientist?* Milton Keynes: Open University Press.

Driver, R. (2015) The teaching and understanding of concepts in science. In N. Entwistle (Ed) *Handbook of Educational Ideas and Practices*. London: Routledge.

Driver, R. & Scanlon, E. (1989) Conceptual change in science: A research programme. *Journal of Computer Assisted Learning*, 5(1), 25-36.

Driver, R., leach, J., Millar, R. & Scott, P. (1996) *Young people's Images of Science*. Philadelphia: Open University Press.

Driver, R., squires, A., Rushworth, P. & Wood-Robinson, V. (1994) *Making Sense of Secondary Science: Research into Children's Ideas*. London: Routledge.

Fisher, R., Myhill, D. & Twist, L. (2011) *Evaluation of Every Child a Writer Report 2: Teaching and Writing in ECaW Classes*. University of Exeter and National Foundation for Educational Research. DfE RR108b.

Frodsham, S. & McGregor, D. (2021) Illustrating aspects of creativity with primary science teaching trust fellows. Available at https://sites.google.com/brookes.ac.uk/illustratingcreativepractice/homepage. Accessed 29.07.24.

Gouge, K. & Yates, C. (2002) Creating a cognitive acceleration programme in the arts: The WIGAN LEA arts project. In M. Shayer & P. Adey (Eds) *Learning Intelligence: Cognitive Acceleration Across the Curriculum from 5 to 15 Years*. Buckingham: Open University Press.

Hamaker, T. & Blackwell, J. (2003) *Cognitive Acceleration through Technology Education: Teacher Guidelines and Pupil Task Pages*. Taunton: Nigel Blagg Associates.

Hendry, G. D. (1996) Constructivism and educational practice. *Australian Journal of Education*, 40(1), 19–45.

Inhelder, B. & Piaget, J. (1958) *The Growth of Logical Thinking From Childhood to Adolescence*. London: Routledge.

Keogh B. & Naylor S. (1999) Concept cartoons, teaching and learning in science: An evaluation. *International Journal of Science Education*, 21(4), 431–446.

Kosnik, C., Menna, C., Dharamshi, P. & Beck, C. (2018) Constructivism as a framework for literacy teacher education courses: The cases of six literacy teacher educators. *European Journal of Teacher Education*, 41(1) 105-119.

McGregor, D., Frodsham, S. & Wilson, H. (2022) The nature of epistemological opportunities for doing, thinking and talking about science: Reflections on an effective intervention that promotes creativity. *Research in Science & Technological Education*, 40(3), 363–388.

McLachlan, T. (2020) *12 Ideas for Teaching Creative Writing*. Available at https://blog.hope-education.co.uk/ideas-for-teaching-creative-writing/. Accessed 22.08.22.

McPhail, G. (2016) The fault lines of recontextualization: The limits of constructivism in education. *British Educational Research Journal*, 42(2), 293-313.

Ofsted (2011) Good practice in primary mathematics: Evidence from successful schools. Available at https://www.gov.uk/government/publications/good-practice-in-primary-mathematics-evidence-from-successful-schools. Accessed 03/03/25.

Piaget, J. (1950) *The Psychology of Intelligence*. London: Routledge.

Piaget, J. (1965) *The Child's Conception of Number*. London: Routledge.

Piaget, J. (1969) *The Child's Conception of Time*. New York: Ballantine Books.

Piaget, J. (1970) *The Child's Conception of Movement and Speed*. New York: Ballantine Books.

Piaget, J. & Inhelder, B. (1974) *The Child's Construction of Quantities*. London: Routledge.

Richardson, K. (1998) *Models of Cognitive Development*. Hove: Psychology Press.

Richardson, V. (2003) Constructivist pedagogy. *Teachers College Record*, 105(9). https://doi.org/10.1046/j.1467-9620.2003.00303.x

Round, R. & McPhail, G. (2019) Using music: From spontaneous to scientific concepts in the primary school writing classroom. *International Journal of Education and the Arts*, 20(5), 1–25.

Seleznyov, S., Adhami, M., Black, A. Hodgen, J. & Twiss, S. (2021) Cognitive Acceleration in Mathematics Education further evidence of impact. *Education*, 3(50), 1-13.

Shayer, M. & Adey, P. (1981) *Towards a Science of Science Teaching. Curriculum Development and Curriculum Demand*. Oxford: Heinemann Educational Publishers.

Shayer, M. & Adey, P. (2002) *Learning Intelligence: Cognitive Acceleration Across the Curriculum From 5 to 15 Years*. Buckingham: Open University Press.

Shayer, M. & Adhami, M. (2010) Realizing the cognitive potential of children 5-7 with a mathematics focus: Post-test and long-term effects of a 2-year intervention. *British Journal of Educational Psychology, 80*, 363-379.

Ugwuozor, F. O. (2020) Constructivism as pedagogical framework and poetry learning outcomes among Nigerian students: An experimental study, *Cogent Education, 7*(1), 1818410, DOI: 10.1080/2331186X.2020.1818410

Rosário, P., Högemann, J., Núñez, J.C., Vallejo, G., Cunha, J., Oliveira, V., Fuentes, S. & Rodríguez, C. (2017) Writing week-journals to improve the writing quality of fourth-graders' compositions. *Reading and Writing, 30*, 1009-1032.

Rosario, P., Högemann, J., Núñez, J.C., Vallejo, G., Cunha, J., Rodríguez, C. & Fuentes, S. (2019) The impact of three types of writing intervention on students' writing quality. *PLoS One 14*(7): e0218099. https://doi.org/10.1371/journal.pone.0218099

Russell, T., Longden, K. & McGuigan, L. (1991) *Primary SPACE Research Report: Materials*. Liverpool: Liverpool University Press.

Von Glaserfeld, E. (1995) A Constructivist approach to teaching. In L. P. Steffe & J. Gale (Eds) *Constructivism in Education*. Hillsdale, NJ: Lawrence Erlbaum, pp. 3-16.

9
CLASSROOM CASES FEATURING ASPECTS OF SOCIAL CONSTRUCTIVISM

CONTENTS

Introduction	211
Interactive Consideration of Perspectives in Science	215
Scaffolding Mathematical Conversations	218
Deliberating About Computers and Books	222
Arguing About Macbeth	227
Summary	230
Additional Reading	230
References	231

Chapter Aims

After reading Chapter 9, you will have considered:

- how the social constructivist theory of learning and associated concepts can be used as 'tools' to think about the ways that policy and practice influence learning;
- a variety of different practices that characterise ways of supporting interaction and dialogic exchange in learning;
- how practice can promote social constructivism in learning;
- how practice can promote or constrain the extent of the ZPD;
- how practice influences the nature and extent of participation within learning interactions;
- how teacher as *modeller, guide* or *scaffolder* influences the agentive opportunities made available for learning and learners.

INTRODUCTION

As explained in Chapter 8, the interest in constructivism prevailed for several decades before the turn of the century. However, more recently, it has been critiqued (Taber 2019) and the focus for educational research has increasingly looked beyond just eliciting learners' ideas and conceptions. It has turned increasingly to exploring and assessing how practice can influence the progression in learners' thinking and understandings about phenomena or happenings. This has influenced a developing concern with dialogue, particularly the ways that teachers employ it (Alexander 2018; Littleton and Howe 2010) as well as the ways that verbal utterances can reflect learners' cognitive development (Mercer 2008; Littleton and Mercer 2013). Consequently, within the last two decades, there has been much study of talk in classrooms that might inform how practice could support and scaffold the many productive (Hennessy et al. 2021) and varied (Alexander 2018; Schillings et al. 2018; Rapanta & Christodoulou 2019; Lord et al. 2021; Macagno 2022; Rapanta and Felton 2022) forms that dialogue can take.

As introduced in Chapter 1 and expanded on in Chapters 4-6, the importance and role of social exchanges in learning was discussed. It was explained how the extent and nature of social interaction can be demonstrated through considering the types of verbal exchanges engaged in. Dialogue between peers, for example, when constrained to just comparing each other's ideas about the same concern (i.e. concept cartoons in Chapter 8), is quite different in nature and purpose to that which emerges between a novice and an expert endeavouring to jointly solve a problem.

Besides this, if you recollect, in Chapter 3, you were introduced to constructivist theory that highlighted how individual action precedes thought and discussion. That is, how individuals construct knowledge 'from within' (Beck 2016: 101) through assimilation and accommodation. In this chapter, contrastingly, the narrative construals that illustrate social constructivist concepts are brought to the fore. In contrast to Chapters 3 and 8, here opportunities for knowledge that emerges 'from without' (Beck 2016: 101) and is generated within the zone of proximal development (ZPD) are considered. These construals illustrate how the social dimensions of learning interactions can vary widely across classes concerned with different kinds of learning objectives within contrasting subject matter.

As was also introduced earlier in the book, how curricular policy is enacted through teachers' practice and the ways that subject matter is communicated about in the classroom can also orient how learners are offered particular kinds of learning experiences.

In considering the narrative construals presented in this chapter, think about how discussion is promoted, guided and supported by the teacher, who else is involved and for what purposes. Also consider the nature and extent of the ZPD supported by the teacher through their practice to promote opportunities for learning.

Social Constructivism and Practice

In contrast to Chapter 8, where pedagogy within the constructivist movement was related to supporting individuals to interact with their environment to assimilate personalised views of reality, practice discussed here is concerned with promoting the social dimension of learning. There are many ways that social interaction can be enacted in teaching practices. One example includes providing learners with creature cards of *Quarks* or *Dufties* with lists of particular mathematical characteristics (Bauersfeld 1992) that students have to compare. Students are subsequently presented with alternate pictures of *Quarks* and *Dufties* to argue about, discuss assumed properties, negotiate what is relevant and resolve whether the presented alternate objects are indeed a *Quark* or a *Duftie* (Bauersfeld 1992: 470).

Question for Consideration 9.1

How far can the dialogue engaged in between people suggest the nature and extent of the ZPD generated through social interaction?

Other kinds of activities that involve learners' extending discussion about their differing understandings and alternate propositions can promote social constructivism. Drama or theatrical techniques, for example, can offer opportunities for students to engage in discussion with other learners and negotiate what is salient (Baskerville et al. 2023). The following is a transcript of a discussion between three girls who are in a primary school. It is a science lesson, where they are considering properties of materials. They are preparing to act out what would happen if they are playing netball in an environment where everything around them was made of sponge. They are deliberating here about how they might 'act out' playing netball in a spongy environment.

Sophie: Netball would be really hard if everything was sponge.

Sarah: Yeah, imagine the court being sponge. If it rained you would like sink

Simone: Okay, so here are our ideas on normal netball. So you pivot, you jump, you throw, you pass, you shoot, that kind of stuff and then if it's sponge, then you'll flop around, trip over.

Sarah: Sinking like quicksand, where you would have to wear snow shoes

Simone: Because snowshoes like spread your weight across the ....

Sarah: The ball would not bounce, would not roll. The ball would get stuck and, and the hoop.

Sophie: Yeah.

Sarah: We would get stuck. [Laughing]

Sophie: We would sink into the sponge. It would be very hard to play netball.

Sarah: Well the sponge could actually be good because it would break your fall.

(Extract from McGregor and Duggan 2016)

This excerpt illustrates how a very different task to the mathematics one, comparing *Quarks* and *Dufties*, can support social interaction that involves dialogic exchanges reflecting the sharing of understandings and conjectures about possibilities. In the netball discussion, it becomes apparent how the utterances offered by each of the students contributes to a see-sawing development of their collective idea about how to 'act out' what playing netball would be like in a world made of sponge. They need to negotiate, that is, exchange dialogically what they think could be done, to reach agreement about what to do. Contrasting these two tasks, to determine whether on object is a *Quark* or a *Duftie* or deciding how to 'act out' moving in a spongy world, serves to indicate how practice, that is, what a teacher chooses to say and do, varies the scaffolding or support students are given to learn in a social constructivist way.

Thinking Further About Dialogue and Social Constructivism

In Chapter 4, you were introduced to 'inner dialogue' and the way that language offers a social means by which internal thoughts of both a communicative and intellectual nature might be shared.

Task 9.1

You were asked to think about (in Chapter 4, Task 4.5) how a father might help a child find a lost toy. Consider further this time what kinds of discussion might take place. What kinds of questions might an adult pose of a child who has lost something? Is the sequence of questions important? How significant are the replies provided by the child to find the lost object? How much might the father adjust his questioning as it takes longer to establish where and when the toy might have last been seen?

Through this kind of verbal exchange, the direction and thought process that the father is following comes into existence. His logic and sequential thinking is likely to become more evident as he discusses with his child where the typical places are that the toy is played with, when was the toy last tidied away, where is the toy normally stored, etc.

> **Question for Consideration 9.2**
>
> What kinds of scaffolds support social construction?

There are a number of studies that discuss the nature of dialogue in general (Littleton and Howe 2010; Mercer 2000; Mercer and Hodgkinson 2009) and nomenclatures (Hennessey 2021; Mercer 2008; Rapanta & Christodoulou 2019) that categorise the nature of talk that emerges in classrooms. You could reflect on which of the following (in Tables 9.1 and 9.2) might best describe how the father and child are likely to talk to each other in their joint endeavour to find the lost toy!

Within school education, 'dialogic teaching' (Alexander 2018) is widely recognised. The oft-acknowledged categories include those listed in Table 9.1. In thinking about these forms of 'teacher talk' that are usually concerned more directly with school curricular matters, consider where they are evident in the excerpts throughout this chapter and elsewhere in the book. You might also wish to reflect back on the excerpts in Chapters 7 and 8 to consider, for example, where rote and recitation prevailed or the forms of talk were evident within constructivist construals.

Returning to social constructivism, in considering how practice affects the nature of dialogue that emerges in classrooms, it is key to consider how interaction is encouraged to support productive verbal exchange. Appreciating the extent to which students are afforded opportunities to practice using linguistic tools of thought (Vygotsky 1981) suggests how the process from inter- to intra-thinking is scaffolded and supported or straitjacketed for learners (Jesson et al. 2016).

Table 9.1 Categories of Dialogic Teaching (after Alexander 2018)

Categories of Dialogic Teaching	Description
Rote	Concerned with memorising times tables, routines and spellings
Recitation	Involves testing recall of knowledge and understanding through questions designed to check recollection of previously explained facts
Instruction	Involves the teacher directing learners about what to do
Exposition	Involves the teacher imparting facts, transmitting what needs to be known
Discussion	Involves the exchange of ideas with a view to sharing information and solving problems

In the girls' discussion about netball played in a spongy environment, you could also consider the extent to which the three forms of talk (Table 9.2) are evident. Consider whether the girls just agree uncritically, or do they make available for each other mental resources they can offer to contribute to joint understanding.

Table 9.2 Categories of (Learner) Talk (after Mercer 2008)

Categories of Learner Talk	Description
Disputational	Discussion is characterised by disagreement and individualised decision-making. There are few attempts to pool resources or to offer constructive criticism or suggestions to or for each other. Characteristic discourse features: short exchanges consisting of assertions and challenges or counter assertions.
Cumulative	Discussion is positive but uncritical. Partners use talk to construct a 'common knowledge' by accumulation. Characteristic discourse features: repetitions, confirmations and elaborations.
Exploratory	Partners engage critically but constructively with each other's ideas. Statements and suggestions are offered by individuals for joint consideration. These may be challenged and counter-challenged, but challenges are justified and alternate hypotheses offered. Characteristic discourse features: Knowledge and reasoning are more visible in the talk.

In the following narrative construals of classroom practice, consider how dialogue appears to be supported. To what extent is modelling, guiding or scaffolding (detailed earlier in Chapter 4) adopted in the teacher's practice.

The subject-related contexts presented to consider concepts within the social constructivist movement are:

- Interactive consideration of perspectives in science
- Scaffolding mathematical conversations
- Deliberating about computers and books
- Arguing about Macbeth

INTERACTIVE CONSIDERATION OF PERSPECTIVES IN SCIENCE

In this narrative construal, the primary teacher concerned, Ms Davey, has devised an activity to enhance different aspects of social constructivist learning. She is concerned with fulfilling the school's requirements to address the National Curriculum for science. Ensuring she is a policy actor (Ball et al. 2011), her practice is designed to address the National Curriculum, which states:

National Curriculum [Policy extracts]

Working scientifically is described separately at the beginning of the programme of study, but must always be taught through and clearly related to substantive science content in the programme of study. Teachers should feel free to choose examples that serve a variety of purposes, from showing how scientific ideas have developed historically to reflecting modern developments in science.

Spoken language

The national curriculum for science reflects the importance of spoken language in pupils' development across the whole curriculum – cognitively, socially and linguistically. The quality and variety of language that pupils hear and speak are key factors in developing their scientific vocabulary and articulating scientific concepts clearly and precisely. They must be assisted in making their thinking clear, both to themselves and others, and teachers should ensure that pupils build secure foundations by using discussion to probe and remedy their misconceptions. (DfE 2015)

There are a variety of drama strategies (McGregor and Anderson 2023) that can support social interaction and social constructivism in many different ways. Ms Davey has selected a drama technique called, *Hot seating* (Farmer 2011), which is a strategy whereby teachers or learners are placed to act as if in a *role*. Others (teacher and/or pupils) can then question the hot seated person about being that character or object. A teacher or child in the hot seat can also 'be' someone reflecting on a particular event or experience. The person (or a group of children) in the 'hot seat' usually sits on a chair at the front of the class and is placed in the 'spotlight' when questioned by the others in the room. Ms Davey has already engaged the class in an active storytelling activity when the teacher has been in-role as a well-known character, the Victorian botanist, Marianne North (McGregor 2021).

As a character from history, Ms Davey is dressed as a wealthy Victorian woman. She is in-role acting as if in an imagined tropical rainforest describing her life in the mid-19th century. She explains to the pupils how she is the daughter of a wealthy parliamentarian and regularly travelled overseas with her father visiting a variety of countries throughout Asia and South America. She was particularly passionate about exotic flowers and realised that it was much better to sketch and paint them rather than dig them up and transport them back (by boat, not plane) to Victorian England. She also explains how her paintings were so well regarded that they ended up on display in a gallery in Kew Gardens, London. Ms Davey then metaphorically sits in the *hot seat* (Farmer 2011: 28), to respond to questions that the students pose. The dialogue develops as transcribed below:

Mark: Why are you painting the plants you see?

Ms Davey: Why am I painting? Because I want people to see things that I can see when I go on my travels. I want to show people parts of the world and what I can see there. Yes.

Sarah: You travel around the world.

Ms Davey: Yes, I've travelled to lots of places.

Paige: How did you get here?

Ms Davey: How did I get here? I walked.

Pupils:	What!
Ms Davey:	Wait, how did I get where? To where I am now or to the rainforests. How do you think I travelled to the rainforest? When Queen Victoria was alive.
Henry:	On a donkey.
Ms Davey:	I used a donkey to get up the mountains.
Hunter:	A carriage.
Ms Davey:	Yes, I used a carriage ... My main way of transport. I did use a carriage to get there. How did I get here?
Layla:	Was it a boat?
Ms Davey:	A boat. I would have gone by boat. Yes.
Georgia:	Why are you going to different places?
Ms Davey:	Why am I going to different places? Because the things I see far, far away in my travels, we don't see the beauties, the colours, the plants.

The discussion in class continues.

> ### Task 9.2
>
> How does the discussion between the Sophie, Simone and Sarah differ to that of Ms Davey's moment in practice? How do you imagine the practice of each teacher in the two classrooms differs to result in the such contrastingly different forms of dialogue? How would you describe the interactions between peers and the teacher and pupils in the two excerpts?

In the first excerpt, arguably the three pupils could be deemed to be demonstrating Alexander's type of talk labelled 'Discussion'. The three peers are exchanging ideas with a view to solving the problem of playing netball on a spongey surface. Interestingly, they each offer constructive suggestions that make available for each other ways of beginning to think beyond just the netball game, but also what would happen if weather conditions changed and it began to rain. This type of talk could arguably demonstrate Mercer's 'exploratory' form of dialogue engaging constructively and rendering their reasoning more visible. The nature of talk in Ms Davey's lesson, however, does not demonstrate such symmetry (or balanced exchanges) between pupils. In Ms Davey's lesson the teacher is more dominant in the learning activity although many pupils are also involved. In this narrative construal the teacher has adopted a drama strategy to teach the subject matter. This is an approach that has recently become popular (McGregor and Anderson 2023). As indicated in the policy excerpts, Ms Davey has interpreted choosing *examples that serve a variety of purposes, from showing how scientific ideas have developed historically to reflecting modern developments in science.* As can be seen from the transcript, a historical dimension of science (McGregor and Precious 2015: 209-210) informs the curricular focus. This scientist was partly responsible for halting the regular practice of Victorians 'collecting' specimens from overseas and bringing them to England for display in museums. Although not in the transcript presented here, this becomes a later focus of the discussion with pupils.

In this narrative construal of practice, there is asymmetry in knowledge relations; the teacher is the more expert other, knowing more about scientific ideas that have developed historically. Her goal, it appears, is to be assisting the thirty-one 10- to 11-year-olds by engaging them in using language that (they) hear and speak to scaffold the development of their scientific vocabulary. The dialogue also contributes to collaboration in joint problem-solving (Wood et al. 1976), that is, making available for all the class collective mental resources, as well as designing the learning task to 'recruit attention [...] maintain "direction" in the problem solving [and] mark critical features' (Wood et al. 1976: 104). The nature of curricular material, both scientific and linguistic, in this episode indicates the beginning of discussion that socially generated a ZPD for the pupils. Ms Davey appeared to value historical and cultural scientific knowledge and acted as a *scaffolder* making available knowing about science in an interactive and imaginative way.

SCAFFOLDING MATHEMATICAL CONVERSATIONS

In mathematics classrooms, social–constructivist practices were first researched and implemented in the 1990s (Cobb and Bauersfeld 1995). However, research and practice in the last couple of decades have expanded the understanding of mathematics education as a more social and cultural activity and the ways that mathematical learning is mediated and language has been considered pivotal in meaning-making (Sfard 2008; Schutte et al. 2019; Planas et al. 2021) have notably increased.

In considering why teachers might be concerned with practice that scaffolds social constructivism, it is useful to review national policy and the extent to which it is required in school classrooms. In reading this extract, it is useful to think about how policymakers are expecting mathematics to be experienced by learners. Some of the aims may more directly relate to the behaviourism and information-processing movement discussed in Chapters 2 and 9. Other aims may relate to the constructivist movement considered in Chapters 3 and 10.

Task 9.3

Consider where the social constructivist movement, or concepts within it, appear to be related to the national policy for mathematics.
Are there any demonstrations of these processes in the narrative construal below?

The following extract is from the National Curriculum for mathematics in England (DfE 2021).:

Purpose of Study

[...] A high-quality mathematics education therefore provides a foundation for understanding the world, the ability to reason mathematically, an appreciation of the beauty and power of mathematics, and a sense of enjoyment and curiosity about the subject.

Aims

The national curriculum for mathematics aims to ensure that all pupils:

- become fluent in the fundamentals of mathematics, including through varied and frequent practice with increasingly complex problems over time, so that pupils develop conceptual understanding and the ability to recall and apply knowledge rapidly and accurately
- reason mathematically by following a line of enquiry, conjecturing relationships and generalisations, and developing an argument, justification or proof using mathematical language
- can solve problems by applying their mathematics to a variety of routine and non-routine problems with increasing sophistication, including breaking down problems into a series of simpler steps and persevering in seeking solutions

Mathematics is an interconnected subject in which pupils need to be able to move fluently between representations of mathematical ideas. The programmes of study are, by necessity, organised into apparently distinct domains, but pupils should make rich connections across mathematical ideas to develop fluency, mathematical reasoning and competence in solving increasingly sophisticated problems.

Spoken language

The national curriculum for mathematics reflects the importance of spoken language in pupils' development across the whole curriculum – cognitively, socially and linguistically. The quality and variety of language that pupils hear and speak are key factors in developing their mathematical vocabulary and presenting a mathematical justification, argument or proof. They must be assisted in making their thinking clear to themselves as well as others, and teachers should ensure that pupils build secure foundations by using discussion to probe and remedy their misconceptions. (DfE 2021)

Students could experience *reason(ing) mathematically by following a line of enquiry, conjecturing relationships and generalisations and developing an argument, justification or proof using mathematical language* if supported or scaffolded in lessons to learn through social interaction. However, as previously discussed, teachers can vary in the ways they support social interaction and sustain opportunities for students to develop lines of argument, provide justification and jointly consider proof.

The requirement, too, for mathematical *language that pupils hear and speak (as) key factors in developing their mathematical vocabulary and presenting a mathematical justification, argument or proof* again is supportable through dialogic exchange and the development of their argumentation.

The following excerpt, taken from a secondary lesson in Cognitive Acceleration in Mathematics Education, remains relevant in mathematics classrooms today (Seleznyov et al. 2021); it 'links mental operations on numbers with pencil and paper algorithms and with a visual model of the number line' (Adhami et al. 1998: 16). Can you 'see' how the teacher supports the development of intersubjectivity more closely related to constructivism, but then encourages the pupils to engage in collectively construing a model that explains how they have all gone about the arithmetic problem given.

Ms Smith, the teacher, introduces the lesson and explains how it is concerned with mental arithmetics and the way that fits with a number line.

Ms Smith:	First do 15 + 13 in your head [she does not write the sum]. How did you do it?
Pupil 1:	I added 3 to 15 and then added 10.
Pupil 2:	I added 10 to the 15 and then counted 3 more.
Pupil 3:	I added the two tens together and then the 5 and the 3 together.
Ms Smith:	What about 16 + 27? How would you do that?
Pupil 4:	I added 4, that's 20 then added 20 then added 3.
Ms Smith:	[Acting puzzled] Why 3?

Several pupils volunteer to explain.

Ms Smith writes the sum on the board.

Pupil 5:	I added 20 first.
Pupil 6:	I have my way. I added 15 to 25, that's 40, then added 1 and 2.
Pupil 7:	I added 7 first, that makes 23 then added 20 more.
Ms Smith:	How did you actually get 23?
Pupil 7:	I just know it.
Ms Smith:	Did you count on and use your fingers?
Pupil 7:	No, it's obvious. If you add 4 then add 3.
Ms Smith:	So you went first to 20, then to 23.
Pupil 7:	Yes, of course.
Pupil 8:	I went 16 and 30 is 46 then took away 3,
Ms Smith:	What is common between all these methods?
Pupil 9:	They are all different.
Pupil 10:	You do what is easier for you, numbers you like.
Pupil 11:	You make easy numbers first then add them.
Ms Smith:	What are easy numbers?

Pupil 11:   10, 20, 30.

Pupil 10:   Numbers with 5s and 0s.

(Adhami et al. 1998: 16)

The dialogic exchanges, or the use of language in this narrative construal, offer a way for individuals to firstly explain their thinking and secondly share how they have each (differently) thought about how to work out the sum of two numbers, then consider their personal strategy to solve the problem and finally begin to reflect on each individuals' contribution to generalise an explanatory model. The teacher scaffolds the activities to finally reach a collective explanatory model.

This particular approach to developing students' thinking is designed around 'construction' whereby activities presented by the teacher offer students opportunities to develop 'strategies' or 'generate' solutions to problems (Adhami et al. 1998: xiii). Shared reflections on each other's cognitive processing required to find resolutions (Seleznyov et al. 2021: 2) demonstrate intersubjectivity. This limited kind of intersubjectivity (explained in Chapters 3 and 4) enables learners to advance their own thinking through reflecting on the ways that others' might solve similar problems differently or even more effectively. However, the teacher subsequently encourages reflection from all pupils to consider their individual strategies to solve the problem and suggest, 'What is in common between these methods?'. At this point all the pupils are involved in a larger collective ZPD involving the whole class (see Chapter 5). Pupils 9, 10 and 11 begin considering how to generalise from the various strategies articulated. This characterises social constructivism rather than intersubjectivity. Practices that can promote rich discussions (Jacobs et al. 2022) have become a much more common focus of recent mathematic educational research.

Mr Cook, another secondary mathematics teacher, recognised his students were always in a rush to achieve the correct answers to problems and that finding the right solution was their motivation in mathematics lessons. He realised that his students did not necessarily consider mathematical evidence that would enable them to better understand concepts. He designed his approach to encourage students to talk and think more deeply about mathematics. He organised groups of students, typically in trios, to work together according to their thinking and verbal capabilities. He encouraged mathematical conversations by presenting dissonance in the form of mathematics solutions that were *not* correct. He provided incorrect solutions to problems for the students to discuss and subsequently agree what they collaboratively thought were the correct solutions. Incorrect solutions to mathematical problems were posted around the room and the students rotated in groups to discuss each in turn. The students had to review the (incorrect) solution, make a claim about disagreeing, provide evidence for disagreeing and then offer a correct solution.

Question for Consideration 9.3

What different kinds of discussions (supported by teachers' practice) promote social constructivism?

In another secondary mathematics classroom, Mr Mathe presented all his students with the same problem to solve, *The sum of three consecutive integers is 81. Find the three numbers.* The students were asked what *integer, consecutive numbers* and *sum* means before they started to clarify the terms being used. They were then asked to attempt solving the problem on their own to find out how many different ways there are to reach a solution. Each student then worked in a group to collectively decide between them the best way to solve the problem and a representative of the group wrote their solution on the white board at the front of the class. The teacher then orchestrated a discussion about how different dimensions of each of their solutions (algebraic, common sense, series of divisions using variables, looking for number patterns) differed.

For each of these approaches, dialogic exchange was engaged in by all of the students, but the extent to which the epistemic outcomes were achieved varied (Rapanta and Felton 2022). Consider, from the descriptions, how far each individual student might have participated in argumentative reasoning, that is to what extent do you think each student contributed their understandings about something. Some educational researchers label this as argumentation (Erduran and Jimenez-Aleixandre 2012), that is evaluating the validity of each speaker's claims and evidence. As Rapanta and Felton (2022) argue, however, not all educational dialogues are aimed at argumentation as a goal. However, as Resnick et al. (2018) suggest, discussion not designed to be argumentative may still achieve epistemic gains as a by-product despite the lack of dialogic objectives. In Mr Cook and Mr Mathe's classes, the teachers both scaffolded social interaction through the ways they organised students to work together (differently), and the ways they communicated discussion and negotiation were important as well as their design of (open) learning tasks that could be resolved in multiple ways.

DELIBERATING ABOUT COMPUTERS AND BOOKS

As you have read earlier in Chapter 5, dialogic exchange in social constructivism is important. Social interaction is critical so that learners can engage with the linguistic tools made available and subsequently act agentively to collaborate and construe shared understandings. It is through verbal exchanges that construction, in the broad sense of meaning-making, takes place (Ford 2012). Remember, as Vygotsky stated:

> Every function in the child's cultural development appears twice: first on the social level, and later, on the individual level. First between people (interpsychological) and the inside the child (intrapsychological). (Vygotsky 1978: 57)

In classroom contexts, through taking turns to engage dialogically with the matter at hand, speakers and listeners can attempt to make sense of each other's ideas to reach a consensus or even agree to disagree. If you recollect in Chapter 4, the concept of intersubjectivity within social constructivism was explained. Where tension exists because understandings differ, engaging in intersubjectivity to negotiate a shared understanding can result in a non-local mind emerging between people.

> **Question for Consideration 9.4**
>
> Does symmetrical participation in discussion matter for social constructivism?

Argumentative dialogue is a discursive activity in which tensions between individuals are addressed. Erduran and Jimenez-Aleixandre (2007: 2) define argumentation as a kind of intellectual discussion through which knowledge claims are individually (and collaboratively) 'constructed and evaluated in the light of empirical or theoretical evidence'. As Osborne (2004, 2007), Erduran et al. (2015) and others suggest, argumentation has become more prominent in secondary education since the turn of the century. It is recognised, though, to be pedagogically difficult (Newton et al. 1999) to promote, not least to ensure, symmetrical (see Chapters 4 and 5) participation by all learners. It is also challenging because assumptions about practice require teacher enactments that are not always clearly specified in teaching materials.

That is, developments in learners' reasoning and *epistemic* understanding, like Collin's assumptions in Chapter 3, could not be assumed to naturally emerge just from 'exchanging' and 'discussing' each other's ideas. More sophisticated patterns of discussion evident in argumentation are based on Toulmin's (1958) notions about arguments that need to include 'claims', 'warrants', 'backings', 'rebuttals', etc. To support teachers developing argumentation in classrooms, a simple 'argumentation' framework (Osborne et al. 2004) could include the following prompts:

why do you think that?

can you think of another argument for your view?

can you think of an argument against your view?

how do you know?

This is the kind of teacher questioning that can scaffold talk whereby the students justify why they have a particular view or belief, consider a polemic perspective and then verify their thinking. This kind of talk can be teacher led, or students can be provided with the prompts written out as a guide so that they can respond to them in smaller groups, thus enabling the opportunity for more participants.

> **Questions for Consideration 9.5**
>
> How much does symmetrical participation in discussion matter for social constructivism?

In a learning sense, this kind of structured talk highlights the nature of *symbolic interactionism* (Blumer 1969) introduced in Chapter 5. It is assumed within discussion that the participants' arguments respond to people, objects and concepts according to the meaning they each, personally attribute to them. The following construal demonstrates how a teacher, like Ms Pessagno, could scaffold young pupils to engage in argumentation that supports learners communicating their ideas about the relative usefulness of computers and books. Ultimately, they have to decide through emulating a political debate whether they would prefer a world with books or computers in it.

Task 9.4

Consider how the following narrative construal detailing primary pupils engaging in argumentation, which could be setup by Ms Pessagno, as a parliamentary style debate engages them in articulating claims, providing warrants, offering rebuttals and finally reaching a resolution of some kind.

You may find it useful to also think about the aspects of the English curriculum policy (below) that could be addressed through adopting this kind of social activity in school.

Policy Extract: National Curriculum: English (DfE 2016)

Purpose of study

English has a pre-eminent place in education and in society. A high-quality education in English will teach pupils to speak and write fluently so that they can communicate their ideas and emotions to others and through their reading and listening, others can communicate with them. [...] All the skills of language are essential to participating fully as a member of society; pupils, therefore, who do not learn to speak, read and write fluently and confidently are effectively disenfranchised.

Extract from National Curriculum: Computing (DfE 2014)

Purpose

Computing also ensures that pupils become digitally literate – able to use, and express themselves and develop their ideas through, information and communication technology – at a level suitable for the future workplace and as active participants in a digital world.

Aims

are responsible, competent, confident and creative users of information and communication technology.

Key Stage 2 POS [includes]:

- understand computer networks including the internet; how they can provide multiple services, such as the world wide web; and the opportunities they offer for communication and collaboration
- use search technologies effectively, appreciate how results are selected and ranked, and be discerning in evaluating digital content
- select, use and combine a variety of software (including internet services) on a range of digital devices to design and create a range of programs, systems and content that accomplish given goals, including collecting, analysing, evaluating and presenting data and information
- use technology safely, respectfully and responsibly; recognise acceptable/unacceptable behaviour; identify a range of ways to report concerns about content and contact.

This narrative construal involves eight primary school pupils sat at the front of their class. Three are positioned to the left representing the proposition team (PT) and three others seated to the right are the opposition team (OT). Other students chair, introduce the debate and adjudicate proceedings. The following narrative construal offers some excerpts from the discussion that indicates how argumentation can be enacted with young people to frame a debate about computers and books.

Setting up the Debate

Chair: Hello everyone. Today we are going to consider whether computers are better than books. Our debate will argue the motion proposed. We have a team of three arguing that computers are better than books [Juliette, Nesta and Reese] and we have a team of three arguing that this is not the case [Sadie, Katy and Neriah].

Beginning the Debate

Juliette: Computers are machines that can multi-task, they can hold more information than a library and can be used to play games and other forms of entertainment. You can also use computers for education.

Neriah: Issue!

Juliette: Yes?

Neriah: Some information may not true, like on answer.com. Sometimes people just give opinions.

Juliette: Mmm, however, some information, can be accurate, like the BBC. Computers can help people of all ages develop their minds.

Secondly computers store a lot of information. Any information can be just a click away.

Computers can also be used for entertainment like videos, games etc.

Vote for our motion that computers are better than books.

All: [Applause]

The Opposition

Sadie: Computers can be hacked, they can be unreliable and may affect good health. Online shopping, for example, can be hacked and credit card details can be abused. Police may find it difficult to track crimes. The unreliability may affect people using information for exams. A friend of mine used online information and did badly in his tests.

Nesta: Issue!

Sadie: Yes?

Nesta: Your friend should have been aware answers may not be accurate. Why was he cheating using a computer?

Sadie: That isn't what I was trying to say. Computers don't always provide reliable information. Needing help for exams people need to be careful. Health-wise, spending a lot of time on computers can result in issues like Repetitive Strain Injury and it becomes difficult to write.

Nesta: There is an app called iBooks, in which pictures are animated and young children find them very interesting. Also computers can limit what children see. Parental guidance can allow parents to check on the history of the children's activity. In books a child could easily hide what they have been reading. Parents can also block inappropriate sites.

Each of the three proposers offer suggestions in turn supporting the motion that computers are better than books and each of the opposition presents counter-arguments. The listeners of the debate also present questions for the proposers and opposers to respond to.

Drawing the Debate to a Close

The chairperson explains how before the vote both the proposers and the opposition teams will summarise their arguments and answer any questions from the audience.

Once the summaries that support and oppose the notion that 'Computers are better than books' have been heard, the chair then asks for a show of hands to demonstrate which argument, the 'for' or 'against' team, the audience agree with.

The narrative construal here of the debate about the pros and cons of books and computers indicates how social constructivist processes can be scaffolded in this way. Although preparation for the debate (informed by Noisy Classroom 2021) is not discussed here, a teacher like Ms Pessagno would have worked to *model* and *guide* the pupils in particular ways to speak and articulate their arguments. The narrative construal suggests how the students were able to offer 'claims', 'warrants', 'backings' and 'rebuttals' (described in Table 9.3). These dialogic moves (Toulmin 1958) indicate how they are attempting to share understandings, evidence dialogically how their perspectives are different, then justify and verify them and finally make judgements about what they think is best. Reflecting on the arguments made available by each of the speakers, the whole class reach a final vote. The argumentation processes demonstrate features of social constructivism.

Table 9.3 Description of Features of TAP

Features of Toulmin's Argument Pattern (TAP)	Description of the Characteristic Feature
Claims	Proposals or propositions are offered concerning the issue to be debated, this constitutes the claim
Data	Evidence supporting the claim is articulated
Warrants	Explanations of the way that evidence supports the claim are shared
Qualifiers	Consideration of particular circumstances in which the claim may be true are presented
Backings	Assumptions or influences that may not be obvious are shared
Rebuttals	Perspectives that contradict the claim, the evidence, particular circumstances or assumptions are aired

Source: Adapted from Simon et al. (2006).

Reflecting, too, on the English and computer curricular policies, the argumentation activity offers opportunities for aspects of these two areas of the curriculum to be addressed. Not only does the argumentative dialogue require participation through speaking, writing (in preparing arguments) and reading fluently and confidently, the pupils also demonstrate how they are digitally literate. They are able to express themselves as active participants in a digital world and they demonstrate how they are responsible users of information and communication technology.

There is much potential in this social constructivist approach to extend across many disciplines in education, much as the *epistemic insights* project has done (Billingsley and Chappell 2024).

In the final construal, 'Arguing about Macbeth', another pedagogic strategy demonstrates how dialogic moves can be scaffolded by a teacher to support social constructivism to achieve a different form of argumentation.

ARGUING ABOUT MACBETH

As you have already read above, the social constructivist movement can be interpreted and supported differently across the curriculum. In thinking about developing practice that English teachers might adopt with 13- and 14-year-olds to teach about characters, play plots and alternative views of protagonists, in this case Shakespeare's Macbeth, consider the following National Curriculum Policy extract for Key Stage 3 students (11-14 years of age).

National Curriculum [Policy extract]: Spoken English KS4

Pupils should be taught to:

- speak confidently and *effectively*, including through:
- using Standard English *confidently* in a range of formal and informal contexts, including classroom discussion
- giving short speeches and *presentations*, expressing their own ideas and keeping to the point
- participating in formal *debates* and structured discussions, summarising and/or building on what has been said
- improvising, rehearsing and *performing* play scripts and poetry in order to generate languages and discuss language use and meaning, using role, intonation, tone, volume, mood, silence, stillness and action to add impact

(Extract from DfE 2014)

Task 9.5

In thinking about the National Curriculum Policy for English, what is it that students are expected to be able to do when learning about plays? What do you infer teachers could do to enact the policy? How does the policy extract indicate the students should engage with play scripts? Does the narrative construal described here fulfil curricular requirements?

Mr Beadle, a creative drama and English teacher, has 'invented' a unique approach at his London school, to engage his class of Y9 boys, whom he thinks are at risk of underachieving. He has devised a way of organising the classroom differently so that eventually it ends up as 'the shape of a tennis court' (Teachers TV, n.d.). The chairs represent the edge of the court and the speakers are positioned as if they are players each side of a virtual net. He has developed this fast-paced approach with different phases where the boys begin arguing as individuals with someone sat opposite, (along two long rows of seats), they then swop seats and discuss their views with another student and then they move again and exchange views with a third person. This means that through their discussions they rehearse debating Macbeth's character from different perspectives (and the influences on his actions) related to different acts and scenes in the play.

Consider this final 'rally' where there are two opponents on the classroom tennis court:

Arlo: He's very confused by the witches coming and telling him all of this, and she [Lady Macbeth] says he should do this, he should do that. and if he gets there every time he should think back, 'I should not do it?' She tells him, screw your courage, you have no courage. Remember [though] he's a brave warrior who fights.

Dean: His wife just bullies him. It's his own fault. He should know that he is wrong.

Mr Beadle praises the two boys for articulating alternate perspectives regarding Macbeth motives to kill the King. He then invites the two boys to continue with their verbal rallies. Arlo reflects further on the role of being King and that particular actions are guided by God and determine his destiny. However, Dean argues from a religious perspective suggesting that as an individual person Macbeth knows it is wrong and he could have rebuffed Lady Macbeth's suggestion. He continues by explaining that killing means he (MacBeth) may go to hell.

Knowledge about the plot to kill the King that develops between Macbeth and his wife are made more explicit through the discussion. Each boy's views are articulated through the 'rallying' discussions that Mr Beadle mediates. What is evil and good, wrong and moral in thoughts and actions are considered through the verbal exchanges emerging to communicate the pros and cons of Macbeth killing the King. The teacher's practice involving scaffolding (for argument tennis) brings about purposeful dialogic exchanges that encourage students inter-mental processes to be made explicit and apparent for the rest of the group. In this excerpt, Arlo and Dean make available for others in their class their understanding of Macbeth. The teacher also encourages and reinforces what is salient to help learners make sense of what has been made available regarding the play plot.

The teacher's practice models for the students how to use words that have precise and unique meanings, meanings that are 'fully encoded in language forms' (Minick, 1996: 355). The teacher affords active opportunities for the students to participate in deliberating over interpretations and meanings so that they are able to think and mentally act. Mr Beadle is metaphorically a *guide* too. His kind of 'contingent' guidance in dialogue, through interaction with agents of the culture (the teacher as English expert), enables intellectual growth from the outside in (Bruner 1996).

As explained in Chapter 4, language is useful for learning in many ways. It can represent or 'label' things, it can convey how different entities are thought about and it can be used to argue about alternate meanings and interpretations of objects and processes. In this case, the teacher scaffolded the dialogic exchanges to extend individual's ZPD concerned with understanding how and why Macbeth kills the King (and the consequences thereafter).

Having considered the various ways that different kinds of argumentative dialogue have been generated between peers (as well as teacher and pupil), this final construal offers an example of a more physical metaphoric scaffold, that of verbal exchanges alternating across a virtual tennis court, supporting social interaction. In this way, the teacher has included more explicitly the use of 'signs', including gestures and language to support learners engaging in social interactions to learn. The teacher has also drawn on the metaphor of arguing as a tennis match to signal that he intends the students should 'bat' around ideas and consider suggestions from other polemic perspectives. In engaging his students to think about why (and how) Macbeth (or others) became responsible for killing the King, he signals how verbal exchange is important, and he intends the boys should feel more confident, to respond to his expectations regarding speaking, listening and participating in active discussions about the main protagonist in the story.

Although the play is formal in the way it is written by Shakespeare, the National Curriculum suggests that students should speak confidently and effectively in their *language use and meaning, using role, tone and action to add impact*. The metaphor of a tennis match generating a very energetic, inter-active and somewhat combative setting appears to be one that the teacher feels is appropriate to mediate invaluable argumentative exchanges between his students.

SUMMARY

This chapter has described how different kinds of practice in classrooms can frame and directly shape the nature and extent of social interaction that influences the development of individual and collective ZPDs and learning in science, mathematics and English. The various narrative construals serve to illustrate a range of concepts associated with social constructivism (see Table 9.4), through interactive exchanges, including dialogue, that are purposely supported and scaffolded for.

Table 9.4 A Summary of the Nature of Practice, Interactions and Social Constructivism Demonstrated Across the Narrative Construals

Narrative Construals	Nature of Practice	Nature of Interaction(s)	Nature and Extent of ZPD
Interactive consideration of perspectives in science	Providing stimulating material to be thought about, questioned and discussed so that collective thinking is developed.	Asymmetrical between teacher (experienced other) and pupils (novices).	Involving all learners in class through extended dialogic exchanges in the collective ZPD.
Scaffolding mathematical conversations	A range of practice, from whole class exchanges to small groups and pairs, deciding how they could solve problems and reach a collective resolution.	Asymmetrical between teacher and pairs of classmates.	Extended from pairs and triads generating small auras of socialness to then a whole class ZPD.
Deliberating about computers and books	Teacher provided the framing for the debate. Proposed motions considered from alternate perspectives for individuals to reach decisions.	Classmates either present or listen, question and vote.	Interactions scaffolded to develop ZPD to involve whole class (debaters, listeners, questioners, voters).
Arguing about Macbeth	Teacher provides tennis metaphor scaffold. Students consider Shakespearean play, Macbeth, from juxtaposed perspectives.	Co-ordinated argumentation: For and against Macbeth killing the King.	ZPD extended to involve whole class. All students involved, collectively and in turn.

ADDITIONAL READING

Adhami, M. Johnson, D. & Shayer, M. (1998) *Thinking Maths*. Accelerated learning in mathematics. Oxford: Heinemann.

Chappell, K. & Craft, A. (2011). Creative learning conversations: producing living dialogic spaces. *Educational Research*, 53(3), 363-385. This article discusses creative learning conversations as a way of contributing to change and moving education towards a future fit for the 21st century.

Knapp, N. F. (2018) The shape activity: Social constructivism in the psychology classroom. *Teaching of Psychology*, 46(1), 87-91. This interesting article discusses how social constructivist processes differ between geometry, physical education and art students given the same task to engage with.

Round, R. & McPhail, G. (2019) Using music: From spontaneous to scientific concepts in the primary school writing classroom. *International Journal of Education and the Arts*, 20(5), 1-25. This paper discusses ways that creative higher order conceptual thinking, exemplifying Vygotskian ideas, is supported.

REFERENCES

Alexander, R. (2018) Developing dialogic teaching: Genesis, process, trial. *Research Papers in Education*, 33(5), 561-598. https://doi.org/10.1080/02671522.2018.1481140

Ball, S., Maguire, M. & Braun, A. (2011) *How Schools do Policy*. London: Routledge.

Baskerville, D., McGregor, D. & Bonsall, A. (2023) Re-thinking theorising about the use of drama, Theatre and performance in learning science. In D. McGregor & D. Anderson (Eds) *Learning Science through Drama*. Cham, Switzerland: Springer.

Bauersfeld, H. (1992) Classroom cultures from a social constructivist's perspective. *Educational Studies in Mathematics*, 23(5), 467-481.

Beck, S. (2016) How we learn. In Qvortrup, A., Wiberg, M., Christensen, G. & Hansbol, M. (Eds) *On the Definition of Learning*. Campusvej: University Press of South Denmark, p. 55.

Billingsley, B. & Chappell, K. (2024) *The Future of Knowledge: The Role of Epistemic Insight in Interdisciplinary Learning*. London: Bloomsbury.

Blumer, H. (1969) *Symbolic Interactionism: Perspective and Methods*. Englewood Cliffs, NJ: Prentice Hall.

Bruner, J. (1996) *The Culture of Education*. Cambridge, MA: Harvard University Press.

Cobb, P. & Bauersfeld, H. (Eds.) (1995) The emergence of mathematical meaning. *Interaction in Classroom Cultures*. Hillsdale, NJ: Lawrence Erlbaum.

DfE (2014) *National Curriculum in England: English Programmes of Study*. Updated 16 July 2014. Available at https://www.gov.uk/government/publications/national-curriculum-in-england-english-programmes-of-study/national-curriculum-in-england-english-programmes-of-study#key-stage-3

DfE (2015) *National Curriculum in England: Science Programmes of Study*. Updated 6 May 2015. https://www.gov.uk/government/publications/national-curriculum-in-england-science-programmes-of-study/national-curriculum-in-england-science-programmes-of-study

DfE (2016) *National Curriculum for English*. Available at https://www.gov.uk/government/collections/national-curriculum. Accessed 03/03/25.

DfE (2021) *National Curriculum in England: Mathematics Programmes of study*. Available at https://www.gov.uk/government/publications/national-curriculum-in-england-mathematics-programmes-of-study/national-curriculum-in-england-mathematics-programmes-of-study. Accessed 03/03/25.

Erduran, S. & Jimenez-Aleixandre, J.M. (2012) Research on argumentation in science education in Europe. In D. Jorde & J. Dillon (Eds) *Science Education Research and Practice in Europe: Retrospective and Prospective*. Rotterdam: Sense Publishers, pp. 253-289.

Erduran, S., Osborne, J. F. & Simon, S. (2004) Enhancing the quality of argument in school science. *Journal of Research in Science Teaching*, 41(10), 994-1020.

Erduran, S., Ozdem, Y. & Park, J.-Y. (2015) Research trends on argumentation in science education: A journal content analysis from 1998-2014. *International Journal of STEM Education*, 2(5), 1-12.

Farmer, D. (2011). *Learning Through Drama in the Primary Years*. Drama Resource.

Ford, M. J. (2012). A dialogic account of sense-making in scientific argumentation and reasoning. *Cognition and Instruction*, 30(3), 207-245. https://doi.org/10.1080/07370008.2012.689383

Hennessy, S., Kershner, R., Cacagni, E. & Ahmed, F. (2021) Suppporting practitioner-led inquiry into classroom dialogue with a research-informed professional learning resource: A design-based approach. *Review of Education*, 9(3). https://doi.org/10.1002/rev3.3269

Jacobs, J., Scornavacco, K., Harty, C., Suresh, A., Lai, V. & Sumner, T. (2022) Promoting rich discussions in mathematics classrooms: Using personalized, automated feedback to support reflection and instructional change. *Teaching and Teacher Education 112*. https://doi.org/10.1016/j.tate.2022.103631

Jesson, R., Fontich, X. & Myhill, D. (2016) Creating dialogic spaces: Talk as a mediational tool in becoming a writer *International Journal of Educational Research*, 80(3), 155-163.

Littleton, K. & Howe, C. (2010) (Eds) *Educational Dialogues. Understanding and Promoting Productive Interaction*. London: Routledge.

Littleton, K. & Mercer, N. (2013) *Interthinking: Putting Talk to Work*. London: Routledge.

Lord, P., Dirie, A., Kettlewell, K. & Styles, B. (2021) *Evaluation of Philosophy for Xhildren: An Effectiveness Trial*. Educational Endowment Fund. Available at https://ripe-tomato.org/wp-content/uploads/2021/03/philosophy_for_children_report_-_final_-_pdf.pdf. Accessed 03/03/25/.

Macagno, F. (2022) Coding relevance. *Learning, Culture and Social Interaction. 36* https://doi.org/10.1016/j.lcsi.2019.100349

McGregor, D. (2021) Stories from History: More Authentic ways of thinking through acting and talking about science. In P. White, J. Rachel & K-V Cuylenburg (Eds) *Science and Drama: Contemporary and Creative Approaches to Teaching and Learning*. Cham: Springer.

McGregor, D. & Anderson, D. (2023) *Learning Science through Drama. International Perspectives*. Cham, Switzerland: Springer.

McGregor, D. & Duggan, A. (2016) *Empowering Learners through a Dramatic Enquiry*. University of Leeds: British Educational Research Association Annual Conference. Accessed 14/9/16.

McGregor, D. & Precious, W. (2015) *Dramatic Science. Inspired Ideas for Teaching Science Using Drama Ages*. London: Routledge, pp. 5-11.

Mercer, N. (2000) *Words and Minds: How We Use Language to Think Together*. London: Routledge.

Mercer, N. (2008) Three kinds of talk. Available at https://thinkingtogether.educ.cam.ac.uk/resources/5_examples_of_talk_in_groups.pdf Accessed 26/3/19.

Mercer, N. & Hodgkinson, S. (2009) *Exploring Talk in School*. London: SAGE.

Minick, N. J. (1996) Teachers' directives: The social construction of "literal meanings" and "real worlds" in classroom discourse. In S. Chaiklin & J. Lave (Eds) *Understanding Practice Perspectives on Activity and Context*. New York: Cambridge University Press.

Newton, P., Driver, R. & Osborne, J. (1999) The place of argumentation in the pedagogy of school science. *International Journal of Science Education*, 21(5), 553-576.

Noisy Classroom (2021) *Computers Are Better than Books*. Available at https://www.youtube.com/watch?v=Hz8i_dTEeC8 Accessed 30/7/24.

Osborne, J. (2004) Ideas, evidence and argument in science. In *In-service Training Pack, Resource Pack and Video*. London: Nuffield Foundation.
Osborne, J. (2007) Science education for the twenty first century. *Eurasia Journal of Mathematics, Science and Technology Education*, 3(3), 173-184.
Osborne, J., Erduran, S. & Simon, S. (2004) Enhancing the quality of argument in school science. *Journal of Research in Science Teaching*, 41(10), 994-1020.
Planas, N., Morgan, C. & Schütte, M. (2021) *Classroom Research on Mathematics and Language*. London: Routledge.
Rapanta, C. & Christodoulou, A. (2019) Walton's types of argumentation dialogues as classroom discourse sequences. *Learning Culture and Social Interaction*, 36(1). https://doi.org/10.10 16/j.lcsi.2019.100352
Rapanta, C. & Felton, M. (2022) Learning to argue through dialogue: A review of instructional approaches. *Educational Psychology Review*, 34, 477-509.
Resnick, L. B., Asterhan, C., Clarke, S. & Schantz, F. (2018) Next generation research in dialogic learning. In G. E. Hall, L. E. Quinn & D. M. Gollnick (Eds) *Wiley Handbook of Teaching and Learning*. Wiley-Blackwell, pp. 323-338.
Schillings, M., Roebertson, H., Sevelberg, H. & Dolmas, D. (2018) A review of educational dialogue strategies to improve academic writing skills. *Active Learning in Higher Education*. https://doi.org/10.1177/1469787418810663
Schutte, M., Friesen, R. A. & Jung, J. (2019) Interactional analysis: A method for analysing mathematical learning processes in interactions. In G. Kaiser & N. Presmeg (Eds) *Compendium for Early Career Researchers in Mathematics Education, ICME- 13*. https://doi.org/10.1007/978-3-030-15636-7_5
Seleznyov, S., Adhami, M., Black, A. Hodgen, J. & Twiss, S. (2021) Cognitive acceleration in mathematics education further evidence of impact. *Education*, 3(5), 1-13.
Sfard, A. (2008) Thinking as communicating: Human development, the growth of discourses, and mathematizing. *Mind, Culture and Activity*, 8(1), 42-76. https://doi.org/10.1017/CBO9780 511499944
Simon, S., Erduran, S. & Osborne, J. (2006) Learning to teach argumentation: Research and development in the science classroom. *International Journal of Science Education*, 28(2-3), 235-260.
Taber, K. (2019) Constructivism in education: Concepts, methodologies, tools, and applications. https://doi.org/10.4018/978-1-5225-7507-8.ch015
Teachers TV (n.d.) *A Lesson from the Best*. Available at https://www.youtube.com/watch?v=aSebl8X0ZlU
Toulmin, S. (1958) *The Uses of Argument*. Cambridge: Cambridge University Press.
Vygotsky, L. S. (1978) *Mind in Society. The Development of Higher Psychological Processes*. Cambridge, MA: Harvard University Press.
Vygotsky, L. S. (1981) The genesis of higher mental functions. In J. V. Wertsch (Ed) *The Concept of Activity in Soviet Psychology*. Armonk, NY: Sharpe.
Wood, D., Bruner, J. S. & Ross, G. (1976) The role of tutoring in problem solving. *Journal of Child Psychology and Child Psychiatry*, 17, 89-100.

10
CLASSROOM CASES FEATURING ASPECTS OF SOCIOCULTURALISM

CONTENTS

Introduction	235
Mathematical Ways of Working	236
Thinking Historically in a Secondary Classroom	239
Appropriating Ways of *Being* a Technological Scientist	243
Activating Agency in a Community Science Project	250
A Different Cultural Norm in the Forest School	252
Summary	257
Further Reading	258
References	258

Chapter Aims

After reading Chapter 10, you will have considered:

- how the sociocultural theory of learning and associated concepts can be used as 'tools' to think about the ways that policy and practice influence learning;
- the ways in which practice extends opportunities to develop sociocultural dimensions of learning;
- ways in which practice positions learners for learning;
- the extent to which dialogue, thought and action are interrelated when learning socially;
- how identity and agency are related and opportunities for development can be afforded by the teachers;
- ways that a classroom, group or community culture influences how mind as distributed emerges;
- ways that learning within and beyond the classroom can extend experiences of learning that are sociocultural in nature;
- how a teacher as a *sherpa, tourist guide or even co-adventurer* offers ways of thinking about the influence of practice in a sociocultural perspective.

INTRODUCTION

As considered in Chapter 6 (and earlier), the relational views of learning, pedagogy and knowledge in a sociocultural perspective of learning are more complex than social constructivism. As Rogoff (2003: 37) explains, 'human development is a process in which people transform through their ongoing participation in cultural activities, which in turn contribute to changes in their cultural communities across generations'. It therefore involves teachers whose pedagogy appreciates the ways that learners need to participate in practice themselves, generates opportunities for all to contribute and recognises how activity can afford positions that learners can take up, which in turn enable emergence of their agency and identity, which in turn influences the culture within which they learn. From a sociocultural perspective, then, teachers need to understand what is salient to learners as they 'engage in activity and develop competence in the practice in question' (Hall et al. 2008: ix). In a school context, pedagogy is concerned with three interrelated aspects of the curriculum: what is specified (that policy directs should be taught or learnt, such as the National Curriculum programme of study); the curriculum as it is enacted by the teacher's practice; and how their (the teacher's) enactment determines learner's experience of the curriculum. In this theorisation of learning, context and interaction, activity, agency and identity are all important concepts. As introduced to you in earlier chapters, context is more than just the subject matter to be studied, interaction extends beyond intersubjectivity and agency and identity emerge through participation rather than being assumed to be innate. The complexity of moments in practice that demonstrate different ways teachers provide affordances that offer opportunities for learners to develop trajectories along each of these dimensions is necessarily interrelated. However, narrative construals are presented here to indicate how some of the concepts within the sociocultural perspective of learning are enacted and could be further developed in:

- Mathematical ways of working
- Thinking historically in a secondary classroom
- Appropriating ways of being a technological scientist
- A different cultural norm in the forest school (FS)

MATHEMATICAL WAYS OF WORKING

In Chapter 5, you were introduced to the features of Lampert's (2009) teaching that she regularly practised in her mathematics classroom. She describes how teaching can be understood as a 'collection of practices' (p. 25). The collection of practices supporting a sociocultural way of working can include a range of practical actions or things that teachers do 'rather than what they think or know' (Lampert 2009: 23). This resulted in her 10-year-old students becoming enculturated into adopting particular routines or ways of interacting (both dialogic and actional) with each other. A particular goal for her practice was to extend or afford opportunities for her learners to develop ways of working that valued mathematical reasoning and problem-solving abilities. Outlined in Chapter 5 are three regular features of the mathematical activity she deliberately aimed to nurture. These included the students thinking about and being able to discuss with peers, the 'conditions' or assumptions made in mathematical problems; the 'conjectures' that were plausible, making them explicit for others to evaluate; and 'revision' of conjectures informed through dialogue with others. These three processes become an integral part of the *classroom culture* as indicated by the frequent and regular use of these practices by both the teacher and the students. She also guided them to working regularly in groups of four and adopt particular interactive practices that were inclusive and productive in these mini-communities. In supporting inclusivity, Lampert was concerned with developing a 'wider lens' that taught 'to difference'. She had previously taught about fractions and recognised that the following topic needed to accommodate students of all skills and different levels of understanding. She already knew that she had some students who needed special help in learning English as a second language, reading and general mental ability. However, with no special needs support available, she decided to adopt a problem-based approach to teaching the whole class mathematics.

Task 10.1

Lampert (Lampert 2009: 369) presented the following problem to her class of 10-year-old students.
Suppose you know that there are 23 classes of students at Kellogg School, and suppose you walked into the third grade and counted 28 in that class.

1. How many students would you think there were in the whole school?
   Experiments: (Draw a diagram if it will help you think about this)
   Conjecture:
   Reasoning:
2. Now suppose you walked into a first grade room, and there were 17 students in that class. Would you change your mind about how many students were in the whole school?
   Experiments:
   Conjecture:
   Reasoning:
3. If you could look into one other classroom to refine your estimate about how many students were in the class, which one would you want to look into? Why?

The ways that this teacher has enculturated her class to engage in mathematical discourse was introduced to you in Chapter 5. If you were to enact 'teacher as a *sherpa*', what would characterise your practice here? How would you ensure *all* the students successfully participated in mathematical dialogue (experiments, conjecture and reasoning) to think about the tasks above? What would 'doing mathematics' look like in this classroom where the social norms of interaction support collaboration? What kind of dialogue would you anticipate and how would you position the students to learn mathematics?

...and finally, how does the nature of learning appear to differ here when contrasting the narrative construal of Ms Ramen's mathematical lesson, for example, where the teacher metaphor aligned more to that of a *watchmaker* or *parent bird*, described in Chapters 2 and 9.

Characterising Ms Lampert as a *'Tourist Guide'* in This Episode

Lampert notes how she reviews her students' 'accomplishments' and considers their 'diverse and unstable levels of performance' before deciding how to go about her teaching. She considers the measures she has made of students' capabilities (through quizzes or tests), and she also reflects that she should learn from her experiences and 'take a retrospective look at what I had done so far about differences and how students responded'. Just as a *tourist guide* might ask about travellers' previous experiences of the locality and the things they have done there, what they thought and what they liked. Ascertaining such information demonstrates taking account of prior experiences of participants about to embark upon a new venture.

Involving all the Students

However, Lampert does not explicitly describe how she acted as a teacher to support the students' learning through solving these particular problems. She has already enculturated them in using notebooks to jot down their thinking about problems posed, then listen to others' explaining their thinking and revise their jottings as appropriate. As described in Chapter 5, they engage in discursive practices (annotating their jottings) that involve recognising 'conditions' or assumptions in a problem, producing 'conjectures' about possible lines of enquiry and then 'revising' the propositions in light of discussion with others. As Lampert reflects, 'this series of problems engendered broad participation and at the same time brought out more different kinds of mathematical performance' (Lampert 2009: 369). She noted in her reflective journal the varied resolutions her students generated, and she explained how one trio of girls generated a visual representation of the problem – a map of 23 classrooms; they speculated that there were 28 pupils in each room and then added up the total number of pupils in the school. Several others indicated how they worked out their solution differently, some by taking 28 ('number of kids in one classroom visited') and multiplied it by 23 ('number of classrooms').

What Would 'Doing Mathematics' Look Like?

In thinking about how to group students to participate in the mathematics class, Lampert (2009: 374) considers encouraging students from very different backgrounds to collaborate to solve problem. She notes that three boys, one deemed 'gifted and talented', another from a different school that followed a contrasting mathematics programme and a third who was quiet with a low reading level, working effectively together. She describes how 'their collaboration brought a new and interesting aspect of the mathematics of fractions to the class. And because each boy needed to learn something different, this was an efficient way to teach them, together'.

Given another task where the students are thinking further about fractions, the routinised way that they articulated their conjectures for sharing with others and engaged in dialogue about each other's assertions was also noted by Lampert. She recollected how a 'mix of ideas' were forthcoming from students because she had not 'grouped the class according to how they performed on the quiz'. She was also surprised by a particular student, Donna, who did not perform well in the quiz and rarely contributed to class debates. However, the task affordances enabled her to 'make a statement accompanied by reasoned evidence about why a particular assertion could not make sense'. It appeared she was able to 'see herself in a more complicated way, and other students were able to regard her differently too' (Lampert 2009: 376). Through participation in the classroom activity, a new dimension of Donna's identity emerged.

Dialogue and Positioning the Students to Learn Mathematics

The teacher, Lampert, successfully positioned students to engage with each other in thinking about mathematical problems collectively by providing problems to solve, which each pupil could relate to, and successfully communicate about to the others to share their thinking (and make available their mental resources). In this way, the zone of proximal development (ZPD) was distributed around the class, that is/ the collective thinking, or mind (Cobb 1999: 135) was extended (or distributed) beyond individual students.

Contrasting the Teacher as a *Watchmaker* or *Sherpa*

In Chapter 7, the mathematics teacher, Ms Ramen, is the controller of what is to be learnt and she tightly orchestrates what the students say and do at specific moments. The drill-and-practice approach is designed to increase students' rapidity of recall. The intention is to ensure that as many learners as possible can recite on demand what the teacher determines they must commit to memory.

In contrast, in Ms Lampert's mathematics lesson considered here, she opens with problems that can be solved in varied ways, she interacts with different groups of pupils, at different levels according to their needs. She often responds to queries with further questions or prompts or engages other students in the dialogue regarding different conjectures, reasoning and revisions of ideas or propositions.

In adopting an approach that presents an open problem, the students can work collaboratively. Lampert extends affordances that can be responded to in differential ways. This generates opportunities for all the students to participate in mathematical practices that enable individual appropriation of mathematical processes and outcomes.

THINKING HISTORICALLY IN A SECONDARY CLASSROOM

Another study, like Lampert's, where a practitioner explored a different approach to teaching is Mr Bird (Bird 2012). He took an action research approach (McNiff et al. 2003) with a sociocultural perspective (Bird 2012: 77) to consider the impact of his changed practice on his students' learning. As a secondary history teacher, he explored how his practice might be developed to reflect the more spontaneous and emergent learning he had observed in other teacher's drama lessons. He reviewed his practice and then set about generating opportunities for his students to become more involved with historical subject matter, see history as a series of ways of thinking and steer students to talk and act more as competent historians. He intended that his students should be afforded opportunities to deeply examine historical data (from Domesday 1066 survey data), engage in dialogic exchanges with each other about it and in doing so reify how they were interpreting, evaluating and synthesising evidence.

Task 10.2

In reading the following construal of Mr Bird's practice in teaching secondary history students the 'Domesday Unit', consider what he does to position the students to think like historians. Also consider how he affords his students opportunities to interpret, evaluate and synthesise historical evidence. To what extent does it appear the students are enculturated into thinking and talking like historians?

In introducing the Domesday unit to the class, Bird asks the students what kinds of questions might they ask about the document if they wished to verify it as a valid source for historians. The kinds of questions different pupils asked included (Bird 2012: 118): 'When was it written?', 'Who wrote it?', 'How old is it?', 'What is it written about?', 'Why was it written?', 'Why is it called Domesday?' and 'How are you going to read it?'.

He provided copies of some entries about the local area in the Wirral (where his school was located); however, despite the named places located in close vicinity, many students did not recognise the names. One student asked about 'Thurstaston', whereas another wanted to know what 'Caldy' was. Other words in the Domesdays entries were also asked about, including: 'hide', 'wapentake', 'waste', 'rider' and 'smallholders'. Other questions that arose in this introductory lesson were 'Why are the common places underlined?', 'What does the Domesday book have to do with the Wirral?' and 'Is it a whole book of everyone's taxes?'.

Bird then introduces an extract from Domesday about the town of Wallasey. It provides information about Robert of Rhuddlan who lived in Wallasey. It also provided information about the land and other things he owned, such as hides, number of ploughs and his small holders. The students verbally share their understandings and dialogically exchange views about what they think these things mean in order to make sense of the information introduced to them in the form of Domesday entries. They begin to compare data (number of hides, ploughs, etc.) for different landowners (e.g. Thurstaston and William Duke of Normandy) and what that means in mediaeval times. In doing so, the students begin to use the Domesday discourse. In developing their thinking and historical dialogue further, Mr Bird invites them to think about the different forms that a rebellion might take in Mediaeval times against William the Conqueror, who was the Norman King of England, who intended on taxing landowners to raise income. This following brief dialogic excerpt (Bird 2012: 122) demonstrates the nature of discussion that takes place about a possible rebellion.

Tom: Refuse to work

Mr Bird: What's that called?

Girl: Standing up to them

Mr Bird: Good. Refusing to work. Standing up to your leaders. What is that called? Strike

Boy: Yes strike there is another word for it though? Beginning with R - means kind of the same thing but with a bit more violence involved? Revolt

Mr Bird: Excellent - yes a revolt or rebellion. What does that mean? What could peasants do if they went on a rebellion. Some Norman knights turn up you are thrown off your land and you are fed up with that what can you do?

Boy: Plan an assassination

Mr Bird: Yes plan to murder him or assassinate him. Yes.

Steve:	You could try and find out who feels the same way and raise some sort of army.
Mr Bird:	Ok Good. Mike, pay attention what are we talking about?
	We are talking about what peasants might do if they lose their land.
	And what specifically are we saying now about what they can do?
Paul:	They could go on a rebellion?
Mr Bird:	Right good! Well done. Anything else peasants might be able to do?
Mike:	They could stop working?
Mr Bird:	They could stop working. And of course people might starve, Martha?
Chloe:	You know 'cos Paul said like have all peasants together. But they frown their own food and like...
Mr Bird:	True so what are you trying to say?
Martha:	If they stopped working then peasants wouldn't have food for themselves.
Mr Bird:	Oh I see, They can't really stop working otherwise they are going to starve so they are in a bit if a bind aren't they.
Chloe:	Couldn't they just poison the food because they all eat from the food the peasants make and they could just poison it?

Later in the unit after further familiarisation with data entries, Mr Bird scaffolds an activity that requires the students to compare information from the Domesday data about different landowners. He provides them with a table in which they can record what they find out about the number of hides, ploughs, peasants and their value in 1066 and (twenty years later in) 1086. The activity was intended to provide practice in collecting data that mapped the location of manors and whether their relative values increased or decreased between 1066 and 1086. The data they collected demonstrated how the value of seven Manors in the Wirral were worth significantly less 20 years later (in 1086) after the first Domesday data was collected in 1066. Immersed in discussing these key features noted in the Domesday entries, the students appropriated very specific terminology regarding the data collected by William I and what they thought it meant. Later in the unit, the students were asked about their understandings about what could have happened between 1066 and 1086 through reading the *Domesday Book* entries about the local areas they had become familiar with. They were organised to work together in small groups to present what they found out.

One group using Domesday data from three regions, Yorkshire, Wirral and around Hastings, compared the areas (manor name), who was (previous and) current land owner, the number of hides, peasants and the value in 1066 and how it changed by 1086. A question posed by one student indicated how she had interpreted that a previous landowner for one manor (in 1066) who had been replaced by King William (the Conqueror), like virtually all the others, could have become a peasant in 1086.

Like this group, all the others also presented what they found from scrutinising the Domesday entries to the rest of the class.

Positioning Students to Think Like Historians

As the Domesday unit progressed, Mr Bird offered different kinds of opportunities for his students to engage with historical data and participate in negotiating meanings about a range of entities related to mediaeval history. Initiating thinking about the origins and purpose of the *Domesday Book* introduced students to the mediaeval context of the classroom activity.

The activity considering the Domesday data differently afforded students opportunities to be active participants in constructing understandings about historical data. Mr Bird drew from Wiske (1999) and assumed a participative view of knowledge whereby the student's understanding could be defined as a 'performance' rather than a 'state of mind' (Wiske 1999: 237).

In seeking understanding through dialogue and working with others, there were many occasions for them to be more agentive (Bruner 1996) and even 'perform' as a historian by deploying intellectual tools that demonstrated how they interpreted, evaluated and synthesised Domesday data.

Enculturation Into Thinking and Talking Like Historians

Offering ongoing activity for *all* students to discuss and think about intriguing and salient information in the *Domesday Book* entries appears to enculturate them in considering what the data mean in a mediaeval context when William the Conqueror invaded England.

Lucy, particularly, in the final dialogic excerpts (above) indicated how she had appropriated the issue of English landowners living in manors who could be evicted by others after 1066.

Identity

Mr Bird questioned some of his students about the perspectives they developed about themselves and their learning as a result of the Domesday activity. The students themselves felt they developed competencies in history and appropriated historical ways of thinking, and through this process their identity has been transformed. The efficacy developed in scrutinising the mediaeval document improved their self-esteem and agency, that is, the confidence with which they could make assertions from the historical data.

Offering Affordances to Interpret, Evaluate and Synthesise Historical Evidence

Specific tasks and interactions with others (including the teacher) mediated the students thinking about mediaeval history, particularly what it meant for landowners and those working the land in the wake of William I invading England. The tasks ranged from initially considering what the *Domesday Book* represented and the information it contained to scrutinising aspects of the Domesday entries. Students then generated comparisons of data collected in 1066 and 1086 that involved students moving around the room to collect information from each other's data entries. This afforded dialogue and required 'asking questions', evaluating, 'expressing surprize and speculating' about the 'evidence they are gathering in the on-going activity' (Bird 2012: 126). All of the tasks culminated in collaborative presentations that offered students different ways of communicating what they had found out.

Practice that Promotes a Sociocultural Way of Working

Mr Bird had successfully enabled his students to interpret and 'see' what the data suggested about how mediaeval England had changed as a result of William I's reign.

He transitioned to a more exploratory style of practice. He guided the pupils across the Domesday data terrain, like a *sherpa*, who is an experienced leader knowing the geography of the area he is leading his travellers through. He realised that this involved a change in questioning technique that valued pupils' voice, strategies to explore their thinking and activities that positioned them as knowledgeable, and he also realising the discipline (history) as a set of social practices rather than a collection of abstract facts. He recognised he provided 'far more opportunities for dialogue' and afforded more opportunities for the students to be agentive through 'performances of understanding' which involved more frequent opportunities for group presentations.

APPROPRIATING WAYS OF *BEING* A TECHNOLOGICAL SCIENTIST

In this narrative construal, the nine- and ten-year-old pupils are engaged in thinking about the technological science of generating carriers that can be used to transport various objects. The whole class is purposively organised as a community of learners (Wenger 1998: 5) by their teacher, Ms Duggan. Similar to the mathematics and history class, the students are progressively introduced to a series of situations (Table 10.1) that allow them to consider salient information that is relevant to the final enquiry.

> **Task 10.3**
>
> What does Ms Duggan *say* and *do* to engage the students in social interaction *and* scientific practices? How is a collective culture generated? What kinds of affordances does she extend that invite them to *talk* and *act* agentively? How does she encourage them to engage collaboratively and participate as learners in a community of beginning or novice knowers thinking about science and technology?

The arena for this activity is a primary school. The setting involves the whole class participating in-role as technological scientists in the Victorian era (1837–1901). There were a series of distinct related tasks that offered ongoing activity and furthered in-depth thinking about technological science for the learners. The historical context for the participatory activity was drawn from the story of Mattie Knight (1838–1914) and her work involving designing and constructing the flat-bottomed brown paper bag. To prepare for the technological science enquiry, the following table (Table 10.1) outlines the participatory tasks engaged in to prepare for the experimentational element of the activity.

Materials and artefacts aligned with the Victorian period were made available for the students. The materials available for creating the carriers included hessian, string, cotton, needles, thread, gummed paper and brass split pins. The artefacts to be transported included books, boules, eggs and strawberries, all objects that might typically need to be carried from a store to home during that era. The five distinct tasks that the students engaged in, in small groups, within the whole class community were:

i Design an original carrier using materials available in the Victorian era that can be used to transport given artefacts, typical of that time;
ii Construct the carrier as designed in task i;
iii Devise tests that show the constructed carrier is 'fit for purpose';
iv Generate a presentation for the 'patent committee' that includes the drawn design and argues how the carrier is unique;
v Take up a role on the 'patent committee' to judge each other's designs and constructions of original carriers.

Table 10.1 A Summary of Ms Duggan's Practice Intended to Position the Students to Collectively Consider Working Like a Technological Scientist (In-role) in *as if* (Andersen 2004) Victorian Times

Sequence of Tasks	Teacher's Practice	Intended Positioning of the Learners
Introduction	Inviting the children who might help carry shopping home, in the Victorian era in a typically cone-shaped bag, to think about the issues of such a design. They are asked questions that focus their consideration of problems in packing heavy and light things together in the same carrier, carrying books, boule, soft fruit and/or eggs all the way home and then struggling to place them on a counter-top at home ready for unpacking without everything spilling out.	As technologists thinking about issues of a cone-shaped bag having a pointed end that can only be laid on its side. Consider possible (re)design of the cone-shaped bag used in the Victorian era.
i	Inviting the pupils to design a carrier (given Victorian era materials) to transport a particular object or artefact.	Collaborating technologists designing an original carrier to solve a 'real' problem.
ii	Inviting the pupils to construct (and amend design if needed) using materials made available for the carrier design generated in step ii.	Collaborating technologists transforming their design into a 'real' working object.
iii	Inviting the pupils to consider how they might 'test' whether the constructed carrier is 'fit for purpose' and can successfully transport the carried objects across the room.	Collaborating science technologists testing whether their constructed design 'really' works.

Table 10.1 A Summary of Ms Duggan's Practice Intended to Position the Students to Collectively Consider Working Like a Technological Scientist (In-role) in as if (Andersen 2004) Victorian Times *(Continued)*

Sequence of Tasks	Teacher's Practice	Intended Positioning of the Learners
iv	Inviting the pupils to generate a presentation (using the diagrammatic design document) that describes what their original design is and how it would work. They explain how their carrier is original, justify the use of the particular materials chosen for different parts of the carrier and demonstrate how it is 'fit for purpose'.	Collaborating science technologists presenting and explaining how their invention works, what is original about it and demonstrating how it is 'fit for purpose'.
v	Inviting the pupils (as patent committee members) to listen to presentations from each group that involves describing and justifying their original designs and demonstrating the successful carrying functionality. The patent committee members (as pupils in role) judge whether each groups' carrier is original and 'fit for purpose' before agreeing to award a 'patent' certificate.	As patent committee members listening to and then judging the originality, functionality and explanatory narratives of each group's invention.

Source: Adapted from McGregor (2016).

In each of the tasks outlined above, pupils work in small groups to collaboratively achieve the sequential steps. They assume working in role as scientific technologists and are oriented by the teacher, like a tourist guide, to participate in tasks i to v.

Task i: Interactional Exchanges Whilst Designing and Constructing the Carrier

Throughout the activity, the pupils collaboratively work together to design and construct their own unique carriers. They are challenged with deciding which materials are appropriate for which parts of their particular carrier, that is, whether they need to ensure eggs are not broken or strawberries are not squashed or boule spheres do not fall out of the bottom of the carrier.

As an excerpt from a group discussion below illustrates, the dialogue reflects the extent to which the pupils are negotiating with each other to create their original carrier to transport boules.

> Pupil 1: ...don't make it look like a normal bag...[referring to the diagram Pupil 3 has sketched] that doesn't look like a normal bag...so is that the inside [pointing inside]?
>
> Pupil 2: that's the walls
>
> Pupil 1: so that's one side

Pupil 3: yeah so this is the inside....and we have literally got to sew the inside
Pupil 1: so...
Pupil 3: ...and that thing on the in-side is ....[pointing]
Pupil 1: so make a hole...then
Pupil 2: take it up like this ... [pointing to where the hessian could be adhered] then carry on through the hole
Pupil 3: Yes
Pupil 1: ...and they can be like compartments on the side
Pupil 3: ...yes, just for extra storage
Pupil 2: Why
Pupil 3: well, so we can have different sections for different types of things
Pupil 1: there could be a big pocket
Pupil 2: so we need...
Pupil 3: there could be a pocket on the front
Pupil 1: okay so...[altering the sketched diagram]
Pupil 2: so we don't need that [crossing out a part of the sketch of the design plan]
Pupil 3: ...so slim things like paper? ...that we don't want crushed
Pupil 1: so we need...
Pupil 3: We need the sacking [...]
Pupil 1: A great idea...we need the card and the [gummed] paper...

The pupils challenged to develop a solution to the problem of designing and constructing a carrier that can transport heavy boules are positioned as potential technological scientists. In generating a design and then transforming it to a material object, that they then test out (to see if it can carry boules across the room), they are demonstrating 'performing their understanding'. All the other triads in the class do the same, but they design and create carriers for different artefacts such as eggs, strawberries, books or shoes. There are 11 different varieties of carriers designed and produced.

In keeping with the Mattie Knight story, the pupils are invited to engage in the role as technological scientists creating something original that could potentially be awarded a patent (like Mattie Knight in the United States). To achieve their patent award, the pupils have to explain why they designed the carrier they way they did, explain how it works, what the functions are of each material and then demonstrate it can successfully transport the object it was designed for by physically carrying it across the room.

Task iv: Explaining Their Designs and Demonstrating That the Carrier Is Fit for Purpose

Working in-role as technological scientists, the triads 'present' their unique prototype plan of their carrier to the rest of the class who assume roles as patent committee members. The teacher explains to the patent committee members that their role is to judge whether each groups' artefacts, designs and justifications are good enough to achieve an award. This again is in keeping with the Mattie Knight narrative, resonating with her presenting her machine designs for patenting, to US committees in 1868).

Ms Duggan: Scientists explain your designs to the patent committee. Patent committee be ready with your questions.

The group of three pupils hold up their carrier design.

Pupil 1: We made our bag for the French boule game

Pupil 2: If you lost the box or someone sold you it without the case, you could just put them in this bag, and then they will roll around in the bag and then you can just take them out and play with them

Pupil 3: This is our design, no one else's

Pupil 1: So we changed our plan a bit when we were actually making it because we realized it wouldn't be so strong if we used cotton for the handles, so we ended up using, erm, rubber bands like a new band [handle]. We used gummed paper to stick all the sides together....We were going to do sewing....but we didn't have the [brass] pins ....

Pupil 2: It was hard poking the needles through the cardboard

Pupil 1: Yeah

Task v: Questions From the Patent Committee

The students rapidly appropriate the way the patent committee works and three pupils (Pupil 4, Pupil 5 and Pupil 6) launch in with various questions, to the boule carrier design triad, about their original created object.

Pupil 4: How did you choose the materials?

Pupil 1: We thought that....the cardboard was the strongest material that that we had there

Pupil 3: If we used paper it would just tear ....

Pupil 2: Yea...shhhhhh [mimicking ripping sound]

Pupil 3: And the [boules would] fall straight through the paper ...and there was no other strong material, but...

Pupil 2: ...because

Pupil 1: Cotton was very expensive!

Pupil 5: What inspired you to make this carrier?

Pupil 1: Mattie inspired us to make this bag. We thought we should make one of our own.

Pupil 2: Yea, and...

Pupil 1: ...and its especially designed for the French boule game

Pupil 2: ...and...we thought of the uses for it and what the bags look like now and we tried to make something new...not like a normal bag

Pupil 6: If you had really heavy boules, wouldn't it smash down on the floor? ...and drag?

Pupil 1: We don't know yet if that would happen, but we tried not to make the handles too long

Pupil 2: Yeah

Interestingly, all 11 carriers are awarded, in turn, their patent certificates. Each carrier design was deemed 'original' and 'fit for purpose', that is, the 'patent committee' (the remainder of the class) agreed that each group's design and transportation testing (demonstrating the carrier could hold the object for at least a minute) in front of the committee were successful.

What Does the Teacher <u>Say</u> and <u>Do</u> to Engage the Students in Social Interaction and Scientific Practices?

The teacher invites the triads of students (as teams of technological scientists) to engage in collaborative problem-solving. Knowing there is no one 'correct' outcome, the challenge can be more engaging as it offers differential outcomes that all pupils can achieve at some level (as Lampert intended in her mathematics lesson outlined earlier).

Invited to think about how they might improve the Victorian cone-like carrier provided the pupils with a concrete affordance they could relate to.

How Is a Community and Technological Science Culture Generated?

Ms Duggan introduced the 'story' of Mattie Knight and invited the pupils to take up a role like her and rehearse how they might be technological scientists within the classroom arena. Provided with materials (split pins, needles, thread, sacking cloth, buttons, etc.) to create a carrier reminiscent of the Victorian era, the students were given a technological opportunity to practise as technical scientists. They practice designing, constructing and testing, the kinds of things that technologists and scientists do.

What Kinds of Affordances Does Mrs Duggan, the Teacher, Extend that Invites Them to Discuss and act Agentively?

Pupils encouraged to work in triads collaborating on a shared endeavour are likely to make available each others abilities and mental resources to succeed as a team of scientific technologists. Enabled to work independently but collaboratively on a specific task involving designing, constructing and testing a carrier extends many opportunities to appropriate how to be a young would-be scientific technologist. Jointly presenting their products requires them to rehearse what they have done, and explain how and why their design worked to the rest of the class. Facing their peers as the 'patent committee' affords another opportunity for joint social activity as they support each other in their presentation and explanatory story they need to provide to achieve their patency award. Questioning from the patent committee is initiated by Pupil 4, who asks about the choice of materials to construct the carrier. Responses are offered in turn by Pupils 1, 2 and 3. This clearly demonstrates they have collectively developed joint responsibility for their technological outcome claiming that the cardboard was the strongest material and that paper would just tear, making a ripping sound.

The dialogues that emerged between all triads as they designed, created and then defended their original carriers evolved as they practised questioning each other, constructing responses and articulating justifications at various points in their discussions.

How Does Ms Duggan Encourage Them to Engage Collaboratively and Participate as Learners in a Community of Beginning or Novice Knowers Thinking About Science and Technology?

All the above opportunities scaffolded for by the teacher combine to encourage active participation by all pupils to create carrier designs, collaboratively construct it, test it and then present the assessment to their peers. All the tasks i – v provide a scaffolded experience for the pupils to engage in ongoing activity that is purposeful, differentiated and achievable by all. As Rogoff (2008) describes, these groups had clearly worked at the personal, interpersonal and community levels and along the planes of apprenticeship, guided participation and even participatory appropriation.

Interviewing the pupils after this classroom experience, three reflections are shared here that indicate the collaborative and scientific nature of the activity they particularly emphasised:

Alice: We acted quite a bit like a scientist cos you had to draw a diagram and send it off and tell people what you needed and then you had to go and get all the stuff, maybe making a few trips back to get more things if you required or needed them and it got you thinking quite a bit – do I need that? Should I put this back? Do we actually need it?

Ted: It made me feel really good drawing our diagram and doing it because usually in science we will draw our diagram, get everything in place, everything we need, make it or half make it and suddenly we will move on to something else which can be quite annoying but here we actually got to finish it and that made me feel like a scientist.

Georgia: It made me feel like a scientist – especially at the end when we were describing what was our own design. It made me feel like everyone was a scientist.

As Calabrese Barton and Tan (2010: 189) describe, 'whether one focuses on the task, the resources, or the networks of individuals involved in [informal] learning settings, there is broad agreement that learning by guided participation or apprenticeship does not happen individually or instantaneously but in "social networks that collectively perform necessary tasks and cognitive work" (Nasir and Hand 2008: 144). Learning is an embodied activity that involves the ongoing re-creation of practices, roles and identities among individuals over time'.

ACTIVATING AGENCY IN A COMMUNITY SCIENCE PROJECT

As outlined in Chapter 6, Calabrese Barton and Tan (2010) investigated the processes and outcomes of a 'voluntary' year-long informal project that 10- to 14-year-olds (referred to as Youth) were involved in. The project was concerned with green energy technologies in a mid-western town in the United States. The group of 20 youths produced three video documentaries entitled, *We're Hot! What about you!*, *We be burnin'* and another one entitled *Where da heat Go?* from their dataset. They were alarmed that most of the people they interviewed for their project were unaware of the local Urban Heat Island (UHI) effect. They also

> espoused a confidence in their knowledge of UHIs and their abilities to act on that knowledge to make a difference. Their situating themselves as individuals who could create 'awareness' and 'educate' the unknowledged [brought] into focus the intersecting roles of knowledge and action critical to these boys' developing knowledge base and sense of self in science. (Calabrese Barton and Tan 2010: 188)

Task 10.4

Involved in a shared project, to what extent could students demonstrate their agency?
What and how might the various influences within their community impact on the emergence of their agency?
What kinds of information would you need to evidence development of their agency?

To consider how the students demonstrated agency through a sociocultural lens, it is appropriate to pay attention to 'what and how the individuals learnt through observation and guidance of knowledgeable others, allowing them to become fluent in the cultural practices of communities' (Calabrese Barton and Tan 2010: 188). To consider only what they do of their own free will neglects the social and contextual influences on agency. An individual's agency does not reside solely within individuals in a specific capacity (Biesta and Tedder 2007) but rather as an emergent enactment that arises as a result of the social, historical and cultural context that people find themselves in. In this case, the students working together on an informal environmental science project, the dynamics in play included the physical arena (Lave 1993) of the urban area and the immediate environment they were concerned with, as well as themselves and the other participants in the local community, and the ways that they could possibly envisage 'doing' something about the situation they were in. As relative novices, they were initially guided to think about their town and whether it was a UHI by asking the questions such as 'Where would you rather be on a hot summer day? Standing in the middle of a mall parking lot or under a shady tree?'

The ensuing debates extended what and how the science was talked about and investigated. The youth hypothesised about temperatures of different parts of the environment and carried out experimental investigations of different parts of the urban area (different buildings, roofs, vegetation, etc.) including indoor and outdoor places in the town. To investigate the UHI phenomena, the students used scientific equipment including temperature sensors, digital thermometers and laser tape devices.

The experienced researchers (as teachers) exercised agency in the way they made decisions about what to *say* and *do* to engage the youth and stir them into self-sustaining activity and action that emerged from and with the local environment. Teacher agency manifests in the ways in which enactments of practice are carried out (Priestley et al. 2015). In this case, this involves the interplay between the environment, the material resources made available and the ways the teachers interact socially with the youth.

Although the youth wished to produce video ethnographies as an outcome of this project, what emerged as a result of joint participation between them and the researchers were the three scientific documentaries. These documentaries reflected their curiosities and desires and involved interviews with each other and members of the wider community as well as data they had generated in the project. Producing the documentaries involved youth participating as interviewers, reporters, researchers, science investigators, film crew members, photographers, journalists, editors, etc. Data produced included images, figures and graphs they generated as well as aspects of youth culture involving IT media such as rap music, tracks with salient lyrics, etc.

The production of the three science documentaries required effective collaboration from the youth (included data-informed presentations; well-conducted and knowledgeable interviews with others'; the appropriation of pertinent music underlining the key messages of the videos).

These evidenced the ways that the Youth were allowed space to:

> take up new identities and practices for tackling [real world] questions [...]. By engaging in the knowledge, practices and identities in the tool of science in embodied ways, youth can also transform the worlds they traverse. [Agentively] they used knowledge, practice and context of science to develop their identities, to advance their positions in the world, and/or alter the world towards what they envision as being more just. (Calabrese Barton and Tan 2010: 195)

A DIFFERENT CULTURAL NORM IN THE FOREST SCHOOL

The use of FSs, at first glance, offers much potential to extend and situate learning beyond the classroom setting. As Waite and Goodenough (2018) indicate, it offers a unique arena for enactment of an alternate pedagogy. This is emphasised by Leather (2016: 1) who highlights the cultural, social and historical dimensions it can offer for education. McCree (2019: 6) explains how a woodland setting can offer learners opportunities to develop 'physical, social, cognitive, linguistic, emotional, social and spiritual' aspects of learning. In contrast to teaching that often prevails in school classrooms, the FS situates learning that is not focused on transferring uncontextualised abstract knowledge. The FS approach emerged and evolved as an adaptation from Scandinavia where the culture was quite different (Cree and McCree 2012: 3). Scandinavia was previously less industrialised and less populated and many more people worked the land. Families were generally more engaged with outdoor lifestyles. However, the transference of the Scandinavian FS cultural approach to the United Kingdom has not been wholly possible because there are limited local woodland spaces, current family lifestyles contrast starkly with those from farming communities and there is variable access to appropriate environmental resources for schools. Despite the challenges, however, many schools value the alternate educational experiences FSs can offer young children. The outdoors are a 'unique instructional setting' Orion and Hofstein (1994) and the 'Forest School programmes lead to different learning experiences and outcomes and the construction of qualitatively different kinds of knowledge to those offered by more formal learning spaces' (Garden and Downes 2023: 1). Arguably FSs are spaces where traditional teaching and learning roles are subverted, and 'familiar actors are required to construct new identities and practices' (Garden and Downes 2023).

The FS principles (McCree 2019: 5) embrace a long-term perspective of learning promoting progressive development over time. The learners are expected to be agentive in their play, explore and interact with the outdoor environment. Ongoing use of the woodland habitat is expected to be monitored to ensure the impact of visitors and their activities are not detrimental to the environment. This requires a collective and collaborative approach involving practitioners and learners to carefully manage usage to sustain an ecological balance. However, despite the potential for learning that involves sociocultural concepts (particularly the emergence of agency and identity of learners), McCree evidences that variation in FS contexts results in practice enactments that can significantly promote or curtail educative potential.

> ### Task 10.5
>
> Given a brief introduction to the philosophy of the FS above, what kind of practice would you anticipate supports learning in this contrasting environment to a school classroom?

> How would you anticipate the distinctly different cultural context might influence practice, especially as education is intended to be 'learner-centred' in the FS. What kinds of different influences come into play in this case on development of the learner's agency?
>
> Can you envisage where the teacher enacts the metaphor of a *tourist guide, sherpa* or *co-adventurer*?

Coates and Pimlott-Wilson (2019) investigated children's views of their learning experiences in FSs; they interviewed 33 children from two schools in the East Midlands area of England. Questioned about their views of the FS, children say they 'see' the FS as a very different setting to the school classroom. One child (Coates and Pimlott-Wilson 2019: 30) suggests that 'You have more choices at Forest School, so when you are at school you don't have any choice but you have to do the lesson; and then at Forest School you have a choice if you want to do it or if you don't want to do it', whereas another indicates that 'we can have a little adventure on our own without a teacher'. As Coates and Pimlott assert, the FS environment offers opportunities for children to make decisions and do what is novel for them.

Activity enables the development of creativity and problem-solving (Beresford 2022). The FS offers a learning space 'that is removed from the physical constraints of the classroom and the pedagogical constraints of the national curriculum to provide a more flexible and responsive environment' (Harris 2018: np) promoting 'physical literacy' and social skills such as 'conflict management and negotiation' (Beresford 2022: 15).

One child (Florence) in the Coates and Pimlott-Wilson (2019: 31) study explains 'it's quite different [from school] because we don't have to do working, maths, like we're doing maths but we're not writing it down anywhere. We needed to know how many ropes and tarps were needed if we were building our den and we needed to use maths for that. So, you're actually out playing while learning'. Although the children can 'see', there are opportunities to apply what they have learnt in the classroom, the physical and tactile nature of learning in the FS offers more context. As Mai articulates, 'you can explore the outer world and nature [at forest school] rather than, inside [the classroom] you can just look outside the window and not like touch the real-life stuff and inside you're like, in like a museum. You're not allowed to touch the real stuff. But you can be creative [in the Forest school] and make your own stuff outside and out of the stuff in nature' (Coates and Pimlott-Wilson 2019: 32). There are also many opportunities for collaborative working too, as Isobel explains 'Our whole group, we made a decision ... we all had one decision so we had, let's say if I wanted it [den] to have a roof that goes like that, like a house, I would have picked that and then Olly might have picked to have a tarpaulin on the floor. So we would all pick one thing and put it together so then it would make a super cool den!' (Coates and Pimlott-Wilson 2019: 35).

> **Task 10.6**
>
> Given the perspectives of 33 children questioned about their experience of FSs, and many of them indicating the unfettered nature of learning there, what would you anticipate the teacher's (or forest school leader's) practice would look like?

Martin-Millward (2020) collates the transcripts of 26 incidents or moments from observations of learning in FS settings. She discusses how these incidents are critical in the sense of 'the teacher's utterances influence the shape and tone of subsequent interaction [...] where alternative choices were available which might have challenged the pupils to engage in a higher level of literate thinking' (Martin-Millward 2020: 82). One such moment involved a forest school leader (FSL), Ms Flow, asking the children about collecting thin twigs for a fire that were not on a tree.

Owen: You have to find them off the floor

Ms Flow: Why do we have to find them off the floor?

Owen: Because it, um, you want the trees to keep on growing, um, if they

Ms Owen: So we want the trees to carry on growing, but what have trees got

inside them, that doesn't burn?

The Ms Flow's brief recognition of Owen's reply is emphasised, but she hasn't had the response she is looking for yet.

Jack:	Oxygen
Ms Flow:	No, oxygen, they haven't got oxygen inside them.
Ms Flow:	[reframing question] They've got a lot of something inside them.
Maya:	Is that water?

(Martin-Millward 2020: 151)

Maya appears to comprehend what Ms Flow is seeking and appropriately suggests the 'correct' reply. The FSL uses the response to explain from her perspective why twigs can't be broken from the trees to be used for a fire. This teacher's practice has limited what is made available for the children to think about as McCree suggests can happen. Rather than encouraging them all to explore the area and consider what might be useful for a fire or asking which materials they can find in the forest that would be good for burning, Ms Flow has narrowed the opportunities for learning. She specifies that thin twigs are needed for a fire and that snapping them off trees is not appropriate.

She directs learners' attention in a very specific way, and she does not discuss and have the children decide how to go about effectively collecting what is needed as a team. She truncates the dialogue and associated possibility thinking of the children. Consequently, there is a missed opportunity to develop a collective ZPD that could involve the whole community of children visiting the FS.

Other communications elicited (Martin-Millward 2020) between FSLs and their children ranged from conversations where the teacher was the authoritative controller of learning (as discussed in Chapters 2 and 7) to interactions where learners were positioned to be agentive (as considered in Chapters 3, 5 and 6). Looking for incidents that positioned children as active participants in the FS community of learners, there were fewer episodes demonstrating agency than anticipated. What is evident from this brief dialogic excerpt is that despite being located in a setting that potentially affords much to involve children in collective participatory learning, an FSL's practice can limit learners' agentive activity curtailing, too, development of their learner identity.

> ### Task 10.7
>
> How can the extent to which learners are afforded agency be determined? What do you need to know about the learning environment and the way in which an FSL's practice is enacted to judge whether practice is affording individuals to be more or less agentive? Consider the following excerpts from various reports of studies of learning in the FS environment. To what extent do artefacts appear to play a role in mediating learners' agency and identity?

Attwood (2010: 12) reported how the same fallen tree was interpreted in many different ways by the children visiting the FS. Initially the log was used as a shelter, then it was transformed to a car and finally a train with which children took turns 'driving'. On another occasion, a further fallen tree was adapted as a boat by a handful of children. They added rocks and sticks to act as 'controls'. Interestingly, the log also became a horse for other children in the group. The imaginative ways that the children collectively engaged with artefacts in the wooded environment arguably reflect the extent to which the setting of the FS afforded them agentive opportunities. Attwood (2010: 14) also notes how other objects found naturalistically in the FS setting afforded children the opportunities to 'create stone circles', experiment with rolling stones down different slopes and even initiate moving a log with a rope.

However, the practice of the FSL is not detailed. The kinds of particular practices that teachers could employ to promote learning that resonates with a more sociocultural experience are suggested in Figure 10.1. These suggestions are accrued from across Chapters 6 and 10. Despite these practices chiming clearly with aspects of the FS principles, detailed illustrations from the field are challenging to find (Table 10.2).

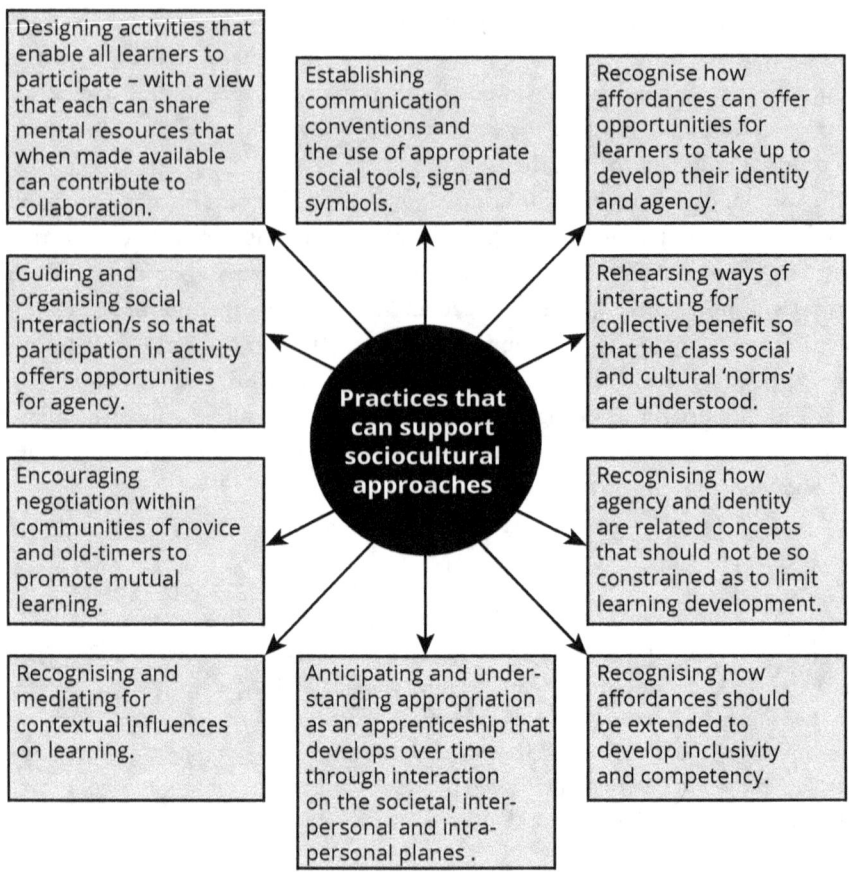

Figure 10.1 Repertoires in Teacher Practice That Enable More Participatory Activity in Learning Thought About as Sociocultural

Table 10.2 Summary of the Different Concepts That are Evident in the Narrative Construals of Aspects of Sociocultural Practice

Classroom Case	Nature of Sociocultural Practice	Nature of Knowing	Process of Learning
Mathematical ways of working	Presenting open tasks. Encouraging enculturated ways of working like mathematicians. Ensuring all students could demonstrate some level of competency.	Competency as a mathematician working out solution to a problem.	Collectively responding to tasks using cultural ways of working like a mathematician.
Thinking historically in a secondary classroom	Encouraging learners to engage in historical practices, particularly the disciplinary	Competency as evidenced through activity and discourse engaged in as a historian.	Collectively working in groups to make sense and communicate understandings to

Table 10.2 Summary of the Different Concepts That are Evident in the Narrative Construals of Aspects of Sociocultural Practice *(Continued)*

Classroom Case	Nature of Sociocultural Practice	Nature of Knowing	Process of Learning
	discourse, in various ways.		demonstrate appropriation.
Appropriating ways of *being* a technological scientist	Immersing learners to work in small groups on an enquiry with multiple outcomes.	Competency as evidenced through activity and discourse engaged in as a scientific technologist to achieve a patent.	Collectively working in groups to generate a solution to problem task and communicate how it was done to demonstrate appropriation.
A different cultural norm in the forest school	Offer opportunities for learners to explore and make sense of the forest environment in their own way.	Developing propositions, recognising how it is different to be in the outdoors.	Demonstrating agency and development of identity through engaging socially in interactive activity with others in the FS environment.

SUMMARY

In this chapter, you have considered various ways in which practice can promote (or even might constrain) sociocultural dimensions of learning within a mathematics, history, technological science and outdoor setting. In each of the narrative construals, different aspects of sociocultural dimensions of learning were brought to the fore. In mathematics, the ways that a teacher can extend opportunities for students to participate in mathematical practices and think like mathematicians (through offering conjectures, reasoning and revisions) were discussed. In history, students were afforded distinct collaborative opportunities to engage in historical discourse enabling critique of *Domesday Book* entries and in doing so were able to appropriate influences on life in mediaeval England. The construal also demonstrated how practice can influence the social, individual, collective and cultural dimensions of learning for learners. In a technological science context, students were shown to be able to act agentively to collectively design, construct and test their own original carriers. They were re-positioned during the activity to consider the extent to which their (and others') creations could have been potentially patented, and in doing so, they appropriated technological ways of being and acting. Finally, the outdoor setting of FSs was considered to explore some of the relational connections between setting, practice and learning. It was highlighted how there were differential opportunities for the participating learners to develop varied forms of agency and discipline-related identity. Potentially, the metaphor of teacher as *co-adventurer* is possible in a FS setting. Exploring, with no prior experience, of an unfamiliar woodland landscape, there is an opportunity for the learners to learn *with* the teacher. Encountering unknown natural artefacts but engaging in collective and symmetrical dialogue that welcomes all propositions, considerations and evaluations could immerse learner and teacher alike in developing a collective ZPD. Contrasting the ways that practice was enacted in these cases with earlier chapters highlighted the ways that a teacher as a *tourist guide, sherpa or co-adventurer* offers learners very different experiential ways of thinking, developing practices and competencies. It also provides illustrations of the ways practice can extend the social, cultural, historical, perceptual and cognitive dimensions of learning.

FURTHER READING

Curnow, J. & Jurow, A. S. (2021) Learning in and for collective action, *Journal of the Learning Sciences*, 30(1), 14-26. DOI: 10.1080/10508406.2021.1880189. This article discusses cognition as distributed, the nature and impact of material and social infrastructure.

Sfard, A. (2016) Ritual for ritual, exploration for exploration. Or, what learners are offered is what you get from them in return. In J. Adler & A. Sfard (Eds) *Research for Educational Change*. London: Routledge. This chapter explains the sociocultural perspective and emphasises explanatory talk and Bernstein's perspective of continuous evaluation.

Roth, W.-M. & Tobin, K. (2007) *Science, Learning, Identity. Sociocultural and Cultural-Historical perspectives*. Rotterdam, Netherlands: Sense Publishers. This book grounded in empirical situations introduces and discusses various dimensions of identity in science.

REFERENCES

Andersen, C. (2004) Learning in 'as if' worlds: Cognition in drama in education. *Theory into Practice*, 43(4), 281-286.

Attwood, J. (2010) *Exploring the Benefits of a Forest School Project in Twerton, Bath*. Accessed on 05/08/2021. Available at: https://docplayer.net/46463482-Exploring-thebenefits-of-a-forest-school-project-in-twerton-bath-summer-2010.html Accessed 13/2/24.

Beresford, K. (2022) *Exploring the Effectiveness of 'Forest School' on the Health and Development of Pre-school Aged Children*. Available at https://sphr.nihr.ac.uk/wp-content/uploads/2022/01/Katie-Beresford_Forest-Schools-Literature-Review.pdf. Accessed 13/2/24.

Biesta, G. J. J. & Tedder, M. (2007) Agency and learning in the life course: Towards an ecological perspective. *Studies in the Education of Adults*, 39, 132-149.

Bird, M. J. (2012). *Rethinking Formative Assessment from a Sociocultural Perspective: A Practitioner Investigation in a History Classroom*. The Open University: EdD thesis. Available at https://oro.open.ac.uk/49115/ Accessed 27/7/24.

Bruner, J. (1996) *The Culture of Education*. Cambridge, MA: Harvard University Press.

Calabrese Barton, A. & Tan, E. (2010) We be Burnin! Agency, identity and science learning. *The Journal of the Learning Sciences*, 19, 187-229.

Coates, J. & Pimlott-Wilson, H. (2019) Learning while playing: Children's forest school experiences in the UK. *British Educational Research Journal*, 45(1), 21-40.

Cobb, P. (1999) Where is the mind? In P. Murphy (Ed) *Learners, Learning and Assessment*. London: Open University Press/PCP.

Cree, J. & McCree, M. (2012). A brief history of the roots of forest school in the UK. Part 1. Available at https://www.outdoor-learning-research.org/Portals/0/Research%20Documents/Horizons%20Archive/H60.History.of.FS.pt1.pdf?ver=2014-06-23-151226-000 Accessed 14/2/24.

Garden, A. & Downes, G. (25 January 2023): New boundaries, undecided roles: Towards an understanding of forest schools as constructed spaces. *Education 3-13*. https://doi.org/10.1080/03004279.2023.2170187

Hall, K., Murphy, P. & Soler, J. (2008) *Pedagogy and Practice. Culture and Identities*. London: SAGE/Open University Press.

Harris, F. (2018) Outdoor learning spaces: The case of forest school. *Area*, 50, 222-231. https://doi.org/10.1111/area.12360

Lampert, M. (2009) Learning Teaching in, from, and for Practice: What do we mean? *Journal of Teacher Education*, 61(1-2), 21-34. https://doi.org/10.1177/0022487109347321

Lave, J. (1993) Situating learning in communities of practice. In L. B. Resnick, J. M. Levine, & S. D. Teasley (Eds) *Perspectives on Socially Shared Cognition* (pp. 17-36). Washington, DC: American Psychological Association.

Leather, M. (2016) A critique of Forest School: Something lost in translation. *Journal of outdoor and environmental Education*. Avaialble at: https://marjon.repository.guildhe.ac.uk/id/eprint/10203/1/Leather_JOEE%2026-Sep-16%20v2.pdf Accessed 14/2/24.

Martin-Millward, T. (2020) *Choices, Choices, Choices: The Nature of Children's Agency Within a Forest School Context*. Unpublished PhD thesis. Oxford: Oxford Brookes University.

McCree, M. (2019) When forest school isn't forest school. In M. Sackville-Ford & Davenport, H. (Eds) *Critical Issues in Forest Schools*. London: SAGE.

McGregor, D. (2016) Using drama within a STEM context: Developing enquiry skills and appreciating what it is to be a scientist! *Journal of Emergent Science*, 12, 16-24.

McNiff, J., Lomax, P. & Whitehead, J. (2003) *You and Your Action Research Project* 2nd ed. London: Routledge.

Nasir, N. S. & Hand, V. (2008) From the court to the classroom: Opportunities for engagement, learn ing, and identity in basketball and classroom mathematics. *Journal of the Learning Sciences*, 17, 143-179.

Orion, N. & Hofstein, A. (1994). Factors that influence learning during a scientific field trip in a natural environment. *Journal of Research in Science Teaching*, 31, 1097-1119. https://doi.org/10.1002/tea.3660311005

Priestley, M., Biesta, G. J. J. & Robinson, S. (2015) Teacher agency: What is it and why does it matter? In R. Kneyber & J. Evers (Eds) *Flip the System: Changing Education from the Bottom up* 1st ed. London: Routledge, pp. 134-148.

Rogoff, B. (2008) Observing sociocultural activity on three planes: Participatory appropriation, guided participation and apprenticeship. In K. Hall, P. Murphy & J. Soler (Eds) *Pedagogy and Practice. Culture and Identities*. London: Open University Press/SAGE.

Waite, S. & Goodenough, A. (2018) What is different about forest school? Creating a space for an alternative pedagogy in England. *Journal of Outdoor and Environmental Education*, 21, 25-44.

Wenger, E. (1998) *Communities of Practice: Learning, Meaning and Identity*. Cambridge: Cambridge University Press.

Wiske, M. S. (1999) What is teaching for understanding? In J. Leach & B. Moon (Eds) *Learners and Pedagogy*. London: Paul Chapman.

CONCLUSION: WHAT IS THE USE OF THEORY AND WHY DOES IT MATTER FOR PRACTICE?

CONTENTS

Summarising the Main Theories	261
Reflecting Back on Enactments of Practice and Teaching Metaphors	264
Reviewing Speaking Metaphorically	269
References	270

Conclusion: What Is the Use of Theory and Why Does It Matter for Practice?

One of the reasons this book came into being was a shared concern about the ways that some terms (or concepts) in education are talked about and understood quite differently. To explain further...

In Chapter 1, you were introduced to different ways that Pritpal and Sally articulated the way they learnt to drive a car. You were then invited to consider how their views might be theorised. Subsequently, you were introduced to the ways that various authors defined learning. Understandings ranged between those that suggest learning is evidenced by 'a change to the individual through experience' (Jarvis 2018:18); is 'conceptual and linguistic' but 'does not have a clear physical or reified identity in the world' (Hodkinson and Macleod 2010: 174); and is a 'process by which one turns into one's own some of the patterns of acting that already exist in society' (Sfard 2016: 333). These contrasting perspectives were discussed further to explore prominent features that characterised the different ways learning is understood to happen. What became apparent was that there is no universally agreed formulation that theorises 'learning', this is because we cannot know exactly how or what another human has learnt from things that have happened to them, both in and out of school.

A simple theoretical model is then introduced to you to enable you to appreciate how learning is related and directly influenced by a teacher's practice and that the nature of knowing or knowledge that can emerge for the learner from that.

You were then introduced to the use of metaphors to help you as a reader relate assumptions people hold about the process and outcomes of learning in the ways they talk and write about it. We drew on Sfard's (1998) acquisition (AM) and participation (PM) models to make more explicit how metaphors, like theories, can help you 'see' more exactly from different perspectives what people mean when they talk about learning.

The subsequent chapters in Part 1 of the book provide an introduction to the nature and origins of long-held theories of learning. The discussions about the concepts associated with each theoretical movement also include consideration of metaphors that could help you as a reader appreciate particular features of each of the theories.

SUMMARISING THE MAIN THEORIES

In explaining the historical development of theories of learning, you are introduced to the difference between theory which emerges from researching into human behaviours and activities and intuitive or 'folk theories' (Bruner 1996: 44) that are developed by people based on their experience of being in the world.

Throughout Chapters 2-6, you are also invited to pause and consider what sense or theorising you might make of your own or others' practice and the impact it may have on learners and learning. Alongside thinking about the impact of different pedagogies as a reader, you are also invited to reflect on the ways that curricular policy directives suggest practice should be enacted in schools, suggesting how what teachers do in classrooms should position learners and shape learning.

In maintaining a theorised approach to discussing the various theoretical movements, the ways that learning, knowledge and pedagogy are linked are borne in mind throughout the book. Reflection is also constantly concerned with *epistemology*, that is, how as humans we come to know the world as we do, and *ontology*, what individuals believe about the world.

Behaviourism

As explained in Chapter 2, this perspective emerged as a scientific approach to learning developed, turning away from psychology. The work by Pavlov (1927) in researching how to control particular behaviours of dogs and Skinner's (1968) theorising about operant conditioning contributed to rise to the behaviourist movement. As explained in the chapter, there were concerns about the application to educational thinking. However, there still remains today a legacy of the drill-and-practice approach, valuing rapid retrieval, rote and recall in learning, particularly in aspects of mathematics and phonics, for example. The teacher controls what is to be learnt and successful learning is that where habits are formed. Transmission views of knowledge are valued and inherent assumptions about learners as passive receivers of information (Table 11.1) do not recognise pupils as agentive problem-solvers. Figuring out how to set up a new mobile phone or cooking a new recipe, for example, are not the kinds of learning acknowledged in this movement.

Information Processing

As explained in Chapter 3, this perspective emerged from behaviourist perspectives during the 1960s and 1970s with the advent of the modern computer. In this movement, the mind was understood differently. Rather than one which should absorb and regurgitate given information in behaviourism, in information processing, the mind is seen to be more akin to the computer, capable of manipulating symbols. The brain (of individuals) is given problems related to existing symbol structures that learners are familiar with. The brain is then assumed to search for correspondence and difference by decoding symbols. Answers are found by identifying and following the rules or algorithms the learner can retrieve and select to resolve that particular kind of a problem. The type of teaching related to this movement would involve learners following and learning step-by-step processes, which are then applied to solve different types of problems. The learners are assumed to be *passive symbol processors* (Table 11.1) responding to pre-defined problems given by the teacher. Successful learning is the acquisition of rules and procedures (external to the knower) and is minds-on only.

Constructivism

As explained in Chapter 3, behaviourism and information processing theories remained challenging (in the late 20th century) for educational psychologists who questioned how drill and practice used in schools could prepare students to solve real-world problems. Pribram, a psychologist who investigated *extrinsic* motivations of monkeys (cited in Woods 1998: 4), revealed the possibility that an activity itself might hold some intrinsic interest for animals. Pribram's work alongside Piaget's (1950) theorising about how children and young people think and understand the world around them gave rise to cognitivism. This resulted in a transition in thinking about learning as a passive activity to one where a learner is *intrinsically* motivated and self-directed to discover things about the world by themselves. You were then introduced to the idea of activity, the source of learning and the variation in the ways that Piagetian ideas are taken up in practice. It was pointed out to you, that if a learner is active, it does not necessarily mean that they are generating their own personal understanding of something. Constructivism involves a person being agentive, that is, they construct their own understandings, realise connections between things and generate meanings. Their knowledge is not given, it is generated or constructed for themselves. It was explained to you how thinking does not precede activity, as in information processing theory, but that knowing and doing co-construct each other. Various interpretations of Piagetian theorising are also discussed in this chapter to demonstrate how a teacher's practice can make quite a difference to way that a child might experience a learning activity and consequently the meaning they make from it. A common challenge for teachers wishing to extend a constructivist experience for their learners is to build on prior knowledge. However, it is the student, who must construct the meaning and move from prior understanding to new understanding. The teacher cannot do that for them, but the teacher assumes that the motivation to do this is there. Another common challenge for teachers is making appropriate use of the elicitation of learners' ideas and thinking to ensure each individual subsequently progresses during an activity once the learner's understandings are known. Another important concept that is widely interpreted in Piagetian constructivism is the nature of social interaction. In Piaget's theory, learners amend their ways of thinking to better 'fit' reality when faced with conflicts or problems (or indeed others' juxtaposed views) that do not align with their existing view of the world.

The terms *equilibrium* and *cognitive dissonance* are also explained to you that relate to social processes.

Intersubjectivity from a Piagetian perspective involves learners making explicit their differing understandings of the same phenomenon. This is not co-construction but a process of translation because only the individual is concerned with another's view.

The nature of co-operation is also discussed, as it depends on *reciprocity* between learners so that they grant each other's propositions *equal status* and share an interest to explore alternative perspectives.

Social Constructivism

As introduced and explained in Chapter 4, in theories of learning that are more social in nature, language and meaning-making are paramount. However, there are many ways that these concepts within constructivism and social constructivism are interpreted and enacted in classrooms. Therein lay many challenges for teachers who wish to support more social dimensions to their constructivist practice. Challenges to Piaget's model of stage development are considered and the ways it is understood and adopted to inform practice are contrasted with social constructivism. Interestingly, the legacy of his model extends to curricular policy even today.

The ways that context matters is introduced in Chapter 4, to expand on explaining why children find it difficult to *perform* in particular kinds of ways expected by teachers.

Within Chapter 4, the development of social constructivism emerging from Vygotsky's theorising about the impact of social, cultural, historical and even political influences on thinking and learning is considered. What is also introduced in Chapter 4 and extended into Chapters 5 and 6 are the different ways that the zone of proximal development (ZPD) is understood and supported in social constructivist perspectives. Vygotskian notions concerning speech, thought and even intersubjectivity are also presented for you to contemplate what they mean for your practice.

Socioculturalism

In Chapter 5, it is explained to you how this is a complex and evolving field. Socioculturalism has emerged from Vygotskian perspectives of the social, historical and cultural influences on learning. For some, tensions remain between the ways that learning, knowledge and mind are understood in constructivism, social constructivism and sociocultural perspectives. For others, rapprochement was possible and pragmatically desirable as the views were considered partially complementary with the potential to illuminate different educational issues (Cobb and Yackel 1996; Smith et al. 1999). More recently, others such as Lave, Wenger, Rogoff, Holland and Sfard have each contributed to the discourse and proffered different dimensions, arguments or even concepts within the sociocultural movement. As is discussed further in Chapters 5 and 6, there are contrasting views of context, the activity engaged with, the extent and distribution of collective participation, the purpose of learning tasks, the role of cultural artefacts, the community practices adopted by learners and the development of identity and agency (Table 11.1). The complexity of different cultures and their participants' ways of *acting* and *being* are considered alongside the relevance and salience for schools and teachers.

REFLECTING BACK ON ENACTMENTS OF PRACTICE AND TEACHING METAPHORS

In Part 2 of the book, the chapters take up quite a different purpose and tone. These chapters are intended to help you, the reader, to understand how the theories introduced in Part 1 might be useful to develop your practice. To enable you to consider what teachers have done, and indeed, could do, you are presented with several narrative construals related to some aspect of each theoretical movement. Each narrative construal usually involves dialogue between the teacher and learners to enable you to appreciate what concepts within the theoretical movement might look like in a classroom.

Inevitably, each narrative construal could not emphasise all aspects of a particular theoretical movement. Remember, too, that although the metaphors applied emphasise teacher enactments, for each of the cases considered, the relational nature of practice, learning and knowledge was also discussed.

Conclusion: What Is the Use of Theory and Why Does It Matter for Practice?

Table 11.1 Key Features, Relating Learning, Practice and Knowledge in Theories of Learning

	Behaviourism	Information Processing	Constructivism	Social Constructivism	Socioculturalism
Nature of (teachers') practice	The teacher is the holder of knowledge/authority.	Teachers are the authority.	The teacher provides the conditions for learning.	The teacher mediates interaction.	Teacher as 'sherpa' or even co-adventurer.
	The teacher solves problems on behalf of the learners.	Problems are given and pre-defined.	Problems are perceived by the learner through misfit and emerge as conflicts and perturbations to be resolved.	Tasks are differential problems to be solved.	Teacher affords opportunities for progressive development within a collective ZPD.
	Teaching is by drill and practice rather than problem-solving.	Problem-solving is a controlled process.	Solutions are created in the head.	Solutions are generated in the ZPD that exists between people.	The teacher is a guide and mediator.
	Tasks are stable, that is, they have the same meaning across learners.	Solutions are pre-given algorithms stored in the head.	Tasks are stable across learners.	Teacher as 'modeller' or 'guide'.	Collaborative activity offers opportunities for learning.
	Metaphors: *Lion tamer, sculptor* or *petrol pump attendant*.	Tasks are stable, that is, they have the same meaning across learners.	Teacher as *'gardener'* or *'facilitator'*.	Teacher is the 'scaffolder' enabling progressive development within the ZPD.	
		Metaphors: *Watchmaker* or *parent bird*.	Teacher is the 'guide on the side' enabling intersubjectivity.		
Assumptions about learners	Passive receivers. All similar.	Learners are passive symbol processors.	Learners are constructors of meaning and problem-solvers.	Learners are active participants in the learning process.	Learners can be agentive in various ways.
	Innate ability determines their potential for learning.	Motivation is intrinsic.	Learners are self-regulated and self-directed.	Learners are social and interact with others to learn.	Learners' agency and identity are influential in learning, and in turn influence the nature of what is learnt.
	Brain is the mind.	Learners solve problems of a particular kind.	Mind is agentive.	Mind emerges through social interaction.	Identity can be positional, dialogic or figurative.
	Motivation is extrinsic.	Innate abilities determine the capacity of the learner to learn.	Motivation is intrinsic.	Motivation is intrinsic.	
	Learners react to the environment (including	Learners see, think and then act.			

(Continued)

Table 11.1 Key Features, Relating Learning, Practice and Knowledge in Theories of Learning (Continued)

	Behaviourism	Information Processing	Constructivism	Social Constructivism	Socioculturalism
How learning is assumed to happen	stimuli provided by the teacher). Identity and agency are not acknowledged. Repetitive practice. Imitative. Forming habits laid down in the brain. Associated with habits.	Identity and agency are not acknowledged. Learning is the acquisition of rules and procedures. Learners act on the environment: learning is minds-on only.	Learning is minds on, hands on. Learners' prior knowledge and experience shape new learning. Learning is by mutual adaptation and internalisation, leading to new associations and self-organisation of knowledge to better fit reality. The development of systems of mental operations marks intellectual revolutions, leading to abstract reasoning and reflection.	Learning is hands on, minds on. Learning is promoted through collaboration. Stand-alone competence is achieved through prior working with more expert others within the ZPD.	Mind is distributed and emerges through different forms of collaboration. Experience is essential for learning. Learning emerges through collaborative activity. Resolutions emerge in the ZPD that exists between people. Learning is influenced by and influences the culture within which learners participate.
Nature of knowledge that is valued	Knowledge is given and abstract, not in context. It is external to the learner.	Knowledge represents how the world is. Language is a system of symbols that are given and mirror reality.	Knowledge is abstract organised sets of mental structures and procedures. Radical constructivism deems that an	Knowing is socially constructed. Competency is associated with subject matter.	Knowledge and knowing are contextualised. Knowledge and knowing are not

It is independent of the situation or context a learner is in.	individual's knowledge is derived from human experience.	transferable between contexts.
Recounting or recalling given information.	Language is a system of symbols that represent the world and exerts no formative effect on the structure of thought.	Knowledge learnt in school is abstract, decontextualised from the real world.
Knowledge is external and independent of situations in which it is learnt.	Thought precedes language and is not determined by it.	Knowledge and knowing emerge through cultural practices.
Knowledge corresponds to physical structures stored in the brain – enabling mental processing and particular forms of problem-solving.	Knowledge can be understood as realist, subjectivist or relativist.	Signs, symbols and actions constitute dialectical ways of communicating.
	Language precedes thought and action.	Knowing emerges from participatory activity.
	Coming to know is semiotic in nature.	Knowledge and knowing are appropriated through collaborative activity with others.
	Signs, symbols, actions and the spoken word constitute language.	
	Knowing emerges from interactional exchanges.	
	Knowledge and knowing are internalised from shared cognitive resources that emerge in joint problem-solving with others.	

Enactments from behaviourist episodes, in Chapter 7, present Ms Jones and Ms Ramen tightly controlling what is to be learnt in primary school phonics and arithmetic. Their practice assumes, like the *petrol pump attendant*, that what they know should be metaphorically *poured* into the pupils' *empty heads*. The pace and expected rapidity of the whole class to remember and recall given information are reminiscent of the *lion tamer* metaphor. Mr Thomas provides symbolic actions that represent the grammatical use of commas in sentences, appropriate for a secondary English class. Like Ms Jones the students are encouraged to mimic the teacher, in this case, how he demonstrates the use of commas.

All three teachers tightly frame the episodes, like a *sculptor*, structuring and shaping the lesson. Each lesson begins with simpler tasks and progresses to more complex activity. Ms Jones begins with the easy recitation of single letters, and then progressing to pairs of letters (and actioning a particular depiction of these phonemes); Ms Ramen begins with times tables or number sets as they are called and progresses to simple problems to be solved, enacting the metaphor of a *watchmaker* or *parent bird*. Mr Thomas also builds the lesson to finish with simple problems about sentence construction to be solved by applying rules learnt earlier, echoing the information-processing *watchmaker* metaphor too.

In Chapter 8, each of the episodes or narrative construals presented provided insight in various ways that constructivism or a teacher as a *gardener* could be enacted. In each case (in science, mathematics and English), the learners were offered different kinds of opportunities to generate their own task solutions. In science, providing a range of materials for individuals to select, handle, interact with and experimentally find out about substances resonates closely with teacher as a *gardener*. Mr Edward's intentions in having the pupils work *independently* resonates with constructivism; however, on closer scrutiny, you may question the extent to which activities are carried out without others' influence. Mrs Pott's intentions to *scaffold* students drawing an *original* image and composing some *unique* prose also echo constructivism. In each of these narrative construals, it is possible to see how the teacher's enactments and intentions to support constructivism do not always align. As McPhail (2016: 294), introduced to you in Chapter 3, suggests, there is a general belief or 'doxic acceptance' of often romanticised and confused perceptions of constructivism. There are, in the construals offered in Chapter 8, some conflicts between the ideology of constructivism and agency.

In Chapter 9, where practice supporting social constructivist learning was considered, each teacher, Ms Davey, Ms Smith, Mr Cook and Mr Beadle all supported social interaction through different practices. They organised students to work together (differently), facilitated communication and negotiation of each other's views or understandings and designed (open) learning tasks that could be resolved in multiple ways. Mr Cook *modelled* how incorrect solutions constrained mathematical thinking so he reorganised the nature of the tasks the pupils worked on together to figure out alternate ways of explaining how particular mathematical solutions could be achieved. Ms Pessagno clearly acted as a *guide* in the ways she prepared her pupils to articulate arguments about books and computers from different perspectives.

In Chapter 10 where practice supporting concepts within the sociocultural movement was considered, you were introduced to a range of situations where context and activity mattered. Agency and identity were evident in the narrative construals. In Ms Lampert's, Mr Bird's and Ms Duggan's classrooms, the pupils practiced mathematical, historical and technological ways of working, respectively. The teachers demonstrated how they were both experienced in their subject disciplines and knew how to act as a *tourist guide* enabling their pupils to progress in a mathematical, historical and technological world, respectively. The community science project and the forest school construals suggested how agency and identity were, and could be, better supported. In the science project, the teachers also demonstrated how they were *sherpas*, knowing the local terrain, offering suggestions about possibilities, empathising with their students' lived experience, ensuring they supported the urban youth to act as environmental advocates. In the forest school setting, the potential to develop a teacher's practice as a *co-adventurer* was also considered.

REVIEWING SPEAKING METAPHORICALLY

Despite the range of metaphors applied, there are nuances in teaching to support learning that are difficult to consider metaphorically. As Sfard suggests, metaphors offer 'reification' (Sfard 2016: 325) that can be related to everyday life. She elaborates describing how they can become a 'tool for creating new discourses rather than just embellishing existing ones' (Sfard 2016: 326). In writing this book, it has become apparent that there is a need to generate more metaphors to make clearer the differences in ways that social construction, for example, discussed at length in Chapter 4, and participation in practices, an important process in socioculturalism, can be distinctly represented. As introduced in Chapter 1, Sfard's AM and PM metaphors help distinguish what acquisitionists value in learning, that is, acquiring knowledge, concepts and mental schemes. In contrast, the PM metaphor suggests how Vygotskians who recognise 'participation in historically established human activities as the main object of learning-induced change' value the development of competency in new practices. These contrasts would not be so starkly explicit if 'the participationist discourse' – producing a totally new discourse on all those phenomena that we consider unique to humans (Sfard 2016: 327) – had not become so widely understood. Another nuance that would be helpful to develop a metaphor for would be Lave and Wenger's (1991) suggestion about the changing nature of participation as people learn and that it is at first termed legitimately peripheral but gradually changes as knowing and practices are developed as participants become more experienced. Representing metaphorically, the reciprocal impact participants have on the communities within which they develop their more expert practice is also challenging. However, for now, the AM and PM go some way into developing metaphors that extend the discourse about 'what changes when a person learns' (Sfard 2016: 327).

Theorising and Practice

Furlong (2013: 184) suggests when teachers 'engage in a complex practical activity such as teaching, [they] reflect on it and begin to theorise it in order to make sense of it'. However, he reiterates Hirst's (1999) view that the issue is not whether teachers engage in theorising their practice, but that they will, either consciously or subconsciously (Van Manen 1995). Furlong emphasises a number of concerns about teachers theorising their practice (and learning). A teacher may, for example, theorise that prefacing any questions they ask of a class with a child's name heightens children's attentiveness to the subject matter that is being presented. This could then develop into a belief that the whole class will improve their learning when question and answer techniques involve the use of learners' names. This is an example of Bruner's (1996) folk pedagogies mentioned in Chapter 2. It is possible that the use of metaphors can help teachers theorise about their practice and that the theories presented here, with the emphases provided through the use of teaching metaphors, provide the tools aspired to at the beginning of this book. As Furlong suggests, I hope that the theories presented here are sufficiently robust to be critically scrutinised by others; they are informed by research evidence and practice from elsewhere so that the inherent values and assumptions associated with them are interrogated.

Rogoff explains how people often take their own community's (or school's) way of doing things for granted. She argues that the most difficult cultural processes to examine are those *confidently* enacted and based on *unquestioned assumptions* in a community. As she states, cultural processes surround us all and often involve 'subtle, tacit, taken-for-granted events and ways of doing things that require open eyes, ears and minds to notice and understand' (Rogoff 2003: 11). This book is intended to help you, the reader, look at practice and learning afresh in schools and consider the assumptions underpinning certain ways of doing things. Remember, a fish out of water doesn't notice until it is!

REFERENCES

Bruner, J. (1996) *The Culture of Education*. Cambridge, MA: Harvard University Press.

Cobb, P. & Yackel, E. (1996) Constructivist, emergent and sociocultural perspectives in the context of developmental research. *Educational Psychologist*, *31*(3), 175-190.

Furlong, J. (2013) *Education – An Anatomy of the Discipline: Rescuing the University Project?* London: Routledge.

Hirst, P. H. (1999) The nature of educational aims. In R. Marples (Ed) *The Aims of Education* (pp. 124-132). London: Routledge.

Hodkinson, P. & Macleod, F. (2010) Contrasting concepts of learning and contrasting research methodologies: Affinities and bias. *British Educational Research Journal*, *36*(2), 173-189.

Jarvis, M. (2018) Learning to be a person in society. Learning to be me. In K. Illeris (Ed) *Contemporary Theories of Learning*. London: Routledge.

Lave, J. & Wenger, E. (1991) *Situated Learning: Legitimate Peripheral Participation*. Cambridge: Cambridge University Press.

McPhail, G. (2016) The fault lines of recontextualization: The limits of constructivism in education. *British Educational Research Journal*, *42*(2), 294-313.

Pavlov, I. P. (1927). *Conditioned Reflexes: An Investigation of the Physiological Activity of the Cerebral Cortex*. Oxford: Oxford University Press.

Piaget, J. (1950) *The Psychology of Intelligence*. London: Routledge.

Rogoff, B. (2003) *The Cultural Nature of Human Development*. Oxford: Oxford University Press.

Sfard, A. (1998) In two metaphors for learning and the dangers of choosing just one. *Educational Researcher, 27*(2), 4-13.

Sfard, A. (2016) Metaphors in educational research. In A. Qvortup, M. Wiberg, G. Christensen & M. Hansbol (Eds), *On the Definition of Learning*. Odense: University Press of Southern Denmark.

Smith, L., Dockerell, J. & Tomlinson, P. (1999) *Piaget, Vygotsky and beyond. Future Issues for Developmental Psychology and Education*. London: Routledge.

Van Manen, M. (1995) On the epistemology of reflective practice. *Teachers and Teaching, 1*(1), 33-50.

Woods, D. (1998) *How Children Think and Learn*. Oxford: Blackwell Publishing.

INDEX

A

Ability, 51, 61-3, 71, 73, 78, 80, 86, 92, 106, 113, 132, 134, 135, 167, 172, 175, 188, 192, 195, 222, 239, 268
  grouping, 21
  innate, xi, 3, 17, 62
  theorising ability, 9, 20, 23, 35-9
Achievement, 5, 23, 49, 74, 92, 100-1, 159-60
Activity, xiii, xiv-xv, 7, 13, 22, 76, 85, 87, 93, 152, 266-72
  in behaviourism, 161, 164, 166
  in constructivism, 45-9, 52, 54-7, 59-60, 62, 66, 185, 187-8, 194, 198, 207-9
  in information processing, 34-5, 173, 177
  in social constructivism, 102-3, 105, 109, 112, 114, 218-21, 226-7, 229-230
  in socioculturalism, 126-8, 133-41, 146-7, 238-9, 241, 244-8, 252-4, 256, 258-260
Activity theory, 136-9
Agency, xiii, xv, 17, 70, 85, 125, 140
  in behaviourism, 29, 164, 269
  in cognitivism, 55-8
  in constructivism, 44-5, 54, 56, 61, 64, 98, 185, 271
  in information processing, 156, 269
  learner, 58, 66, 98, 109, 112, 260
  in social constructivism, 82, 112, 237-8
  in socioculturalism, 126-7, 133, 137-8, 140-2, 145-7, 245, 253-6, 258-260, 267-8, 272
  teacher, 29, 98, 109, 119, 254
Alexander, Robin, 3, 214, 217
Appropriation, 139, 242, 252, 254, 259-260
Argumentation, 107, 114, 220, 222
Assessment, 2, 7, 36, 60, 73-5, 78-80, 87-8, 91-2, 100, 118, 138, 152, 192, 252
Attainment, 2, 75, 158-9, 209
Authority, 89
  teacher as authority, 30, 39-40, 106-7, 116, 177, 268
Autonomy, 107, 120

B

Bakhtin, Mikhail, 85-6, 93, 103
Ball, Stephen, 151-2, 159, 165, 172, 218
Bauersfeld, Erik, 101-6, 112, 119, 215, 221
Behaviourist theory, xiv-xv, 15, 17, 19-43, 45-6, 48, 55, 72, 119, 155-183, 208, 221, 265, 268
Brain, xi, xiv, 12, 22-4, 55, 59, 268-270
  development, 71-2, 79

as mind, 22-4, 29-30, 32-4, 36, 39-40, 45, 49, 265. *See also* Mind
Bruner, Jerome, xii, 20, 24, 41, 45, 67, 70, 84, 86, 89-90, 94, 114, 122, 140, 147, 151-2, 156, 164-5, 179, 232, 245, 264, 273

C

Classroom contexts
  arithmetic, 127-8, 131, 166-9, 178, 220, 268
  drama, 175, 183, 187, 216, 228
  English, 24, 49-54, 75, 83, 236, 268, 137, 144, 165, 175-6, 188, 197, 224-5, 227-8, 236, 252-4, 257
  forest school, 47, 50-1, 53-4
  history, 112, 140, 216, 239, 257, 242-3
  mathematics, xv, 14, 35, 50-2, 62, 74-5, 81, 102-5, 107-8, 112, 117, 120, 130, 135-6, 145, 166, 173-5, 178, 182-3, 187-8, 192, 190, 213, 218-22, 230, 236-9, 243, 248, 257
  phonics, 14, 28, 31, 33, 74, 157-9, 164-7, 175-8, 205, 262, 268
  science, xv, 57, 62-3, 72, 74-5, 78, 102, 109-14, 116-8, 142, 184-193, 206, 215-7, 230, 239-1, 243-5, 248-9, 250-1, 257, 268-9
  technology, 117, 129, 190, 192-3, 224-5, 243, 249
Classroom practices, xiii, xvi, 87, 118, 207, 218
  behaviourist, xiv-xv, 15, 17, 19-45, 48, 55, 72, 119, 155-183, 201, 208, 221, 265
  cognitivist, xiv, 45, 48, 208, 266
  constructionist, 31, 60, 103-5, 107, 116-9, 185, 217, 224, 225, 255, 266
  constructivist, xiv-xv, 17, 45, 49, 63, 65, 101, 106, 114, 184-212
  information processing, xv, 15, 35, 40, 155-183
  social constructivist, 8, 93, 97, 99, 101, 104, 115-6, 121, 213-236, 271
  socioculturalist, 101, 108-11, 121, 237-262
  symbolic interactionist, xiv, 105, 215-6, 227, 271
Cobb, Paul, 48, 99, 103, 106-7, 109, 115, 186, 221
Cognitive development, 45, 64, 66, 87, 128, 188, 190, 211
Cognitive demand, 64, 188, 193
Cognitivism theory, 207, 265. *See also* Classroom practices; Theories
Collaboration, 13, 91, 106, 121, 146, 221, 228, 240-41, 254, 259, 269
Community, xi, xiii, xv-i, 31, 104-5, 117, 127, 137, 139-40, 142-3, 147
  of enquiry, 13

of knowledge, 107, 114-5
of learners, 136
of practice, 83, 133-4, 143-4
within school, 143-5
Conditioning, 26, 29, 265
Constructionist, 10. *See also* Classroom practices; Theories
Constructivism, xvi, 8, 10, 49, 52-5, 57, 59, 61-7, 70, 76, 79-80, 86, 88, 93-4, 98-100, 184-212, 266
radical, 70-3. *See also* Classroom practices; Theories
Context, xv-i, 8, 13, 25, 49-50, 52-4, 72, 75, 79-80, 86-8, 94, 97, 99-102, 113-5, 121-2, 147, 157, 160, 162, 164-6, 177, 197, 208, 238, 245-6, 254, 256, 267, 269-270, 272
children as contextualists, 77-9, 93
cultural, 75, 82, 112, 126-35, 138, 140-3
and learning, 104, 115
Cooperation, 60-1, 74, 91, 106, 266
Creativity, 48-9, 186, 196, 256
Culture, xiii, xv-i, 41, 82, 90-1, 93, 101, 105-6, 108, 114-5, 122, 126-50
and activity, 135-7
of a community, 130-8
and context, 127-9
and learning, 106, 132
microculture in the classroom, 101, 103, 106-10
ways of working, 130-1
West African Tailors, 129
Yucatec Midwives, 129
Curriculum, 14, 25, 45, 49-54, 60, 62-5, 100, 117-8, 120, 135, 166, 172, 186, 230, 232, 238, 256
critique, 14
English national curriculum, England, 31, 33, 49-53, 157-9, 174-5, 200, 227, 231
history national curriculum, England, 49-54
mathematics national curriculum, England, 49-53, 118, 166-7, 195-7, 222
and Piaget's stage model, 74-7
and the role of instruction, 89-9
science, national curriculum, England, 117, 192, 218-9
teachers as policy actors, 151-2, 165, 167, 172, 218

D
Dewey, John, 70, 80, 82, 84, 89-90, 104, 139
Dialogue, xi, xiii, xvi, 6, 13, 61, 84, 86-7, 89-90, 114, 156-7, 161, 164, 185, 193, 214-21, 226, 230, 232-3, 238-48, 258, 260, 267
Driver, Rosalind, 113-6, 118, 120, 189-91, 193

E
Educational policy, 7, 17, 20-1, 26, 30-3, 39, 41, 49, 54, 56, 66, 74, 98, 100, 117-9, 122, 151-2, 156-9, 165-7, 172, 175, 178, 185-6, 195-7, 200-201, 214, 218, 220-21, 227, 230-31, 238, 264, 267
Enactment, 74, 235, 251-2

Engestrom, Yrjo, 136-7, 139
Epistemology, 20, 31, 52, 105, 119-20, 138, 163, 179, 209, 265
Everyday learning, 2-7, 35

G
Gender, differences in learning, 24-5, 110-2, 129, 241
Greenfield, Susan, 79

H
Hands-on, 8, 57, 65

I
Identity, xiii, xv, 9, 17, 38, 126-7, 133-4, 138, 141, 143-7
and agency, 138-41
dialogic, 114, 127, 141, 146, 268
figurative, 146, 268
positional, 142-3, 164, 173, 200, 231, 241, 246, 249, 258, 260
Illeris, Knud, 9, 11
Intelligence, 35-7, 61
Interaction, 91-2, 101-3, 105, 107-11, 126, 130, 133, 136, 138-41, 164, 173-4
social, xiv, 4, 9-10, 12, 60-1, 66, 81-2, 85, 89-90, 93, 98-9, 107, 113, 121, 185, 222, 225, 232-3, 238, 240, 246, 251, 259, 266, 268, 271
symbolic, xiv, 105, 136, 227
Ivory tower, 35

J
Jigsaw, learning as doing a jigsaw, 31, 172-3

K
Knowing, xiii, 6-7, 13, 32, 56, 62, 82, 107, 119-21, 126, 129, 135, 146, 159, 174, 177, 209, 221, 246, 251, 259-260, 264, 266, 269-270, 272
ways of, 76, 93, 113-4, 118-21
Knowledge, xiii, 2-3, 7, 9-11, 13-5, 20, 22-36, 39-41, 45, 47-55, 57-9, 61-66, 70-3, 75-6, 89-91, 93-4, 98-101, 105, 115-6, 118-122, 126, 128-9, 133, 135, 138-40, 142-3, 146, 157-8, 173-5, 177-9, 186-7, 189, 194-5, 201, 207-9, 214-5, 217-8, 221-2, 226, 232, 238, 245, 253-5, 264-270
in behaviourism, 27-33, 39, 157-8, 164, 178
in constructivism, 45, 47-55, 57-9, 61-66, 70-3, 75-6, 89, 94, 186-7, 189, 194, 201, 207-9, 214-5
in information processing, 33-6, 39-40, 157, 166-7, 173, 178
representations of, 22, 26
in social constructivism, 90-1, 93-4, 98-101, 115-6, 118-122
in socioculturalism, 98-101, 105, 111-3, 119-122, 126, 128-9, 133, 135, 138-40, 142-3, 146, 238, 245, 253-5, 264-7

Index

L
Lave, Jean, 24, 35, 100, 105, 126-9, 131, 133, 135, 140, 142-4, 254, 267, 272
Learning
  definition of, xi-ii, 1-16, 263-73
  by doing, 48, 55
Lessons, 6-7, 24, 30, 155-262
  case illustrations
    driving, 5-7
    English, 24, 160-66, 175-78, 201-7, 234
    forest school, 255-8
    history, 243-7
    mathematics, 168-75, 178, 198-200, 223-33, 242
    science, 110, 193-4, 216, 219-220, 233
    technology, 246-51

M
Mediation, 65, 81-3, 91, 101, 135
Mercer, Neil, xii, 16, 20, 80, 156, 214, 217-8
Metaphors, xv, 13-4, 23, 25, 29, 31, 45, 47, 60, 64, 66, 70, 76, 92-3, 98, 116, 126, 139, 147, 157, 165, 172-3, 177, 185, 188, 232-3, 240, 256, 260, 271-2
  AM and PM, 13-4, 272
  co-adventurer, 126, 146-7, 238, 256, 260-61, 268, 272
  gardener, xv, 45, 47, 60-6, 76, 93, 116, 185, 188-9, 194, 268, 271
  lion tamer, xiv, 27, 39, 156, 164-5, 172, 178, 268, 271
  parent bird, xiv, 29, 40, 76, 156, 171-3, 177-8, 240, 268, 271
  petrol pump attendant, xiv, 29, 39, 164-5, 178, 268, 271
  scaffolding, 92, 192, 201, 207, 214, 221, 227, 233
  sculptor, 27, 39, 156, 165, 178, 268, 271
  sherpa, 98, 115, 122, 126, 146-7, 268
  tourist guide, xv, 98, 115, 122, 126, 147, 238, 240, 248, 256, 261, 272
  watchmaker, 31, 40, 76, 156, 172, 177-8, 240
Mind, xii, 11-2, 17, 20-30, 32-7, 40-1, 44-60, 65-6, 71-3, 79, 81, 84-9, 98-9, 109, 113, 120-1, 126, 133, 135-7, 146, 192, 208, 225, 238, 241, 245, 265, 267-9. *See also* Brain
  minds-on, 40, 56, 65, 121, 265, 269
'Move learning forward,' 30
Murphy, Patricia, 23-6, 37, 63-4, 78, 110, 118, 127, 141, 145

N
Narrative construal, 165, 177, 201, 207, 218, 220-21, 224, 227-31, 240, 246, 267

O
Ontology, 20, 119-20, 209, 265

P
Participation, 13, 88, 101, 105, 116, 126-7, 139-41, 143, 145, 214, 226, 238, 240, 241, 252
Pedagogy, xiv, 7, 20-1, 24-5, 29, 30-2, 39-40, 45, 53, 56, 59, 63-6, 73, 76, 90, 98, 104, 114, 117-8, 120-1, 146, 151-2, 156-7, 175, 178, 209, 215, 238, 255
  one size fits all, 32
  'sage on the stage,' 35
  same size fits all, 30
Piaget, Jean, 17, 45-61, 64, 66-7, 70-9, 82-3, 87-94, 99-100, 137, 140, 185, 187, 189-96, 266
Policy. *See* Educational policy
Practice, xi-xvi, 7-8, 11, 13-14, 20-2, 24-5, 27, 35-40, 56-9, 61-6, 70, 72, 74, 83, 87, 98-100, 151-262. *See also* Classroom practices

R
Realism, 122
Recall, 3, 9, 48, 66, 84, 157, 165-7, 171, 173, 177, 195, 198, 217, 222, 242, 265, 271
Reflection, xiii, 10, 13, 24, 48, 57, 59-60, 62, 65, 102, 104, 108, 114, 119, 151, 186, 188, 201, 208, 224, 265, 269
Relativism, 120, 122, 190
Rogoff, Barbara, 58, 60, 81, 83, 86-7, 100, 126, 129, 130, 139-40, 147, 238, 252, 267, 273
Rote, 10, 28, 217, 265
Routine, 102, 128, 159, 167, 195, 197, 222

S
Salience, 112, 267
Scaffolding, 70. *See also* Metaphors, *scaffolding*
School
  primary, 8, 14, 74-5, 157-8, 166-73, 189-92, 197, 200-210, 216, 218-9, 227, 246-51
  secondary, 8, 14, 61, 75, 81, 157, 174-5, 189-190, 192, 223-6, 242-3, 253-4, 259, 271
Self-directed, 47, 63, 65, 76, 81, 106, 186, 266, 268
Sfard, Anna, 9, 12-4, 66, 126, 136, 145, 221, 264, 267, 272
Skinner, B. F., 26-9

T
Tasks, 24-5, 28, 36, 56, 60, 77-9, 88, 90-3, 101-4, 110-2, 130-1, 135, 168, 172-3, 187, 198, 216, 221, 241, 247-251, 260
  and nature of understanding, 104-6
  task stability, 33, 76, 102
Teachers, 76, 87-94, 98, 101-3, 106-7, 113-5, 151-275. *See also* Classroom practices; Metaphors
  teacher as strategist, 29
Teaching, 1-16, 155-275. *See also* Classroom practices; Metaphors
Theories, xii-xv, 2, 4-7, 20, 45

of learning, 17-8
   behaviourism, xiv-xv, 15, 17, 19-45, 48, 55, 72, 119, 268-270
   cognitivism, xiv, 45, 48
   constructionism, 31, 60, 103-5, 107, 116-9
   constructivism, xiv-xv, 17, 45, 49, 63, 65, 184-212, 268-270
   information processing, xiv-xv, 15, 17, 19-45, 155-183, 266, 268-270
   radical constructivism, 65, 70, 72, 80, 102, 269
   social constructivism, xiv-xv, 98-124, 213-236, 268-270
   socioculturalism, xv, 17, 99-121, 126, 238-260
   symbolic interactionism, xiv, 227

V

von Glaserfeld, Ernst, 70, 72-3, 196
Vygotsky, Lev, 61, 70, 80-94, 99-100, 114, 135-9, 217, 225

W

Wenger, Etienne, 126-9, 132-5, 139, 140, 142-5, 246, 267
Wood, David, 28-9, 46, 70, 75, 88, 92-3, 221

Z

Zone of proximal development (ZPD), xv, 70, 90-3, 99-101, 116, 121-2, 136-7, 146, 201, 214-5, 221, 224, 233, 241, 261, 267
   first interpretation, 91-3
   second interpretation, 99-101, 116, 121
   third interpretation, 136-7

www.ingramcontent.com/pod-product-compliance
Lightning Source LLC
Chambersburg PA
CBHW051350070526
44584CB00025B/3706